Development in Theory and Practice

Development in Theory and Practice

Paradigms and Paradoxes

SECOND EDITION

Jan Knippers Black
Monterey Institute of International Studies

Westview Press
A Member of the Perseus Books Group

Copyright © 1999 by Westview Press, A Member of the Perseus Books Group

Published in 1999 in the United States of America by Westview Press, 5500 Central Avenue, Boulder, Colorado 80301-2877, and in the United Kingdom by Westview Press, 12 Hid's Copse Road, Cumnor Hill, Oxford OX2 9JJ

Find us on the World Wide Web at www.westviewpress.com

A CIP catalog record for this book is available from the Library of Congress.
ISBN 0-8133-3446-2 (paperback)

The paper used in this publication meets the requirements of the American National Standard for Permanence of Paper for Printed Library Materials Z39.48-1984.

10   9   8   7   6   5   4   3   2   1

*To my mentors at American University,
including Ted Couloumbis, John Finan, Glynn Wood,
Larman Wilson, and particularly Brady Tyson and
the late Harold E. Davis*

*The law condemns the man or woman who steals
the goose from off the common, but lets the greater villain
loose who steals the common from the goose.*

—*Old English folk saying*

Contents

Part Two Development in Practice: Actors and Strategies

Part Three   Development in Focus:
Contemporary Issues and Themes

Part Four   The Process and the Protagonists:
                 Paradoxes of Development

Illustrations

Figures

Photos

India: Women work longer hours than do men
India: In the village of Mudichur, a clinic run by the YWCA is
       the only source of health care for babies
India: Women's organizations in Bangalore protest dowry-abuse
India: Cultivation of kat consumes large portions of Yemen's scarce
       water and land
Burkina Faso: This village explores the advantages of solar-heated
       water
Togo: Survival is a constant struggle for children
Zimbabwe: NGOs seek to help communities
       sustain local markets
Mozambique: Fishermen compete for dwindling fish stocks

Morocco: Small businesses in Fez are seeking assistance from
       development agencies
Zambia: The expansion of tourism has served to sustain indigenous
       crafts
Tibet: When women control resources, children are healthier

China: "Appropriate" technology for modernizing agriculture
and industry
Fiji: The most modernized of the South Pacific island states
Tibet: Indigenous culture is threatened by Chinese occupation
Ecuador: In the Ecuadorean Sierra, peasants participate
enthusiastically in their local cooperative
Chile: The people of Población Victoria San Miguel demonstrate
self-sufficiency though subject to military repression

Venezuela: In modern Caracas, large sectors of the population
arc left behind
Asunción: Growing income gaps mean luxurious housing
alongside shantytowns
El Salvador: Peasants tend fields on the slopes of the volcano
Guazapa
Brazil: Focus on the informal sector has inspired microenterprise
Amazon rain forest: Deforestation has accelerated dramatically
in the 1980s and 1990s
Ecuador: Quechua speakers in the Ecuadorean Sierra prepare
a musical program for a radio station
Mexico: In maquiladoras, young women are expected to give
more and demand less
Albania: Donkeys remain an important part of the transportation
system around Druja

Acknowledgments

Much of the credit for this revised and expanded second edition is due to the intellectual stimulation and hospitality of St. Antony's College, Oxford University, where I was a senior associate member in 1997–1998. The first edition benefited particularly from the assistance of the Fulbright-Hays Program and the Mellon Foundation. I am, as always, in debt to my husband, Martin C. Needler, who first suggested the paradox format for organizing my thoughts. Errors and irreverences are, of course, my own.

Jan Knippers Black

1   *Introduction: In Pursuit of Appropriate Theory*

Talleyrand, asked for a definition of nonintervention, said it was a term used in politics that meant intervention. The problem with using a term common in public affairs is that such terms are adopted and adapted in accordance with particular needs and may in fact be employed by different spokesmen or at different times to convey contradictory meanings.

Development is such a term. It has no precise meaning, no generally accepted definition. Metaphors aside, society is not an organism with a genetically programmed innate potential. We cannot say of a society, as a gardener might of a flower, that it has become what it should be.[1] Like other terms that have acquired a positive connotation, *development* is user-friendly: It means whatever one wants or needs it to mean.

Why, then, should we bother to study it? For academics, the answer is simple. A term or concept in such common and yet multifarious use may be liberating. It gives us license to poach—to bring intellectual and scholarly traditions to bear on a broad range of issue and policy problem areas without becoming trapped by disciplinary, jurisdictional, cultural, or geographic boundaries.

There are more compelling reasons, however, for studying development. One is that, for better or worse, a lot of things are being done in its name that any well-informed person should know about. Another is that given the ambiguity and generally positive connotation attached to the term, useful things can be done in the name of development. Finally, the very open-endedness of the study of development gives us an incentive to elaborate our visions of what might be—a wagon to hitch to a star.

For the most part, however, it has not been the study of development and underdevelopment that has led to a mushrooming of official development assistance programs; rather, the latter has given rise to the former. In fact, the study of development has flourished in recent years, but its very currency has in some ways made the study of it more difficult. The more public attention in the wealthier countries has been focused on the ravages of poverty and the maldistribution of the world's bounty, the more elaborate, abstract, and jargonized have become our rationales for

what we do or fail to do about it. And the more the literature has proliferated, the more strained has become communication among those who
approach it from different perspectives, disciplines, and professions. Let
us deal briefly with each of these obstacles.

Useful Fallacies

It should not be surprising that along with a wealth of insight and information, the flourishing of development studies has also brought forth misinformation, disinformation, and new conceptual vehicles for ethnocentricity and prejudice. In the first place, there has been a serious disjuncture
among field practitioners, theoreticians, and policymakers. In the design
of theories and policies, informational vacuums tend to be filled by prejudice. In the second place, policymakers routinely invoke widely shared
moral ideals to justify the pursuit of cruder interests. And finally, national-
ities and classes clearly favored by global inequality seek relief from impotence or guilt through the resolution of cognitive dissonance. That resolution is likely to take one or more of the following general forms: (1) there is
no problem; (2) there is a problem, but it is not *our* problem; (3) there is a
problem, but it is not our fault; (4) there is a problem, but we are solving it;
or (5) there is no solution. These circumstances of ignorance, interest, and
psychological need have nurtured a number of useful fallacies.

Assuming Progress

India's progress since independence in increasing life expectancy has
been truly remarkable; the figure has risen from an average of twenty-
seven years upon independence in 1947 to sixty-one years in 1994.[2] Population has more than doubled during that period, with food production,
overall, keeping pace—a consequence largely of the so-called green revolution. Food and other amenities, however, have not been efficiently distributed. In fact, there has been increasing inequality and pauperization
in the rural areas. Whereas in 1947, 25 percent of the rural population
was landless, by 1988 that proportion had risen to 40 percent. The landless were continually swelling the population of urban areas, placing severe strains on municipal governments. In Madras, slums or shantytowns accounted for 25 percent of the population in 1961, 33 percent in
1971, 40 percent in 1981, and 50 percent in 1988.[3]

For the developing countries as a whole, it is certainly clear that
progress has been made in the period since World War II in some areas
(e.g., life expectancy), but there has been slippage in others (e.g., self-
sufficiency); and it is not clear that progress or development, by any
definition, is inevitable. Immanuel Wallerstein, who has identified 75-to
100-year cycles of "expansion" and "contraction," or prosperity and

depression, in the capitalist world economy over several centuries, has written that we are slipping into the downside of a cycle.[4]

At any rate, there does not appear to be any felicitous unidirectional locomotion, fueled by divinity or fate, that lets us off the hook. Nor is there convincing evidence that the thrust of policy to date on the part of rich countries and areas with respect to the less fortunate has been to the benefit of the latter. And while outcomes are not necessarily attributable to the intentions and efforts of policymakers and implementers, they are not wholly independent of them either.

Furthermore, although none would claim that there are easy ways for the "unpowerful" to influence policy, it remains true that "if enough people beat their heads against a brick wall, that wall will fall."[5] In short, there is no legitimate rationale for escape—through either complacency or despair—from concern about the planet and its passengers.

Patenting Modernism

In one version of a perhaps apocryphal story, a visitor to India asked Gandhi what he thought of Western civilization. Gandhi replied, "It would be a good idea."

Contrary to the ethnocentric and tempocentric impression sometimes conveyed by development literature, modernism was not invented by the West, much less by the United States. Nor is there anything particularly new about the essence or the major components of international development. One should not need a stroll through Egypt's Valley of the Kings or through the Mayan temples of Mexico's Yucatan Peninsula or along China's Great Wall to be reminded that the contribution of "the West" to modernity and its diffusion is a thin veneer, most likely soon to fall beneath another Asian layer.

Technology transfer is probably as old as trade, certainly as old as empire. Economic planning was presumably in effect in Egypt when the Pharaoh reacted to Joseph's dream by storing grain from the years of abundant harvest for the anticipated seven lean years; and the planning and social-welfare systems of the Incas were apparently in many respects superior to those of their contemporary Andean counterparts. The ambitions of larger or richer states with respect to their neighbors have always been coated with the rhetoric of higher cause—spiritual or material uplift. And as for unsolicited advice, we need no carbon 14 dating to judge it timeless.

For the affluent of the First World, as well as for the Westernized elite of the Third, a major obstacle to understanding the challenges facing less-affluent peoples has been a tone pervading official pronouncements, and even much of the academic literature, of self-congratulation on the one hand, condescension on the other.

The dichotomous use of the terms *modern* and *traditional* is generally more pernicious than a mere lack of definition. It may mean that we have lumped together under a single derogatory heading all cultures other than our own. As the opposite of modernism, tradition is the essence of the national self-determination and cultural identity that is everywhere under assault. And the culture of which modernization, and now global-ization, is a carrier is not necessarily a real culture—rooted either in pop-ular or in elite tradition—from anywhere. It is now more likely to be a "virtual" culture, deriving from the needs and imaginations of advertis-ers and reflecting the capabilities of the communications revolution—a composite caricature of real culture that exacerbates the disjuncture be-tween learning and experience.

Furthermore, while there can be little doubt that the past several decades have seen an unprecedented diffusion of some of the values and life-styles of some of the most highly industrialized Western states and the near suffocation of many less-aggressive cultures, there is some doubt as to whether that diffusion is unavoidable and much doubt as to whether it is desirable or universally desired.

Any assessment of the achievements of the "West" must surely weigh in the balance its failures and self-destructive tendencies as well. Anthro-pologist Johannes Wilbert has pointed out, for example, that observance of the loving care with which some of the so-called "primitive" peoples of the Amazon Basin attempt to protect their ecological systems makes us look quite primitive by comparison.

Blaming the Victim

A director of the U.S. Agency for International Development in northeast Brazil, justifying the agency's efforts in 1963–1964 to undermine Brazil's regional development agency for the severely depressed Northeast, said, "They didn't see their problems as clearly as we felt we did."[6] All too of-ten, U.S. officials in the post–World War II period have structured events in the Third World on the assumption that the problems in Africa, Asia, and Latin America lay in the quality of Africans, Asians, and Latin Amer-icans. The blame for poverty and powerlessness has been placed squarely on the poor and powerless. It has followed, then, that the impo-sition of foreign models on their societies has been for their own good.

The tendency to blame the victim is by no means peculiar to the field of development. Means of explaining inequality so as to justify it were sys-tematized in religion and philosophy long before such was undertaken by modern social science. Conservative Catholic thought, which has pre-vailed in Iberia and Latin America, at least until recently, and has enjoyed a revival in Eastern and Central Europe in the 1990s, held that the exist-ing social hierarchy was an expression of divine will (rather than, say, the outcome of a bloody conquest). Hindu rationalization was even more to the point: The higher castes were being rewarded in this life, as lower castes and outcastes were being punished, for their behavior in a previous incarnation.

The rationalization most common in the contemporary United States—an adaptation of the so-called Protestant Ethic—is even more devastatingly effective, more emboldening to the rich and demeaning and debilitating to the poor; it is that one's station is reflective of virtue or shame (e.g., of industriousness and thrift versus laziness and profligacy) in *this* life.

The business of explaining and promoting development probably has more than its share of the selfless and empathetic. Even so, traces of this ethic are sprinkled among the terms that have come into common usage. A number of perfectly good words have been devalued as a consequence of their use as euphemisms. Ideology, for example, has been used to designate the pursuit of self-interest by "have-nots." The pursuit of self-interest by "haves," on the other hand, has been labeled pragmatism.

Words like *secularism* and *rationalism,* used to distinguish modern societies from traditional ones, are often defined in circular fashion, thinly veiling the implication that they refer to the thought processes of clear-headed folks like us. Any attempt to define them in more precise terms runs the risk of making self-serving theories susceptible to empirical testing. Secularism in its most limited formulation connotes low receptivity to religious and ideological appeals, hardly a characteristic of the supposedly modern contemporary United States.

Rationalism is sometimes clarified by reference to such poles of Parsonian pattern variables as value instrumental action.[7] In theory, instrumentality should be an operationalizable concept, but even psychiatrists and clinical psychologists are hard put to determine whether the behavior of their patients is instrumental. And yet, we presume to know enough about the values and options available to a few billion people to determine whose behavior is instrumental and whose is not.

While there is an obvious correlation between national levels of wealth and industrialization and levels of formal education and literacy, formal education is not the only kind of education and illiteracy is not the same as ignorance, much less irrationality. Our assumption that non-Westernized folk are less rational than we are says more about our rationality problems than about theirs, and our assumption that the illiterate are ignorant is a projection of our own ignorance of them.

Certainly a glance at folklore challenges the view that the poor are ignorant of their own needs or of why they are not being met. The "Juan Bimbo" of Venezuelan rural folklore and the "roto" of Chilean shantytown humor are not subservient, grateful clients; they are shrewd operators who feign humility while trying to outsmart their patrons.

It may well be true, as Brazilian educator Paulo Freire has claimed, that "self-depreciation is a characteristic of the oppressed, which derives from their internalization of the opinion the oppressors hold of them."[8] But there is a very important shade of difference between self-esteem and sense of efficacy. The "fatalistic" conviction so often noted among the Third World peasantry that efforts to organize in pursuit of class interests would be dangerous and probably futile is empirically well grounded. It might be that a sense of efficacy on the part of the severely and systematically repressed would be beneficial to the society as a whole in the long run, but, as John Maynard Keynes said, "In the long run we're all dead"; and in the short run it could be quite suicidal.

Limiting the Options

In the late 1980s, U.S.-born Jesuit economist Peter Marchetti, who had been among the intellectual pathfinders of the Nicaraguan revolution, hosted an informal gathering in Managua for students and young Sandinista activists. The group's discussion generally centered on means of dealing with the country's dire economic problems. One of the guests, a middle-aged foreigner, tended to dominate the conversation with suggestions of expensive, highly centralized, high-tech approaches that the young Nicaraguans viewed as absurdly inappropriate. After he left, the local guests asked Marchetti why he had invited "that American businessman." Marchetti replied that that was no American businessman; that was a Soviet technical adviser.[9]

A Third World perspective that virtually equates First and Second World approaches to development, that views those approaches not as alternative ones but as the same inappropriate one, becomes increasingly widespread as the world shrinks and as the failures of large-scale development programs mount. Such a perspective must be disconcerting to many development theorists, policymakers, and practitioners of the overdeveloped world. The Cold War worldview, which has supplied the overriding rationale for most major programs and disbursements of foreign assistance by major First World donors, particularly the United States, has held that Third World countries have two options, and only two—dog eat dog or all eat dog—for organizing their societies and their economies. Those who would reject whatever is being marketed at a given moment as "private enterprise" are opting, by definition, for a "centrally planned economy," or "communism." At times, spokesmen of the Second World have appeared to be projecting the same message.

The end of the Cold War has actually sharpened the edges of that dichotomy, as those who would take exception to the arguments and policy implications of the prevailing neoliberalism are portrayed as opting for the model employed by failed and discredited Communist regimes. The same phony dichotomy is employed to discount both locally appropriate and promising experiments in developing countries and tried and true social democratic mixed economy models in the highly developed European states.

For most of the Third World in the postwar period, modernization has meant exposure to the influences, if not the dictates, of the First World. Such exposure has not, on balance, contributed to a narrowing of the gap either between rich and poor nations or between rich and poor within Third World nations. Per capita income in the poorest region of the world, Sub-Saharan Africa, dropped from $560 in 1980 to $450 (in 1980 dollars) in 1988. During the same period, per capita income in the industrialized countries increased from $11,000 to $13,000.[10]

True, the 1980s was a decade of devastating recession for much of the Third World, and particularly for Africa and Latin America, where economies shrank by 20 percent and 8 percent respectively. But the growth spurts, in some cases quite dramatic ones, of the 1990s have served only to widen income gaps. In 1994, the ratio of income of the richest 20 percent of the global population to that of the poorest 20 percent was 78 to 1, up from 30 to 1 in 1960. The number of billionaires worldwide increased between 1989 and 1996 from 157 to 447. The net worth of the world's ten wealthiest individuals amounts to one and one-half times the total national income of the forty-eight countries designated by the United Nations Development Program to be the least developed.[11]

Moreover, in the 1980s and 1990s the gap within was widening relentlessly in the First World's most recent colonial and neocolonial centers—Great Britain and the United States—and those two states exhibited other strong indicators as well of "de-development."[12]

While the U.S. economy boomed in 1997 and the richest 5 percent of the population gained an average of $6,400 (not counting capital gains), the poorest 20 percent of families saw their incomes decline by an average of $210.[13] Even so, staggering under unanticipated burdens of environmental contamination, resource depletion, inflation, unemployment, and, above all, debt, Third World nations may have little choice but to look to the First World for loans, credit, or "relief." And the leveraged policy changes on which aid and credit have been conditional have meant little choice also as to where to look for policy guidance. What path Third World leaders might choose if they had real choice remains an open question.

Then what of the model so recently offered by the Second World? Did it not promise a means more just and more readily sustainable of escaping underdevelopment? But alas, true socialism had no more of a reign in the Second World than did true liberalism in the First; as the twentieth century draws to a close, true socialism is utterly without a forum and the only true liberals to be found are bearing the socialist standard. As liberalism was to provide a platform for a previously excluded middle class, socialism was to be the vehicle for drawing the working class into political participation. As it turned out, the concept of a working-class state was not left devoid of all meaning; but as a new bureaucratic class assumed responsibility for major decisions, workers were left with control only of their own workplaces. The upshot, as a Polish sociologist expressed it to this author, was "a massive conspiracy by Poles as workers against Poles as consumers."[14]

Even if a Second World model remained intact, such a model, with its assumption that bigger is better and its stress on centralized decision-making and on production for its own sake, without regard for environmental constraints or for consumer preferences, would hardly be attractive to the contemporary Third World. Though many of the elements of that model remain intact—e.g., large-scale bureaucracies and centralized decision-making—the major actors are increasingly private rather than public and responsible to markets and managers even farther removed from the local populations. From the People's Republic of China through the shards of the ex–Soviet Union and what used to be its East European bloc, regardless of the labels and histories of national leaders, "capitalist roaders" have the road all to themselves. Already, though, these newly overhauled vehicles must negotiate not only the bottlenecks of the model they are fleeing but also the washouts of the world system they would join. Most are mired in debt and sinking under inflation or austerity or both. The question now that the Second World has closed down is which of its peoples will succeed in attaching themselves to the First World and which will tumble helplessly into the Third.

The smugness of the First World's cold warriors at this turn of events is inappropriate to say the least. The winners, if there are such, of the Cold War are not those countries that fought it but those that avoided its extremes, that were able to make the most of both free-market competition and government intervention in the public interest to generate dynamic economies underpinned by comprehensive social-welfare systems. Meanwhile, the worst of both worlds—of bureaucratic rigor mortis coupled with the utter unavailability or unaffordability of essential goods and services for large sectors of the population—is all too familiar in the Third World. But that is not to say that all options have been exhausted. There remain as many options as there are people with ideas and commitment to the common good.

Speaking in Tongues: The Communication Problem

Despite the fact that no single discipline can lay exclusive claim to the study of development, the potential for escape from disciplinary shackles and reintegration of the social sciences afforded by the topic has not been fully exploited. Most studies falling under the rubric of development have found their points of departure in a single discipline and have failed to deal adequately with the interactions among cultural, social, economic, and political phenomena or have failed to take advantage of the insights that might be drawn from work in other disciplines. It seems, in fact, that the greater the volume of literature devoted to development, the more it gets pigeonholed into subcategories.

In addition to the gaps among disciplines, the gap that most needs to be bridged is that between theory and practice. Most of our theoretical approaches are pitched at a level too abstract—too global in purview, too dependent on aggregate data, in general too far removed from the workaday world of the would-be beneficiaries—to be much help to those who would actually design and/or implement projects in areas steeped in poverty. At the same time, there is an accumulated wealth of folk wisdom derived from on-the-job training that has yet to inform the theoretical literature. For the most part, theoreticians and practitioners appear to occupy different worlds and perhaps even speak different languages; at any rate, they are too infrequently found talking to each other.

There is also a breach between those who deal in the hardware of development (that is, the technology, appropriate or otherwise) and those who deal in the software (techniques of management and training); and there is a further breach between both of those categories and those who concern themselves, as scholars or practitioners, with the sociocultural, political, or environmental impacts of those technologies and techniques.

This is not to say that specialization is a negative development; it may be, in fact, a very necessary one. But with it comes an ever greater need for reintegration and cross-fertilization. This book does not pretend to satisfy that need; it does aspire, though, to call attention to it, to move the discourse in the indicated direction, and to make a modest contribution to the development of "appropriate" theory.

Appropriate Technology and Appropriate Theory

Appropriate technology has sometimes been misconceived by advocates of Third World interests as necessarily referring to an older or lower order of technology. Such advocates have bristled at the idea of their countries being locked permanently into a lower order of productivity and their people subjected to unnecessary rigors in the accomplishment of potentially simple tasks. But the concept of appropriate technology does not apply to a particular level of technology; rather, it applies to a particular attitude about technology.

It rejects the "law of the instrument" approach to the selection of technology, whether the instrument be of high technology or low, in favor of selection based on a well-informed assessment of need and sustainability.

Such an assessment would take into account shortage or surplus in the labor force; the particular roles and needs of the prospective employees or consumers; the availability of the resources needed for its operation; the impact of the new technology on community integrity and on the environment; and a host of other factors.

Perhaps the best indicator of the appropriateness of a particular technology or tool is its adoption, spontaneously, by a client or beneficiary community. The Kayapo Indian town of Gorotire, in the Brazilian Amazon, was selected by nonindigenous Brazilian investors in the 1980s to be the site of a gold mine. In the course of gaining access to the site and acceptance in the community, the visiting Brazilians recorded local dances on videotape and played back the tape to the villagers. As to the proceeds of the mine, the bargain struck, after extensive negotiation, was that the Brazilians would turn over to the Indians 10 percent of the returns for a designated period. After the mine began to produce, the Brazilians delivered 0.10 percent rather than 10 percent, telling local community leaders that they had misunderstood, or were misrepresenting, the outcome of their negotiations. When the Brazilians returned to Gorotire some time later for a subsequent bargaining session, they found that the session was being videotaped by the Kayapo.[15]

By the same token, the appropriateness of a theory with respect to development might be judged, to some degree, by its usefulness to those most in need—particularly organizers and members of low-income communities in the Third World and in pockets of poverty in the First and Second Worlds. Just as an inclination to appropriate technology does not imply rejection of high technology, the pursuit of appropriate theory does not imply the rejection of grand or macro theory but rather calls for the development of linkages that would facilitate cross-fertilization.

A new body of midlevel theory might bring more of the findings of the various social sciences to bear on the work of planners and make implementers, or field agents, less vulnerable to blindsiding—to seeing their projects sabotaged by sponsoring agencies, local leaders, or supposed beneficiaries. Likewise, such theory might strengthen local leaders in their dealings with high-pressure donor agencies. At any rate a theory, like the now-prevailing neoliberalism, that merely justifies the generalization and deepening of poverty and inequality, offering only the ahistorical promise of convergence through market-regulated trickle-down over time, is of little use to those waiting to be trickled on.

The social sciences, like the supposedly harder ones, have often succumbed to the law of the instrument. The availability of aggregate data and machines for crunching it has led us to portray human needs and governmental or societal performance in excessively compartmentalized ways. We may then take satisfaction in increases in aggregate income that in fact come at the expense of disaggregated community. We may fail to understand why target populations are less than enthusiastic about new opportunities extended by donor agencies or why benefits never seem to reach those sectors for whom they are allegedly intended.

Furthermore, those who deal in grand theory are understandably, perhaps necessarily, drawn to models that reduce actors to ideal types and predict behavior on the basis of a very limited number of factors. As anyone who has ever worked in development at the village level knows, the unexpected always happens. That is surely unavoidable; no model could possibly encompass all the factors. It makes a very great deal of difference, however, which factors are included and which excluded and how the predilections of actors are assessed. Economists in particular have tended to hold politics as a constant and to assume a profit-motivated "rationality." Greater familiarity by the theorists with the experience of the practitioners might lead to a more useful choice of factors and more realistic expectations of actors.

Have the theoreticians and planners alike failed to note that the greater the sums of money that have been spent on development in a particular locale, the less promising have been the prospects that any gains for the majority of supposed beneficiaries will be sustained? The fact that such sums in themselves generally denote inappropriate technology and inadequate planning only partially explains the frequency of spectacular failures. Nor do the inordinate overhead costs and the inevitable corruption that attach to big money projects provide sufficient explanation. Since the biggest investments in development kick in only when vested interests are perceived to be threatened, some skepticism as to the veracity of the stated goals of donor organizations might be in order. There would remain, of course, the very important questions as to whether donors', planners', and implementers' goals are in harmony and whether any of those goals are likely to be reflected in outcomes. And for the locale in question, even making benign and optimistic assumptions on other aspects of motive and outcome, there remain the legacies of dependency and debt.

Given all the factors likely to impede the development process, perhaps it is the occasional success that should most spark our curiosity. At any rate, if we are to push back the frontier of our ignorance and to find new patterns in the seeming chaos of development, we might start with a new order of questions, one that builds on what we know about interest and power relationships and organizational behavior, that idealizes neither supposed benefactors nor supposed beneficiaries—in short, one that addresses the real world, warts and all. Moreover, if we are to have any positive impact on the ongoing development process, we would do well to position ourselves at the intersection between the real world and the official world and to ask how we might cut down the number of wrecks at that intersection.

Such questions and, in general, the nature of interests and interactions among the many categories of protagonists in the development process will be dealt with in Part 4 of this volume. In the meantime, however, we will address ourselves also to a broader set of questions: What is meant by development? How is it explained? How is it measured? How is it planned, promoted, funded, and implemented by First World donors? By Third World governments? How is it sustained? And finally, what are its limits?

Notes

1. As noted by Leonard Frank, "The Development Game," *Granta* 20, winter 1986, pp. 229–243.

2. United Nations Development Program [UNDP], *Human Development Report 1997* (Oxford: Oxford University Press, 1997), p. 165.

3. Data compiled by the Madras Institute of Development Studies, 1988.

4. Immanuel Wallerstein, ed., *World Inequality: Origins and Perspectives on the World System* (Montreal: Black Rose Books, 1975), pp. 12–28.

5. One of the columnist Ashleigh Brilliant's "pot-shots," or "unpoemed titles," syndicated 1975.

6. Peter D. Bell, "Brazilian-American Relations," *Brazil in the Sixties*, ed. Riordan Roett (Nashville: Vanderbilt University Press, 1972), chap. 3.

7. Talcott Parsons, *The Evolution of Societies*, ed. and with an introduction by Jackson Toby (Englewood Cliffs: Prentice Hall, 1977).

8. Cited in Coleman McCarthy, "Thinkers and Their Thoughts: Paulo Freire and Educating the Oppressed," *Washington Post*, July 31, 1972.

9. As told to the author by Peter Marchetti, Managua, January 1987.

10. Clive Crook, "The Third World: Survey," *Economist*, September 23, 1989 (special section, p. 3).

11. UNDP, 1997, Chapter 2.

12. The Washington, D.C.-based Center on Budget and Policy Priorities reported that in 1990 the top 1 percent of the U.S. population would have almost the same after-tax income as the bottom 40 percent. The report also noted that the share of the national income going to middle-income Americans had fallen to the lowest level since the end of World War II.

13. Editorial, *The Nation* 266, no. 2, January 12–19, 1998, p. 3.

14. Pawel Spiewak, sociologist and editor of *Republica* (Warsaw), June 1987.

15. The British Broadcasting Corporation aired a documentary feature on the Kayapo on June 3, 1987.

PART ONE

Development in Theory:
Meanings and Models

2 Defining Development and Its Nemesis

Development, it has been noted, is a user-friendly term, having virtually as many potential meanings as potential users. If there is a commonality among its many uses, it might be in denoting enhancement, that is, increasing value or desirability; but that leads us once again back to subjectivity. The business of the land developer may be seen in very negative terms by community leaders or environmentalists. Likewise, the very limited concept of economic development now current among city and state governments in the United States and elsewhere—an elaborated version of the "cargo cult" designed to attract industry[1]—may be anathema to organized labor; pliable labor is assumed to be a prerequisite.

What so complicates the study of international, or Third World, development, however, is that the most commonly adopted meanings (and thus explanations and strategies) do not simply differ; from diagnosis to prescription, they are almost diametric opposites. Development is a standard borne by those who would promote the interests of the affluent and the powerful as well as by those who would serve the unaffluent and the unpowerful; by those who would expand the reach of the most-industrialized states and those who would shield the least-modernized from nefarious influences; by those who would stress the virtues of entrepreneurship and individualism and those who would nurture community and collective concerns; by those who would pursue strategies of top-down initiative and decision-making and those who advocate a bottom-up, or grass-roots, approach; and finally, by those who would exploit and maim Mother Nature for the benefit of either business or labor in today's world, as well as by those who concern themselves with a bountiful and livable environment for future generations.

The divergence of interpretations begins with the diagnosis of the central problem. In the late 1950s and early 1960s, when international development assistance was becoming a major enterprise and the academic community was laying out the rationales that were to support it, it was generally assumed that traditionalism was the problem and modernization was the solution. Dealing now with the flotsam of modernization, more-recent generations of theorists and practitioners are tempted to search for grounding in tradition.

Identifying the Problem

When much of the now-designated Third World was beginning to emerge from colonialism and poverty was becoming "underdevelopment," the problems seemed more than obvious to First World scholars. In some countries, the sharp skewing of land distribution resulted in poor land use as well as in concentration of profit and economic power. In others, the soil lacked nutrients, farming techniques had not changed since biblical times, and social and political organizations were highly fragmented. Subsistence farming and handcrafting of consumer goods generated no surplus for investment or for insurance against nature's tantrums. The most basic elements of infrastructure, such as roads, bridges, and dams, were primitive or nonexistent, and productivity was further stymied by the lack of health care and education. The solution seemed equally obvious: a transplantation of the clearly superior technologies (modes of production, e.g., industrialization), institutions, and ultimately habits and values from West to non-West, or First World to Third.

By the late 1960s and to a far greater extent by the late 1990s, the thrust of late industrialization and other manifestations of the diffusion of "Western" culture had brought about dramatic changes. In demographics, one of the most consequential changes was urbanization. According to United Nations (UN) figures, the world's urban population, which had stood at 28.9 percent of the total in 1950, had risen to 45 percent by 1994 and was expected to reach 47 percent by 2000. Another change was the population explosion, which owed much to the diffusion of modern sanitation and medicine. World population continued to grow by some 80 million a year in the late 1990s. Estimated at 2.9 billion in 1960, it had almost doubled by 1994 and was expected to double again, to more than 11 billion, by 2045.[2]

In social organization there had been a considerable breakdown of extended family or tribal ties and a partial regrouping in such organizations as unions and parties. Social structure was also transformed, as the expansion of commerce and the growth of government itself generated middle classes, and industrialization gave rise to urban working classes.

In political organization, social and technological changes led generally to a weakening of regional caudillos or tribal leaders and to a greater concentration of power in the central government of the state. New patterns of trade, new modes of production, and increased productivity transformed the traditional market basket, resulting in the availability of a greater quantity and variety of consumer goods. And changes in attitude were manifest in rejection of communal ties and values and the embracing of consumerism.

What Price "Progress"?

There is no denying that the diffusion, or recycling, of the products and attendant social features of the vanguard of technology has brought many blessings to the Third World. But those are mixed blessings, to say the least, and the mix has often favored only a minority. Let's start with demographics. Although the provision of sanitation facilities and health-care services remains woefully inadequate in most countries, modern medicine has truly changed the face of the earth, bringing about dramatic improvement in infant- and maternal-mortality rates and thus in life expectancy. For the less-developed countries (LDCs) as a whole, life expectancy has risen over the past half-century from forty-one years to about sixty-three. One of the upshots, of course, of this modern miracle is what has come to be known as the population explosion. The explosion is often allotted the lion's share of the blame for the failure of development, or the failure of development to benefit the teeming masses of the Third World. (It is usually overlooked that rapid population growth was probably a precondition for the rapid economic growth that is seen by so many as the primary goal and manifestation of development.) The draconian measures for reducing the growth rate instituted briefly in India and over a longer term in China had many negative consequences, including exacerbation of the practice of female infanticide. Such measures are not likely to serve as models for other countries. Population growth drops somewhat with urbanization, but urbanization, with all its attendant problems, is hardly to be encouraged. The only benign formula we know of for dramatically reducing the growth rate is widely shared prosperity with greater opportunities, in particular, for women.

Urbanization has made possible the provision of such amenities as electricity and running water and such service institutions as hospitals and public schools. Indeed, as in health, gains in education, and particularly in literacy, have been impressive. The frantic pace of urbanization, however, and the sheer size of urban concentrations in some Third World countries have placed a severe strain on municipal governments, resulting in extensive pockets of urban anarchy. And the population explosion has meant that on a global basis, while the absolute numbers of well-fed, literate persons rise, so do the numbers of the hungry and illiterate. The World Health Organization reported in 1989 that 1 in every 5 persons on earth—about 1 billion people—is suffering from malnutrition or disease. And the United Nations Children's Fund (UNICEF) estimated that 50 million infants will die of hunger and malnutrition in the 1990s. The United Nations Development Program (UNDP) found that while the proportion of the world's population classified as income poor, trying to get by on less that U.S. $1 a day, declined between 1987 and 1993 from 34 to 32 percent, the absolute numbers increased from 1.2 billion to 1.3 billion. And 100 million of them were in the relatively affluent industrialized countries.

Urbanization, along with technological advances, has facilitated the spread of the communications media, enhancing the distribution of information, but also of misinformation and of propaganda. It has also led to traffic congestion, pollution, and street crime. Progress in curing such respiratory diseases as tuberculosis has been offset by the development of new respiratory ailments resulting from the constant inhaling of gasoline fumes, particularly from diesel fuel, and other pollutants.

Changes in social organization have weakened the constraints imposed by family and community on individual behavior, dissolving patron-client networks, mitigating such practices as nepotism, and freeing the individual to choose his or her own locales, associates, and professions. But the same change process weakens also the socialization and security provided by extended families and traditional communities without necessarily generating enough jobs or social-welfare services to compensate for the loss. In fact, late industrialization, typically capital intensive, has scarcely begun to absorb the workforce so rapidly being pushed off the land or pulled by the attractions of the metropolis and swollen by the population explosion. Thus the new freedom may well be of the sort that means "nothing left to lose"—freedom to wander jobless, homeless, and hungry in alienated isolation. The streets of Bogotá, Bombay, and so many other cities have become cruel homes and schools for untold thousands of urchins, and this aspect of the Third World increasingly lurks beyond the gilded gates of the First World as well.

Socioeconomic changes have made possible new, more effective forms of political organization, resulting, in some cases, in the dissolution of feudal patterns; reinforced central governments have acquired greater capabilities for public service but also, given the expansion of military, paramilitary, and police forces, for surveillance and repression.

The new consumerism may have accelerated production and the creation of jobs. In fact, such attitudinal change may have been a necessary concomitant to the expansion of domestic markets, but it also increased demands for imports and contributed to burgeoning debt. Furthermore, it has generated an array of new problems. In India, for example, the new materialism is generally credited with the phenomenon of dowry abuse (see discussion in Chapter 8).

The spread of the new consumerism has not necessarily been reflected in the generation of a correspondingly large category of new consumers. The economic development strategy popular in the 1950s and 1960s that featured import-substitution industrialization was generally characterized by a simple transfer of technologies and product lines from First World to Third. Technologies thus were capital intensive and product lines catered to the middle and upper classes. The combination of production geared for the few and increasing demand by the many fed inflation and frustration and, in general, contributed to a climate of crisis.

Development planners might have met this crisis by increasing the range and volume of products to cater to the working classes and by taking other steps to accelerate the expansion of domestic markets, but the political and economic implications of such a commitment were generally frightening to elites. Thus, the most common reaction was that of dampening effective demand—in some cases so abruptly and by measures so harsh that military dictatorship seemed called for. Subsequently, planners, prodded by the International Monetary Fund (IMF) and other public and private creditors, turned again to an emphasis on production (often highly mechanized) for export, a strategy wherein the masses streaming into the cities were needed neither as workers nor as consumers. Meanwhile, land previously devoted to subsistence farming had been converted for export production.

Increasing landlessness is a particularly acute problem in much of the world, and development programs have done little to remedy it; in fact, such programs have sometimes made it worse. Richer farmers more readily have access to newly available products, technologies, and credit; and the enhanced value of the land tempts those richer farmers to buy out or push out their struggling tenants or neighbors. The alienation of the land—whether by force of arms or by market forces—has led, in many countries, to scarcity of basic foodstuffs and inflation of food prices. It has led to bloated urban labor forces and to ever-larger and more-desperate pools of migratory farm laborers. It has contributed to famine in Africa and to insurgency in Central America. Finally, it has contributed, in overdeveloped and underdeveloped states alike, to the ultimate, most profound kind of dependency, in which only a privileged or isolated few have the option of producing what they would consume or of consuming what they produce.

The Reckoning

For many Third World countries modernization has brought spurts of rapid economic growth. For a number of them—especially the so-called NICs (Newly Industrialized Countries)—it has brought about a major transformation in the nature of goods produced and exported, from unprocessed primary goods to processed ones, for example, or from primary goods to manufactured ones. A few countries that at midcentury were strictly dependent on wildly fluctuating markets for primary goods are competing now with the major powers in the marketing of state-of-the-art military hardware and other high-tech products. A few—but fewer still (Asia's "gang of four" [see Chapter 6], for example)—have even experienced rapid growth and economic transformation and at the same time achieved a more nearly egalitarian distribution.

For the great majority, however, modernization has been accompanied by chronic unemployment, chronic inflation, unpayable debts, denationalization of resources, environmental degradation, and a deepening of dependency. In the case of dependency, direct political ties between colony or client state and the metropole may have become attenuated and economic ties of investment, trade, and aid may have been diversified, but subsistence farming, almost everywhere under assault, threatens to go the way of subsistence hunting and fishing, and handicrafts have become virtually dependent on tourism for their survival. The world capitalist system has penetrated the steepest mountain ranges, the steamiest jungles, and the loneliest islands; and the community, in First World or Third, that does not depend for its livelihood on decisions made in faraway places by people unconcerned about its welfare is very rare indeed.

Empowerment and Sustainability: An Alternate Vision

The mainstream of development professionals, pursuing the path of least resistance, continues to treat development—in practice if not always in rhetoric—as a top-down process. That implies control of decision-making by major donors in centers of established power; the diffusion of technology and other attributes of modernization from those centers to areas less fully integrated into the international economic system; the assumption of trickle-down of material benefits from those best positioned to profit from public or private investment to the neediest; and enhanced productivity as the goal and the evidence of development. Productivity, in turn, is measured in the currency values attached to goods and services.

The tendency to measure value, and thus development, in monetary terms is hardly surprising, given the fact that, at least in the most direct and immediate sense, money is what most of us work for. Nevertheless, as the United Nations First Development Decade (1961–1971) gave way to the second, a growing number of theoreticians and practitioners of development were concluding that material product is the wrong goal and the wrong measure.[3] They refused to see socioeconomic change as developmental unless it proves to be nurturing, liberating, even energizing to the unaffluent and unpowerful. The focus, they said, should be on the animate rather than the inanimate—on human rather than material resources. The measure of enhanced value should be in the quality of life, including not only creature comforts and productive and creative capacity but also self-reliance and capacity to interact effectively with one's physical and social environment.

The bottom-up approach, designated in the 1980s in its most elaborated and ambitious form as empowerment, calls for attention to health and education, of course, but also to more effective locally based problem-solving techniques. Like some programs of the 1960s—generally meagerly funded ones—the approach encompasses the promotion of community development through self-help, but with greater emphasis on the process itself rather than on the completion of particular projects. Also, in the 1980s and 1990s, emphasis has been on the sustainability of the process enabling collective decision-making and collective action as well as any labor-saving or income-producing outcomes of such action.

Theoreticians and practitioners of bottom-up, or grass-roots, development note that environmental sustainability requires not only the guardianship of nature's regenerative capacity but also full support for the forward guard. The only reliable guardians of any ecological system are the people who know it, depend on it, and do not have the option of leaving.

The role of the development practitioner or change agent in such an approach is that of catalyst and information broker rather than of decision-maker or information giver, that of promoting self-reliance rather than dependency. It is not an easy role. Seeing promise in the recultivation of traditional ways, development specialists often feel that they are swimming upstream; the attractiveness to Third World peoples of modern ways and gadgets makes for a powerful current.

Notes

1. In the modern elaborated version, localities, states, and nations seeing economic development as an exogenous force to be attracted build not only landing strips (airports) but also golf courses, convention centers, industrial parks, and the like. Strategies for attracting investment usually also include tax holidays or other fiscal incentives and various means of assuring that labor will be cheap and cooperative.

2. United Nations Development Program, *Human Development Report 1997* (Oxford: Oxford University Press, 1997), pp. 194–195.

3. See Jorge Nef, "Development Processes: Contradictions Between Theory and Practice," *Worldscape* (Center for International Programs, University of Guelph, Ontario, Canada) 3, no. 1, spring 1989, pp. 7–9; and Lester B. Pearson et al., *Partners in Development: Report of the Commission on International Development* (New York: Praeger, 1969).

Suggested Readings

Adelman, I., and C. T. Morris, *Economic Growth and Social Equity in Developing Countries* (Stanford: Stanford University Press, 1973).

Barnett, Tony, *Social and Economic Development: An Introduction* (New York: Guilford Press, 1989).

Chomsky, Noam, *World Orders Old and New* (New York: Columbia University Press, 1994).

Deacon, Bob, with Michelle Hulse and Paul Stubbs, *Global Social Policy: International Organizations and the Future of Welfare* (London: Sage Publications, 1993).

George, Susan, *How the Other Half Dies: The Real Reasons for World Hunger* (Montclair, N.J.: Allanheld, Osmond and Co., 1977).

Goulet, Dennis, *The Cruel Choice: A New Concept in the Theory of Development* (New York: Atheneum, 1973).

Harrington, Michael, *The Vast Majority: A Journey to the World's Poor* (New York: Simon & Schuster, 1977).

Harrison, Paul, *Inside the Third World: The Anatomy of Poverty*, 2nd ed. rev. (Harmondsworth, UK: Penguin Books, 1987).

Hayter, Teresa, *The Creation of World Poverty: An Alternative View to the Brandt Report* (London: Pluto Press, 1982).

Hirschman, Albert O., *Journeys Toward Progress* (New York: Twentieth Century Fund, 1963).

Independent Commission on International Development, Willy Brandt, Chairperson, *North-South: A Program for Survival* (Cambridge: MIT Press, 1980).

Isbister, John, *Promises Not Kept: The Betrayal of Social Change in the Third World* (West Hartford, Conn.: Kumarian Press, 1993).

Khor, Martin, *The Future of North-South Relations: Conflict or Cooperation?* (Penang: Third World Network, 1992).

Nef, Jorge, *Human Security and Mutual Vulnerability: An Exploration into the Global Political Economy of Development and Underdevelopment* (Ottawa: International Development Research Center, 1995).

Safa, H. I., ed., *Toward a Political Economy of Urbanization in Third World Countries* (New Delhi: Oxford University Press, 1982).

Saul, John Ralston, *The Unconscious Civilization* (London: Penguin Books, 1997).

Thomas, A., and H. Bernstein, *The Third World and Development* (London: Open University Press, 1983).

Uphoff, N., and W. Ilchman, *The Political Economy of Development* (Berkeley: University of California Press, 1972).

3 Explaining Development: Theories and Models

Any attempt to characterize competing models of development is handicapped by overlap and underlap and fuzziness at the margins. Most dichotomies coincide to some degree with what might be labeled First World and Third World perspectives. Such a division, however, fails to account for the fact that Third World elites, pursuing class interests as well as individual economic and political interests, often adopt First World perspectives, and that a great many scholars and practitioners of development from the First World choose to identify with the nonelites of the Third World.

We might circumvent the fallacies of a territorial approach by speaking of concentrational versus redistributive, or elitist versus egalitarian, approaches, but such categorization would call for imputing to some players motives and values that are not acknowledged. We will begin therefore by segregating models and approaches into two very broad categories having their modern theoretical and philosophical roots in Europe in the eighteenth and nineteenth centuries. The categories had in common the assumption that progress, or development, was possible and desirable, but they differed in that one viewed the economic interests of nations and classes as being in harmony while the other viewed those interests as being in conflict. Not surprisingly, the states promoting the view of harmonious interests have been those that were expanding their economic horizons and seeking to penetrate markets previously closed by colonial arrangements or nationalistic protectionism. Those same states, however, have not been averse to placing pragmatism over principle when their own interests called for protecting domestic markets or colonial or neocolonial relations. In fact, due to the fierce trade competition the United States encountered during the 1980s and early 1990s from Japan and the so-called Asian tigers, the familiar call for "free" trade was often supplanted by a call for "fair" trade.

Assuming Harmonic Interests

Liberal Internationalist School

The Liberal Internationalist School attributes its paternity to Adam Smith, author of *The Wealth of Nations* (1776). Developed in reaction to mercantilism, which held that the maximization of a nation's wealth called for strict governmental control of international trade and investment and other economic activities, the new theory was a progressive one, holding that wealth and opportunity then monopolized by courts and colonizers should be redistributed through free and competitive enterprise to a new class of merchants and entrepreneurs operating their own businesses. Smith, however, recognized the danger of the evolution of monopolies and advocated strict governmental regulation to prevent such a development.

Like persons and places and religions, theories that acquire celebrity status—and thus usefulness to the powerful—become caricatures of themselves or their original versions; liberalism was no exception. As the theory came to be championed by an expansive Great Britain in the nineteenth century and by the United States in the twentieth century, its qualifiers faded and its progressive features were transformed. The surviving core of the theory held that states had a common interest in the free flow of goods, services, and capital across national borders. Smith's laissez-faire principle was reinforced by David Ricardo's theory of comparative advantage. That theory posited that states should take advantage of their raw materials, low labor costs, technologies, or other strengths in order to specialize in those goods they could produce most efficiently while trading for goods in which other states had the advantage. In colonial and neocolonial systems, the advantage accrued, of course, to mother countries, not colonies.[1]

Development and Modernization Theorists

In the late 1950s and early 1960s, a group of scholars inspired by what appeared to be the virtually limitless opportunities and responsibilities of the United States in the postwar period began to build upon the principles of liberalism to explain economic growth and social change, or the lack of it, in the Third World. The approach posited that Third World states willing to eliminate trade barriers and other obstacles and to welcome investment and technological transfers from the industrialized states would be able to accelerate the development process. One of its proponents, Walt Rostow, even held that after achieving a stage he labeled "take-off," the process would be irreversible.[2]

Those approaching the issue from the discipline of economics chose to define development primarily in terms of economic growth and to measure it through aggregate data on gross national product (GNP) or per capita income, data that were blind to the skewing of income distribution. The accumulation, or concentration, of capital seen as necessary to promote growth was, at any rate, expected to be mitigated by a trickle-down effect. Other social sciences stressed the beneficial effects of the spread of Western-style education and communications and the attitudinal traits thus transmitted, such as rationalism, instrumentalism, and consumerism. The "revolution of rising expectations" was expected to accelerate social mobility, drawing more and more individuals previously steeped in tradition into the modern sector.

Political scientists weighed in with particular concerns for participation and institutionalization and their consequences with respect to stability. Samuel Huntington, for example, championed institutionalization, fearing that in its absence increasing participation would be destabilizing. Others saw structural differentiation, increasing governmental efficacy, or egalitarianism as more appropriate indicators.[3]

The scientific validation sought by scholars of the period eluded them, however, in part because their optimism, even implicit determinism, often led them to see what they wanted to see or to label whatever they saw as progress or development. Furthermore, their hesitance to acknowledge bias meant that arguments over values were generally presented as if they were over facts.

The optimism of that generation of scholars has been tempered by subsequent events: the spreading militarism of the 1970s, the economic deterioration of the 1980s, and, in the 1990s, the accelerating growth of inequality of wealth and income gaps between and within states. Nevertheless, paradigms underpinned by the assumption of harmonic interests continue to guide the major development programs of Western governments and international agencies.

Cultural Causation

One consequence of disappointment with political and economic trends in the Third World and of disillusionment with paradigms predictive of attitudinal and institutional change has been a reversion to emphasis on the explanatory power of culture as an independent variable. Cultural causation may well be the most common assumed or explicit explanation for differential reward and punishment in multicultural societies—local, national, or global. It predates the heyday of development and modernization theory and underpins much of the latter. In the case of orthodox economic models employing the "rational actor," cultural causation becomes a means of explaining why some actors seem more rational than others. Thus the assumption is made that some cultures are more conducive to democracy and to economic dynamism and prosperity than others. For elites in highly unequal societies, the approach has the virtue of directing explanation, and thus blame, for growing income gaps and attendant social disorder toward the presumed cultural weaknesses of disadvantaged groups.

Perhaps the most influential convert to theses of cultural causation is Samuel Huntington. Huntington, who had earlier professed that Third World modernization was both desirable and inevitable, in the 1980s suggested that non-Nordic cultures may prefer austerity, hierarchy, and authoritarianism to wealth, equity, and democracy. In the 1990s Huntington was arguing that the most important distinctions among people are cultural, that the newly emerging axis in world politics is between the West and the rest, and that the greatest threat to world peace in the foreseeable future will be that of a clash of civilizations. The civilizations he sees as most likely to pose future threats to the West are the Islamic and the Chinese.[4]

Interdependence

As we shall see, much of the turf of harmonious and discordant approaches alike was swallowed up in the 1980s by the encroachment of the new amalgamated discipline of international political economy. The concept of "interdependence," however, appears to encapsulate the tempered perspectives of the contemporary current in the harmonic interest approach. Deriving in part from attempts by Robert O. Keohane and Joseph S. Nye, among others, to deal with relations among industrialized states in the process of economic integration, the model (known in international relations theory as "transnational relations and complex interdependence") notes that many categories of actors other than nation-states—multinational corporations and transnational banks, for example—have gained importance in the international arena, and that economic issues and tools have become at least as important as national security issues and military force in molding relations among states.[5]

In analyzing relations between industrialized and developing states, theorists have noted a boomerang effect—that is, a new vulnerability on the part of the industrialized states to economic problems in the Third World. For example, although the high interest rates of the early 1980s in the First World, particularly the United States, were more devastating to the Third World than to the First, the consequent debt crisis in the Third World threatened the solvency of U.S. banks and closed markets for U.S. manufacturers. Likewise, Western creditors felt highly threatened by Mexico's peso crisis of 1994 and by the "meltdown" of East and Southeast Asian currencies in 1997.

Assuming Discordant Interests

Marxism and Marxism-Leninism

Karl Marx was not the first philosopher to call attention to social injustice; even among scholars who consider themselves non-Marxist or anti-Marxist, however, he is given a prominent place among the founding fathers of social science, since so many of the concepts and analytical tools he introduced or elaborated have come into general usage for discussing inequitable social relations.

Marx posited that the manner in which individuals and society meet their basic material needs takes primacy over religious, philosophical, cultural, and other considerations in determining the broad outlines of social organization and ideology. Differing material interests, based on how one earns a living—e.g., whether through ownership of land or other assets or only through labor—result in differing perceptions of social reality and relegate individuals and families into social classes. Class conflict, in earlier times between feudal landlords and a rising class of industrialists and in modern times between those lords of industry and finance, the ruling "bourgeoisie," and workers, or the "proletariat," then becomes the driving force underlying political and social strife.[6]

Drawing from Hegel the principle of historical dialecticism, Marx theorized that any mode of production would have built-in contradictions or self-destructive tendencies that would undermine it until eventually it was replaced by a mode that was more efficient. The most important contradiction he saw in the capitalist system was the draining off of "surplus value"—the gap between what workers earned for their labor and what they paid for goods and services—into profits. This gap would lead to overproduction and underconsumption—thus to economic depression—as workers became less and less able to buy what they produced. Eventually a desperate working class would rise up in spontaneous revolution and destroy capitalism, replacing it with a socialist system, in which the workers themselves would collectively own the means of production. After a transitional period in which the working class would control the state, the state would wither away, unneeded in a classless "communist" society.

Vladimir I. Lenin, an impatient activist as well as an intellectual, did not anticipate a "spontaneous" uprising of the working class. Rather, he believed it was the responsibility of a "vanguard" of professional revolutionaries to educate and organize the proletariat and to lead them in the assumption of their historic role.

More important, though, to future analysts of unequal relations among states was Lenin's theory of imperialism. Building on the work of J. A.

Hobson, Lenin asserted that capitalism had been able temporarily to circumvent the problem of overproduction through the conquest of foreign peoples and the establishment of overseas colonies. These colonies served as captive markets for the absorption both of surplus production and of surplus capital. According to his formulation, finance capital would become increasingly crucial to the process and would come to control manufacturing in the global economy.[7]

Dependency Theory

Whereas the Marxist-Leninist theory of imperialism seeks to explain why and how the dominant classes of the dominant capitalist powers expand their spheres of hegemony or control, dependency theory examines what this relationship of unequal bargaining and multilayered exploitation means to the dominated classes in the dominated countries. And whereas development and modernization theorists elaborated what they viewed as the *promises* of the diffusion of Western culture, technology, and money, dependency theorists (*dependentistas*) have seen such diffusion as an impediment to development, at least to development defined in terms of inclusiveness and egalitarianism.

Dependency theory, in a sense, represented the coming of age of a social science paradigm by and for the Third World. Its roots are to be found in the work of the UN Economic Commission for Latin America (ECLA) in the early 1960s, under the leadership of Argentinean economist Raúl Prebisch. He called attention to the deterioration in the terms of trade for producers of primary products and sought redress in Latin America through economic integration.

The search for means of understanding modern processes of perpetuating exploitative relations between First World and Third was carried on by other Latin Americans, notably Brazilians Fernando Henrique Cardoso and Teotonio dos Santos and Chilean Osvaldo Sunkel, along with German-American Andre Gunder Frank, who resided for many years in Chile.[8] It soon spread also to other Third World regions and to academic circles in the developed states. Whereas modernization and development theorists have been criticized for failure to concede biases and for confusing facts and values, *dependentistas* have been criticized for straightforward advocacy of radical social change.

The assumptions that underpin dependency theory are in many ways opposites of those that underpin development and modernization theory. They include the following: First, economic interest has primacy over culture or attitudes in determining the distribution of power and status in national and international arenas. Second, the causes of underdevelopment are not to be found in national systems alone but must be sought in the pattern of economic relations between hegemonic, or dominant, powers and their client states. The perpetuation of the pattern of inequality within client states is managed by a clientele class, which might be seen as the modern functional equivalent of a formal colonial apparatus. Third, both within and among states, the unfettered forces of the market-place tend to exacerbate rather than to mitigate existing inequalities. The dominant foreign power benefits at the expense of its client states, and the clientele class benefits at the expense of other classes.

Implicit here are the convictions that development will not take place through the trickle-down of wealth or through the gradual diffusion of modern attitudes and modern technology; that the upward mobility of individuals expressed by their gradual absorption into the modern sector is no solution to the problem of the impoverishment of the masses; and that stability is no virtue in a system of pronounced inequality.

Whereas modernization and development theorists see foreign invest-ment and foreign aid as critical to development in the Third World, de-pendency theorists see such investment and aid as means of exploitation, that is, of extracting capital from client states. Even where such transfers from the developed states generate economic growth, *dependentistas* would expect it to be a distorted pattern of growth that exacerbates in-equalities among classes as well as among regions within client states.

The Center-Periphery Model and World Systems Theory

The relationships hypothesized or described by dependency theorists have been incorporated by Norwegian scholar Johan Galtung into a model of elegant simplicity. According to the Center-Periphery Model, elites of the center, or metropolis, draw bounty from the periphery of their own state system (through taxes, for example) in order to be able to nurture and support co-opted elites of client or "peripheral" states. In turn, elites of those client states, dependent upon elites of the center for assistance in exploiting and suppressing their own peripheral popula-tions, have no choice but to allow center elites to participate in or share in the product of the exploitation of the peripheral peoples of the peripheral states.[9]

World systems theory, pioneered by Immanuel Wallerstein, also views the world economy as segmented into core and periphery areas. Rather than focusing on interactions among governments, however, this ap-proach calls attention to the transnational interactions of nonstate actors, particularly multinational corporations and banks. The international economy is said to be driven by economic elites, particularly of the devel-oped capitalist states, whose governments normally do their bidding. The control centers of the world economy are then the financial rather than the political capitals. The farther one lives from such a center, the slower the trickle-down of its wealth.[10]

Wallerstein, who sees the ideas of *dependentistas* as generally falling within the world systems perspective, takes issue with more traditional Marxists and liberals alike for what he calls a rigidly developmentalist approach. That is, both schools assume that each nation-state must pass through the same set of stages, or modes of extracting surplus, in the same order. As he sees it, the nation-state system, which came into being in part as a convenience to economic elites of an earlier era, has ceased to be the institutional base of the global economy. The essential struggle, then, is not between rich and poor states, but rather between rich and poor classes in a global society.

International Political Economy

The field of international political economy (IPE), which came into prominence in the 1970s and 1980s, has been said to constitute a synthesis of modernization and dependency approaches. Whether or not such a claim can be justified, IPE does embrace aspects of both approaches, particularly of their more modern Third World-focused versions, and it serves to diffuse, or perhaps confuse, what might otherwise appear a sharply polarized debate. At least in addressing Third World issues, the focus of international political economy theorists, like that of dependency theorists, tends to be on groups whose interests are defined with reference to social structure rather than on aggregate data relating to individual preferences. They seek to explain variation in class strength and behavior through comparative studies of agrarian production systems, industrial infrastructure, timing of development, and position in the world political economy. Drawing upon such class analysis, international political economy theorists generally accept the assertion of modernization theorists of a positive relationship between development and democracy. They accept also, to a point, the *dependentista* assertion that Third World countries have been disadvantaged by their participation in the global economy, but with the proviso that positive results have on occasion been achieved where Third World governments had the capacity to negotiate the conditions of their participation.

Thus the international political economy agenda recaptures the scope of nineteenth-century social concerns for the purpose of addressing contemporary policy issues. International political economy is not so much a new field as the resurrection of, or reestablishment of continuity with, an older one, one born of concerns about industrialization not only of the Third World but also of the First; one that recognizes the necessary interaction of economic and political factors. The artificial and inconvenient separation of social insights and data into disciplinary cubicles is, after all, a fairly recent expedient.

Rediscovered works in comparative historical development revealed that the sequenced stages modernization theorists expected to see transplanted from First World to Third had not even been characteristic of the First World. Gerschenkron's 1962 study of European trends, for example, noted that development took very different paths depending on the timing of industrialization.[11]

The observation that development follows no preordained sequence of stages is one that international political economy holds in common with the World Systems School. International political economy, however, faults the world system approach for underestimation of the role of the state in determining economic outcomes. Rejecting both the liberal preference for an unfettered market and the Marxist choice of state dominance of economic decision-making, international political economists contend that both state and market have important roles to play and that on occasion they are mutually reinforcing. Effective operation of the market may in fact be dependent upon the vigilance of a strong state, prepared to intervene where necessary. If, however, the state lacks autonomy from private economic elites, as Bates (1981) found to be the case in his study of African agriculture policies, its interventions are likely to subvert the market in developmentally detrimental ways.[12] Ultimately, the consequences of state intervention must depend to a considerable extent on the political character of the intervening state.

Like dependency theorists, adherents of the international political economy approach concern themselves in particular with "the contradiction between the geographic character of state power and the transnational character of economic power." Unlike most *dependentistas*, however, international political economy theorists argue that the penetration of foreign capital does not necessarily result in the contraction of the economic role of a Third World state. Studies by Peter Evans of petrochemical and iron industries in Brazil, by Frank Tugwell of the oil industry in Venezuela, and by Theodore Moran of the copper industry in Chile have shown that foreign-owned extractive sectors may provide sites for the expansion of state entrepreneurial activity.[13] Evans pointed out, however, that expansion of the state's role does not necessarily advance other categories of development, such as improved living standards for the majority.[14]

The End of Debate

It seems safe to assume that so long as there has been inequity there has been dissent, or heresy. But public debate requires a forum, and, in the aftermath of decisive social struggles, one of the things that the have-nots have not is a forum. The end of the Cold War is not, as suggested in the title of Francis Fukuyama's influential article, "the end of history."[15] But it has been in a sense, for the time being, the end of the debate.

The great debate between those who assume harmonic interests—that what is sauce for the goose is sauce for the gander—and those who see the gander getting more than his share little by little acquired a forum. Increasingly, after the great depression of the 1930s and World War II, popular, or nonelite, interests aggregated through labor unions, suffrage, civil rights, and independence movements, and broadly based political parties found grounding in national governments.

For a time, particularly in the 1960s and 1970s, the needs of the disadvantaged in the Third World appeared to coincide with those of would-be nation builders and of national industrialists who sought protection from transnational competitors. That coincidence of interests constructed a forum for those in academia as well as in government and nongovernmental development agencies who took exception to the prevailing paradigm, that of liberalism interpreted by First World elites and marketed as in the interest of all. Contrarian theories, assuming discordant interests, began to lose their Third World patrons with the military counterrevolutions of the 1960s and 1970s and were further disabled by the recessions of the 1980s, but the collapse of socialist regimes that signaled the end of the Cold War was their coup de grâce. Right too late or too soon, those who warned against resource and policy denationalization and the globalization of systematized inequality were left without defensible turf on which to take a stand.

The Neoliberal Monologue

With the collapse of the Soviet Union and of what passed for socialism elsewhere, so-called U.S. Cold Warriors were quick to claim victory. The winner in this case, however, was not a country or a set of countries but an economic system. That system was a socially premodern version of capitalism bulwarked by postmodern technology. The system has demanded unconditional surrender, not just of socialism in its extreme forms but also of most traces of popular economic decision-making, of the many variations of state planning and regulation, state-run enterprise, and protected domestic industry and of social services and benefits and other elements of the welfare state—products of more than a half-century of political development engineered by national governments. And surrender has generally been forthcoming. It seems that no array of weapons has been quite as threatening to governments as the trillion dollars sloshing around changing hands every day in global currency markets, beyond the control of any government. Every currency is thus left vulnerable to speculative manipulation. Capital operates in a sellers' market, with fixed conditions as to its availability, and governments are forced to compete for its favors.

Such globalization of economic power and planning has meant also a level of hegemony in the realm of ideas unprecedented perhaps since the era of scholasticism. It is not in spite of the importance of a general development paradigm or of the serious implications of the growing gap but rather because of them that most literature on the subject remains so arid, so nearly devoid of debate.

It has commonly been argued that wealth and income gaps are not problems in themselves so long as the losses of the poor are in relative terms only, not in absolute ones. But at least since Aristotle, political scientists have been pointing out that political power and distribution of wealth are interdependent. As power is relational, a relative loss of income means an absolute loss of power and an ever more uphill struggle for the deprived and oppressed, of the First World and Third, in the pursuit of effective participation and social justice. The ever-increasing concentration of economic power includes the power to limit the parameters of public debate.

Dissidents, Heretics, and Outliers

For the political Right, the end of the Cold War meant the loss of its cover story—that is, its rationalizations for supporting antidemocratic forces—but the Left had lost something harder to come by and to replace: its dream of a world more just. In the new order, debate on economic issues has been muffled not because it appears treasonous but because it appears futile. Resource allocation is perceived to have been snatched away by the inexorable forces of the global marketplace.

The economic devastation that followed the final cataclysms of the Cold War in the region of its epicenter got a long head start in Latin America. The debt crisis of the early 1980s left Latin American leaders at the mercy of creditors and currency speculators. The state itself, as a representative of a sovereign people, was so weakened that any line of policy, or even rhetoric, that smacked of economic nationalism threatened to set off a stampede of fleeing capital. Although the surrender of economic policy-making seemed not to be a matter of choice, it nonetheless demanded explanation and justification, which was scripted in neoliberal terms. Dependency theorists might claim that this turn of events had validated their analysis of the problem, but in a global economy—that is, one without economically defensible borders and without an alternative market or credit source—they were left without politically feasible solutions.

The school of dependency theorists has not vanished, though some might argue—since Fernando Henrique Cardoso, one of its founders, was elected president of Brazil as a born-again neoliberal—that it has gone under deep cover. Others, including Osvaldo Sunkel, have argued in the 1990s that while a strategy of export promotion may be unavoidable, a healthy economy, resistant to the effects of global market volatility, demands priority attention to the development of the domestic market.[16]

Some have looked to regional arrangements for the kind of defensive coalition building that no longer seems possible at the national level.

Globalization Theory. Many theorists of international politics and development have come to focus in the 1990s on some aspects of economic globalization—its nature, causes, and consequences; its beneficiaries and its victims; and in particular the ways in which it has changed the relationship between public and private sectors. Most of those drawn initially to the study of globalization had been identified with dependency or world systems models or with the field of international political economy. Leaders in this trend, such as Susan Strange and Barry Gills, have been concerned primarily with the loss of political accountability, with growing income gaps, and with other effects of the process they saw as detrimental to society generally. But the new focus has more recently drawn economists and others whose interests and concerns lie elsewhere and who take a more benign view of globalization and its consequences.

Some are concerned that, as in the case of most weddings and mergers, the remarriage of political science and economics in globalization theory may turn out to be an unequal one, one that is drawn toward safety in the seemingly technocratic economic side of the equation, tending to the political only in its willingness to ask embarrassing questions. Dedicating a special issue of *New Political Economy* to the politics of globalization, Gills says, "We seek to reclaim the terrain of the political, sometimes lost in the first phase of the globalization debate, and indeed to make concrete strategies and concepts of 'resistance' central to our analysis of 'globalization.'"[17]

Development Practitioners and Political Activists. A great body of scholarly and normative literature inspired by needs and interests running counter to those advanced by neoliberalism has been produced in the 1990s. This intellectual flourishing, however, on the part particularly of environmentalists, feminists, community organizers, and human rights monitors has yet to generate a great debate. Between these concerns and neoliberalism as now advanced there is little common ground, and economists who now enjoy unchallenged disciplinary primacy in the business of theoretical legitimation have generally ignored them.

Environmentalists. Environmentalists warn that the global village is being stripped of resources by a feeding frenzy set off by deregulation and the openness of markets and fueled by hard currency debt service requirements. Globe-hopping investors take what they can of depletable resources and then move on, leaving communities and ecosystems devastated.

The late economist Kenneth Boulding once said, "Anyone who thinks exponential growth can go on forever is either a madman or an economist."[18] The environmental perspective might in fact pose a great challenge to neoliberalism since its thesis of absolute limits is directly contradictory to that of an absolutely unlimited requirement of growth. It also has the advantage of a large and highly committed constituency, crosscutting classes and generations. But the two approaches' arguments are not articulated. For the most part they are played out in different arenas, coming together only in greenwash—corporate public relations gimmicks to demonstrate concern for the environment. In other words, it is not through straightforward debate but only through greenwash that the money movers and their apologists acknowledge the existence of an environmental challenge to their position.

The Women's Movement. Scholars engaging in gender analysis, along with chroniclers and supporters of the international women's movement, have noted that the front-line victims of economic restructuring now sweeping the global village are women. At the same time that shrinkage of the public sector has cost women their best professional jobs, the loss of family services, pensions, and benefits has expanded their responsibilities. While some women are being squeezed out of the better-paying formal economy, others are being drawn in ever greater numbers into exploitative informal sector work. Moreover, it is not only women's interests that have suffered in this new order but also the public policy expressions of women's values, those of nurturing versus punishing, of cooperation versus competition, of collective responsibility versus individualized self-indulgence. Major public and private institutions have made a point in recent years of making room for women but not of listening to them or reversing policies so damaging to their families and communities.

Community Empowerment. Globalization—the alienation or distancing of decision-making about priorities and livelihoods—presents a dire threat to the ideal of the individual and collective self-sufficiency or "empowerment" that is the philosophical foundation of community development. David Korten has summed up the contradiction as follows: "A globalized economic system has an inherent bias in favor of the large, the global, the competitive, the resource-extractive, and the short-term. Our challenge is to create a global system that is biased toward the small, the local, the cooperative, the resource-conserving and the long-term—one that empowers people to create a good living in balance with nature."[19]

As governments, bound first to distant creditors, default on their debts to their own citizens, the newly displaced and deprived are discovering what the long-suffering have always known—that the last bastion of security is the community, a community organized and aware of the need for general commitment and mutual support. Theorists of grass-roots development note that such awareness and commitment run directly counter to the neoliberal ideal of individualism.

Human Rights Advocates. Though human rights consciousness has not woven about itself, or become embedded in, a theoretical model, it has become a major focus of concern, a point from which to affix to the mind's eye a wide-angle lens. When human rights concerns generated popular mobilization, particularly among students and religious communities in Europe and North America, in the 1960s and 1970s and thus became a focus of intellectual and policy debate, the concept of such rights was rather narrowly drawn. The objective of the human rights movement was to stop the torture, execution, and other physical and psychological means of repression practiced by dictatorships and standing in the way of redemocratization. A government of the people should then be able to assure the protection of other basic rights.

The 1948 Universal Declaration of Human Rights, however, had sought to establish a far more encompassing view of the rights deserving universal protection. And activists from the poorest countries early on urged human rights organizations to adopt a broader view of their mission. That argument carried weight as local chapters proliferated in the Third World.

With the spread of democratization or redemocratization in the post–Cold War era of economic globalization, the broader mission previously assigned to democracy has reverted to the defenders of human rights. That is, as decision-making has been removed from the province of state government and as democracy has come to be defined in narrow terms of electoral process, basic economic and ecological rights—to food and shelter, potable water and breathable air—increasingly come to be seen as human rights issues. It follows, then, that deprivation of such rights cannot be legitimated by government no matter the rationale and no matter how such governments may have been conceived. Protection of such rights cannot be entrusted to individual governments but must be the concern of the international community.

Mary Robinson, UN high commissioner for human rights, commented in 1997 that the gap between civil/political and socioeconomic interpretations of human rights stood as a major obstacle to the effectiveness of UN programs. She has committed her office to the promotion of a broad interpretation, embracing economic, social, cultural, and gender rights along with the civil and political rights more traditionally acknowledged in the West.[20]

Notes

1. See Adam Smith, *An Inquiry Into the Nature and Causes of the Wealth of Nations* (New York: P. F. Collier, 1901; first published 1776); and David Ricardo, *Works and Correspondence,* ed. Piero Sraffa, with the collaboration of M. H. Dobb (Cambridge, UK: University Press for the Royal Economic Society, 1951–1957).

2. Walt W. Rostow, *The Stages of Economic Growth: A Non-Communist Manifesto* (London: Cambridge University Press, 1960).

3. Gabriel Almond and G. Bingham Powell, *Comparative Politics: A Developmental Approach* (Boston: Little, Brown and Co., 1966); and Samuel Huntington, *Political Order in Changing Societies* (New Haven: Yale University Press, 1968).

4. Samuel Huntington and Myron Weiner, eds., *Understanding Political Development* (Boston: Little, Brown and Co., 1987), pp. 21–28; Samuel Huntington, "The Clash of Civilizations?" *Foreign Affairs* 72, no. 3, summer 1993, p. 22.

5. See Robert O. Keohane and Joseph S. Nye, *Power and Interdependence: World Politics in Transition* (Boston: Little, Brown and Co., 1977).

6. Karl Marx, *Capital* [first published 1867], *The Communist Manifesto* [first published 1848], *and Other Writings*, ed. and with an introduction by Max Eastman; with an essay on Marxism by V. I. Lenin (New York: Modern Library, 1932).

7. Vladimir I. Lenin, *Imperialism: The Latest Stage in the Development of Capitalism* (first published in Petrograd 1919), trans. J. T. Kozlowski (Detroit: Marxism Educational Society, 1924); see also Lenin, *Collected Works* (Moscow: Progress Publishers, 1960–1970).

8. See, for example, Fernando Henrique Cardoso and Enzo Faletto, *Dependencia y desarrollo en América Latina* (Mexico City: Siglo XXI, 1969); Teotonio Dos Santos, *El nuevo carácter de la dependencia* (Santiago de Chile: Facultad de Ciencias Economicas y Sociales [CESO], 1968); Andre G. Frank, *Development and Underdevelopment in Latin America* (New York: Monthly Review Press, 1968); Osvaldo Sunkel, "Política nacional de desarrollo y dependencia externa," *Estudios Internacionales* 1, April 1967.

9. See, for example, Johan Galtung, *Essays in Peace Research* (Copenhagen: Eilers, 1975); *Development, Environment, and Technology: Toward a Technology for Self-Reliance* (New York: UNCTAD Secretariat, 1979); and *The True Worlds: A Transnational Perspective* (New York: Free Press, 1980).

10. Probably the best known of several books and articles in which he has elaborated his theory of development is Immanuel Wallerstein, *The Modern World-System: Capitalist Agriculture and the Origins of the European World-Economy in the Sixteenth Century* (New York: Academic Press, 1974).

11. Alexander Gerschenkron, *Economic Backwardness in Historical Perspective* (Cambridge: Harvard University Press, 1962).

12. Robert H. Bates, *Markets and States in Tropical Africa* (Berkeley: University of California Press, 1981).

13. See Franklin Tugwell, *The Politics of Oil in Venezuela* (Stanford, Calif.: Stanford University Press, 1975); Theodore H. Moran, *Multinational Corporations and the Politics of Dependence: Copper in Chile* (Princeton: Princeton University Press, 1975); and Peter Evans, *Dependent Development: The Alliance of Multinational, State and Local Capital in Brazil* (Princeton: Princeton University Press, 1979).

14. Peter Evans, "Foreign Capital and the Third World State," pp. 319–352 in Huntington and Weiner, eds., op. cit.

15. Francis Fukuyama, "The End of History," *The National Interest*, no. 16, summer 1989, pp. 3–18.

16. Oswaldo Sunkel, *Development from Within: Toward a Neostructuralist Approach for Latin America* (Boulder: Lynne Rienner Publishers, 1993).

17. Barry Gills, editorial, "Globalization and the 'Politics of Resistance,'" in Barry Gills, ed., *New Political Economy*, Special Issue, 2, no. 1, March 1997, pp. 11–15.

18. Kenneth Boulding, cited in Harold Gillian, "The World's Biggest Problem," *This World (San Francisco Chronicle)* February 16, 1992.

19. David Korten, *When Corporations Rule the World* (West Hartford, Conn.: Kumarian Press, 1994), p. 270.

20. Mary Robinson, "Realizing Human Rights," The 1997 Romanes Lecture, Sheldonian Theater, Oxford University, November 11, 1997.

Suggested Readings

Boulding, Kenneth, "The Economics of the Coming Spaceship Earth," pp. 3–14 in Henry Jarrett, ed., *Environmental Quality in a Growing Economy* (Baltimore: John Hopkins University Press, 1968).

Cardoso, Fernando Henrique, and Enzo Faletto, *Dependency and Development in Latin America* (Berkeley: University of California Press, 1979).

Chilcote, Ronald H., *Theories of Development and Underdevelopment* (Boulder: Westview Press, 1984).

Daly, Herman, and John Cobb, *Toward the Common Good: Redirecting the Economy Toward Community, the Environment, and a Sustainable Future.* 2nd ed. (Boston: Beacon Press, 1994).

Evans, Peter B., Dietrich Rueschemeyer, and Theda Skocpol, eds., *Bringing the State Back In* (New York: Cambridge University Press, 1985).

Evans, Peter B., and John D. Stephens, "Development and the World Economy," chap. 22 in Neil F. Smelser, ed., *The Handbook of Sociology* (Newbury Park, Calif.: Sage Publications, 1988).

Frank, Andre Gunder, "The Development of Underdevelopment," in James D. Cockcroft et al., *Dependence and Underdevelopment: Latin America's Political Economy* (New York: Doubleday, 1972).

Frank, Andre Gunder, and Barry K. Gills, eds. *The World System: Five Hundred Years or Five Thousand?* (New York: Routledge, 1996).

Galtung, Johan, *The True Worlds: A Transnational Perspective* (New York: The Free Press, 1980).

Galtung, Johan, "A Structural Theory of Imperialism," *Journal of Peace Research* 8, no. 2, 1971.

Heilbroner, Robert, *The Worldly Philosophers.* 6th ed. (New York: Simon and Schuster, 1992).

Kay, Geoffrey, *Development and Underdevelopment: A Marxist Analysis* (New York: St. Martin's Press, 1975).

Korten, David, *Getting to the Twenty-First Century: Voluntary Action and the Global Agenda* (West Hartford, Conn.: Kumarian Press, 1992).

Petras, James, *Critical Perspectives on Imperialism and Social Class in the Third World* (New York: Monthly Review Press, 1978).

Prebisch, Raúl, *Change and Development: Latin America's Great Task* (Washington, D.C.: Inter-American Development Bank, 1970).

Rodney, Walter, *How Europe Underdeveloped Africa* (London: Bogle-L'Ouverture Publications, 1972).

Seligson, Mitchell A., and John T. Passi-Smith, *Development and Underdevelopment: The Political Economy of Inequality* (Boulder: Lynne Rienner Publishers, 1993).

Smith, Adam, *An Inquiry into the Nature and Causes of the Wealth of Nations* (New York: Modern Library, 1937).

So, Alvin Y., *Social Change and Development: Modernization, Dependency, and World-System Theories* (Newbury Park, Calif.: Sage Publications, Inc., 1989).

Strange, Susan, *The Retreat of the State: The Diffusion of Power in the World Economy* (Cambridge: Cambridge University Press, 1996).

Tinker, Irene, *Persistent Inequalities: Women and World Development* (New York: Oxford University Press, 1993).

Wallerstein, Immanuel, *The Politics of the World-Economy: The States, the Movements, and the Civilizations* (Cambridge: Cambridge University Press, 1984).

4 Measurements and Findings

Saint Augustine, the original confused social scientist, reportedly said, "For so it is, oh Lord my God, I can measure it, but what it is that I measure I do not know." The empirical problems encountered in any attempt to move competing models and theories of development from the drawing board to a real-world testing ground are myriad.

Just as there are no universally accepted means of defining or explaining development, there are no value-neutral means of measuring it. Choices of definition and of explanatory models must determine how the process is to be promoted and how achievement will be assessed. Though the logic of such a sequence is clear enough, field operations may be guided by another logic entirely.

Aggregate Data and the Law of the Instrument

It has been said that the way of least resistance makes men and rivers crooked; it can also make assessments of levels of development or evaluations of the results of development efforts unreliable or meaningless. At times the availability or acceptability of instruments of measurement is more readily apparent than is the guiding paradigm or the overriding goal. In such cases, the law of the instrument is likely to become the prevailing logic. Phenomena that are not measurable by the available instrument are then disregarded. In practice, what that ordinarily means is that the researcher wants something to count—items that can be aggregated.

The tendency to reliance on aggregate data calls for several precautions. In the first place, despite the seeming authoritativeness of numbers, it must be remembered that like other kinds of research and reporting, number-crunching not only is susceptible to human and machine error but is subject as well to intentional manipulation for political or bureaucratic advantage. A case in point involved the campaign in Great Britain to get motorists to switch to unleaded gas. An official of the Environment Ministry reported that the potential market for unleaded was 80 percent of the cars on British roads. At the same time, the minister for roads and traffic, having a different constituency and set of bureaucratic interests, put the proportion at 43 percent. What made this case particularly interesting was that the two officials were husband and wife.[1]

Furthermore, if we focus exclusively on aggregate indices or on means rather than ends, we easily lose sight of the central problem. Commenting in 1970 on Brazil's "economic miracle," President Emilio G. Medici said, "The economy is doing fine, but the people aren't."[2] This ultimate abstraction of the economy has by no means been uncommon in the literature of development, because the requirements of growth and those of redistribution are different and often contradictory. While some economists have included redistribution and generalized standards of living in their indices of development, many others—those who define development primarily as economic growth—have been content with such national aggregates as growth in GNP and per capita income. Countries engaged in a serious attempt to redistribute income and raise the standard of living of the majority generally have a poor showing in such indices. Thus international agencies have been more supportive of governments that gleefully announce their soaring GNP growth rates to the hungry masses.

For those who see development primarily in terms of egalitarianism or redistribution, aggregate data may also be an essential tool. The best known of the various indices providing summary measures of inequality, for comparison from state to state or from period to period in a single state, is the Gini Coefficient, based on the Lorenz Curve. The researcher may, however, wish to delve more deeply into the distribution of income within a particular population, in which case she might compare the income shares of groups of individuals or households with their population shares or compare the income shares of deciles of the population from the poorest to the richest. For example, at the same time U.S. economists were hailing the Brazilian miracle, Brazilian economist Celso Furtado was pointing out that the richest 900,000 Brazilians had the same total income as the poorest 45 million.[3]

In addition to measures of relative inequality, the researcher might want to examine absolute levels of deprivation and compare them country to country or over time in a single country. Indices useful for that purpose are more varied and perhaps less reliable. It has become common for countries to establish a poverty line based on income or consumption. For purposes of international comparison, the World Bank has set the equivalent of U.S. $1 (1985 purchasing power parity [ppp] $) in consumption per person per day as the line of absolute poverty. Other measurements might include caloric or protein intake, the number of doctors or health practitioners serving a particular segment of the population, or the number of hours of work required to purchase some basic commodity. An index that has proved informative—despite obvious drawbacks—is the physical quality of life index (PQLI) devised by the

Overseas Development Council of Washington, D.C. It combines in a single number life expectancy, infant mortality, and literacy, each being assigned equal weight.

The United Nations Development Program in 1990 released a report ranking 130 countries according to a new human development index (HDI). Like the PQLI, the index uses a combination of criteria to measure the quality of people's lives. It also measures inequalities within countries as well as between classes, regions, rural and urban areas, age groups, and sexes. The HDI adopts a "conglomerate perspective," focusing on advances made by all groups in each community. The index uses three variables: life expectancy, educational attainment (adult literacy and combined primary, secondary, and tertiary enrollment), and real gross domestic product (GDP) per capita. The UNDP's *Human Development Report* for 1997 ranks 175 countries in accordance with that index as well as with indices of gender-related development—that is, gender disparity within the HDI—and gender enpowerment, focusing on participation in economic and political decision-making. The 1997 edition also introduces a Human Poverty Index, which approaches comparison from a "deprivational perspective." As variables, it uses the percentage of people expected to die before the age of forty, the percentage of adults who are illiterate, the percentage lacking access to health services and safe water, and the percentage of underweight children under five.[4]

The use of any data, however, may serve to befuddle rather than to clarify if it is incorrectly analyzed, a particular danger if researchers are dealing in data on countries or areas with which they are otherwise unfamiliar. A study indicating declining infant- and child-mortality rates in Chile in the 1970s, for example, might be doubly confusing. For one who had known Chile in earlier decades but knew nothing of Chile's political apocalypse of the 1970s, such findings might appear simply a continuation of earlier progress. Or the nonspecialist, unaware of the deterioration of living standards for the poorest after the coup d'état of 1973, might assume that the military dictatorship had pursued an enlightened social-welfare policy. In fact, even among the poorest in Chile there is considerable understanding of population planning. Thus the decline in mortality reflects in part a decline in the birthrate among the poor, owing to high levels of unemployment.[5]

Another problem associated with the law of the instrument has been the tendency of researchers to undertake an unwarranted leap in logic from what the instrument can reveal to what it cannot. It is far easier, for example, to establish correlation than to trace cause and effect. Thus correlations found to hold for a particular point in time have been assumed to be necessary and to suggest a causal relationship. A number of cross-national statistical studies, beginning with that of Seymour Martin Lipset in 1959, established a positive relationship between high levels of economic development and democracy, and it was assumed that that correlation reflected a functional interdependence between the two attributes.[6]

Such studies fell into disrepute in the 1960s and 1970s when the most highly developed of the Latin American states fell victim to brutal military-led counterrevolutions and when a few East Asian states achieved remarkable strides in economic development without a corresponding move toward democracy. More recent studies have fallen back upon the more modest claim that industrial capitalism creates conditions that facilitate organization among middle and working classes, thus making it more difficult for elites to exclude them from political participation. It must be conceded, however, that elites may respond by reinforcing mechanisms of repression rather than by liberalizing, especially if they are able to count on external political and economic support. It must also be noted that class interests that coincide at one stage of development may not coincide at the next. The interests of middle and working classes, for example, tend to coincide early in the process of industrialization but to come into conflict at a later stage.

The Challenge of Intangibles

If the measurement of economic growth and of income distribution and inequality has proved challenging, measurement of nontangible attributes has been even more so. We have seen that since economic development was easier to measure than political development, some scholars have sought to impute the latter from the former. Likewise, in the 1960s, scholars hooked on number-crunching tried to measure the progress of democracy or "modernization" by attaching numerical values to attitudes or by counting whatever was available to count and drawing conclusions about attitudes from the results. Peter Ranis, for example, sought to correlate democracy and political stability with such "civilizing paraphernalia" as TV sets.[7]

Modernization

Problems encountered in assessing causes, levels, or consequences of "modernization" have arisen from the general fuzziness of the concept or at least the lack of consensus among users as to its meaning. There has also been considerable confusion as to whether the indices employed are intended to represent cause or effect or both and as to whether they are meant to represent a syndrome or alternative responses to Western influence.

Indices vary, but among those most commonly used have been (1) secularism and/or rationalism—that is, openness to the scientific and technological, accompanied by rejection of the religious and ideological;

(2) individualism and/or achievement orientation—that is, rejection of extended family or other collective interests in favor of unfettered pursuit of personal advancement; (3) consumption orientation; (4) geographic mobility and preference for urban living; (5) participation—that is, motivation and ability to organize, vote, and otherwise cooperate in active pursuit of individual and group interests; (6) egalitarianism and/or integration—that is, recognition of equal rights and provision of equal opportunity within families, among classes, and across multicultural or multiracial societies; and (7) expansion of literacy, education, and access to communications media. Political and sociological indicators have also included structural differentiation, stability, and organizational efficacy or institutionalization.

I suggest that this supposed "syndrome" exists only in the minds of wishful thinkers. To the extent that all of these attributes are characteristic of a single society at a given time, the conjuncture is surely an aberration. Many of these orientations, in fact, tend to be countervailing. A striving for personal advancement defined in consumer terms surely undermines a societal predilection toward egalitarianism and integration. Rapid urbanization places a heavy strain on national resources, and as Martin C. Needler has noted, increasing social mobilization and participation has a destabilizing effect on societies with limited resources.[8] The pooling of indices by scholars with underlying but unaddressed differences in values was bound to result in confused or contradictory findings as to relative levels of modernity and development.

Furthermore, it is questionable in the first place whether or to what extent these indices represent the so-called developed countries today, much less in the era when they were developing, and in the second place whether each of these values or attitudinal orientations is in fact contained in the package of influence diffused from West to non-West. Finally, it must be asked again whether each of these attitudes and trends is actually conducive to economic growth or redistribution or any of the other goals commonly associated with development.

Whether the rugged individualism of the pioneering spirit or the close ties to family and community and the cooperation that the frontier demanded bore more responsibility for development in the United States is an open question, but the "Protestant ethic," much touted as an engine of development, was hardly a secular code. Although a headlong pursuit of personal gain and avid consumerism may be more common in the United States today than pursuit of the common good and frugality, it is arguable that those orientations are detrimental to the continuing development process, and it is most unlikely that they constituted an unmixed blessing in earlier stages of development.

That the highly industrialized countries value science and technology is apparent enough, but that that orientation is accompanied by a rejection of religion and ideology is not equally apparent. The supposedly modern United States continues to rank very high in indices of religious belief and church attendance. Furthermore, while the anticommunist orientation that the United States marketed so assiduously during the Cold War hardly qualified in breadth or depth as a full-fledged ideology, it certainly ran against the current of social science. For its true believers, anticommunism had all the affective qualities that modernization theorists ascribe to ideology.

The diffusion of Western culture has contributed in various ways to urbanization, but there is considerable question both in the United States and in poorer countries as to the extent to which this demonstrates a preference for urban living. The exodus from rural areas, in North America and elsewhere, has come about not only and not necessarily because of the pull of job opportunities and cultural stimulation, but also because of the push of rural stagnation and the increasing control of land by agribusiness.

As for egalitarianism and integration, the United States hardly stands as a worthy model of those traits, and the attitudes on the subject that the country has marketed and displayed abroad have probably been even worse than the standards set in the domestic arena. Integration of the native population is not the major issue in the United States that it is in many other countries of the New World because the native population was almost obliterated, but the surviving Native Americans have by no means been integrated. The United States was among the last countries to give up outright slavery, and wherever it exercised police powers in the hemisphere in the early decades of the twentieth century, it introduced forms of discrimination previously unknown. There are many who argue that the lack of respect for human life demonstrated by the United States in Vietnam, or more recently in Panama and Iraq, was indicative of the continuing force of racial prejudice.

Part of the problem in assessing the content of the cultural diffusion that has been labeled modernization derives from the fact that programmed and unprogrammed influences have not necessarily been in the same direction. In fact, they have sometimes been quite contradictory, and in those cases the programmed ones have usually been overriding. Consumerism in areas under Western influence has no doubt been spurred by the demonstration effect of material wealth and technological gadgetry in patron states but has also been generated as a matter of consistent policy in order to expand markets for Western-based firms.

Social mobilization and participation are a different matter entirely. In the first place, participation in the United States, of late, has hardly been exemplary. Voter turnout in the U.S. presidential election of 1996 was less than 50 percent, the lowest since 1924. In the second place, the programmed influence of colonial and neocolonial states has been brought to bear, on balance, on containing rather than promoting participation in the Third World. Certainly the U.S. and French constitutions and, more recently, European parliamentary systems served as models for newly independent states. Nevertheless, First World states have normally been hostile to social mobilization in the Third World and have continually thwarted attempts to expand participation and give substance to the form of democracy. When the American empire was young, that great crusader Woodrow Wilson sent in the marines to Central America and the Caribbean to impose free and fair elections, but marines writing of their experiences put "free and fair" in quotes.[9] Little wonder that official U.S. rhetoric of the 1980s and 1990s had a familiar ring. Meanwhile the French, touting a strong democracy at home, have resisted the threat of democracy in the South Pacific. The islanders were not very happy with the French choice of their neighborhood as a site for nuclear-weapons testing until 1996, when international public opinion, aroused by Greenpeace activism, forced a policy change.

The role of Western cultural diffusion in the expansion of literacy, education, and access to the communications media in the Third World is also a mixed bag. Direct foreign assistance for those efforts has often had more to do with attempting to influence content than with promoting learning for its own sake. The *concientização*, or consciousness-raising, approach to literacy training that was launched by Paulo Freire in Brazil in the early 1960s was denounced by U.S. officials as subversive. On the other hand, the commander of the U.S. military group in Brazil in the late 1960s praised military involvement in primary education "because people can't operate complex machines, such as computers, if they can't read the instructions."[10] Because of their overall socioeconomic orientations, the Third World governments most dedicated to the promotion of literacy and education have often been those most strongly opposed by the First World.

Formal education is not necessarily a prerequisite to other aspects of development, much less a panacea. There is considerable evidence, whether as a consequence of content or structure, that it may even serve to delay the presentation of majority demands. Formal education provides yet another channel for misinformation as well as for information. The process is not necessarily humanizing, nor does it necessarily confer self-esteem and a sense of efficacy. Rolland Paulston noted that Quechua-speaking Indian children in Peru subjected to education about alien traditions taught in Spanish by whites learned to depreciate themselves and their own culture.[11] Furthermore, advanced training for nonexistent jobs contributes to the brain drain.

Likewise, the consequences of the expansion of the communications media are largely dependent upon flow and content. Expansion of the media facilitates communication from the top down, but it need not facilitate communication from the bottom up. On the contrary, it may contribute to "massification" as an alternative to association. As the political, socioeconomic, and even cultural content of communications in many Third World countries has been censored by dictatorships supported by First World governments, the most salient role of the media has been demand creation, or the dissemination of consumerism, which, as Alejandro Portes argued, is hardly conducive to development. Defining national development as (1) sustained economic growth and generation of self-sustained industrial growth centers; (2) income redistribution on an egalitarian basis; and (3) emergence of an enhanced national self-image, Portes saw consumerism as a serious threat to development goals. He noted that the capital accumulation and investment necessary for launching the development process calls not for individual fulfillment expressed in consumption but rather for collective discipline and sacrifice.[12] Demand by the privileged few for technologically advanced gadgetry and other durable goods generally perpetuates the drain of resources from the underdeveloped to the overdeveloped world and defers any national attempt to meet the more basic needs of the larger population. Furthermore, even when "modern" industry moves to the so-called Third World, it tends to be capital-intensive (thus offering little employment) and geared to the production of durable goods that only a small sector of the population can afford.

Portes also notes that in psychosocial terms it has been not the supposed attributes of modernity but rather ideology and the revival of some aspects of tradition, generally in combination, that have actually contributed to development. Ideology has served to justify the sacrifices required, and retention of tradition has contributed to legitimation of wide-ranging transformation.

Daniel Lerner asserted in 1965 that social change everywhere was a function of the number of individuals adopting the attitudes and behavior patterns associated with modernity.[13] Social change by individual cooptation would be at best a 500-year plan. But if this social change is meant to incorporate such goals as redistribution and democracy, the available evidence suggests that the change promoted by "moderns" tends to be in a different direction.

This "modern man," having adopted the tastes, material needs, and attitudes of the stereotyped West, and finding himself awash in a sea of "traditionals," becomes alienated from, and perhaps even contemptuous of, the majority of his countrymen. (Businessmen linked to multinational corporations and military establishments dependent on foreigners for training and equipment are by definition in the modern sector.) In a context of scarce resources, modern man is likely to see popular demands for a larger share of the pie as a threat to his lifestyle. If this modern man were really the rugged individualist he is purported to be, and if the traditional majority were as strongly oriented toward collective pursuit of interests as they are alleged to be, modernity might pose no great danger. In fact, however, if the poor were so collectively oriented, they might not be poor in the first place. And modern man, far from depending on his own devices, unites with other individuals and entities—national and foreign—whose interests are threatened and plots to protect his lifestyle, at whatever cost to the nation as a whole.

It appears, then, that the consequences of modernization have more often been the opposite of those hypothesized by modernization and development theorists. Undeterred, however, many who planned or implemented development programs on behalf of major donor institutions in the 1990s, now under the banner of neoliberalism, proceeded in accordance with the same assumptions and blueprints. A major element of continuity, with consequences often devastating but little known, is the assumption that a surviving non-Western or nonmodern culture is a problem to be overcome rather than an asset to be nurtured and employed.

Empowerment

The concept of empowerment, which gained popularity in the 1980s, particularly among village-level practitioners, applies primarily to a strategy rather than to a theoretical model. For that reason and also because of the chasm generally separating theoreticians and practitioners, the concept has been less vulnerable than those associated with theoretical models to awkward attempts to operationalize and measure it with pretense of numerical exactitude. Most efforts to identify contributing factors and to assess levels of achievement have been subjective.

Albert O. Hirschman, one of the few major theoreticians of development who has focused on process at the grass-roots level, has noted that "the whole venture of grass-roots development has arisen in good measure from a revulsion against the worship of the 'gross national product' and of the 'rate of growth' as unique arbiters of economic and human progress." He also observes that those who engage in the venture see it as intrinsically worthwhile, without regard to macroeconomic consequences.[14]

It should be possible to come up with indices of empowerment no less reliable than those that have been used in the past to measure modernization and other such abstract concepts, but that really is not saying very much. It should be possible, for example, to count, if not on a global scale, at least on a national or regional one, the number of organizations springing from or responding to nonelite communities and to track the increase or decrease in their numbers over time. Such an effort would bog down immediately, however, in disagreement, both in principle, or definition, and in fact, over which organizations were genuinely representative of grass-roots interests as opposed to representing efforts by elites to manipulate development at the grass roots.

Measuring the effectiveness of such groups on any kind of macro scale would be even more difficult. It would run the risk of slipping into some of the fallacies that crippled modernization and development approaches—for example, assuming a kind of omniscience on the part of researchers that would allow us to know what constitutes self-reliance and successful problem-solving among peoples and environments unfamiliar to us, and falling back upon economic criteria for measuring essentially psychological, sociological, and political phenomena. That is not to say that attempts to refine indices and to measure progress toward empowerment would not be worthwhile but just to point out that at best the results would be far from precise; and whatever the results, they would be unlikely to change any minds about the value of grass-roots efforts and the appropriateness of empowerment as a goal.

While noting the dubious utility of seeking to assess the "overall" impact of grass-roots development, Hirschman has made a number of observations that should be useful to those who would understand its dynamics or seek to promote it. Among them: (1) Social energy may be conserved and transformed. Invested unsuccessfully in a particular kind of collective action, social energy is likely to reappear in a different form. Hirschman's example is that of a group frustrated in a "radical" undertaking—a land takeover—remobilizing some years later to form a successful cooperative. I would add that examples of the reverse—remobilization for more "radical" undertakings—are also common. (2) Social action projects having only economic goals initially may give rise to explicitly political activism. (3) A cooperative must break even in order to survive, but economic success is not the only kind of success; any sort of collective enterprise should serve educational purposes and may well spin off other such enterprises. (4) There is no preordained sequence in development; education, for example, may precede collective action in pursuit of economic goals, but economic pursuits may also set in relief the need for literacy or other fruits of education. (5) Grass-roots development does not necessarily require the prior seizure of the central power of the state. (6) Authoritarian or elitist rule requires that subjects concern themselves exclusively with their own welfare and that of their immediate family, distrusting their neighbors. Thus empowerment, or grass-roots development, is by nature collective or communal.[15]

Many of the ideas and ideals that characterize the concept of development as empowerment have been expressed as goals of international organizations. The idea of "integrated rural development," for example, as promoted in the 1960s and 1970s by the World Bank and the United

Nations, rejected conventional planning methods in favor of an approach involving local communities in every step of the process, from expression of needs and setting of priorities to implementation of projects. The approach also called for comprehensiveness, for interrelated actions on various fronts, i.e., community organization, education, curative and preventive medicine, innovation in irrigation and water purification, and enhanced agricultural productivity.

In practice, however, the required integration of efforts rarely took place. The bureaucracies involved, international or foreign and domestic alike, generally resisted pooling personnel and funds and sharing responsibilities and credit or blame. At any rate, large bureaucracies seem incapable of genuinely involving people at the community level in decision-making. The upshot was that almost any project undertaken in rural areas fell under the rubric of integrated rural development, and the label served to confer legitimacy and a progressive cover on some very conventional projects that contributed to the further concentration of wealth in rural areas and the out-migration of peasant populations.

A report prepared by the UN Research Institute for Development in 1974, pursuant to resolutions adopted by the Economic and Social Council and the General Assembly, called for a new "unified" approach emphasizing various kinds of structural and institutional change.[16] Success should be measured not in aggregate indices of growth, like GNP, but in the involvement of the entire target community in the development process, in the enhancement of social equity, in the cultivation of human potential, and in the capacitation of the community to set and meet its own goals. The UNDP, in the late 1990s, continued to urge attention to such intangibles. Even as the organization sought means of drawing meaningful comparisons through aggregate data, it pointed out that human development was about choices and capabilities, about freedom and security, about creativity and participation, about dignity, self-respect, and the respect of others. The empowerment approach, running counter to the interests of political and economic elites, was not likely to be pursued by many governments. Empowerment, however, has been the motivating vision of a great many small nongovernmental organizations based in the First World or the Third.

Even now, in these oh-so-material times, many seasoned practitioners of community development see the material products or outcomes of their projects—items marketed or money circulated through microenterprise, for example—as mere indicators or means toward more important but intangible ends, such as the nurturing of cultural pride or community solidarity, that is, the accumulation of communal and organizational bonds that Robert Putnam has dubbed social capital.[17] Sustainability of ecosystems—a tangible goal, measurable in principle in terms of nature's regenerative and assimilative capacities—will ultimately be dependent upon the less tangible or less readily measurable sustainability of community.[18]

Notes

1. *Economist,* March 18, 1989, p. 59.

2. Cited in Dan Griffin, "The Boom in Brazil; An Awful Lot of Everything," *Washington Post,* May 27, 1973.

3. Cited in Eduardo Galeano, "The De-Nationalization of Brazilian Industry," *Monthly Review* 21, no. 7, 1969, pp. 11–30.

4. United Nations Development Program, *Human Development Report 1990* (London: Oxford University Press, 1990 et seriatim).

5. David F. Hojman, "Neoliberal Economic Policies and Infant and Child Mortality: Simulation Analysis of a Chilean Paradox," *World Development* 17, no. 1, January 1989, pp. 93–108.

6. Seymour Martin Lipset, *Political Man: The Social Basis of Politics* (New York: Anchor Books, 1963).

7. Peter Ranis, *Five Latin American Nations: A Comparative Political Study* (New York: Macmillan Co., 1971).

8. Martin C. Needler, *Political Development in Latin America: Instability, Violence, and Evolutionary Change* (New York: Random House, 1968), chap. 5.

9. The attitudes and methods of the U.S. "enforcers" of "democracy" in Latin America in the early twentieth century are revealed in Ronald Schaffer, "The 1940 Small Wars Manual and the 'Lessons of History,'" *Military Affairs* 36, no. 2, April 1972, pp. 46–51.

10. Mayor General Richard J. Seitz, commander of the U.S. Delegation to the Joint Brazil-United States Military Mission, October 1968–July 1970. Interview, Washington, D.C., June 4, 1973.

11. Rolland G. Paulston, "Estratificación social, poder y organización educacional: el caso peruano," *Aportes,* no. 16, April 1970, pp. 91–111.

12. Alejandro Portes, "Modernity and Development: A Critique," *Studies in Comparative International Development* 9, no. 2, spring 1974, pp. 247–279.

13. Daniel Lerner, *The Passing of Traditional Society: Modernizing in the Middle East* (New York: Free Press, 1965), p. 83.

14. Albert O. Hirschman, *Getting Ahead Collectively* (New York: Pergamon Press, 1984).

15. Ibid.

16. Claude Ake, *A Political Economy of Africa* (Lagos: Longman Group, Ltd., 1981), pp. 152–156.

17. Robert D. Putnam, "The Prosperous Community: Social Capital and Public Affairs," *The American Prospect,* no. 13, spring 1993, p. 35.

18. Means of promoting, measuring, and evaluating participation, a crucial building block in the construction of community sustainability, receive thoughtful attention each week at the Participation Forum, organized by Diane LaVoy, senior policy adviser for participatory development at the U.S. Agency for International Development (USAID). Forum summaries, an invaluable tool for advocates of participatory development, are available through the Environmental Health Project of USAID's Office of Health and Nutrition.

Suggested Readings

Anand, Sudhir, and Amartya Sen, *Gender Inequality in Human Development: Theories and Measurement*, Human Development Report Office Occasional Paper 19 (New York: UNDP, 1995).

Atkinson, Antony B., "On the Measurement of Inequality," *Journal of Economic Theory* 2, no. 3, 1970, pp. 244–263.

Atkinson, Antony B., and François Bourguignon, "The Comparison of Multi-Dimensional Distributions of Economic Status," *Review of Economic Studies* 49, 1982, pp. 183–201.

Basu, Kaushik, "Achievements, Capabilities, and the Concept of Well-Being," *Social Choice and Welfare* 4, 1987, pp. 69–76.

Brown, Michael Barratt, *Models in Political Economy: A Guide to the Arguments* (Boulder: Lynne Rienner, 1985).

Deininger, Klaus, and Lyn Squire, "A New Data Set Measuring Income Inequality," *The World Bank Economic Review* 10, no. 3, 1996, pp. 565–591.

Gills, Barry, ed., "Globalization and the 'Politics of Resistance,'" *New Political Economy*, Special Issue, 2, no. 1, March 1997.

Herman, Edward S., "The Economics of the Rich." *Z Magazine* 10, no. 7/8, July–August 1997, pp. 19–25.

Lindblom, Charles, *Politics and Markets: The World's Political Economic Systems* (New York: Basic Books, 1977).

Our Global Neighborhood. The Report of the Commission on Global Governance (Oxford: Oxford University Press, 1995).

Seligson, Mitchell A., ed., *The Gap Between Rich and Poor: Contending Perspectives on the Political Economy of Development* (Boulder: Westview Press, 1984).

United Nations, *World Economic and Social Survey, 1996* (New York: United Nations, 1996).

United Nations Research Institute for Social Development, *States of Dismay: The Social Effects of Globalization* (London: Kegan Paul/Earthscan, 1995).

World Bank, *World Development Report 1997* (Oxford: Oxford University Press, 1997).

Photos

All photos were taken by the author.

In India, as in most LDCs, women start work younger, work longer hours, eat less, and have less access to health care, education, and credit than do men.

In the village of Mudichur, in the Indian state of Tamil Nadu, a clinic run by the YWCA is the only source of health care for babies. Legislation provides for comprehensive public health care, but implementation is spotty. In India, as elsewhere, health care professionals resist living in poor rural villages.

In India, dowry-abuse—harrassment of a bride by the groom's family to provide more gifts from her own family—has been getting worse since the 1970s, not in spite of modernization but because of it. Such abuse is seen as deriving from the new materialism, or consumerism, of the urban middle class. In this scene women's organizations in Bangalore demonstrate at the home of a groom whose bride committed suicide.

Underemployed men in Yemen spend long hours chewing kat; this cultivation of kat, a mild narcotic, consumes ever larger portions of Yemen's scarce water and arable land.

Sunshine is about the only thing not in short supply in the north African Sahel region. With assistance from a Canadian NGO, this village in Burkina Faso (formerly Upper Volta) was exploring the advantages of solar-heated and water-and solar-powered cook stoves.

Survival is a constant struggle for children such as these in an Ewe village in Togo. Togo's population continues to grow at an annual rate of 3 percent, but infant mortality averages 109 per 1,000 births, and life expectancy is only 48 years. Most people are undernourished, and there is only one physician for each 18,000 persons.

In Zimbabwe, as elsewhere in the Third World, NGOs seek to help communities sustain local markets threatened by globalization.

Fresh fish in local markets, like this one in Mozambique, are becoming more scarce as foreign-based factory trawlers compete with community fishermen for dwindling fish

PART TWO

Development in Practice: Actors and Strategies

5   *Donor Strategies and Programs*

As noted in Chapter 1, international development as such is by no means an exclusively modern or Western phenomenon. Nevertheless, the contemporary infrastructure and modus operandi, based on globally systematized divisions into donor and client states and institutions, is an expression of the severely skewed post–World War II allocation of resources and ambitions on the one hand, needs and vulnerabilities on the other. In the aftermath of that war, with Europe and much of the Orient laid waste, U.S. economic and military superiority seemed beyond challenge.

U.S. Development and Foreign Assistance Policy

The United States emerged from that war with three-fourths of the world's invested capital and two-thirds of its industrial capacity. The national neurosis resulting from recognition of such a skewed distribution was perhaps less one of guilt than one of paranoia. Diplomat George Kennan, noted as the author of the policy of containment, observed in 1948:

> We have about 50% of the world's wealth but only 3.6% of the population. Our real task in the coming period is to devise a pattern of relationships which will permit us to maintain this position of disparity. . . . We need not deceive ourselves that we can afford today the luxury of altruism and world-benefaction. . . . We should cease to talk about vague and unreal objectives such as human rights, the raising of living standards, and democratization. . . . The final answer might be an unpleasant one, but . . . we should not hesitate before police repression by the local government.[1]

The extent of U.S. dominance of the international capitalist system at that time dictated that the strategies and tactics characterizing the broader development game would conform, at least initially, to U.S. business and bureaucratic interests, and that the rhetoric would reflect the fears and passions—as perceived or inflamed by policymakers—of the tuned-in U.S. public. On the client or supplicant side of the equation,

Third World states, individually or collectively, have on occasion countered with development programs of their own design, but for the most part the less-developed countries (LDCs) have had little choice but to conform or react to blueprints drawn up elsewhere.

There were a couple of catches, however, to this general scheme. In the first place, the skewing of resources in this case was so severe that without remedial action the United States would be left virtually without trading partners. Thus was born the program of massive support for European reconstruction known as the Marshall Plan. The other catch, as seen by policymakers, was that the U.S. public would be insufficiently supportive of a policy premised upon the maintenance of empire for its own sake. The remedy for that problem was supplied by the dissembling and general nastiness of Joseph Stalin, the Soviet acquisition of the atomic bomb, and the success of the Chinese Communist revolution. A set of policies designed in part to maintain and expand U.S. economic supremacy could be premised upon an all-encompassing threat to U.S. survival.

For the United States, then, and by extension for donor entities in general, the idea of development as a process and a goal for the Third World toward which the First World should be of assistance grew out of the felicitous experience with the Marshall Plan in Europe and out of Cold War fears and ambitions. Within that framework, moreover, development strategies, even more than theoretical models, have been closely associated with larger economic and political trends.

Major changes in U.S. development strategy have not always coincided, however, with changes in administration. Sometimes they constitute a part of the changing climate of opinion that is a harbinger of political change. And owing to bureaucratic inertia or sabotage, among other things, there is often a considerable lag between the announcement of a new policy, or the rise or peaking of a policy's popularity, and the beginnings of implementation. Furthermore, whatever the intentions of a president or administration, development policy, in the course of moving through the U.S. Congress, the U.S. bureaucracy, then client country governments and institutions, and finally interacting with supposed beneficiaries, is certain to become an amalgam of varied, and even in some cases competing, enterprises. From an empowerment perspective, that is not necessarily disadvantageous, as we shall see in Part 4.

Security and Economic Interests

Along with reviving the economies of Western Europe, the Marshall Plan, through which some $13 billion was transferred between 1948 and 1951, was seen as serving to block the spread of Soviet influence and to undergird free-market economies in the area. Thus when it began to appear that other countries and areas were slipping out from under U.S., or "Western," control and veering toward socialism, economic aid and development programs were seen as logical accompaniments to military aid and training programs.

Initially in support of the Truman Doctrine of 1947,[2] under guise of which the United States supplanted British hegemony in Greece, Turkey, and Iran, the Truman administration initiated the Point IV foreign assistance program. The authorizing legislation, called the Act for International Development, passed in 1950, created the Technical Cooperation Administration (TCA) to direct technical assistance to developing countries. Whereas capital alone sufficed to generate reconstruction and revive economies in Europe, it was assumed that the less-developed states would require training and the transfer of the latest in Western technology as well. The appropriateness of the most advanced technology was scarcely even questioned until the mid-1960s.

The Mutual Security Act of 1951 replaced both the TCA and the Economic Cooperation Administration, which had supervised the Marshall Plan, with the Mutual Security Agency (MSA). The agency's primary responsibilities were political and military, and its economic development component was intended also to serve those ends, above all to counter the spread of Communist influence in the Far East. By the time the MSA was replaced, in 1955, by the International Cooperation Administration (ICA), the focus of concern—and about half of the MSA's $600 million economic aid disbursals—had shifted to the Middle East and South Asia. Meanwhile, in 1954, Public Law 480 had created the Food for Peace program, to be administered in part by the Department of Agriculture. It was intended to ease world hunger as well as to expand overseas markets for U.S. agricultural commodities, especially grains.

The approach to development that was undertaken in the 1950s and that in most particulars survived at least through the 1960s stressed the promotion of increased production and productivity, especially through macroeconomic planning; institution-building; public investment in large-scale infrastructure projects (e.g., highways, dams); training and technical assistance, stressing First World technologies and bureaucratic procedures; and the facilitation of private trade and investment abroad.

Planning stressed attention to comparative advantage, which for most LDCs was seen to lie in the export of primary products, and to infrastructure projects that enhanced the feasibility of foreign investments. Foreign assistance was not normally tied to specific projects but was often tied to the purchase of capital goods from the United States and to the elimination of tariffs or regulations viewed as obstacles to trade and investment. Where Third World governments resisted such pressures and continued to protect nascent industries, or where cheap labor offered an obviou advantage, U.S. and other foreign investors moved from a concentration on plantations and mineral extraction to manufacturing and service industries in and for domestic Third World markets—so-called tariff-jumping industry.

Development plans drawn up with U.S. assistance often called for new taxes. The nature of the power structure in most client states meant that taxes would be regressive and any new tax burden would be borne by the nonaffluent. Resulting new revenues were not to be spent on the non-affluent, however; it was argued that benefits would eventually "trickle down" to low-income sectors, but that short-term requirements of capital accumulation called for the minimization of public spending on general services and social welfare.

The Promising Ambivalence of Camelot

The advent of the 1960s brought relief from the worst of 1950s Cold War paranoia—and with it a certain intoxication with power; in some quarters, it even brought a new spirit of generosity and openness to the interests of other peoples. Above all, Camelot, the abbreviated administration of John F. Kennedy, brought into public life the profound ambivalence that is so often the mark of liberals.[3] The primacy of Cold War advantage and of economic growth fueled by foreign investment remained unchallenged, but it was argued that those objectives would be best served through the promotion of social reform.

Young Americans were challenged to "ask not what your country can do for you, but what you can do for your country," and the Peace Corps was born. A new Agency for International Development (AID—now US-AID), created by the Foreign Assistance Act of 1961 to supersede the ICA, was mandated to promote reform in such areas as education, health, housing, and land-tenure policy without losing sight of the requirements of U.S. business interests. At the same time, a program of aid and training for Third World police forces begun in 1954 was greatly reinforced and the U.S. military undertook new roles, including the training and equipping of Third World military establishments for "civic action" and counterinsurgency.

The cross-purposes of the reformist thrust were most clearly manifest in the Alliance for Progress, a program of aid and incentives directed toward Latin America. Military cooperation between the United States and the Latin American states had been stressed in the postwar period, but the United States had been relatively deaf to Latin American pleas for economic assistance until the triumph of the Cuban revolution. Latin American leaders did not fail to note that Kennedy's *Alianza* proposal preceded the abortive U.S.-sponsored invasion of Cuba at the Bay of Pigs by a single month.

The ambivalence of Camelot was soon to be resolved. By the early 1960s, Third World elites and their U.S. allies were finding that they could not promote technological and economic modernization—even to the extent necessary to expand markets for local and U.S. manufacturers—without at the same time promoting education, mass communication, and new forms of social organization, thus amplifying demands for broader political participation. The Kennedy administration tried to have it both ways: to promote development—even political and economic reform—but within limits, limits guaranteed by reinforced military and paramilitary forces. In insisting on the exclusion, and in some cases even active repression, of the Marxist and/or populist Left, this strategy left the relatively new centrist or moderately reformist political forces without bargaining power and dangerously exposed. In some cases the frustration of newly mobilized groups led to a collapse of the political center and polarization. In any case, the political fluidity alarmed Third World and U.S. business elites and the U.S. government. After Kennedy's assassination, the ambivalence was resolved in favor of an approach featuring fewer carrots and more sticks.

Fewer Carrots, More Sticks

By the late 1960s, most of the aspects of development policy that had reflected the idealism of the early 1960s had vanished, at least from the official utterings and undertakings of major donor institutions. Social reform as an objective ceased to enjoy even rhetorical currency. Community development, involving local participation, organization, and self-help—as undertaken, for example, by Peace Corps volunteers in Latin America and parts of Asia and by other organizations having field agents—came to be increasingly difficult, if not dangerous, and ultimately uncommon.

In Latin America, in particular, as more and more governments fell under right-wing dictatorships supported by the U.S. government, Peace Corps volunteers working directly with the poor found themselves in something of a sandwich. The communities they worked in were likely to hold them in suspicion of serving surreptitious U.S. government purposes, and it was more likely still that the host governments that ultimately supervised them would regard them as hostile interlopers—being used, at least, by the Left. Even other agencies of the U.S. government often appeared to regard them as troublemakers or agents of insurrection. When the volunteers were finally ejected from most South American countries in the 1970s, it was as much for their successes as for their failures.[4]

In the United States, the idea of foreign assistance became less popular, even among liberals, as abuses and failures were revealed and as the country polarized on the issue of the Vietnam War. Bilateral development assistance was cut sharply, as funds were transferred to multilateral programs or shifted into military and security support categories. Program funds usable for general budgetary support took precedence over aid for specific projects, and loan funds increasingly edged out grants. Remaining funds were tied more tightly to trade and investment requirements or security interests.

The thrust of development policy for the period of the late 1960s and early 1970s is well represented by the establishment of the Overseas Private Investment Corporation (OPIC). Authorized by Congress in 1969, OPIC was given a mandate to provide public insurance for private overseas investment—a guarantee, in the event of unremunerated expropriation, of the socialization of losses.

A harbinger of change, however, was legislation adopted in 1969 that after a three-year period of gestation gave birth to the Inter-American Foundation. Like a number of other foreign assistance programs, the foundation is the offspring of strange bedfellows: in this case, Democrats distrustful of the existing foreign affairs apparatus under the Nixon administration and Republicans distrustful of AID as the incarnation of spendthrift Democratic do-gooding. Almost miraculously, the Inter-American Foundation survived as an island of non-partisan professionalism after AID was taken over by the Reagan administration and increasingly made to serve conservative purposes.[5] The foundation's budget has always been modest, but, standing apart from the Department of State and relatively unencumbered by short-term foreign policy and private economic interests, it has managed to provide small loans and grants directly to organizations representing the poor. It has also, more recently, strengthened intermediary organizations in Latin American countries that nurture networks of organizations representing the poor.

"New Directions" for the 1970s

Although U.S. development assistance policy has seen as many convolutions in strategy and rhetoric as has any other aspect of foreign policy, the "New Directions" amendments of 1973 represent the only major legislative overhaul to date of the still-governing Foreign Assistance Act of 1961. The amendments, redirecting attention (if not a great deal in the way of resources) to "basic human needs," reflected a general liberalizing of the national mood resulting in part from the "greening of America"— the coming of age of the baby boom population bulge and the widespread mobilization of young people in opposition to the Vietnam War. It also reflected the incorporation of a new generation of development specialists into public and private development institutions and into academic and lobbying roles; these specialists had been exposed, through

Peace Corps or other field experiences, to real people and real problems among the Third World poor.

Finally, the overhaul responded to the emergence of a new development paradigm (dependency) and an accumulation of empirical studies that challenged the trickle-down assumption of prevailing theories. The studies indicated, for example, that the fruits of previous policy successes—e.g., an average 5.5 percent annual GNP growth rate and a 3.2 percent annual per capita GNP growth rate during the 1960s for the LDCs as a group—had been stingily dispersed. The poor, in most LDCs a majority of the population, had been excluded from the benefits of growth. The poor, then, had lost ground in relative terms as the distribution gap grew, and in many countries, especially those undergoing very rapid growth, they had been disadvantaged in absolute terms as well. An International Labor Organization (ILO) study of 1960s trends also found that per capita economic growth was accompanied in many countries by rising rates of unemployment. The exceptional cases were also instructive; a few East Asian states—South Korea, Taiwan, Hong Kong, and Singapore, in particular—had been able to increase growth and decrease income disparities at the same time. This appeared to be due in part to government planning, protection of and export promotion for domestic industry, regulation of foreign investment, high levels of domestic savings, large-scale investment in education, and strategies maximizing employment and directing the benefits of agrarian reform to small-scale producers.

The New Directions amendments, therefore, were intended to channel assistance directly to the poor, particularly the rural poor. Actual capital transfers were to be modest, but technical assistance would become more readily available. This new focus was adopted simultaneously by the World Bank. Its president, Robert McNamara, told the bank's Board of Governors in 1973 that whereas less than $1 billion of some $25 billion in previous loans had been devoted to subsistence agriculture, increasing productivity in that sector would henceforth be a high-priority objective. (Even so, as late as 1977 only 23 percent of the commitments of the World Bank and its sister institution, the International Development Association, were financing projects that benefited primarily the poor.)[6]

The 1973 amendments channeled development assistance into functional budget categories, originally: Food and Nutrition, Population Planning and Health, Education and Human Resources Development, Selected Development Problems, and Selected Countries and Organizations. Subsequent reorganization incorporated an energy category. For the rural areas, simultaneous attention to these several needs was to be addressed through "integrated rural development" (IRD) programs. The IRD concept, advanced by the World Bank in the mid-1960s but coming into its own only in the 1970s, was intended, above all, to promote coordination.

IRD projects often combined the efforts of more than one external donor (e.g., AID and World Bank) and an array of host country ministries and agencies. Effective coordination generally proved an elusive goal.

The new approach to technical assistance, intended to maximize employment opportunities and project sustainability, came to be known as "appropriate technology." While some LDC leaders saw in this an intent to deny them the fruits of high technology, adherents of the approach stressed that the concept was comparative and situational, that "appropriate" did not necessarily mean low, and that indeed the assessment of appropriateness should lie with the prospective users. Indeed, like the community development thrust of the early 1960s, the New Directions strategy emphasized self-help and the participation of prospective beneficiaries at every step from planning through evaluation.

The concept of institution-building was revived and given new meaning as the earmarking of funds for a plethora of individual projects gave rise to a multitude of contract agencies, both profit and nonprofit, from both First World and Third. The institutions to be built also included those of would-be beneficiaries at the village or community level. As in the heyday of community development in the 1960s, the kind of institution most often promoted was the credit, consumer, or production cooperative.

New public investment was to focus more on human resources than on material ones. Along with renewed attention to education and health care, there was a particularly strong emphasis on family planning and population control as well as on the incorporation of women (heretofore generally excluded) into sponsored development programs. The energy crisis, however, hitting hard in 1973–1974 and again in 1978–1979, turned attention once again to material resources and resulted in a new emphasis on conservation, alternate energy sourcing, and, in general, resource management.

The New Directions aid legislation preceded by several years the major swing of the U.S. political pendulum it foretold. It was not until the inauguration of the Carter administration in 1977 that some in the upper echelons of the executive branch shared the concerns for the Third World poor that had been expressed by Congress. With respect to some countries, the Carter administration also paid heed to legislation passed in the mid–1970s denying military assistance to the regimes that most systematically violated human rights. But attention both to human rights and to human needs began to fade a couple of years into the new administration.

Meanwhile mounting congressional frustration with State Department foot-dragging spilled over into legislation in 1978, creating the International Development Cooperation Administration (IDCA). The IDCA was to have jurisdiction over AID, thus taking it out from under the State

Department. AID's great escape was never realized, however. The IDCA continues to exist, but inconsequentially; its offices, along with the preexisting AID ones, are housed in the State Department. Thus, while the New Directions were taken seriously by meagerly funded nongovernmental organizations, they were never more than marginal to the major donor agencies.

The limited results of the New Directions thrust need not be attributed to hypocrisy, though to be sure there were many in high places whose espousal of it was poorly grounded in commitment. There was commitment to spare among some who promoted and drafted the legislation and who pursued its implementation in the field. But catalyzing self-help is not a role that comes naturally to large bureaucracies, and a mandate for such bureaucracies to penetrate to the grass roots may well serve to undermine local initiative and spread corruption. More important, the New Directions mandate amounted to swimming upstream against a strong current of political and economic interest, both in donor states and agencies and in client states. Little wonder, then, that in many areas a modicum of success sufficed to generate a fearsome backlash.

Privatization and Militarization

The demise of New Directions had less to do with either the successes or the failures of its attendant policies, or of any other development in the Third World, than with inflation in the First World. Inflation and consequent middle-class discontent coincided in the United States with a strong reaction to the "loss" of Indochina and to what appeared to be retreat and defeat in subsequent foreign policy. Thus the coterie that came to power with Reagan in 1980 was one drawn together by frustrated chauvinism. The advent of the Reagan administration was immediately reflected in a shifting of foreign assistance funds away from development and into military and security support assistance (by then known as Economic Support Funds [ESF]), mainly in the form of grants rather than loans. There was also a sharp swing away from focus on the poor and on social infrastructure to promotion of private enterprise, domestic and foreign. The new buzz-word was *privatization*. Unlike the liberalizing trends of the 1970s, privatization was backed by far more than rhetoric. It coincided with the Third World's debt crisis and with the efforts of creditors (mainly private banks in the First World), through the IMF, to maintain a flow of interest payments that was costing many LDCs half or more of their annual export earnings. The upshot, along with foreign public assistance for private export industries in the Third World, has been a virtual fire sale by Third World governments of publicly owned assets.

The privatization thrust was multipurpose, but a companion policy, intended also to enable debt repayment, was the promotion of austerity—

that is, primarily, the rechanneling of Third World government resources away from social programs. In dramatic contrast to Reagan administration free-market rhetoric, this called for extensive donor institution involvement, once again, in macroeconomic planning.

Likewise, while administration rhetoric condemned foreign assistance in general, and while development and humanitarian assistance as a share of all foreign aid fell from about 50 percent to less than 40 percent during Reagan's first term, the total amount of foreign aid almost doubled during that period.[7] And much of the funding that remained in the bilateral economic category, as opposed to military and ESF ones, was allocated to large-scale, private-sector initiatives administered by the new Bureau for Private Enterprise. Institutional development was once again favored, but, again, there was a change in the kind of institution to be cultivated. Now the favored institutions were to be those supporting the interests of big business, like Peru's Instituto Libertad y Democracia, to which USAID allocated some $9 million in 1989.

Since Congress (a predominantly Democratic House during Reagan's first term and a Democratic Senate as well during his second term) was never enthusiastic about the Reagan administration's basic foreign policy thrust, the New Directions amendments to the Foreign Assistance Act were never repealed; they were simply ignored. Highly publicized famine in Africa resulted in a new economic program for that continent and in funding for the new autonomous agency, the African Development Foundation, patterned after the Inter-American Foundation, but at congressional initiative and over executive opposition. It was established by Congress in 1980 and commenced operations in 1984. Also in the 1980s, new categories of development assistance were added for environmental concerns and for AIDS prevention and control.

The administration's 1985 aid "blueprint" retained a special initiative on women in development. Most major programs, however, continued to ignore women, and policy on family planning was turned inside out, so that U.S. funding was withdrawn from all nongovernmental organizations that promoted it.

Along with the general promotion of private enterprise and privatization of public assets, the Reagan administration reemphasized the primacy of economic growth and productivity. Even so, economic interests were subordinated to military ones. This was particularly apparent in the case of the much-heralded Caribbean Basin Initiative (CBI). The CBI, unveiled in 1981, ostensibly has as its primary mission the generation of export industry in the Caribbean. This is done by offering incentives to U.S. industry to invest or relocate in the area and by the removal of tariffs, quotas, and other obstacles to U.S. importation of their products. In addition, the CBI in the 1980s proved to be one of many covers for channeling funds into the pursuit of a military solution to conflict in Central America.

In time, many of the Reagan administration programs and objectives were incorporated into the Foreign Assistance Act, so that AID and other agencies are authorized—in fact, instructed—to pursue the top-down strategies of the Reagan administration as well as their virtual opposite— the bottom-up strategies of the New Directions amendments. Furthermore, the legislation had been weighted over the years with the pet projects of a host of congresspersons. With such a confusing mix of projects and mandates, direct-hire aid employees had been forced to contract out most of the fieldwork and spend their time writing obfuscatory reports.

Thus, the U.S. foreign assistance program served many purposes in the 1980s—some of them mutually contradictory—but the fact that the Reagan administration found it useful was manifest in its defense of the program against sharp cuts made in the FY 1987 budget by liberals. A 1987 USAID newsletter highlighted the benefit of the program to U.S. business and industry, noting that 70 percent of the funds appropriated for bilateral assistance were being spent in the United States, rather than overseas, as was half of the U.S. contribution to multilateral programs.[8]

A Post–Cold War Face-Lift

The end of the Cold War coincided, more or less, with an economic downturn in the United States, leading in turn to a change in the political climate. The change was manifest, in elections in 1992, not only in the return of the Democratic Party but also in the ascendance of a new generation. The "baby-boomer" generation of President Bill Clinton and Vice President Al Gore had not "invested" politically in the Cold War and had no need to cling to its vestiges. But they soon found that the power system that had underwritten it, and particularly its budgetary implications, remained unshaken.

The new team initially launched an effort to rewrite the Foreign Assistance Act of 1961, inviting participation by a multitude of nonprofit development and antipoverty advocacy organizations. This approach, much like the "new directions" of 1973 and the community development of the early 1960s, would have emphasized sustainable, participatory, community-based, environmentally friendly programs focusing on small-scale farmers, traders, and artisans. But that effort was cut short by the "angry white men" backlash registered in the congressional elections of 1994, which left both houses of Congress under Republican leadership. Thus a largely experienced, creative, and equity-oriented team at USAID was left to play out a defensive strategy against adversaries, particularly Senator Jesse Helms (R.–N.C.), chairman of the Foreign Relations Committee, who saw USAID's policies as insufficiently self-serving and sought to gut its budget, consolidating the remnants into the State Department.

In fact, between 1993 and 1994 the agency closed twenty-six missions, and six more were scheduled for closure by 1999. Senior management ranks were reduced by 38 percent, and the overall staff lost 2,700 employees.[9] Such reductions were intended to project the image of a lean and efficient organization, but some insiders observed that the result was an agency that seemed rudderless, as program initiative was increasingly assumed by major contractors rather than by agency officials.

Many of the programs funded in this reduced budget were relatively new, at least in nomenclature, and were in keeping with trends elsewhere in bilateral and multilateral agencies and nongovernmental organizations. These included support for small-scale or "micro " enterprise; disaster relief and food security assistance, a "partnership" initiative that called for drawing together public and private, business and nonprofit organizations in common purposes and pursuits at the municipal level; support for elections and "good governance," including efforts to expose and discourage corruption; and, above all, carrots and sticks to accelerate privatization and investor-friendly reform legislation on business and finance. Leveraging economic restructuring drew major new funding to the former Soviet sphere, but it became an important USAID objective in many other client states as well.

For USAID, as for other national, international, and nongovernmental organizations, many of these initiatives represent a compromise or, more accurately, a double con, between decision-makers, implementors, and constituencies with very different interests and goals. Final accounting as to whether those who stand to gain or lose most would be the more or less affluent or the more or less honest will depend on how the competition is played out in the field, site by site. In general, in the 1990s as before, the odds are that where there is perceived to be less at stake in terms of strategic or material interests there is greater prospect of success for those promoting equity, or empowerment of poor communities.

Even so, the portion of the budget subject to such ongoing contests was quite small. In the USAID budgets for 1996 and 1997, the subtotal categorized as development assistance, and including disaster relief, was only $2.3 billion out of a total of $6.6 billion to be administered by AID. The largest single funding category continued to be ESF, reserved for the sacred cow of "security" interests.

Testifying in support of the administration's foreign assistance budget request for fiscal 1998, USAID administrator Brian Atwood stressed that the proposed funding advanced America's interests "in three direct ways: by helping to prevent crises; by generating dynamic opportunities for expanded trade; and by providing protection from specific global health threats." But he noted also that in the absence of the Cold War, strength alone was no substitute for leadership. "America's position in the 21st century," he noted, "will depend more and more on the quality of our leadership; on the perception that we understand and appreciate the broad interests of the international community, and that we act with these interests in mind."[10]

President Clinton's budget request for fiscal 1998 for programs in international affairs, including State Department, U.S. Information Agency (USIA), Peace Corps, and other agencies as well as contributions to regional and multilateral institutions, amounted to $19.4 billion—just over 1 percent of the federal budget. Of that amount, 37.5 percent, $7.158 billion, was requested for USAID programs and programs administered by USAID for other agencies, an increase of $476 million over the appropriations for USAID-managed programs in 1997 (Figure 5.1). New funding requests included an additional $292 million for programs in Central and Eastern Europe and the Newly Independent States, with emphasis on reconstruction in the Balkans; $135 million more in ESF, the bulk of it directed to the Middle East; and $65 million for Sustainable Development Assistance, about half of it destined to promote food security in Africa.

The USIA suffered deep cuts in the mid-1990s, particularly in its international exchange programs, such as the Fulbright-Hays scholarly exchanges. The Peace Corps also suffered cuts in the mid-1990s. Peace Corps volunteer numbers had peaked in 1966 at about 15,600 but had dropped to about a third of that number in the 1970s and remained at that level for most of the 1980s and 1990s. The program's popularity with governments, including the U.S. government, has followed a zig-zag course, but it appeared to have enjoyed a steadier course of popularity with U.S. and foreign publics than most other U.S. foreign affairs programs.

At the beginning of 1998, there were some 6,600 volunteers serving in about eighty-five countries. Volunteer assignments and destinations had changed steadily over the years in response to changing domestic political climate, evolving needs and conditions in receiving countries, and trends in business or development. In the late 1990s, volunteers were responding in particular to the exploding demand for training teachers of English, for promoting micro-credit and micro-enterprise, for containing deforestation and other environmental damage, and for limiting the spread of AIDS and other epidemics, new and recurrent. The Clinton administration sought to expand the Peace Corps budget of $222 million by 21 percent in 1999 and to field 10,000 volunteers by 2000.

U.S. Development Policy in Perspective

Since 1946, the U.S. Congress has appropriated more than a trillion dollars in foreign aid, including military aid, security support assistance, and food aid, as well as assistance intended for development purposes (Figure 5.2). The largest annual expenditures, both for economic and for military purposes, were those of the early years, associated with the Marshall

Summary

"Every dollar we devote to preventing conflicts, to promoting democracy, to stopping the spread of disease and starvation brings a sure return in security and savings."

—President William Jefferson Clinton
State of the Union Address February 4, 1997

The president's Budget Request for FY 1998 includes $19.4 billion for programs in international affairs. The U.S. Agency for International Development will manage $7.2 billion (37.5%) of those funds, which includes both USAID programs and programs administered by USAID in cooperation with other agencies. USAID works with developing nations and countries in transition to support viable democracies and market economies. America's fastest growing export markets are in developing countries—U.S. exports to countries receiving USAID assistance grew by $98.7 billion from 1990 to 1995, supporting roughly 1.9 million jobs in the U.S. By the year 2000, four out of five consumers in the world will live in developing nations.

USAID's programs advance both our foreign policy goals and the well-being of some of the world's neediest people. The FY-1998 funds will:

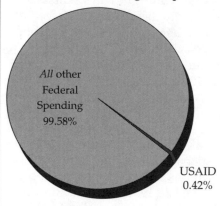

Fiscal Year 1998 Budget Request

All other Federal Spending 99.58%

USAID 0.42%

- Help eradicate polio globally by the year 2000, saving American taxpayers $230 million a year in domestic immunization costs;
- Save more than 3 million lives through immunization programs;
- Help developing nations build their capacity to open their markets and tear down barriers to U.S. trade;
- Extend family planning services to more than 19 million couples around the world who could not otherwise afford them, thus averting thousands of needless deaths of mothers and children;
- Provide assistance to millions of victims of flood, famine, conflict and other crises around the globe.
- Combat worldwide environmental degradation, including global climate change, biodiversity loss and natural resource depletion; and,
- Provide credit to hundreds of thousands of women "microentrepreneurs" starting small businesses.

The request for FY 1998 USAID managed programs represents an increase of $488 million over FY 1997—including, principally:

- An additional $292 million for programs in Central and Eastern Europe and the NIS;
- $135 million more for the Economic Support Fund; and
- An increase of $65.5 million in USAID's Sustainable Development Assistance.

FIGURE 5.1   U.S. Agency for International Development Fiscal Year 1998 Budget Request   *Source:* U.S. House of Representatives, 105th Congress, 1st Session, Committee on International Relations, *Hearing on the Administration's Fiscal Year 1998 Foreign Assistance Budget Request, Feb. 25, 1997* (Washington, D.C.: GPO, 1997), Appendix, p. 50.

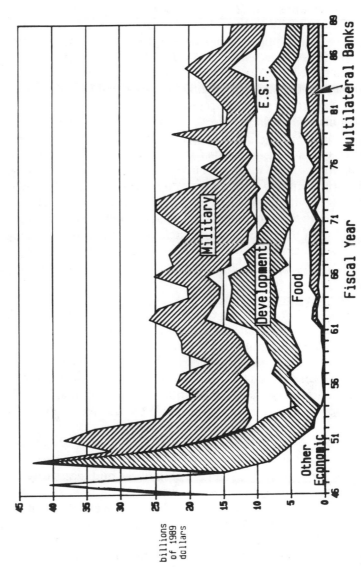

FIGURE 5.2 U.S. foreign aid, 1946–1989, by major program. *Source:* U.S. House of Representatives, 101st Congress, 1st Session, Committee on Foreign Affairs, *Background Materials on Foreign Assistance*, Report of the Task Force on Foreign Assistance, February 1989 (Washington, D.C.: GPO, 1989), p. 145.

Plan. Since that time, the largest expenditures for development and outlays of food aid came in the early- to mid-1960s. Overall, U.S. aid has been
dropping fairly steadily, both in total outlays and as a proportion of GNP,
since the late 1940s and early 1950s (Figure 5.3). During most of that period, outlays for military and security support purposes have exceeded
those for development and relief purposes.

From the late 1950s to the mid-1970s, most U.S. aid was directed to
Asia as a corollary of the wars in Korea and Vietnam. Since the late 1970s,
most aid has been directed to the Middle East, about half of it to Israel
and Egypt. In the late 1980s, more than 60 percent of the total U.S. foreign
assistance budget of about $15 billion was allocated to military and secu-
rity (ESF) categories. Bilateral economic assistance ranged between $2
and $3 "billion."[11]

In time, the use of the Cold War to maintain and expand U.S. economic
supremacy boomeranged, as the Machiavellians lost out to the true believers. In arming itself against all imaginable contingencies and fighting
proxy wars on multiple fronts, the United States weakened its own economy, leaving it with more sticks but fewer carrots with which to pursue
its goals. Moreover, as the implementation of foreign policy devolved increasingly upon the intelligence agencies and the armed forces, so too
did the making of that policy, and the economic interests that were to be
pursued or protected came to be overshadowed or even undermined by
the interests of the "security" bureaucracy.

In his waning years, Kennan, to his credit, declared the Cold War over
and allowed that it need not have gotten so out of hand in the first
place.[12] Even so, at the end of the 1980s, U.S. policy with respect to international development continued to flow largely from Cold War premises,
and as Western European countries increasingly challenged U.S. guidance in development strategy and Japan surpassed the United States as a
donor of economic assistance, the United States continued to expend a
major portion of its shrinking aid budget in the trashing of its own neighborhood.

With the dissolving of the Soviet Union at the end of 1991, however, it
became necessary to draw up new rationales for foreign policy generally,
including development assistance. The tone, if not necessarily the content, of policy rationales at the end of the Cold War has been remarkably
akin to that following World War II. Regions that were so recently enemy
turf have been subject to something on the order of an occupation
regime, though ostensibly a friendly one—no khakis and tanks, only pin-
striped suits and laptops. As in the 1940s, the instigators of economic restructuring are messianic in their conviction that publics want to un-
dergo this transformation, whatever the cost.

In the aftermath of World War II, however, the victorious allies chose to
punish "war criminal" leaders of the defeated states while promoting

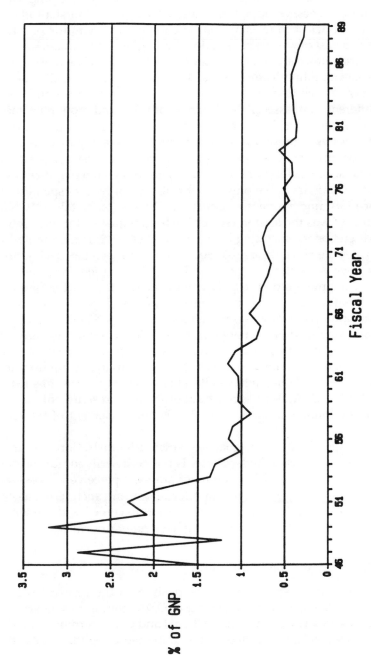

FIGURE 5.3 U.S. foreign aid, as a % of GNP, FY46–89. *Source:* House of Representatives, 101st Congress, 1st Session, Committee on Foreign Affairs, *Background Materials on Foreign Assistance,* Report of the Task Force on Foreign Assistance, February 1989 (Washington, D.C.: GPO, 1989), p. 147.

relief and recovery for ordinary citizens. Not so this time around. The most readily corruptible leaders of the vanquished evil empire have been dealt into the immediate benefits of reform while long-suffering citizens are left to wonder how to live without wages or pensions and who to blame for currencies stripped of value. In lieu of the Marshall Plan, the new Eurasia has seen foreign assistance opening doors for private investors to a vast new market of national going-out-of-business sales.

As in the aftermath of World War II, post–Cold War leaders and foreign assistance administrators speak of a mandate for global leadership, and as before such leaders represent different constituencies and operate from different compasses. All speak now of trade and growth promotion on the one hand and humanitarian aid and poverty reduction on the other, but between those sets of priorities there lies a gaping chasm.

The most unmistakable difference between this postwar period and the last is the allocation of public funding to foreign development needs. International affairs is the only major category of federal spending that has since 1980 undergone real reduction. The approximately $419 billion spent in 1997 was the least in real, or inflation-adjusted, terms in international discretionary spending in any year since 1979; it represented a 50 percent decline since the mid-1980s and an 11.7 percent decline in the previous two years alone (Figure 5.4). It might be argued that people-centered development stood to gain from drastic cuts in a foreign affairs budget tilted toward "security" interests. But development assistance as such has declined by at least one-third since the mid-1980s. At a gathering of the nongovernmental organization (NGO) community early on in the Clinton administration, Vice President Gore pledged that 40 percent of the AID budget would be devoted to humanitarian and environmental concerns. USAID claims to have allocated about 31 percent to such concerns. But the USAID-managed budget itself represents only a minor portion of a foreign affairs budget that is only 1 percent of the federal budget.[13]

Such meager funding for goals to which administration and agency leaders profess to assign high priority is not necessarily indicative of dissembling. It is precisely when administrators are perceived to be serious about humanitarianism or equity, rather than using such terms as cover for other purposes, that funding will be hard to come by; those who expect to have the last word on spending have other priorities.

Other Donor States and Institutions

In the immediate postwar period, the position of the United States as a donor of official development assistance (ODA) completely dwarfed that of all other states as well as of international and nongovernmental entities. As recently as 1982, the United States continued to be the largest single

53 Percent Decline in Real Terms from 1984 to 1997

International affairs spending is barely one percent of total federal spending and less than one-third of one percent of Gross Domestic Product. Since 1984, funding for international affairs (in budget authority) has declined by more than 50 percent in real terms.

Bold numbers are the BUDGET AUTHORITY FIGURES IN 1994 DOLLARS
Italic numbers are the ACTUAL budget authority figures congress passed

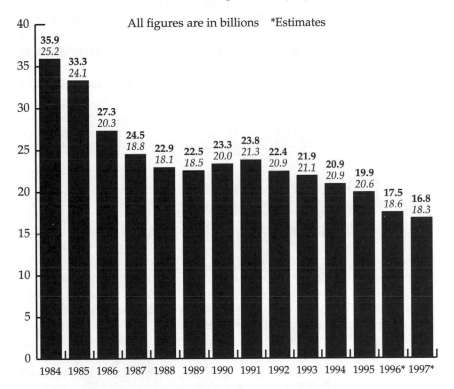

FIGURE 5.4   Decline in U.S. international affairs spending, 1984–1997.   *Source:* U.S. House of Representatives, 105th Congress, 1st Session, Committee on International Relations, *Hearing: New Thinking on Foreign Assistance, Feb. 26, 1997* (Washington, D.C.: GPO, 1997), Appendix, p. 85.

contributor, accounting for 22 percent of ODA—almost double the portions of either Japan or Saudi Arabia, the two second largest contributors.

Overall disbursements of ODA have increased substantially since the 1960s. They have grown since the mid-1970s at a rate of more than 4 percent a year, reaching some $36 billion in the mid-1980s and peaking at $59 billion in the mid-1990s. Counting nongovernmental and multilateral sources along with bilateral ones, there are now more donors than there are recipient countries. As the number-one donor of nonmilitary aid, the United States was eclipsed in 1989 by Japan. And while the United States retained second place in terms of absolute amounts of funds transferred (about $8 billion in 1989), its contribution as a proportion of GNP had dropped to last place among the eighteen countries represented by the Development Advisory Committee (DAC) of the Organization for Economic Cooperation and Development (OECD)[14] (Figure 5.5).

By 1995 the United States had been eclipsed by France and Germany in terms of absolute amounts transferred, and its contribution had dropped to half that of Japan. The United States continued to rank last in aid disbursement as a proportion of GNP among the twenty-one OECD nations in 1995. U.S. contributions had dropped in absolute as well as relative terms since the mid-1980s. While OECD contributions had increased in absolute terms, they had dropped as a proportion of GNP from about 0.35 percent in 1985 to 0.26 percent in 1995.[15] Thereafter contributions dropped in absolute terms and as a proportion of collective GNP.

The Organization for Economic Cooperation and Development (OECD)

In the post–World War II period, OECD member states, growing in numbers (twenty-nine by 1998) and wealth, have always been the mainstay of overseas development assistance. The group contributed up to two-thirds of overall transfers during the Cold War and almost all major transfers since the implosion of the Soviet Union at the beginning of the 1990s. They have never approached, however, their collective goal of contributing 1 percent of GNP, or even the 0.7 percent goal set by the United Nations. Their contributions amounted to 0.35 percent of their combined GNP in 1970, rising slightly to 0.38 in 1982 and dropping back to 0.36 in 1985 and to 0.26 in 1995. Total OECD contributions rose from about $7 billion in 1970 to about $30 billion in 1985 and $59 billion in 1995.

The OECD listed its largest donors in 1995, in descending order, as Japan ($14.5 billion), France (8.4), Germany (7.5), and the United States (7.3). The Netherlands and the United Kingdom followed with 3.3 and 3.2, respectively, and Canada and Sweden with 2.1 and 2.0. For contributions as a percentage of GNP, Denmark led with 0.97, followed closely by Sweden with 0.89, Norway with 0.87, and the Netherlands with 0.80. (UNDP figures for 1995 varied only slightly except in the case of Sweden, which was listed at 0.77.) The United States trailed at 0.10. The European Union on its own account was becoming an increasingly important player, budgeting $8.3 billion for Third World development in 1998.[16]

At the economic summit of industrialized states in Paris in July 1989, coinciding with the bicentennial of the French Revolution, Japanese Prime Minister Suzuki Onu stunned donor and LDC leaders alike by

U.S. No Longer Top Aid Giver

The U.S. ranked fourth in overall official development aid in 1995, after decades as the world's top aid donor. When official development assistance is viewed as a percentage of gross national product (GNP), the United States ranked last among the 21 member countries of the Development Assistance Committee* (graph at bottom).

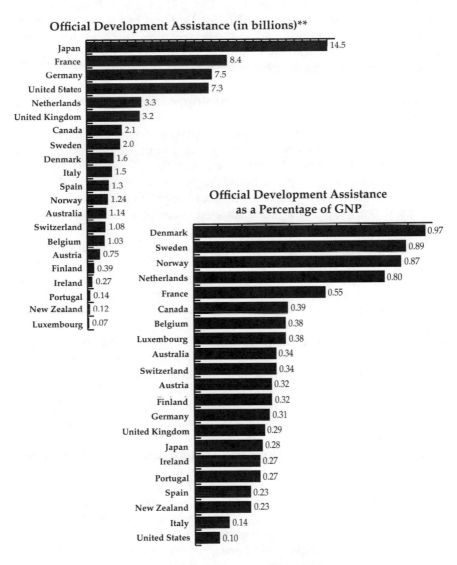

FIGURE 5.5   Official development assistance, 1995.   *Source:* U.S. House of Representatives, 105th Congress, 1st Session, Committee on International Relations, *Hearing: New Thinking on Foreign Assistance, Feb. 26, 1997* (Washington, D.C.: GPO, 1997), Appendix 3, p. 86.

pledging a new economic aid package amounting to $43 billion to be expended by 1992. Much of Japanese aid, like that of other OECD members, has been linked to the promotion of the products and investments of their nationals.

In fact, criticism of the Japanese aid program by Third World countries, other OECD members, and Japanese opposition groups sounds much like the criticism leveled earlier at the U.S. aid program. It has been argued that too much Japanese aid is in the form of loans rather than grants, that it is too tightly tied to the purchase of Japanese goods and technologies, and that too much emphasis is placed on the development of material infrastructure, such as roads, dams, and power plants. Moreover, Japan's development professionals are quick to acknowledge that the rapid buildup in aid projects far outstripped their own acquisition of development expertise.

The Japanese aid program places considerably fewer staff in the field than do those of other donor states. Japan International Cooperation Agency (JICA) spokesmen boast of high performance per person but acknowledge that their personnel are seriously overloaded. Like the United States and several other OECD countries, along with the United Nations and the Vatican, Japan also fields its own corps of volunteers. Between 1965 and 1990, approximately 10,000 Japanese, mostly young men, served overseas under the auspices of the Japan Overseas Cooperative Volunteers (JOCV). Some 2,000 Japanese volunteers were serving in thirty-eight countries in 1989.

The general concept of foreign aid has been more popular and less controversial in Japan than in the United States. Domestic critics have argued for more attention to human needs, for greater effectiveness, and for more independence. Historically, Japan has generally followed the U.S. lead in deciding where to place its aid—often giving precedence to countries where the United States claimed major strategic interests. That accommodation has been fading since the mid-1980s as Japan goes its own way, particularly in expanding programs in Africa. Unlike the United States, Japan rarely places strictly political conditions on the extension of aid.[17]

From 1990 through 1996, Japan provided more than $70 billion in foreign assistance, 20 percent of the world's total. Japan continued to be the world's largest aid donor through 1997, but its contributions as a percentage of GNP dropped from 0.31 in 1985 to 0.28 in 1995. After several years of recession, Japan prepared to slash its ODA budget in 1998 by some 10 percent, a move particularly damaging to African countries and UN projects that had benefited disproportionately from Japanese donations.

An OECD review of public opinion polls in member states between 1960 and 1983 indicated general public support for some forms of foreign assistance, particularly those directly addressed to the amelioration of hunger and poverty. A 1989 report of the Overseas Development Council (ODC) noted that in Canada, the Netherlands, and Sweden, in particular, and to a somewhat lesser degree in the Federal Republic of Germany (FRG), parliaments, parties, and the public are consistently supportive of foreign aid programs. This was in stark contrast to the cases of the United Kingdom (UK), where support has recently been unenthusiastic, and the United States, where the program has often been plagued by partisan and intragovernmental conflict.

According to the ODC report, the countries where foreign assistance enjoyed the greatest public support were the ones that had made the greatest commitment to public education on development issues. They were also the ones whose programs clearly stressed development objectives over political or commercial interests.[18]

The Council for Mutual Economic Assistance (CMEA)

The overall amount of Soviet and East European economic assistance to the Third World (coordinated by the CMEA) was never highly significant. Soviet assistance from 1954 to 1981 totaled a little more than $22 billion, while East European commitments for the period amounted to $12 billion spread among sixty countries. East Germany (GDR), with the strongest economy, was the largest contributor. Assistance from the CMEA group as a whole in 1982 represented 0.17 percent of collective GNP. It was crucial, however, to a few countries, particularly those most in need because of credit freezes imposed by Western countries and institutions.

Such politically responsive aid was particularly important in the Middle East, to Egypt and Syria in the mid-1950s; in Latin America, to Cuba since the early 1960s and to Nicaragua in the 1980s; in Africa, to Angola and Mozambique in the mid-1970s and in the late 1970s to Ethiopia. Aid to India had political significance but was important commercially as well.

Like most other donor states, however, the Soviet Union and its East European allies extended credits to LDCs as a means of promoting exports, and economic assistance as a whole was increasingly neutral with respect to Cold War alignment. Technical assistance was also an important aspect of Soviet bloc programs, engaging more than 100,000 technicians in about seventy-five countries in the early 1980s. At the same time the CMEA states were hosting more than 70,000 students in their universities, half of them from Africa and half of them on scholarship in the USSR.[19]

The Organization of Petroleum Exporting Countries (OPEC)

The OPEC donor category was a fleeting one. In 1970 total ODA from OPEC member states amounted to only $40 million. After petroleum prices rose sharply in 1973–1974, however, foreign assistance from OPEC states also rose dramatically—to $6.24 billion in 1975 and $9.59 billion in 1980. Their contribution in 1980 amounted to 16 percent of total ODA. From the early 1980s until 1990, when oil prices were dropping, however, OPEC development assistance fell by more than 40 percent.

Like other donor states, the OPEC countries used foreign assistance, particularly credits, as a means of promoting trade, but they also used it to strengthen political and cultural ties. Middle Eastern OPEC states, in particular, cultivated Moslem leaders and communities in Africa and Asia and sought to strengthen ties among predominantly Moslem states.

As a percentage of GNP, the contributions of OPEC states were much greater than those of the OECD members, reaching 8.5 percent in 1975 and dropping to 2.79 percent in 1982. Saudi Arabia's contribution in 1982 amounted to 3.53 percent of GNP and that of Kuwait to 4.46 percent. Qatar's contribution for 1975 was up to 15.6 percent of GNP.[20] It should be noted, however, that not all the OPEC states benefited in the long run from the cartel's price hikes. Apart from the Gulf states, most petroleum producers saw the brief period of prosperity run up unpayable debts and uncontrollable inflation without generating additional productive capacity. Some of the wealthier Gulf states, particularly Saudi Arabia, have continued to underwrite major projects, particularly the construction of mosques in Moslem states, but those were not generally projects of a type or funding on a scale that would be characterized as development assistance.

Multilateral Financial Institutions

The most important international financial institutions of the postwar era, the International Monetary Fund (IMF) and the International Bank for Reconstruction and Development (IBRD), more commonly known as the World Bank, created at the Bretton Woods Conference of 1944 by representatives of forty-four states, were designed in large measure to meet the needs of the United States. The role of the IMF was to be that of stabilizing currency exchange rates, while the World Bank's role was to promote development through project loans to governments that facilitate foreign investment. The United States was particularly interested in eliminating colonial (especially British) and nationalistic (particularly Latin American) barriers to profitable trade and investment. To guard against the intrusion of real internationalism, it was decided that voting would be weighted in accordance with size of national contribution.

Those institutions have remained responsive to U.S. interests, or more precisely, to banking interests represented by the U.S. government, since it is the Department of the Treasury that represents the country in their decision-making bodies. The regional development banks, in existence since the early 1960s—Inter-American, Asian, and African—operate under similar rules, including weighted voting, with similar results. Such institutions maintain that their decisions are based entirely on economic criteria and are politically neutral. Setting aside the question, however, as to whether there can be such a thing as politically neutral economic criteria, it remains clear that U.S. political or "security" arguments, when pursued with sufficient vehemence, have almost always carried the day.

The IMF, for example, has claimed that its loan decisions were apolitical except for a general hesitancy to extend loans to unstable governments. Nevertheless, in the fall of 1980, while Jamaica's democratic socialist government, under Prime Minister Michael Manley, suffered a virtually complete banker's boycott, the IMF approved loans to the shaky juntas of El Salvador and Bolivia. The loan to Bolivia was approved despite the fact that a member of the IMF's own team was detained by the drug-dealing generals. The loan to El Salvador had to be approved without on-site inspection because the level of civil strife was such that the government could not guarantee the IMF envoy's personal safety.[21] Similarly, policymakers of the Inter-American Development Bank overrode staff recommendations on several occasions in the 1980s and denied loans to Nicaragua, and the World Bank overrode its own staff professionals to support major engineering projects in the Amazon.

Worse, perhaps, than these extreme examples of caving in to pressure was the fact that for some time, at least in areas under U.S. hegemony, those institutions systematically favored authoritarian governments over democratic ones. That is hardly surprising when one considers the kinds of options faced by leaders of debt-ridden LDCs. Since new loans, of late, are most often extended to enable the repayment of old loans, and since the funds required for debt repayment are most often squeezed out of wages and salaries and services, the leader whose tenure is not dependent on popular approval was apt to be seen then as a better bet.

Liberals in the U.S. Congress, emboldened in the 1970s, attempted to deal with the problem by introducing considerations of human rights and human needs into the votes cast by U.S. representatives to the international financial institutions. They succeeded in 1980 in passing the requisite legislation, but they were never able to ensure its implementation.

With the breakdown in 1971 of the fixed currency exchange rate system, the IMF was left temporarily without a job—at least without the well-defined job of monitoring that system on behalf of the economically dominant states and ensuring that there was sufficient international liquidity to tide countries over temporary balance-of-payment shortfalls. With a debt crisis emerging, however, the IMF was soon reassigned the role of primary collection agency on behalf of First World bankers, thus relieving First World governments of that awkward task.

As the debt crisis of the 1970s became a debt system in the 1980s and the accelerating trend to globalization (the liberation of capital from popular, or governmental, control) became virtually complete in the post–Cold War 1990s, the IMF assumed as well the role of global macro-economic policy coordination. Its role was still championed by U.S. and other OECD governments, though the banking and corporate interests served were now stateless. The institution's ability to impose its policy package—essentially the same one for countries large and small, modern and traditional, relatively prosperous and destitute—is not based simply on the leveraging clout of its own loan funds but on its "better business bureau" role of assigning credit ratings. A country denied credit by the IMF is essentially frozen out of international trade, as it is shunned also by other multilateral, bilateral, and private institutions.

In the post–Cold War era, that is, in the absence of any alternate market, it has become unnecessary for the IMF and other multilateral institutions and their constituencies to cater to authoritarian regimes because national leaders have at any rate been stripped of the role of economic policy-making. In fact, it is advantageous to have in place elected leaders who, lacking options, nevertheless share the blame for a system that continually pushes sacrifice and responsibility downward on the social pyramid while lifting authority, privilege, and economic resources upward and outward to global money movers.

By the late 1990s, the original professed goals of the Bretton Woods institutions had been turned virtually inside out. The IMF, entrusted with maintaining stability, had been charged, in the aftermath of the East Asian financial meltdown, with encouraging reckless lending and investment by sporadically bailing out investors at the expense of taxpayers, workers, and consumers and ultimately with setting off a dangerous round of competitive devaluation. Even major currency spectators became alarmed, and the biggest of them, George Soros, has called for a new comprehensive system of international regulation.

Austerity, or doing without, once recognized as the problem, is now touted as the solution. The World Bank and its regional affiliates, tasked with "development" (in effect pump priming for the Third World), joined forces in the 1980s and 1990s with the IMF and with bilateral and private sector funding sources in leveraging policy changes punishing to the poor and crippling of government authority and capacity to respond to public need. They were called to account in the early 1990s as more than two hundred NGOs—national and international nonprofit development, advocacy, religious, and popular organizations—joined forces in a campaign designated "50 years is enough." It was successful at least to the degree of calling considerable attention to the need to reconceptualize the now twisted missions of those institutions.

Perhaps that campaign strengthened the voices of those within the World Bank and its affiliates who were genuinely committed to making more constructive use of the institutions' resources and energies as well as those tasked with projecting a more enlightened image. In his keynote address to the annual meeting of the World Bank and the IMF in 1997, World Bank president James Wolfensohn put the fight against global inequity at the top of the development agenda. He said that without greater equity there would be neither peace nor global stability and that prosperous nations ignore the gap between rich and poor at their peril.

The Inter-American Development Bank (IDB), comprising, along with 30 Western Hemisphere states, 16 European ones, Israel, and Japan, has recognized that poverty, claiming at least a third of the Latin American population, is on the rise largely owing to mounting unemployment and job insecurity—this despite average annual growth rates exceeding 5 percent. IDB president Enrique Iglesias noted at the bank's annual assembly in March 1998 that unemployment, poverty, marginalization, and soaring violence were putting fragile new democracies at risk.

It is also likely, however, that the new face appearing on the development banks represents recognition of a need to shore up their constituencies on the left, or public interest, side of the equation, as their role becomes less relevant to private sector interests. The World Bank, with 5,400 full-time employees in 1998, remained the fountainhead of development assistance, but it was lending at little more than half of capacity. Its net annual lending of $7.4 billion represented only 2 to 3 percent of the total flow of capital to developing countries.[22]

One may hope that unlike the disappointing results of the World Bank's mood swing under the leadership of Robert McNamara in the early 1970s, the recent change of heart or rhetoric will result in a serious redeployment of resources. Thus far, however, serious effort to remove the blight of poverty has been seen only in the vicinity of the conference hotels where multilateral lenders are scheduled to meet.

Meanwhile, development lending as such becomes increasingly invisible, as some 93 percent of the capital flowing to the Third World is private. Little wonder, then, that development banks, along with bilateral and nongovernmental development agencies, are promoting the idea of building partnerships in the Third World. The problem, however, is that when business deploys its resources it is to the same ends as the bilateral and multilateral institutions—to leverage changes in the interest of the benefactor.

Trade and Investment Regimes and Rules

Trade and investment are motivated by the pursuit of profits. They can be expected to generate economic growth in one or more countries; they may or may not promote development in a broader sense that addresses the public interest. Nevertheless they are increasingly treated as indispensable to development strategy, and they certainly impact, for good or for ill, the prospects for development.

A third pillar of the international institutional structure conceived at Bretton Woods in 1944 was to have been the International Trade Organization, but the U.S. Congress failed to ratify the bill creating it. As a fallback, the General Agreement on Tariffs and Trade (GATT), designed to regulate trade and minimize barriers through negotiated rounds of tariff reductions, was drawn up only two years after the Bretton Woods conference establishing the IMF and the World Bank. The trajectory of GATT, like that of the Bretton Woods institutions, has followed the zigs and zags of power competition among states and classes, institutions, and sectors; like those institutions, conferences, and mechanisms, the GATT has been employed increasingly to pry open markets in the Third World, even as First World markets became ever more restrictive.

An organization on the order of the one aborted in 1944 finally came into being in 1994. The World Trade Organization (WTO), which subsumed the GATT, is an international body that facilitates negotiation and makes rules relating to cross-border trade that are assumed to be binding on contracting parties. It also mediates disputes. The activities of this body do not necessarily favor richer or more powerful countries, but they can be expected to favor private interests over public ones, the generalizable interests of corporations over the particular interests and laws of individual countries.

Much of what used to be the budgetary authority and regulatory power of government had already in practice fallen under the jurisdiction of the IMF, the GATT, and, in the 1990s, the WTO, but the Multilateral Agreement on Investment (MAI), nearing completion in early 1998, appeared to wrest from government the last vestige of a bargaining position vis-à-vis multinational capital. The MAI eliminates all restrictions and conditions on the movement of capital across national frontiers and all advantages that might be retained by national businesses. The agreement gives multinational corporations the power to sue governments for loss of past or potential profits due to discrimination.

The twenty-nine states of the OECD met in Paris in late February 1998 to put final touches on the agreement. At that meeting, Renato Ruggiero, director-general of the WTO, commented, "We are writing the constitution of a single global economy."[23] Once the treaty has been signed by the governments of the richest states, governments of the developing states, who were not consulted in drawing up the agreement, will be offered the chance to sign on. It will be an offer they cannot refuse, because refusal would mean being frozen out of capital markets.

The United Nations and Its Affiliates

Paralleling the case of the multilateral financial institutions, power relations in the United Nations in the early postwar period reflected the preeminent position of the United States on the world stage. As the process of decolonization continued, however, and as some countries ordinarily aligned with the United States began to behave more independently, the United Nations—at least its General Assembly and its specialized and affiliated agencies—came more nearly to reflect the interests of the Third World. Since the late 1960s the United Nations has increasingly been used by Third World countries as a major forum and it has taken initiatives to promote Third World development.

The United Nations created the regional economic commissions that were so influential in the early 1960s and gave shelter and legitimacy to the nonaligned movement. In the UN Conference on Trade and Development (UNCTAD), the Group of 77 (G–77) caucusing Third World countries, generally suffering from deterioration in the terms of trade for their primary products as well as from other forms of discrimination in trade, technology, and investment, found a forum in the 1960s and 1970s for collectively airing their grievances. UNCTAD remains open to the concerns of the G–77, but First World governments and multinational corporations are increasingly unresponsive.

Among the older UN agencies and affiliates whose responsibilities include some aspect of development are the United Nations Educational, Scientific, and Cultural Organization (UNESCO); Economic and Social Council (ECOSOC); UN Children's Fund (UNICEF); Food and Agriculture Organization (FAO); World Health Organization (WHO); International Labor Organization (ILO); and, of course, the UN Development Program (UNDP). The UNDP, launched in 1965, operates a volunteer program, on the order of the Peace Corps or Papal Volunteers, with tours of duty limited to two years. The United Nations volunteers, usually better trained than their Peace Corps counterparts, work at the community level in some of the world's poorest and most strife-torn countries. The functions and the significance of the UNDP have been growing steadily in the 1990s as the agency has assumed the role of supporting implementation of UN social development programs. It recently was tasked with serving as the central office, or clearinghouse, of the United Nations operations country by country. In 1997 it was operating in at least seventy countries.

For its part, the UNDP has made the eradication of poverty its overriding priority; it has devoted considerable energy and resources to tracking global progress—or the lack of it—toward that goal and to orienting politics to the idea that poverty eradication can and must be done. In April 1998, the UNDP and the European Union (EU) established a joint steering group for their aid programs. This should further strengthen the UNDP, but since the EU's priorities include the promotion of private enterprise and its budget ($8.3 billion) was much greater than that of the UNDP ($2.7 billion), the UNDP might find its focus on poverty eradication blurred.

More recently the United Nations has spawned other programs with developmental implications, including a special development fund for women, a fund for addressing population issues, an education and training program for southern Africa, an institute for Namibia, an environment program, a center on human settlement, and a center for science and technology for development. An older agency, the UN High Commission for Refugees, has taken on increasing responsibilities in the 1990s as the number of displaced persons grows. UN peacekeeping operations have proliferated and have proved crucial in many cases to sustaining relief, refugee, and development programs. The Center for Human Rights was absorbed by the Office of the High Commissioner for Human Rights, established in 1997. The commissioner, former president of Ireland Mary Robinson, sits on the Executive Committee of UN secretary general Kofi Annan.

Regional organizations of general competence, such as the Organization of American States (OAS) and the Organization of African Unity (OAU), also maintain development programs. Such programs have thus far been meager, however, as the priorities of those organizations have lain elsewhere.

The United Nations has always had its share of critics, and its development programs have not been spared the heat. The United States has increasingly taken an adversarial stance vis-à-vis the organization. After Third World nations acquired a voting majority in the General Assembly, U.S. representatives to that body began to speak of the tyranny of the majority and of the irresponsibility of the small states. The Nixon and Reagan administrations, in fact, were vitriolic in their criticism, and the Reagan administration, in 1984, withdrew the United States from participation in (and funding for) UNESCO. The administration of George Bush, himself a former chief delegate to the United Nations, retreated from the Reagan position, but was unable to take his party with him. The Clinton administration, through U.S. ambassador to the UN Bill Richardson, popular former congressman from New Mexico, made a concerted effort to educate the U.S. public on the many crucial roles of the United Nations. It has also sought—thus far in vain—a formula acceptable to the Republican Congress for covering the unpaid U.S. assessment to the UN, which amounted to $1.45 billion in 1998.

The United States has yet to ratify the Convention on the Elimination of all Forms of Discrimination Against Women (ratified by 161 countries) and the Convention on the Rights of the Child (ratified by 191 countries). Some U.S. parliamentarians even found something sinister in UNESCO's designation of twenty U.S. landmarks as World Heritage sites and forty-seven U.S. sites as Biosphere Reserves.

When an investigator visited the United States in 1997 under the auspices of the UN High Commission on Human Rights to monitor the use of the death penalty, he found the United States to be second only to

China in its expanding use of the death penalty. He was given less than an enthusiastic welcome. In fact, Senate Foreign Relations chairman Jesse Helms called the mission "an absurd U.N. charade." The UN Human Rights Commission report on the investigation, released in April 1998, found that the United States, in applying the death penalty unfairly, was in violation of international standards and practices and called for a moratorium on further executions.[24]

From the Left, critics have charged that UN professionals, like other international civil servants, earn too much and live too well to be able truly to empathize with the Third World's poor. Furthermore, some argue that the business of the international development establishment, including the United Nations, is merely to attend to the welfare aspects of global capital accumulation and to ensure compliance with international agreements and procedures favoring the affluent.[25]

Supporters of UN programs maintain, however, that although top-down approaches to development appear to be unavoidable for large bureaucracies, UN development agencies show greater sensitivity than most to Third World needs and perspectives and reach many countries and population sectors that other agencies, focused on business or political interests, shun. Moreover, major conferences that combine intergovernmental and NGO forums—such as those on the environment, human rights, sustainable development, women, population, and housing that took place in the 1990s—play an essential part in molding the consciousness of national leaders and opinion makers. Perhaps more importantly, the UN has provided both an amplification system for the voices of transnational NGOs and an organizational nucleus for the promotion of their networking and interest aggregation.

It stands to reason that the trends and contradictory tendencies being played out in the 1990s within and among its 185 member states would register on the international barometer: the United Nations. On the one hand, the importance of the UN role in representing Third World states has been diminished in the 1990s both by a weakening of the position of those states vis-à-vis richer ones and by the weakening of states as such vis-à-vis the private sector. The role of the UN in representing disadvantaged peoples has by no means diminished, however, and may in fact have been enhanced, as the UN has come to be seen as the only promise of direct popular participation at the global level, the protector and nurturer of globally oriented nonprofit NGOs. Though it might not be visible to the naked eye, it was clear that a major struggle was being waged at the turn of the twenty-first century for the soul of the United Nations.

Nongovernmental Organizations

In contemporary development literature, the terms *nongovernmental organization* (NGO) and *private voluntary organization* (PVO) are used descriptively and interchangeably, even though in original usage their meanings were distinct and precise. The United Nations introduced "nongovernmental organization" into the literature in reference to organizations recognized as having consultative status to the UN and receiving some support from that body. The term *private voluntary organization* was reportedly coined by AID to categorize private-sector nonprofit organizations receiving AID contracts or grants.[25]

Both terms have come to be used more generally to refer to private or community-based organizations that may receive funding from governments or international organizations but are not direct appendages of them. PVO remains the more common usage, however, for U.S.-based groups, while NGO is more often used elsewhere. Thus I will use NGO as the more general term and PVO to specify U.S.-based groups. The terms may be used for organizations having purposes other than development, but we are referring here to those having development functions. Some of the literature makes a distinction as well between PVOs/NGOs as service, consultative, or intermediary funding organizations and "popular organizations," representing fund-seeking or problem-solving national or local communities. But such distinctions are not always easy; therefore, unless otherwise indicated, "popular organizations" will be subsumed in this chapter by NGOs.

There has been a remarkable proliferation of nongovernmental organizations in the past three decades. More than four hundred PVOs have registered with USAID and participated directly or through the Advisory Committee on Voluntary Foreign Aid (ACVFA) in a continuous dialogue on its programs. The ACVFA aspires to represent the entire PVO community on a broad range of issues ranging from development assistance strategy to the federal procurement process for grants and contracts.

Another coalition of U.S.-based PVOs, the American Council for Voluntary International Action (InterAction), draws together some 160 organizations working in development and humanitarian assistance for purposes of information exchange and policy advocacy. These organizations are supported by more than 40 million donors and many thousands of volunteers. But there are many thousands of additional NGOs in the United States, Europe, Japan, and other OECD countries. Aid from NGOs amounted to 0.03 percent of the combined GNP of the OECD countries in 1995 compared to 0.26 percent of the GNP as the official ODA outlay.[27]

Meanwhile, the growth of Third World NGOs has been even more impressive; tens of thousands of them are now working with First World counterparts. At the village or neighborhood level, very casual or partial surveys, such as those compiled by the Worldwatch Institute in the late 1980s, identified hundreds of thousands of self-help organizations. The United Nations quit counting in the 1990s after their numbers went over a million.

This proliferation has many causes—among them the growth of international exchange and area studies programs beginning in the 1960s and the massive expansion in the 1990s of internships as academic degree or job placement requirements. NGOs have offered the more adventurous, idealistic, or independent-minded a means of serving peoples without necessarily or directly serving governments. Some such organizations, in First World and Third, are composed of professionals who had served governments but were removed or chose to resign when turnovers at the top resulted in sharp changes in policy direction.

Proliferation of NGOs has resulted also from a relative shrinkage in the 1990s in official development assistance, coinciding with mushrooming evidence of need. Growing need results not only from natural and man-made disaster, such as drought and war, but from the trend of governments both in First World and Third to discard responsibilities and to discontinue service and relief programs.

A more obvious reason for this proliferation, however, has been the recent inclination of government aid agencies to contract out their field-work. By 1988, 62 percent of USAID employees, for example, were nondirect hires, or contractees (compared to about 25 percent in the early 1960s). Some of those were from university faculties or from for-profit engineering or consulting firms, but a great many represented PVOs. US-AID funds channeled through PVOs have increased by about 3 percent each year since 1993.[28]

The Canadian government and a number of European governments also contract out much of their development effort to NGOs. The Dutch government, for example, has worked through an NGO coordinating body to support the efforts of both religious and secular organizations operating overseas. The coordinating bodies serve as independent intermediaries, funding up to 75 percent of the project costs of Dutch groups meeting established criteria, and also fund Third World NGOs directly.[29] The Canadian International Development Agency (CIDA), a governmental body, allocates several million dollars annually to NGOs for use in development education.

Official support for NGO/PVO programs has come about in part because government agencies have recognized the cultural sensitivity, innovativeness, and dedication of many such groups and the advantages of decentralizing, debureaucratizing, and lowering the official profile. Contracting out also broadens the aid constituency and leaves official agencies less vulnerable to "bloated bureaucracy" epithets. For NGOs, however, and particularly for U.S. PVOs dealing with USAID, government support usually means a very considerable erosion of PVO independence; it increases dependency and regimentation and thus decreases innovation and responsiveness to beneficiary communities.

Nonprofit organizations and, in general, the ideal of volunteerism now have the advantage of political support (rhetorical that is, not necessarily material) from both ends of the political spectrum. This offers some advantages for those who would promote the interests of the unpowerful, but it should also raise concerns. Bipartisanship is generally a conspiracy of the elected against the electorate. In this case it represents for governments good cover for making a great escape from responsibility. But the nonprofit sector is not and cannot be a substitute for government services. Government downsizing, in fact, has meant retreat not only from services provided directly but also from crucial support for the nonprofit sector.

The maintenance of a strong nonprofit sector in fact requires the support of a strong government. In addition to the necessary allocations from the public budget, donations from the private sector will not be forthcoming in adequate amounts unless tax and other incentives are established by governments and unless the threat of regulation inspires big business to cultivate an image of social responsibility. Finally, if governments are unable to protect the nonprofit sector, those aspects of it that might be seen as competitive with business will come under attack. That is, if business can see profit potential in a service offered on a nonprofit basis, it will move to eliminate the competition.[30]

NGOs come in many categories, from those having large memberships and bureaucracies and global and comprehensive approaches to development, to those limited in size, in area addressed, and in function. Some of the major organizations with global reach, such as CARE, OXFAM, or Catholic Relief Services, were initially intended to deal with such disasters as flood and famine but have since refocused their efforts so as to concentrate on community development. Some, such as Planned Parenthood or Volunteers in Technical Assistance, limit their efforts to particular problem areas or types of assistance. Others, such as International Volunteer Service (IVS), concentrate on building local organizations and networks capable of identifying needs and addressing them. A few, like Futures for Children, make a point of eschewing government funds. Some agencies, however, that claim to accept no government funding, like World Vision (of fundamentalist religious inclination), nevertheless make a point of funding communities and projects favored also by US-AID.

Religious organizations, long prominent among care givers in the Third World, have increasingly redefined their missions so as to promote income-producing activities, self-help, community organization, and other aspects of development. Liberation theology and the preference for the poor inspired by Pope John XXIII and reinforced by the Medellín Conference of 1968 have had a profound influence on the role of the Catholic church, particularly in Latin America and the Philippines, but notable in other areas as well, including the southwestern United States. In organizing *comunidades de base,* or Christian base communities, where individuals were encouraged to take collective approaches to their problems, and in supporting the organization of rural co-ops, priests and nuns based in poor communities and members of religious orders began to occupy the forefront in movements for social change—or at least to occupy a buffer zone between elite-based governments and mobilized poor communities.

The older, more established Protestant sects have followed the Roman Catholic lead in favoring the poor and challenging an order based on elite privilege. Working through the World Council of Churches, they have been particularly active in Africa. Meanwhile, newer fundamentalist sects, particularly those that mastered fund-raising through televangelism, have moved in to accommodate elites feeling threatened by the new directions of the traditional religious institutions. Such sects have also competed, often with development agendas and very considerable resources and sometimes with local government collaboration, for the souls of poor communities. In Guatemala, for example, fundamentalist sects had a great deal to do with the spread of Protestantism from about 5 percent of the population in 1960 to about 30 percent in the 1990s.

Notes

1. Cited in Saul Landau, *The Dangerous Doctrine: National Security and U.S. Foreign Policy* (Boulder: Westview Press, 1988), p. 33.

2. In a speech delivered to Congress in March 1947, President Harry S. Truman declared, "I believe that it must be a policy of the United States to s⸂.pport free peoples who are resisting attempted subjugation by armed minor⸃.ies or by outside pressures." Cited in ibid., p. 36.

3. Professor Brady Tyson, of American University in Washington, D.C., defined a liberal as "one whose interests are not at stake."

4. The program reached its low point in the 1970s but began to rebound in the 1980s. At the beginning of the 1990s, the Peace Corps was once again in vogue, enjoying bipartisan support. In early 1990, it was functioning in seventy countries, with about 6,100 volunteers and trainees.

5. This reflected a general difference of approach between the two administrations. Nixon tended to accept the Democrat-inspired federal government as it was and work around it, while Reagan tended to bend it to his own purposes.

6. U.S. House of Representatives, 101st Congress, 1st Session, Committee on Foreign Affairs, *Background Materials on Foreign Assistance*, Report of the Task Force on Foreign Assistance, February 1989 (Washington, D.C.: GPO, 1989), p. 247; Stephen Hellinger, Douglas Hellinger, and Fred M. O'Regan, *Aid for Just Development* (Boulder: Lynne Rienner Publishers, 1988), p. 27.

7. Hellinger, Hellinger, and O'Regan, op. cit., p. 27.

8. Ibid., pp. 30–31.

9. U.S. House of Representatives, 105th Congress, Committee on International Relations, *Hearing: The Administration's Fiscal Year 1998 Foreign Assistance Budget Request, Feb. 25, 1997* (Washington, D.C.: GPO, 1997).

10. Ibid. and *Hearing: New Thinking on Foreign Assistance, Feb. 26, 1997,* p. 42.

11. U.S. House of Representatives, 101st Congress, 1st Session, Committee on Foreign Affairs, op. cit., pp. 152, 228.

12. No partisan of peace would want to discount Kennan's conversion, but it should be recognized that, at least since the beginning of the McCarthy era, policymakers in the United States have dared to become statesmen only after they were permanently "out of the loop," or irretrievably retired.

13. U.S. House of Representatives, *Hearings,* Feb. 25 and 26, 1997, op. cit.

14. Elliott R. Morss and Victoria A. Morss, *The Future of Western Development Assistance* (Boulder: Westview Press, 1986), pp. 4–6.

15. United Nations Development Program, *Human Development Report, 1997* (New York: Oxford University Press, 1997), p. 214.

16. U.S. House of Representatives, *Hearing,* Feb. 25, 1997, op. cit., pp. 67–86.

17. Paula Hirschoff, "Yen for the World," *Worldview* (National Council of Returned Peace Corps Volunteers) 2, no. 2, summer 1989, pp. 16–19.

18. U.S. House of Representatives, 101st Congress, 1st Session, Committee on Foreign Affairs, op. cit., p. 19.

19. U.S. Department of State, *Soviet and East European Aid to the Third World, 1981,* Department of State Publication 9345, Bureau of Intelligence and Research, February 1983.

20. Morss and Morss, op. cit., pp. 5–6, 70.

21. *Latin America Weekly Report,* October 10 and 24, 1980; *Central America Report,* November 8, 1980.

22. David Vines, "The Fund, the Bank, and the WTO: Functions, Competencies and Reform Agendas," Global Economic Institutions Working Paper Series 26, Institute of Economics and Statistics, Oxford University, 1997. See also *The Manchester Guardian Weekly,* October 5, 1997, and *The Nation,* March 23, 1998.

23. David Rowan, "Meet the New World Government," *The Manchester Guardian Weekly,* February 22, 1998, p. 14.

24. *Manchester Guardian Weekly,* April 12, 1998.

25. James H. Mittelman, *Out from Underdevelopment* (New York: St. Martin's Press, 1988), pp. 45–57.

26. Denise A. Wallen and Gerald R. Kinsman, "Focus on Funding: Information About U.S. Philanthropy for the Non-U.S. Grantseeker" (unpublished), December 1989.

27. U.S. House of Representatives, *Hearing,* Feb. 25, 1997, op. cit.

28. U.S. Agency for International Development, *Strategies for Sustainable Development* (Washington, D.C.: USAID, 1994), p. 47.

29. Hellinger, Hellinger, and O'Regan, op. cit., p. 115.

30. Clothing retailers in Britain were seeking relief in 1997–1998 from the competition from OXFAM's very successful nonprofit marketing of used goods. In the United States, the for-profit Colombia–Hospital Corporation of American was being criticized for driving out or buying out the nonprofit competition in city after city.

Suggested Readings

Arnold, Stephen H., *Implementing Development Assistance: European Approaches to Basic Needs* (Boulder: Westview Press, 1982).

Arnson, Cynthia, and William Goodfellow, "OPIC: Insuring the Status Quo," *International Policy Report* 3, no. 2, September 1977.

Ayers, Robert L., *Banking on the Poor: The World Bank and Poverty* (Cambridge: MIT Press, 1983).

Barnet, Richard, and John Cavanagh, *Global Dreams: Imperial Corporations and the New World Order* (New York: Simon & Schuster, 1994).

Bello, Walden, with Shea Cumminham and Bill Rau, *Dark Victory: The United States, Structural Adjustment, and Global Poverty* (Oakland, Calif.: Institute for Food and Development Policy, 1994).

Chomsky, Noam, and Edward S. Herman, *The Washington Connection and Third World Fascism: The Political Economy of Human Rights*, vol. 1 (Boston: South End Press, 1979).

Danaher, Kevin, *Fifty Years Is Enough: The Case Against the World Bank and the International Monetary Fund* (Boston: South End Press, 1994).

Development Assistance Committee, *Twenty-five Years of Development Cooperation: A Review* (Paris: Organization for Economic Cooperation and Development, 1985).

George, Susan, and Fabrizio Sabelli, *Faith and Credit: The World Bank's Secular Empire* (Boulder: Westview Press, 1994).

Hayter, Teresa, *Aid as Imperialism* (Baltimore: Penguin Books, 1971).

Hayter, Teresa, and Catherine Watson, *Aid: Rhetoric and Reality* (London: Pluto Press, 1985).

Kolko, Gabriel, *Confronting the Third World: United States Foreign Policy, 1945–1980* (New York: Pantheon Books, 1988).

Korten, David, *When Corporations Rule the World* (West Hartford, Conn.: Kumarian Press, 1995).

Lewis, John, Richard Webb, and Devesh Kapur, *The World Bank: Its First Half Century*, 2 vols. (Washington, D.C.: The Brookings Institution and the IBRD, 1998).

Lewis, John P., and Valeriana Kallab, eds., *Development Strategies Reconsidered* (Washington, D.C.: Overseas Development Council, 1986).

Massachusetts Institute of Technology, Center for International Studies, "The Objectives of United States Economic Assistance Programs," study prepared for the Special Committee to Study the Foreign Aid Program, United States Senate, 85th Congress, 1st Session (January 1957).

Morss, Elliott R., and Victoria A. Morss, *The Future of Western Development Assistance* (Boulder: Westview Press, 1986).

Morss, Elliott R., and Victoria A. Morss, *U.S. Foreign Aid: An Assessment of New and Traditional Development Strategies* (Boulder: Westview Press, 1982).

Please, Stanley, *The Hobbled Giant: Essays on the World Bank* (Boulder: Westview Press, 1984).

Rich, Bruce, *Mortgaging the Earth: The World Bank, Environmental Impoverishment, and the Crisis of Development* (London: Simon & Schuster, 1991).

Scheman, Ronald L., ed., *The Alliance for Progress: A Retrospective* (New York: Praeger, 1988).

Scholte, Jan Aart, "The International Monetary Fund and Civil Society: An Underdeveloped Dialogue," presented at the International Conference on Non-State Actors and Authority in the Global System, University of Warwick, October 31–November 1, 1997.

Underhill, Geoffrey R. D., ed., *The New World Order in International Finance* (London: Macmillan, 1997).

United Nations Development Program, *Human Development Report 1997* (New York: Oxford University Press, 1997).

U.S. Agency for International Development [USAID], *Strategies for Sustainable Development* (Washington, D.C.: USAID, 1994).

U.S. Department of State, *Report of the Carlucci Commission on Security and Economic Assistance* (Washington, D.C.: GPO, 1985).

U.S. House of Representatives, 105th Congress, Committee on International Relations, *Hearing: The Administration's Fiscal Year 1998 Foreign Assistance Budget Request, Feb. 25, 1997* (Washington, D.C.: GPO, 1997).

U.S. House of Representatives, 105th Congress, Committee on International Relations, *Hearing: New Thinking on Foreign Assistance, Feb. 26, 1997* (Washington, D.C.: GPO, 1997).

U.S. House of Representatives, 105th Congress, Committee on International Relations, *Hearing: Oversight: US Agency for International Development, May 9, 1996* (Washington, D.C.: GPO, 1997).

Vines, David, "The Fund, The Bank, and The WTO: Functions, Competencies and Reform Agendas," Global Economic Institutions Working Paper Series 26, Institute of Economics and Statistics, Oxford University, 1997.

Whitehead, Laurence, *The International Dimensions of Democratization: Europe and the Americas* (Oxford: Oxford University Press, 1996).

Willetts, Peter, ed., *The Conscience of the World: The Influence of NGOs in the United Nations System* (London: C. Hurst, 1996).

6   *Third World Strategies*

It has long been an article of faith in the West that the underdevelopment of the non-West is a consequence of its failure to become—or delay in becoming—a part of the world system. Opinion leaders of the non-West were until recently outspoken in their conviction that the opposite is the case—that their underdevelopment is a consequence of the nature of their relations with the West. Thus, while rarely lacking in advice from the First World, some Third World leaders, movements, and regional organizations devised their own strategies for promoting growth and/or equity, for protecting their industries, expanding their markets, and even competing with First World producers. Some such strategies have been successful at times and in places, but over time First World powers have ordinarily found ways either to frustrate such strategies or to turn them to their own advantage.

Most of the creative strategizing and experimentation in pursuit of development for the benefit of the many that was underway at the close of the twentieth century was taking place at supranational or subnational levels. These activities will be addressed in later chapters. It would be very difficult in the late 1990s to identify in any part of the world a major national development strategy that might be said to represent Third World rather than First World interests, or for that matter popular versus elite interests. Even Cuba, last redoubt of popular revolution, has been forced to adopt measures offensive to revolutionary standards of fairness in pursuit of hard currency. The Chilean model, long favored by international financial institutions, is still in most particulars a counterrevolutionary one, imposed only through the suppression of popular participation.

The momentum of the thrust to globalization—the fettering of government—is such that even within the most progressive governments debate runs only to how best to defend against it, that is, which of the rights and benefits of the previously negotiated social contracts must be forfeited to save the rest. Thus, national government appears at least temporarily disabled, an unpromising arena for progressive social initiatives at the close of the twentieth century. Even so, whether one sees the pursuit of equity that has punctuated all history and that gathered a good head of steam in the middle decades of the twentieth century as an aberration or as the vocation of civilization, it is important that we revisit and record what was learned from the experience of decades of purposeful struggle.

Import-Substitution Industrialization

The Latin American states, independent—or at least nominally so— longer than most other Third World states, got a head start in testing locally generated strategies. This was not merely by choice; it was sometimes by necessity, as in the case of import-substitution industrialization (ISI). When the devastation of World War I, followed in short order by worldwide depression, deprived those countries of the markets for their primary products and their sources of credit and manufactured goods, they had little choice but to fall back on their own devices. The strategy they adopted was one that dealt directly with the newly unmet demands, thus minimizing dislocations in the existing economic systems. That is, Latin American governments, particularly those of the more developed South American states, began to encourage domestic entrepreneurs to manufacture the products that had been imported but were now unavailable.

As elaborated later through the efforts of the UN Economic Commission for Latin America (ECLA), this strategy called for nurturing the national markets. Light industry was broadly promoted, and a few countries were able to establish heavy industries as well. Low-interest loans from government banks and financial institutions were among many fiscal incentives employed, and fledgling industries were protected by tariffs, quotas, licensing, and exchange controls. Public enterprises sprang up to support private ones, and regional development commissions sought to integrate more-backward areas into national economies.

Foreign producers, frustrated by trade barriers, began to invest directly in the manufacturing sector and produce for local markets. They were often resistant, however, to government regulation designed to promote forward and backward linkages, local reinvestment of profits, employment of nationals, protection of labor, and sharing of ownership and control with nationals. In such cases, nationalization was sometimes threatened or, more rarely, carried out.

Along with its very positive features, ISI as generally practiced in Latin America (and similar strategies undertaken subsequently in Africa and Asia, particularly in India and other states having well-developed middle classes after they gained independence) had some serious drawbacks. For one thing, such rapid industrialization called for major outlays for capital goods. In the face of chronic shortages of hard-currency reserves, this led to heavy foreign borrowing and consequent debt and inflation. For another, the technologies employed, drawn from the First World, were capital-intensive. Thus, even as the manufacturing sector grew, the proportion of the urban labor force able to find work soon began to decline. Furthermore, new industries were often unable to take advantage of economies of scale, and protective tariff barriers were conducive to inefficiency and monopoly. And given the unequal bargaining position of Third World states, the companies taking advantage of tax incentives, governmental infrastructure support, and tariff protection were all too often foreign ones anyway. Finally, production in many countries remained geared to the fortunate few—those who could afford TVs and stereo sets, washing machines and cars—while demand was growing on the part of the many for affordable shoes and building materials and bicycles—thus accelerating inflation.

One response to the mounting problems with ISI was experimentation with regional integration, as we shall explore below. The challenges of the ISI approach had never been narrowly economic, however; they were also political. And it was in the political arena that its collapse was most dramatically manifest. The real crisis of the ISI strategy was felt when it became clear that continual growth would be dependent upon expansion of the domestic market, and that such expansion implied a far-reaching redistribution of wealth and power. This recognition served to unite and mobilize elites—both domestic and foreign—who saw their interests threatened. The upshot was the suppression—in many countries through armed force—of effective demand and the adoption of a new strategy. This development will be discussed under the heading "Counterrevolutionary Strategies."

Export-Led Growth

The Third World success stories most widely touted in the 1980s and most of the 1990s by major donor agencies and multilateral financial institutions were those of the countries variously referred to as the dragons, the Asian tigers, or the "gang of four": South Korea, Taiwan, Singapore, and Hong Kong. Their success and the somewhat lesser but still impressive success of Thailand, Indonesia, and Malaysia in raising GNP per capita over recent decades had been seen as validating the export-led growth model, especially as compared to an approach featuring import substitution.

The "official story," as carried by media and international financial consultants to publics and economic planners elsewhere in the world, was that the economic strategy underlying the boom in East Asia was one of open arms and open markets to foreign capital and goods—the antithesis of ISI and other expressions of economic nationalism. As late as July 1997, international bankers were praising those countries for sound fiscal and macroeconomic management. It is curious, then, that after their economies began to plunge, one after another, in the great East Asian financial meltdown of late 1997, the same creditors were censuring them for "crony capitalism," protectionism, and excessive government regulation.

The fact is that in the case of the "tigers" (and to a much lesser extent the tiger cubs), export promotion was erected upon domestic economies already integrated and fortified by a policy mix including import-substitution, government planning, regulation, subsidy, targeted investment in physical and social infrastructure, and many other inspirations of economic nationalism as opposed to internationalism, or globalization. In the 1990s, however, many companies had become too large and politically powerful and too reckless in incurring foreign debt for ill-conceived investment—a problem not of too much regulation and too little foreign capital but of the reverse.

The East Asian Tigers and Cubs

The case of the first generation tigers is complicated by strained comparability: Only two—South Korea and Taiwan—have the general attributes of states, including both rural and urban sectors, and only one of them has formally recognized sovereignty. The other two are really cities—entrepôts, or international trade centers. Of these, only Singapore has formal sovereignty. Hong Kong, a British colony until July 1997, has since changed masters. Like Taiwan, it is now claimed by China; unlike Taiwan, however, it is also occupied, or reoccupied, by China. Even so, until late 1997, with the qualified exception of Hong Kong each of the so-called tigers had planned and protected economies and the basic trappings of a welfare state. None approximated the model marketed by creditors and the multilateral financial institutions.

From 1972 to 1982, the "gang of four" had experienced per capita growth rates ranging from 79 percent to 97 percent and increases in world export market shares ranging from 500 to 1,270 percent; even more remarkably, that growth had been accompanied by a diminishing gap between rich and poor. Such growth and export performance took place despite relatively modest national resource bases, but with the impetus of very considerable amounts of foreign investment and development assistance.

In promoting throughout the Third World an "adjustment" package based on export expansion, but including also monetary stabilization, trade liberalization, privatization, and deregulation, spokesmen of First World creditors (i.e., the United States, the IMF, and the World Bank) have highlighted these East Asian successes. Critics of the proposed adjustment package point out, however, that extreme stress on export promotion can lead to runaway inflation, and that Japan and Korea showed concern for bringing their postwar inflation under control before placing great stress on exports. They also became powerful exporters while resist-ing import liberalization and maintaining controls on foreign investment.

It was not until long after their competitive export positions were well established, critics of the creditor approach maintain, that the most suc-cessful East Asian countries turned to import liberalization, and they never accepted the now-prescribed reduction of state intervention. Fur-thermore, these countries had gained policy flexibility through the prior elimination of concentrated landholdings and, in general, through con-cern for employment and income in both rural and urban areas.[1]

Korea: The Prototype Tiger.   For South Korea, the prototype of the East Asian tiger, it was to a large extent a policy of industrial self-sufficiency that built its economy into the world's eleventh largest. The country's eco-nomic prowess was recognized in 1997 by its admission to the OECD, the global country club of rich nations. Savings were for the most part domes-tically generated, largely through equity enhancing policies such as the land reform act of the 1950s and through a rigorous system of taxation.

Companies nurtured in a protected domestic market in the 1960s and 1970s were propelled successfully into the international markets in the 1970s and 1980s. But by the 1990s, Japanese and U.S. counteroffenses were taking their toll, and more importantly, China's capitalist roaders had hit the road. Trade balances shifted. Business tried to maintain shrinking profits and liquidity in the mid-1990s by downsizing, U.S.-style, and by domestic and foreign borrowing. In November 1997, unable to maintain the servicing schedule on a foreign debt of $100 billion, Ko-rea surrendered to the IMF.

The Extraordinary Case of Taiwan.   The Taiwanese case is particularly interesting in that it seems to defy all the development models. Taiwan experienced dramatic annual growth in per capita income, from about U.S. $70 at the end of World War II to about $6,000 in 1988. Meanwhile population was growing at the rate of 3.5 percent annually until the 1960s and about 2 percent thereafter. Real GNP growth averaged 9.2 per-cent over those years, with exports increasing from 9 percent of GNP in 1952 to 49 percent in 1980. These developments were given impetus by massive infusions of foreign investment and aid.

Surprisingly, though, this growth has been accompanied from the be-ginning by a trend toward reduction in income inequality. The income of the poorest 20 percent of the population rose from 3 percent of the total in 1953 to 7.7 percent in 1964, while that of the richest 5 percent dropped from 32.6 percent to 16.2 percent. Great improvement was also seen in housing, health, and education. This combination of rapid growth and diminishing inequity has been explained in large part by the land reform program undertaken between 1949 and 1953. Redistribution of the land was not in this case a revolutionary development; rather, it was a multi-purpose project of a conquering new elite—the Chinese Nationalists flee-ing the mainland. Thus, in redistributing the land, they not only chan-neled a new infusion of money into industry but also broke the power base of the native Taiwanese oligarchy. Public lands formerly held by the Japanese were also sold to farmers on reasonable terms. Along with timely attention to rural income and agricultural productivity, govern-ment policy favored technological developments that made use of abun-dant labor and saved land and capital.[2] The government also invested heavily in education at all levels.

Even more surprising, however, is the fact that these economically pro-gressive policies were undertaken by a rigidly authoritarian and socially elitist government. Through almost four decades of martial law, first un-der Chiang Kai-shek and later under his son Chiang Ching-Kuo, the na-tive Taiwanese, who make up 80 percent of the population, had precious little representation or participation in the country's political life. Never-theless there had been a mushrooming of so-called self-help groups that were taking popular demands into the streets. There were some 1,800 street demonstrations in 1987 alone.

At the end of the 1980s, Taiwan's legislative bodies were still domi-nated by 1949 escapees from the mainland, claiming to represent places like Szechuan and Inner Mongolia, but upon the death of Chiang Ching-Kuo, the presidency and leadership of the Kuomintang passed to a native Taiwanese; and a new opposition party, the Democratic Progressive Party, finally accorded legal recognition in 1989, was rapidly gaining in popularity. In the late 1990s, it held about a third of the seats in the na-tional legislative body, the legislative Yuan, in what had become a com-petitive multiparty system.

At the same time, however, China has become surly in advancing its claims to Taiwan and in punishing states that openly challenge that claim. To the extent that sovereignty had any meaning at the close of the twentieth century, Taiwan is surely a state as independent as any other and, with the world's fifth-largest foreign exchange reserves, far more than most. In the short run at least, with minimal debt exposure, Tai-wan's economy has been relatively unshaken by the Asian meltdown. Its prospects of gaining formal recognition through the UN, however, have receded.

Southeast Asia: The Tiger Cubs.   Like the more mature tigers, the cubs entered the 1990s with pretensions to self-sufficiency in some sectors or products and intentions to regulate some investment flows and markets. International money movers were annoyed by cautious approaches in In-donesia to an industrial policy and by limited efforts in Thailand to curtail foreign ownership of financial firms and land, and in several countries to regulate portfolio investment. Unlike the tigers, however, the cubs had never enjoyed highly integrated and protected domestic economies and did not seriously tax their own constituencies.

Lifted by the rising tide in East Asia, particularly by investment from Japan and the tigers, Southeast Asia boomed from the mid-1980s to the mid-1990s, with GNP growth rates between 6 and 10 percent. But cheap exports from low-wage China were setting off a chain reaction, cutting first into the markets of the high employment, relatively high wage economies of Japan and the tigers. When Japanese direct investment began to taper off in the early 1990s, the cubs looked elsewhere, including to the international banks and speculative institutions. A strategy introduced by the Thais but adopted also by Malaysia, Indonesia, and the Philippines called for the liberalization of the financial sector, maintaining high domestic interest rates and pegging currencies to the dollar.[3]

The new strategy drew the blessings of the IMF and the World Bank, and it drew capital. In Thailand some $24 billion was amassed as net portfolio investment in less than four years and another $50 billion was loaned to Thai banks and enterprises. Such investments never reached productive sectors of manufacturing or agriculture. They were drawn to high-yield, quick turnaround sectors like the stock market, consumer financing and real estate.

By 1996 a glut in real estate was visible to the naked eye. Commercial banks and finance companies were overexposed, the current account was deeply in deficit, and foreign portfolio managers were edgy.

The Meltdown of 1997 and Its Lessons

Thailand was to become ground zero for the great East Asian financial meltdown. The open door for foreign investment turned out to be a revolving door, and streaker capital lunged for it. Thai attempts in mid-1997 to ward off devaluation by dumping dollar reserves and buying back baht proved costly (some U.S. $9 billion) and futile. The value of the baht had fallen 49 percent by October.

The stampede soon spread to Malaysia, Indonesia, and the Philippines, whose currencies were stripped of value. Interest rates, debt service cost, and the prices of imported goods soared. A chain reaction ensued, leaving consumers without affordable choices and laid-off workers defenseless on ever meaner streets. By October the sinkhole was pulling the tigers down as well. The Hong Kong stock market took a dive, and panic rippled through stock markets elsewhere around the world.

Newly Mixed Economy: Privatized Gains, Socialized Losses. By the end of the year the bailout—more than $129 billion—was in place, but it was to be of no apparent benefit to the people of East and Southeast Asia.

On the contrary, they were to bear the brunt of paying off old and new debts and mitigating risk to old and new foreign investors. Those who were to be bailed out through the sacrifices of Asian workers and the good graces of Western taxpayers were those international financiers who had placed their bets on the wrong horses, who in pursuit of quick and easy profits had engaged in or underwritten risky, speculative ventures, and the governments whose policies had encouraged such investment.

Western bankers asserted that there would be no more credit for Korea unless the Korean government retroactively guaranteed their nonperforming loans to the private sector. Thus loans for golf courses, unneeded even in the sense of market demand, and unfinished, instant-ruin skyscrapers became national debt, to be paid directly by taxpayers and indirectly by the same and other citizens deprived of needed services and benefits when government revenues were diverted to debt service.

U.S. officials made it known to Korean and other East and Southeast Asian leaders that no direct aid would be forthcoming until IMF demands were met. The IMF prescription for stabilization? Hair of the dog: liberalization, deregulation, and privatization, a detailed package of major and minor policies designed to make Asian resources and labor cheaper, more accessible, and more profitable to foreign investors.

Korea will see a major erosion of workers' rights and wages. It had already dropped restrictions against foreign access to its guaranteed corporate bond market and direct takeover of Korean enterprises by multinational corporations. Credit Lyonnais Securities calculated that 566 of the country's 653 nonfinancial listed companies were vulnerable to foreign takeover. Indonesia, where the currency had lost 70 percent of its value, will have to abandon attempts to manufacture its own cars and passenger jets. Thailand had already removed all restrictions on foreign ownership of financial firms and was moving forward with legislation to allow foreigners to own land.[4]

Meanwhile, Malaysia was preparing to deport a million foreign workers, many of them to Thailand, where up to two million jobs were being lost, and to Indonesia, where unemployment was expected to rise some six million in 1998. The Thais might, in turn, expel desperate Burmese, Cambodians, and Filipinos, but for the most part Indonesians could be expected to turn their wrath once again on ethnic Chinese merchants.

Vulnerability of Eucalyptus Economies.   In the aftermath of the meltdown, with no options open, the economies of East and Southeast Asia have finally become what the standard bearers of globalization earlier mistakenly or deceptively portrayed them to be: wide open, devoid of protections and restrictions, supplicants of foreign credit and investment on its own terms, to its own purposes. Such openness, along with competitively deflated currencies, will draw the opportunistic capital back, as to a fire sale, and this will be deemed a success for stabilization—maybe even a miracle.

But in fact these economies will be more vulnerable than ever. To an even greater extent than was true of the cubs on the eve of the meltdown, they will be characterized by high-yield, fast-turnaround ventures, transplants that like the eucalyptus put down shallow roots but achieve extraordinarily fast growth by soaking up all the available nutrients from the surrounding environment and starving older, native enterprises. And when the nutrients are diminished, or richer ones appear elsewhere, those ventures, that capital, will slip back out with the greatest of ease through that open door.

Neoliberal doctrine notwithstanding, common sense suggests that the most vulnerable and unstable economies are not those with too little foreign capital but those with too much. Why would the institutions entrusted with the bailout everywhere of troubled economies prescribe therapies that open doors and markets and options only to foreign investors? Like the capitalist roaders of the ex-Soviet sphere who found themselves mowed down on their own freeways, East Asians are learning that when the therapies are the same for ills as diverse as those of Haiti, Russia, and South Korea, chances are the needs being met are not those of the patients but rather those of the doctors.

Implications for Export Promotion

For the East Asian tigers and cubs, a strategy of export promotion was in itself neither the sole source of the boom nor the sole culprit of the bust. It is clear, however, that its most sustained successes were built upon the bedrock of a relatively self-sufficient domestic economy and that international trade initiatives were supported but also regulated by the government. Export promotion will now more than ever be the dominant strategy of these countries, but for the time being it will be a defensive one, harnessing available labor and resources to a demanding debt service schedule rather than to any vision of national development. And it will be undertaken without the nurturing base of a robust domestic economy and a watchful government.

Unlike import substitution, export promotion is not limited by the size of the domestic market, and it is less likely to protect inefficiency—at least of domestic monopolies and oligopolies as opposed to regional and international ones. Its prospects are limited, however, by external demand. This is a particularly vexing problem when most Third World states are pursuing the same strategy, even, on the advice of the same multinational consulting firms, exporting the same "diversified" set of products to the same "niche" markets, and when First World countries are increasingly protecting their own markets. According to the World Bank, Western protectionism reduces the Third World's GNP by a full 3 percentage points, an amount equivalent to twice the foreign aid now provided by the industrialized nations.

The greatest rewards for export promotion accrue to those countries and companies that first pursue the strategy. Later entries must contend with more nearly glutted markets. Once all players in a global system are pursuing the same strategy, rewards accrue to those with the lowest costs, which generally translates into the leanest work forces and lowest wages. It seems clear now that the greatest boon to Western capitalism in the mid-twentieth century was the success of the Communist revolution in China, which for several decades removed the potentially most formidable player from the table.

Obviously, a system in which all players seek growth through exports but protect their own economies is untenable. But unprotected labor means a race to the bottom in wages, unprotected local provisioning of basic commodities and services means abject dependence, and unregulated money markets lead to flash floods and droughts of capital and unaccountable borrowing. The upshot is exportation as debt service servitude. Trinkets, even high-tech ones, may become cheaper even as, for so many, the essentials of housing, utilities, transportation, and health care become unaffordable. In a global system, the long term may be very long indeed, but a system that continually exerts downward pressure on wages and salaries, if it does not exhaust resources first, will eventually run out of consumers.

In fact, in the 1990s, most Third World countries were placing the highest priority on export promotion. It was not normally seen as a matter of choice, however; rather, it was dictated by the crushing weight of foreign debt and the obligation of maintaining debt servicing as a precondition for obtaining further credit. The strategy as promoted by creditors and the IMF differed in little more than product mix from that characteristic of an earlier period of direct colonial rule. Even where growth had been dramatic, the fruits of that growth were not normally redistributed in any form. It was the failure of that strategy to promote balanced and equitable growth in most of the Third World countries that set the East Asian experience in relief. The failures or limits of both ISI and export promotion for countries acting alone led some strategists to promote moves toward economic integration.

Economic Integration

The trend to economic integration in the early 1960s was inspired in part by fear of saturation (at least under existing economic and political conditions) of domestic markets for industrial output. It was hoped that such integration—eliminating intraregional tariff barriers and erecting common external ones, for example—would produce economies of scale and give the ISI process a new lease on life. Like the elaborate and rationalized versions of ISI itself, the trend to economic integration, at least as it evolved in the Western Hemisphere, was largely an initiative of ECLA, under the leadership of Argentinean economist Raúl Prebisch, although it was inspired as well by the early success of the European Economic Community (EEC).

The Post–World War II Phase

The European Union was inspired by a grand vision—that particularly of French statesman Jean Monnet—but constructed in modest segments, beginning in 1940 with the European Coal and Steel Community and evolving in the early 1950s into the EEC. From the beginning its trajectory was political as well as economic, and it was assumed that to be successful it would have to deal with regional and national imbalances and ensure that integration promised benefit to popular majorities in all member states. Labor was to move freely, along with merchandise and capital, protected by unions and legislation.

In the Western Hemisphere, 1960 saw the establishment of both the Central American Common Market (CACM) and the Latin American Free Trade Association (LAFTA), linking Mexico and the South American states. Both areas saw marked increases in intraregional trade. Trade among LAFTA states increased by 100 percent from 1961 to 1968. CACM results were even more impressive. Intraregional exports as a percentage of total Latin American exports rose from 6.5 percent in 1960 to 23 percent in 1970.[5] Nevertheless, serious problems plagued both organizations from the beginning. Although there were special concessions for the poorer member states, the benefits of integration accrued disproportionately to the more-developed ones. Furthermore, although the United States had resisted fiercely the trend to integration, foreign-based multinationals soon maneuvered to take advantage of the expanded markets.

The coup de grâce for the CACM was the so-called Soccer War, which broke out between El Salvador and Honduras in 1969. LAFTA's disintegration, also in the late 1960s, was less dramatic, resulting primarily from the frustration of other states with the disproportionate advantages reaped by Argentina, Brazil, and Mexico. The Andean states—Bolivia, Chile, Colombia, Ecuador, and Peru, later joined by Venezuela—formed their own Andean Common Market (ANCOM). ANCOM's most interesting innovation, watched closely by other Third World states, was its approach to foreign investment. Economic plans directed foreign investors to sectors where capital was most needed. The repatriation of profits was limited. Parent companies were not allowed to restrict exports by their subsidiaries, and subsidiaries and other foreign-based enterprises were eventually (generally in fifteen years) to turn over majority control to locals. ANCOM was brought down by the early 1980s, primarily by political changes in member states, beginning with the military takeover in Chile in 1973.

LAFTA stumbled on as form without much content until it was replaced in 1980 by the even less promising Latin American Integration Association (LAIA). In the Caribbean Basin, the early measures undertaken through the Caribbean Free Trade Area (CARIFTA) proved less than impressive. The organization was superseded by the Caribbean Community and Common Market (CARICOM), which continues to exist, though without seriously transforming trading patterns in the area.

Aspects of economic integration for other Third World regions have been proposed and discussed but have generally fallen victim to sabotage by neocolonial powers, intraregional feuds, or political and economic crises in individual states. Kwame Nkrumah's Pan-Africanist blueprint, for example, included progress in continental monetary integration as part of a larger economic and political integration process. Along with an African monetary zone, Nkrumah's plan included an African central bank and an African payments and clearing union.[6] Nkrumah was ousted from the presidency of Ghana in 1966, but his ideas have reappeared from time to time.

In fact, several regional organizations for economic cooperation in Africa have been formed at various times, but their memberships and objectives have been limited and their successes even more so. Disparities among member states in size and levels of development have been a major obstacle to economic integration in Africa, as in Latin America. Unequal gains for Kenya, for example, to the detriment of Uganda and Tanzania, contributed to the collapse of the East African Community. Similar problems have plagued the Communauté Economique de l'Afrique de l'Ouest (CEAO), in which Ivory Coast has monopolized benefits, and the Economic Organization of West African States (ECOWAS), dominated by Nigeria. And the Customs Union of Swaziland, Botswana, Lesotho, and South Africa was an obvious case of "horse and rabbit stew" (i.e., equal parts of horse and rabbit: one horse, one rabbit).

Furthermore, export-oriented primary producers do not normally experience much demand for each other's products, and even where processed or manufactured goods are available, member states of a customs union might have to be willing to import relatively crude, inefficiently produced goods and even to give them tariff protection. Finally, the former colonial powers whose trade and aid continue to loom so large in African economies will not likely be supportive of cooperative efforts among African states unless European-based companies are the major beneficiaries. And given the political weakness and economic dependency of most African states, it does not seem likely that any regional project could long withstand concerted European opposition.

Nevertheless, the UN Economic Commission for Africa continued throughout the 1970s to promote regional economic integration as a means to collective self-reliance. The Organization of African Unity (OAU) has also lent its support to the idea. The Plan of Action drawn up at the OAU's 1980 meeting in Lagos called for the establishment of an Africa Payments Union by the end of the decade. The decade, however, turned out to be a grim one for most of Africa, scarcely lending itself to bold regional initiatives.[7]

The Post–Cold War Phase

The 1990s have seen a new wave of interest in economic integration, but its promotion and underlying motives derive from quarters quite different from those that gave rise to the earlier phase. Even the European Community, which in 1993 became the European Union, had been drawn away from a Keynesian, demand-driven approach to economic planning to a strict monetarist, trickle-down approach. Despite hardships, most countries of the now fifteen-member body adopted a system of fixed exchange rates on January 1, 1999, in preparation to convert to the euro by the beginning of 2002. A major condition for entering into the monetary union was holding budget deficits to under 3 percent of GDP, so governments were under pressure to deflate economies and cut jobs and services even as unemployment rose to record postwar levels. It stood at 12 percent in the beginning of 1998, including the economically dominant economies of Germany and France.

Elsewhere, the driving force behind the building of new trading blocs was multinational financial and corporate interest in removing barriers to the free flow of goods, services, and, more importantly, capital and incidentally in overriding national legislative protections of labor, community, resources, and ecological systems. In general, movement of people was restricted ever more tightly. Though rhetoric would suggest a trend running counter to globalization, in most cases such regionalism was rather yet another assault on national protections, thus supportive of broader trade agreements and organizations, such as GATT and WTO, and, in general, of globalization.

The North American Free Trade Agreement (NAFTA) was the prototype of the new regional arrangement, both the most promising and the most threatening, depending less on national than on class and sectoral interests. An agreement eliminating most economic barriers between the United States and Canada was signed in 1988; Mexico was added after the signing of a document in 1992 and after legislative ratification in 1993. The agreement generated transnational coalitions, as it was favored by business and banking and opposed by labor and environmentalists in all three countries. Capital, and jobs, headed south first from higher-wage Canada to the United States. At the end of 1994, less than one year after the treaty with Mexico had gone into effect, much of that capital—the portfolio kind—made a sharp U-turn, leaving a collapsed Mexican peso.

Most assessments of gains and losses from NAFTA are of dubious reliability, as they have been drawn up by parties with interests at stake. But at any rate most have focused on gains and losses in national terms, which are of dubious relevance. Mexico, which by various calculations had benefited by 1997 by the shifting of some sixty-six thousand to several hundred thousand jobs from the United States, had also seen a 50 percent plunge in real wages. The remarkable improvement in social indicators registered in the 1960s and 1970s had been lost by the mid-1990s, as average living standards dropped back to the level of 1960. Not all Mexicans suffered, though; in 1997, Mexico placed seventh among nations in numbers of billionaires, with at least twenty-four. The wealth of the richest one of them, $6.6 billion in 1995, was equal to the combined income of the 17 million poorest Mexicans.[8]

Leaders of thirty-four countries meeting under U.S. initiative in the Summit of the Americas in Miami in 1994 agreed in principle to the creation of a free trade zone for the hemisphere within ten years. The initiative bogged down early on, though, as the Clinton administration, seeking to enlist Chile into NAFTA, was unable to overcome bipartisan opposition to the "fast-track" pursuit of subsequent trade agreements.

The Southern Cone Common Market (MERCOSUR, the acronym for Mercado Común del Sur), launched at the initiative of Brazil in 1991, might be seen to a degree as a competitor with NAFTA. The initial members, Brazil, Argentina, Uruguay, and Paraguay, were joined in 1996 by Chile. Bolivia, an associate member, seemed headed for full membership. At the beginning of 1998, MERCOSUR had a market of 210 million with a combined GDP of $712 billion. Meanwhile, the Andean Common Market, stripped of all innovative protective features, continued to exist as a free trade organization, expanding intraregional commerce, and Colombia, Mexico, and Venezuela had entered into an agreement, known as G3, serving the same purpose.[9]

In 1997, there were four Arab and seven Sub-Saharan trade groups in existence, most of which had been organized more than a decade earlier. By the late 1990s they had been weakened by political friction or deep poverty and were of little consequence. In southern Africa, however, after several decades in which cooperation could only mean the hegemony of White South Africa over its neighbors or the cooperation of Black-ruled states in resisting such hegemony, there was finally, since the inception of Black rule in South Africa, a multifaceted movement is underway. Encompassing concerns about health—especially AIDS—education, crime, migration, and many other social and political issues as well as economic ones, the movement had little structure in the late 1990s but considerable momentum.

Since the implosion of the Soviet Union in 1991, some of its shards have sought to establish terms for cooperation. Russia, Belarus, and the Ukraine agreed in 1993 to move toward economic union. The following year, Belarus began talks with Russia about currency conversion to the Russian ruble; for an isolated dictator in Belarus, it appeared to be a move of desperation.

Apart from Europe and the Western Hemisphere, the most ambitious regional movements in the 1990s have been underway in Asia. The Association of Southeast Asian Nations (ASEAN) was established in 1967 by Brunei, Indonesia, Malaysia, the Philippines, Singapore, and Thailand. Successor to a U.S.-inspired security pact, it has become increasingly important in trade promotion. In the 1990s, the association absorbed Vietnam and Burma and opened negotiations with Laos. The incorporation of Burma in 1997 incurred the displeasure of the United States and the European Union because of Burma's repressive military government.

The most ambitious trade promotion initiative is that of Asian Pacific Economic Cooperation (APEC). Meeting regularly since 1989, its membership, accounting for about half of the world's GNP and its merchandise trade, has grown to twenty nations—all those of ASEAN plus China, Japan, South Korea, Taiwan, Hong Kong, Australia, New Zealand, Papua New Guinea, the United States, Canada, Mexico, and Chile. There has been agreement in principle to remove all trade barriers by the year 2020, but few of the other major players share U.S. enthusiasm for the establishment of a Pacific Rim free trade zone. The organization showed a certain timidity in the face of Asia's financial crisis of 1997, preferring to leave rescue packages and thus rule making to the province of the IMF.

Multilateral Bargaining

During the 1960s and 1970s LDCs sought to defend their economic interests through the formation of bargaining blocs within regional and global organizations. The most important exchanges in what became a North-South confrontation took place within organs of the United Nations, particularly the General Assembly and the Economic and Social Council (ECOSOC) and in special ongoing UN conferences like the Conference on Trade and Development (UNCTAD) and the Law of the Sea Conference (UNLOS III).

The LDC Caucus

Raúl Prebisch became the first executive secretary of UNCTAD, which met in 1964 in Switzerland, in 1969 in India, and in 1972 in Chile. The

LDC caucus, G–77 (which actually claimed more than 120 adherents in the 1980s), found UNCTAD a receptive forum, at least in principle. The developed states accepted the G–77 proposal of granting trade concessions on a nonreciprocal basis. The concept was later incorporated into the General Agreement on Tariffs and Trade (GATT) and adopted by the EEC in the Lomé Convention of 1975.

The G–77 promotion of commodity agreements for the purpose of stabilizing primary product prices drew a mixed response. Proposals that developed states devote 1 percent of their GNP to Third World aid and that transnational corporations be subjected to a code of conduct were accepted only on a basis of voluntary compliance; thus, states and corporations with the most at stake were not likely to be accommodating.

In 1974, nevertheless, the United Nations created a commission to monitor the conduct of transnational corporations. A Mexican proposal at the 1972 UNCTAD resulted in the drafting of the UN Charter on the Economic Rights and Duties of States, which was approved by the General Assembly in 1974. Along with preferential treatment without reciprocity and stable prices for Third World exports, the charter stressed the right of expropriation of foreign assets. The charter was to be the first step toward the establishment of the New International Economic Order (NIEO). What with famine in Africa, staggering debts in Latin America, and political and ethnic strife in much of Asia, the dream of a new order receded after the 1970s, but the NIEO remained an important expression of common vision and purpose.

The Law of the Sea conferences were a response to patterns of conflict between the United States and a number of Latin American countries that claimed a 200-mile expanse of territorial waters for the purpose of regulating tuna fishing. The claim, first made by Ecuador, Peru, and Chile in the 1950s, spread through Latin America in the 1960s and from there to Africa and Asia. From the first session of UNLOS III in Venezuela in 1974 until the final one in New York in 1982, the Third World caucus presented a virtually united front. Most G–77 positions were adopted, including the 200-mile exclusive economic zone (EEZ). The United States objected vehemently, however, to the deep seabed mining provisions and voted against the convention at the United Nations in 1982. The USSR and most European states abstained. Major power governments, representing industries that covet seabed resources, belatedly reached agreement on regulation through an International Seabed Authority. An implementation agreement was signed in July 1994. The Clinton administration sent the 1982 convention along with the newly signed agreement to Congress, but the Republican leadership appeared uninclined to move on it.

By 1989, as a consequence of the debt crisis and the efforts of Third World countries, at the urging of First World agencies and bankers, to promote exports, many of those Third World countries had begun to participate very actively in the negotiations of the GATT and subsequently of the World Trade Organization (WTO). They found, to their dismay, that after giving in to First World pressures to open their own markets and to expand exports, the First World was rapidly erecting barriers to keep out their products.

In industrialized countries, average tariffs on imports from the least developed countries in the 1990s were 30 percent higher than the global average. On balance, developing countries were losing about $60 billion annually from agricultural subsidies and barriers to textile exports in industrialized nations.[10]

NGO Networks

Initiatives on issues of trade and resource distribution as between countries of global North and South shifted decisively back to the North in the 1980s. After the implosion of the Soviet Union in 1991 and the demise of an alternative set of trading partners and credit sources, initiative shifted away from states and other representative bodies entirely, whether of North or South, and toward the transnational private profit-seeking sector.

In the aftermath of the East Asian financial meltdown of 1997, as the IMF proceeded to bail out foreign investors who had taken ill-conceived risks and the private lenders who had backed them while imposing crushing sacrifices on popular governments and their constituencies, no government or intergovernmental organization presumed to challenge the wisdom or justice of the course. It fell to an unlikely player to issue that challenge. George Soros, whose Quantum Fund has amassed the best performance record of any investment fund over the past quarter-century, has called for constraints on players like himself. He has proposed the international regulation of money markets and harmonization of some economic policies, including those on taxation, as the only means of correcting inequities and preventing a breakdown of the system.

Such timidity on the part of most governments and intergovernmental organizations left a representational vacuum. Thus bargaining—or more accurately, persuasion—at the global level on behalf of localized populations and nonelites or disadvantaged categories of people has been taken up by networks of nonprofit, nongovernmental organizations operating with the support and under the protective umbrella of the United Nations.

Aspects of this development are discussed elsewhere in this book, but it might be pointed out here that NGO networks dealing with otherwise neglected peoples and issues have been growing, under UN cultivation, for several decades, culminating in a pattern of global conferences in which governmental and nongovernmental forums legitimate and reinforce each other. The most influential—or at least the most celebrated—of these conferences in the 1990s have been ECO '92, the UN Conference on Environment and Development that met in Rio de Janeiro in 1992, and the Fourth UN International Conference on Women, which met in Beijing in 1995. Other important conferences have dealt with social development, population planning, housing, human rights, and the rights of indigenous populations.

Such conferences typically produced documents, resolutions binding in principle on signatory governments. Genuine compliance has been hard to come by, as the Rio plus Five meeting noted in reviewing in 1997 compliance with the commitments made at ECO '92. But such conferences produce more than documents, and the process of building popular coalitions at the global level can be a long-term one.

Many of the approximately thirty-five thousand women who descended on Beijing in 1995 were unsatisfied with the accords finally documented, but the usefulness of the conference did not hinge on its paper trail alone. The most important work of the conference may have been the mobilization, networking, and idea exchange that proceeded from and followed it. A barrage of regional preparatory meetings beginning in 1994 had drawn representatives from 163 countries, and follow-up forums were still being organized around the world in 1997. Such activism has seen clear resonance in gains for women over the past decade in political representation. Twenty-four of the thirty-two women who have served as presidents or prime ministers around the world during the twentieth century were in power in the 1990s.[11]

Resource Management and Commodity Cartels

The Organization of Petroleum Exporting Countries (OPEC)

For a few Third World countries—the dozen or so members of OPEC— the commodity cartel has proved a most useful strategy. The fortuitous experience of OPEC, however, is not likely to be replicated for producers of other commodities. In the first place, the petroleum cartel was not created by OPEC. The producer states had only to cut themselves into the management and the reward systems of a private cartel, the "Seven Sisters" international petroleum companies,[12] that had already proved its potential.

Before World War II, and as recently as the late 1950s, the seven international majors, controlling at least 80 percent of oil production outside of North America and the Soviet bloc, kept the industry wildly profitable through understandings on market shares and pricing policies. The minimal cost of production, especially in the Middle East, meant that despite dramatic growth in the industry in the postwar period, the companies were able to keep prices and profits high. As economic nationalism spread through the Third World, however, and host governments began to demand more in the way of royalties and regulation, the majors began to expand into new areas, playing off one country against another. Such maneuvers, plus a potential oil surplus and a reduction in prices posted by the companies for crude oil, led to the formation of OPEC in 1960.

Thus, the impetus for the creation of OPEC was the need to present a common front and enhance government bargaining power vis-à-vis producer companies. Ultimately, however, it was the commonality or symbiosis of interests between OPEC and the companies vis-à-vis oil consumers, along with the clout major companies enjoyed with governments of consumer countries, particularly the United States, that led to such spectacular success.

The global "energy crisis" of the 1970s was introduced abruptly with the Arab oil embargo following the Egyptian invasion of Israel on October 6, 1973, but the enduring effects were economic more than political; the embargo was accompanied by an explosion in prices. The OPEC countries had established, with the collaboration of the major companies, a means of controlling production, and the fourfold rise in oil prices of 1973–1974 was maintained thereafter.[13] It was not until after the additional sharp price increases of 1979–1980 that market forces struck back. With those increases, the producers had overreached; conservation measures and alternate energy sourcing came into play, but it was to a far greater extent the consequent global recession and the debt crisis that seriously suppressed demand and weakened prices.

In the interim a number of countries, particularly Saudi Arabia and the Emirates and other Persian Gulf ministates, had moved from client to donor state categories in the ODA, or development enterprise, equation. For some of the OPEC states, however, the bust that followed the boom was worse than the preexisting poverty. There was a tendency for higher levels of public spending to be maintained even as the boom was ending, and public borrowing was promoted by bankers frantic to unload petrodollars. The Nigerian public deficit, for example, rose from 1.1 percent of gross domestic product (GDP) in 1979 to 9.17 percent in 1981, even as the country borrowed $1 billion a year in 1979 and 1980. Nigerian imports increased from $9.7 billion in 1977 to $19 billion in 1981, only to fall back sharply to $4 billion by 1986 as credit dried up.[14] The major Latin American producers, Mexico and Venezuela, also fell into debt, deficit, and deep economic crisis in the 1980s and 1990s.

Other Producer Associations

Even before the boom years of OPEC, other Third World countries had experimented with producer associations and many more were inspired by the fairy-tale success of some OPEC members. In the 1980s, such associations included: African Groundnut Council, Association of Natural Rubber Producing Countries, Asian and Pacific Coconut Community, Association of Iron Ore Exporting Countries, Intergovernmental Council of Copper Exporting Countries, Cocoa Producers' Alliance, Group of Latin American and Caribbean Sugar Exporting Countries, Inter-African Coffee Organization, International Bauxite Association, International Tea Promotion Association, Organization of Wood Producing and Exporting African Countries, African and Malagasy Coffee Organization, Pepper Community, and Union of Banana Exporting Countries.

Achievements of such associations, however, have been modest and generally short-lived. Consumers willing to endure long lines at gasoline pumps and to pay outrageous prices for relief from such lines would not behave in a similar manner with respect to peanuts or bananas. Nor does the power of transnationals dealing in those commodities compare with that of the Seven Sisters.

Real commodity prices in general went into a deep plunge in the later half of the 1980s; they were 45 percent lower in the 1990s than in the 1980s, in fact 10 percent lower than the lowest level during the great depression, reached in 1932. For the least developed countries the terms of trade have declined a cumulative 50 percent over the past quarter century, that is, since the early 1970s. General deterioration in the terms of trade for developing countries, however, was not due only to the volatility of commodity prices. Terms of trade for manufactured goods also fell by 35 percent between 1970 and 1990, indicating that a weak bargaining position was itself the root of the problem (Figure 6.1).[15]

Harnessing Energy: The Latin American Experience

By the 1970s the state petroleum corporation had become the rule in Latin America, being found in Mexico and nine of the countries of South America (all of Latin America, that is, except Central America and the Caribbean, Paraguay, and the Guianas). Argentina established the first state corporation, the Yacimientos Petrolíferos Fiscales, or YPF, in 1922. Although Uruguay had no proven reserves, it followed suit in 1931 with the establishment of a state corporation to manage importation, refining, and distribution. Bolivia's state corporation was established in 1936, Colombia's in 1948, Chile's and Brazil's in 1950. PEMEX, the giant Mexican corporation, Petróleos Mexicanos, was established with the nationalization of foreign companies in 1938.

The nationalizations and establishment of state corporations were not simply expressions of nationalism in the abstract but took place often in response to specific instances of unacceptable behavior on the part of the foreign companies, which have long been notorious as poor corporate cit-

Average annual rate of change

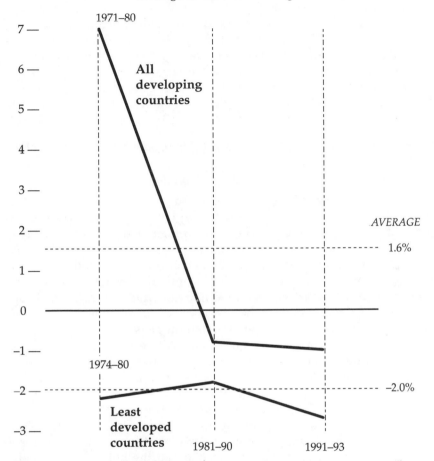

FIGURE 6.1   Declining Terms of Trade for Developing Countries, 1971–1993.
Source: United Nations Development Program [UNDP], *Human Development Report 1997* (New York: UNDP, 1997), p. 85.

izens. It is generally believed in Latin America that oil company ambitions were behind the initiation of war by Bolivia on Paraguay in 1936 and by Peru on Ecuador in 1944. The International Petroleum Company, a Standard Oil subsidiary, defied the Peruvian government's tax claims against it until its expropriation in 1968. It is even likely that rivalries between U.S. and British oil companies played a part in the Mexican Revolution. The son of the dictator Porfirio Díaz was a member of the board of directors of the major British-owned oil company in Mexico, El Aguila. The leader of the revolution against Díaz, Francisco Madero, was reputed to have been financed by Standard Oil and other U.S. companies jealous of the position of British interests, and after the revolution was successful, Madero's legal adviser went to work for a subsidiary of Standard Oil.[16]

Thus in much of Latin America foreign oil companies were not welcome. At the same time, obstacles have been placed in the way of the exploitation of oil resources by state-owned corporations. Even under Democratic administrations, the U.S. Export-Import Bank long refused, out of loyalty to free-enterprise principles, to make credit available to state corporations. Other creditors, including the World Bank, generally followed suit.

Those circumstances changed somewhat after the energy crises of the 1970s. The heavy role taken by the state in Latin American oil exploration and the limitations placed on foreign corporations were no longer as unusual as they once had been. The increase in prices rendered of little consequence the greater costs of production in Latin America as opposed to the Middle East. And the prospects of shortage made it necessary to exploit resources wherever they could be found. But the increased assertiveness of governments and state oil corporations, and the expertise that government petroleum specialists acquired, did not mean that the international companies had adjusted to a new role as benign and cooperative good citizens, despite the efforts of public relations firms to portray the companies as disinterested philanthropists.

The Latin American governments remained wary of the power of the companies and preferred to do without them. The problem was that the companies could still make themselves indispensable, sometimes for innocent technical reasons, sometimes by more heavy-handed manipulation. Thus when, in 1969, President Alfredo Ovando nationalized Gulf's holdings in Bolivia, the company organized a worldwide boycott of Bolivian oil. The control of marketing networks by the international companies, at least at that time, was so effective that the Bolivians eventually had to give in and come to terms with the company (although the attempt was made to disguise the surrender by having it handled by the company's Spanish subsidiary, whose name did not reveal its connection with the parent corporation). Gulf followed similar tactics in its 1976 dispute with the government of Ecuador, suing in California courts to take possession of a shipment of oil consigned to Atlantic Richfield Company by the Ecuadorean state oil corporation. On that occasion the even-handed mediation of the U.S. ambassador, Richard Bloomfield, was successful in reaching a settlement generally acceptable to both sides.

The international companies' control over marketing networks was also responsible for their securing a very favorable financial settlement from the Venezuelan government at the time of the 1976 nationalization of the foreign companies.[17] Venezuela subsequently renegotiated the disadvantageous marketing and technical assistance agreements it was forced to accept because of its weak bargaining position at that time.

In addition to their control of marketing, what the companies had that state corporations often lacked was technology and capital. Thus the technically most competent state corporation, PEMEX, which was capable of handling the technical requirements of on-shore petroleum production, found it necessary to form joint companies with Houston-based U.S. drilling concerns in order to drill offshore in the Gulf of Mexico.

Where most of the state corporations were remiss was in the feebleness of their exploratory drilling programs. The capital requirements of getting drilling equipment into the relatively inaccessible regions where oil is likely to be found, and the inherently risk-laden nature of oil exploration, are responsible here. Governments in Latin America are normally hard-pressed for funds to deal with even the most urgent demands being placed on them and are generally in no position to commit extremely large amounts of capital in ventures whose short-term success is not assured. Thus some specialists now believe the appropriate time to nationalize an oil industry is when the national territory is fully explored, all the risks have been taken, and production is going full blast. This was more or less the point in their national petroleum development at which the Venezuelans chose to nationalize. The Ecuadoreans, unfortunately, inspired by the Venezuelans' example, proceeded to nationalize Gulf's holdings when only a fraction of the national territory had been explored. The government oil corporation, Corporación Ecuatoriana de Petróleos (CEPE), did not itself have the capital to engage in further exploration, and other companies were discouraged from entering Ecuador by the example of what had happened to Gulf. The goose was killed before all the golden eggs had been laid. The government recognized its tactical error, and attempts have since been made to attract foreign companies.

By the 1990s, debt crisis, which in turn owed much to the previous energy crisis, had so beggared the hemisphere and weakened the autonomy of governments that the national petroleum corporation had almost been rendered a mythological beast and national regulation of energy policy had lost its teeth. The skeletons of national companies remained intact in most cases, but they were being picked by the vultures. Privatization became a condition for debt relief, and the petroleum industry was the most coveted of investment opportunities. First, doors were opened wide for participation and competition in prospecting and drilling, then in petrochemical industries and wholesale marketing for the domestic market.

At the end of the twentieth century, national resource management was a receding goal, but it remained an ideal nonetheless. Given the folly of current rates of resource depletion on a global scale, it seemed likely that whether or not national governments were enabled to reenter the game as uncompromised players, the issue of popular participation in resource management would be raised forcefully once again in the twenty-first century.

Notes

1. See Vittorio Corbo, Morris Goldstein, and Mohsin Khan, *Growth-Oriented Adjustment Programs* (Washington, D.C.: International Monetary Fund and World Bank, 1987).

2. Shirley W. Y. Kuo, Gustav Ranis, and John C. Fei, *The Taiwan Success Story: Rapid Growth with Improved Distribution in the Republic of China, 1952–1979* (Boulder: Westview Press, 1981).

3. Walden Bello, "The End of the Asian Miracle," *The Nation* vol. 266, no. 2, January 12–19, 1998, pp. 16–21.

4. John Cassidy, "Taging J. P. Morgan: Who Should Pay Korea's Bills," *The New Yorker*, January 19, 1998, pp. 4–5. See also Mark Atkinson, "No Bargain for Korea in This Sale," *Manchester Guardian Weekly*, January 11, 1998, p. 12.

5. William P. Glade, "Economic Aspects of Latin America," chap. 9 in Jan Knippers Black, ed., *Latin America, Its Problems and Its Promise* (Boulder: Westview Press, 1984).

6. Claude Ake, *A Political Economy of Africa* (Lagos: Longman Group, Ltd., 1981), pp. 160–172.

7. Guy Martin, "The Franc Zone, Underdevelopment and Dependency in Francophone Africa," *Third World Quarterly* 8, no. 1, January 1986, pp. 205–235.

8. United Nations Development Program [UNDP], *Human Development Report 1997* (New York: UNDP, 1997), p. 38.

9. James Lee Ray, "International Relations in Latin America: Conflict and Cooperation," chap. 14 in Jan K. Black, ed., *Latin America, Its Problems and Its Promise*, 3rd. ed. rev. (Boulder: Westview Press, 1998).

10. UNDP, 1997, op. cit., p. 9.

11. Jane S. Jacquette, "Women in Power: From Tokenism to Critical Mass," *Foreign Policy* 108, fall 1997, pp. 23–37.

12. Exxon, Texaco, Gulf, Standard of California, Mobil, Royal Dutch Shell, and British Petroleum.

13. See John M. Blair, *The Control of Oil* (New York: Pantheon Books, 1976), p. 293; and Peter R. Odell, *Oil and World Power*, 4th ed. (Harmondsworth, UK: Penguin Books, 1975), pp. 9–20.

14. World Bank, *World Development Report, 1988* (New York: Oxford University Press, 1988), pp. 71–74.

15. UNDP, 1997, op. cit., p. 9.

16. Richard B. Mancke, *Mexican Oil and Natural Gas* (New York: Praeger, 1979), p. 26.

17. Interview with Humberto Calderón Berti, then director, Venezuelan Institute of Petroleum Technology, and subsequently minister of mines and hydrocarbons, June 9, 1977, Caracas.

Suggested Readings

Augustine, John S., ed., *Strategies for Third World Development* (New Delhi: Sage Publications, Inc., 1989).

Bello, Walden, and S. Rosenfeld, *Dragons in Distress: Asia's Miracle Economies in Crisis* (San Francisco: Food First, 1992).

Bennis, Phyllis, and Michael Moushabeck, eds., *Altered States: A Reader in the New World Order* (Brooklyn, N.Y.: Olive Branch Press, Interlink, 1993).

Bideleux, Robert, and Richard Taylor, eds., *European Integration and Disintegration: East and West* (London: Routledge, 1996).

Byres, T., and B. Crow, with Mae Wan Ho, *The Green Revolution in India* (London: Open University Press, 1983).

Corbo, Vittorio, Anne O. Krueger, and Fernando Ossa, *Export-Oriented Development Strategies* (Boulder: Westview Press, 1986).

Furtado, Celso, *Accumulation and Development: The Logic of Industrial Civilization*, trans. Suzette Macedo (New York: St. Martin's Press, 1983).

Haggard, Stephen, *Developing Nations and the Politics of Global Integration* (Washington, D.C.: Brookings Institution, 1995).

Heady, Ferrel, *Public Administration: A Comparative Perspective*, 2nd ed. (New York: Marcel Dekker, 1979).

Helleiner, G. K., "Conventional Foolishness and Overall Ignorance: Current Approaches to Global Transformations and Development," in C. Wilber and K. Jameson, eds., *The Political Economy of Development and Underdevelopment*, 5th ed. (New York: McGraw-Hill, 1992).

Hewlett, Sylvia Ann, *The Cruel Dilemmas of Development: Twentieth Century Brazil* (New York: Basic Books, 1980).

Hyden, G., R. Jackson, and F. Okuma, *Development Experience: The Kenyan Experience* (Nairobi: Oxford University Press, 1970).

Mittelman, James H., *Out from Underdevelopment: Prospects for the Third World* (New York: St. Martin's Press, 1988).

Nader, Ralph, ed., *The Case Against Free Trade* (San Francisco: Earth Island Press, 1993).

Nef, Jorge, and H. Wiseman, "The Second World: A New Periphery?" *Worldscape* 4, no. 1, 1990, pp. 1–4.

Nyerere, Julius K., *Freedom and Development* (Dar es Salaam: Oxford University Press, 1973).

Papanek, Gustav F., *Lectures on Development Strategy, Growth, Equity, and the Political Process in Southern Asia* (Islamabad: Pakistan Institute of Development Economics, 1986).

Ranis, Gustav, "Can the East Asian Model of Development be Generalized?" *World Development* 13, no. 4, 1985, pp. 543–546; and William R. Cline, "Reply," ibid., pp. 547–548.

Rifkin, Jeremy, *The End of Work: The Decline of the Global Labor Force and the Dawn of the Post-Market Era* (New York: G. P. Putnam's Sons, 1995).

Serra, José, "Three Mistaken Theses Regarding the Connection Between Industrialization and Authoritarian Regimes," in David Collier, ed., *The New Authoritarianism in Latin America* (Princeton: Princeton University Press, 1979), pp. 99–163.

Sheahan, John, *Patterns of Development in Latin America: Poverty, Repression, and Economic Strategy* (Princeton: Princeton University Press, 1987).

7 Political Counterparts and Consequences

The Cold War that so dominated behavior and discourse over the last half of the twentieth century acquired a military and ideological super-structure that need not be addressed here. Fundamentally, however, it was about access to markets and resources, and the engagement that mattered most was not between the geopolitically demarcated East and West blocs but rather between North and South.

It was the cover story of a no-holds-barred permanent global war be-tween good and evil that for both sides in the East-West neighborhood le-gitimated a brazen and brutal struggle for control of political forces, thus governments, thus resources in the newly decolonizing, technologically backward, but in many cases resource-rich bulk of the world. That strug-gle, for all of its unspeakable costs, had the virtue of maintaining two models and two markets, neither of which in undiluted form had great appeal but which in their polarization allowed for compromise and exper-imentation along the continuum of the political and economic spectrum.

The dynamic of that competition, centering on control of states, al-lowed for—in a sense even nurtured—the extension of the nation-state system throughout the Third World. The state, in turn, became an arena for the more nearly timeless struggle between accumulation and redistri-bution, or between elitism and equity.

Since the nineteenth century, a movement to redress some of the worst social depredations of the industrial revolution had been gaining mo-mentum. Through the organization of labor and of other oppressed or concerned groups and eventually of broadly based, interest-aggregating political parties, progress was being made, as discussed in Chapter 2, on many fronts. Rights and benefits for the more vulnerable elements of populations were finding their way into constitutions and laws and in some cases were even being enforced and funded. The central venue for competition, decision-making, and implementation was the state, and struggle for control of the state engaged ever broader constituencies.

Though conscious global strategy did not necessarily govern the major moves of popular forces during the Cold War, a strategist would have kept in mind that he was operating in the context of a four-way grid: of North versus South and West versus East blocs. Revolutionary movements that if successful would dislodge major players, including foreign ones, from the top of the social pyramid normally pitted South and East against North and West, as did counterrevolutionary ones, which aimed to weed out political participants from the lower rungs of that pyramid. The coalitions generated by the pursuit of change through elections were not necessarily so clear-cut, as it was sometimes presumed that such pursuit dampened the prospects of a revolution, but all too often the elected leader found the mantle of office was a straitjacket.

Revolutionary Strategies

There is no single revolutionary blueprint adequate or appropriate to inform the undertakings of Third World leaders generally. Each new revolution draws lessons from earlier ones but builds also on local needs and experience and on the dynamics unique to its own national revolutionary process.

Each is also a product of its own times. Just as most rebels at the turn of the nineteenth century drew upon the ideals of liberalism and the French enlightenment, most rebels since the turn of the twentieth have drawn to some extent upon the ideals and the analysis of Marx, as elaborated by Lenin. But the guidance to be drawn from Marx has been limited by his miscalculation as to the level of development at which a society is most susceptible to revolution.

Developments of the twentieth century have shown that it is not at the stage of advanced capitalism, but rather in the early stages of transition to capitalism—when subsistence farmers are being displaced and when the middle class seeks allies among the lower classes—that social upheaval may give rise to revolution. Once the middle class has acquired a certain size and status and has been co-opted by the power structure, the outcome of social upheaval is more likely to be counterrevolution. Thus, a strategy that assumed the irrelevance of the peasantry and the hostility of the middle class would be off on the wrong track from the start.

Strategy and Circumstance

The actual course a society in revolution pursues in its quest for development depends on at least three factors: (1) strategies consciously adopted by leaders; (2) more or less spontaneous popular initiatives; and (3) the domestic and international context, including a generally predictable but nonetheless awesome obstacle course laid down by external powers and business and banking interests. The course pursued—and it sometimes seems a zigzag one—grows out of the interplay of these factors.

The extent of redistribution, and thus the success of a revolution, depends in large part on how much wealth there is to redistribute. It also depends on maintaining the unity of the revolutionary coalition and, in general, the politicization of the population. Revolution is the ultimate bottom-up development strategy, and just as top-down strategies call for the minimization of political involvement, revolution calls for the maximization of it. There is no such thing as a technocratic approach to revolution. The only programs that stand much chance of success are those that spring from the aspirations, the imagination, and the capabilities of the common people.

While most spokesmen of Third World interests charge that those interests are continuously damaged by the more powerful forces that calibrate the workings of the international capitalist economic system, few such spokesmen—whether of revolutionary or of more conventional bent—would actually seek to withdraw their countries from participation in that system. Tendencies toward autarky are more likely to be imposed than chosen.

Even the Chinese of the People's Republic, who should have been better able than most to go it alone, opted to maintain commercial and other ties with the West. Those ties were severed early on by the United States and its allies. The Soviet Union extended technical assistance in the early years, particularly in the start-up stages of heavy industry, but after the mid-1950s, the Soviets also pulled out, leaving the Chinese without access even to spare parts and with little alternative to "self-reliance."

Soviet assistance proved crucial and more reliable for a number of other revolutionary regimes subjected to trade and credit embargoes by the West. But such rescue operations brought the Soviet Union few tangible rewards, and the all-out supporting role it undertook in the case of Cuba was not repeated elsewhere. Meanwhile, being forced into self-reliance has had marginal benefits for some countries. Nicaraguans rediscovered traditional remedies, for example, that are just as effective and far less costly than equivalent drugs previously imported. Such benefits, however, have generally been heavily outweighed by the economic and political costs of trade disruption.

Soviet credit and technical assistance, incidentally, did not necessarily incline revolutionary regimes to adopt Soviet development models. Mozambique's revolutionary party, the Mozambique Liberation Front (FRELIMO), found Chinese and Yugoslav approaches more relevant to its needs, and Nicaragua's Sandinistas drew particularly from the experiences and institutions of Mexico.

Since Third World rebellion has generally been against colonial and neocolonial powers as well as against domestic elites, most revolutionary ideology has been infused with economic nationalism, and revolutionary strategy has included some measure of nationalization or expropriation. Initial targets have included public utilities, the communications media, banking, and extractive or plantation industries that dominated exports and unfairly exploited labor. The extent of socialization actually carried out, however, has often had more to do with military or political developments than with economic planning. In Mozambique, for example, about 90 percent of the Portuguese settlers had left the country within a year of independence; thus the new revolutionary government was compelled to take control of small businesses, shops, garages, and such, which it had no preparation or desire to manage. It has since invited former residents to return and invest in the private sector.[1]

Land reform has commonly been a high priority for revolutionary governments, but approaches have varied widely. In Mexico and Bolivia, the displacement of the landowning classes was not a plan of the middle-class revolutionary leadership. Rather, it was an initiative of the peasants themselves, which the national leadership had little choice but to embrace. The brutality and counterproductivity of Stalin's forced collectivization limited the appeal of that approach for most subsequent revolutionaries. The most notable exception was Mao Zedong; he turned to forced collectivization only in the mid-1950s after concluding that a gradualist strategy for rural transformation, based primarily on cooperatives, had failed to promote equity or to generate a surplus for diversion to industry. His turn to collectivization so offended Nikita Khrushchev, who was attempting to de-Stalinize, that it became one of the several factors generating a Sino-Soviet rift.

Elsewhere direct state control of agriculture has generally been limited to plantations expropriated from foreigners, colonial powers, or, as in the case of Nicaragua, friends and relations of the deposed tyrant, and to marketing arrangements. Some measure of redistribution of land has been common, however, either to individuals or to village or tribal cooperatives or communes (e.g., communal *ejidos* in Mexico, *Ujamaa* cooperative villages in Tanzania). The extension of credit and services to new landowners has generally been programmed, but scarcity of technicians and resources has often prevented follow-up.

Having suffered from dependence on imported manufactured goods with continuously escalating prices, countries undergoing revolutions have often sought to abandon reliance on primary commodities with unreliable markets and to industrialize rapidly. That strategy has generally bogged down early on due to capital flight and shortage of hard currency for the purchase of capital goods. In the face of trade embargoes, it has proved difficult enough just to acquire the spare parts to keep existing industries operating. A common fallback strategy has been that of promoting low-tech processing or other light industry, building upon available raw materials.

Innovations in industry have often involved some approach to worker self-management. The most elaborated and successful experiment of that sort was that of Yugoslavia, the only East European country apart from the Soviet Union and Albania to experience its own home-grown revolution. The strategy contributed for more than two decades to raising living standards and to maintaining popular participation. Over the years, however, as conflicts arose between the directives of central authorities and the decisions of self-managed units, they were increasingly resolved through the circumscription of the jurisdiction of the latter.

Making the Most of Motivation

Ironically, perhaps, the greatest successes of revolutionary governments have been in the delivery of services—services that popularly elected governments promise but are usually unable to deliver: health care, education, recreation, and better wages and working conditions, at least initially, for labor. This is because, while revolutionary governments are sorely lacking in material resources—they were poor to start with and are then subjected to military and economic warfare—what they have in abundance is highly mobilized and motivated citizens, committed to a common vision. Such a citizenry can do little, in the absence of material resources or external markets, about building heavy industry; but it can accomplish near miracles in the promotion of literacy or the eradication of disease. When the population ceases to be so mobilized and motivated, it is safe to say that the revolution has run its course.

Characteristics often attributed to revolution—dogmatism, centralization of decision-making, and rigid bureaucratization, for example—are indicative either of simple tyranny masquerading as revolution or of the onset of a postrevolutionary reconcentrational phase. The essence of revolution is the presence of common purpose in the absence of centralized control. People who have so recently risked life and limb in the pursuit of personal and national dignity will not easily be shunted aside when decisions affecting their livelihoods are to be made. In fact, dealing with a mobilized population and with the usual crises of external assault and material deprivation makes pragmatism and flexibility on the part of leadership absolutely essential.

In Nicaragua in the 1980s, policymakers and managers, far from being immobilized by centralization, were still struggling to coordinate the activities of ministries, each of which had undergone its own self-contained revolution. Lacking the resources to promote change in the orderly manner they might have preferred, Sandinista leadership had the good sense to be supportive of popular initiatives that showed promise, to give way where they had to—as in holding back the tides of new squatters pouring into already overcrowded Managua—and to revise their own policies when they confronted strong popular resistance.

Cuba: The Last Holdout

Through most of the 1980s, while the rest of Latin America witnessed a negative per capita growth of 8 percent, Cuba enjoyed unprecedented prosperity. Moreover, it was a prosperity built on the values and achievements of the revolution. Advances in education, particularly in science and technology, allowed mechanization of the sugarcane harvest and freed Cubans to work instead in such high-tech fields as biotechnology and informatics. Cuba was meeting some 70 percent of its own pharmaceutical needs and was exporting state-of-the-art drugs for treating cancer, AIDS, and other scourges of the times. But the more modernized the economy, the more dependent it becomes on raw materials, spare parts, and, above all, energy. Thus the disintegration of the Soviet bloc, marketplace for more than 80 percent of Cuba's trade at the end of the 1980s, delivered an awful shock, shrinking the economy by some 40 percent in about three years.

For the generation who made their own history, there is pride still in holding out—even in being the last holdout—against a particularly virulent strain of capitalism. But that generation complains that its children don't understand what was won through the revolution, or what they have to lose, because they have never been without it. Those coming of age in the 1990s are especially taunted by cousins from Miami who bring Nintendo games and cellular phones and other marvels of modern-day consumer mania. And the pride of Cubans, young and old, is shattered by the privilege extended to hard currency–toting tourists and denied to them. The urgency of the need for foreign reserves is such that the best of the country's resorts, hotels, restaurants, and nightclubs, wrenched from foreigners with such gratification in 1959, have once again been set aside for foreigners. Such "apartheid" tourism adds poignancy to the question that has haunted friends of the revolution since its inception: Is the worst of the system the price that must be paid for the best of it? Must universal literacy always be punished by an absence of anything worth reading? Is there an unavoidable trade-off between material equity and cultural and political creativity? Architects of the Cold War, on both sides, were bent on proving that there is. The Castro government has yet to meet the challenge of disproving the thesis.

The Cuban economy has been damaged, of course, by a U.S. embargo in place for thirty-seven years and tightened particularly in the 1990s. But the worst of the Cuban plight is to some degree obscured by that embargo. Were it to be lifted, Cuba would still have to come to terms with a world economic system hostile not only to socialism but even to mixed and regulated economies and socially responsible government.

Cuba is already undergoing far-reaching change. Foreign investment from Europe, Canada, Japan, and Latin America is being welcomed in the form of mixed enterprises, particularly in tourism and energy generation. Dollars now circulate freely, and remittances from expatriates in Miami have proved to be a powerful stimulus to economic growth, if nonetheless an irritant to social harmony. In fact, in terms of the indices that matter most to economists, Cuba has already recovered from its crisis. Economic growth registered 7.8 percent in 1996, the second highest in the region according to the UN Economic Commission for Latin America and the Caribbean.

Meanwhile, Cuban economists are dropping the language of Marxism and talking instead of neostructuralism, development from within—that is, competing internationally on the basis of a healthy domestic market—and mixed economies, Western European style. Political reform, though, will encounter more resistance. Members of Cuba's National Assembly have been elected directly since 1993 rather than by provincial assemblies. One encounters talk of moving from a one-party exclusive system to a one-party dominant one. But the revolutionary generation will not be easily sold on the idea of a multiparty system. They knew it all to well, as one diplomat has said, and knew it to be in the Cuban context a "laced product."

Can Cuba succeed where all other Third World states have failed—in integrating the world capitalist system without loss of national sovereignty and, in particular, without loss of the social gains of revolution? Maybe. The Cubans are certainly a remarkable people. Of the "special period" of hardship, Alberto Faya, musical director of Casa de las Americas, says it is not so special, not so different from what globalization has done to most of the peoples of the Third World. The really special period that Cuba experienced was an earlier one, when it was able for a time to get a fair price for its products. And the earnings of that period have been invested in intellectual development that will help Cuba find a way through its troubled transition.[2]

Options Closed, Lessons Learned

Successful revolution is probably at least as much a product of paranoia and overreaction on the part of the haves as of strategy and mobilization on behalf of the have-nots, and for a number of reasons it seems a most unpromising option for the foreseeable future. In the first place, the economic growth and modernization that have occurred at least in spurts in so much of the world in recent decades have swelled the middle classes and made the crucial coalition of middle and working classes less likely.

Moreover, the popular commitment to risk and sacrifice essential to successful revolution will not be forthcoming unless all peaceful means of the pursuit of change have been foreclosed, and the haves with the most at stake have discovered or rediscovered that an elected leader unable or unwilling to follow through on a popular mandate is a more effective hedge against social change than a brutal dictator. Finally, in the post–Cold War global village, where economic policy-making is centrally controlled by a transnational private sector creditor cartel, conquest of the state would no longer be much of a prize.

Even so, it should be remembered that violence is not the defining feature of revolution. Violence—or the threat of it—is implicit in all political processes. And the nation-state is not the only appropriate arena for political organization. The most important lesson to be learned from revolution is that a population organized and united and committed to a common purpose can sometimes overcome formidable odds and achieve miracles.

Counterrevolutionary Strategies

It might well be argued that counterrevolutionary strategies are not of the Third World but of the First. Since they are played out in the Third World, however, they will be dealt with briefly here.

The basic counterrevolutionary strategy has been less often a response or reaction to a revolutionary one than to a populist strategy featuring economic nationalism and political liberalization. That is in part because populist regimes and policies have been more vulnerable to overthrow and reversal than revolutionary ones.

Political Demobilization

The counterrevolutionary strategy outlined here is essentially one that characterized military dictatorship in South America's Southern Cone— Argentina, Uruguay, and Chile—and Brazil between the 1960s and the 1980s. With some variations, however, the strategy has been adopted by regimes in all major Third World areas—for example, since the 1960s, those of Mobutu Sese Seko in Zaire, Ferdinand Marcos's Martial Law in the Philippines, Suharto's "New Order" in Indonesia, the shah in Iran, and Colonel Sitiveni Rabuka in Fiji. In some of these cases, the counterrevolutionary strategy shaded into kleptocracy, or government as theft. The strategy seeks not merely to freeze socioeconomic relationships and maintain the status quo but rather to promote accumulation or reconcentration—that is, to redistribute assets and income from the bottom up. Its political component, which will not be elaborated here, calls for the elimination of the means of participation by the nonaffluent through the dissolution of parties, unions, and other organizations representing them.

Economic Restructuring

The process of reconcentration has generally begun with a dampening of inflation through cutting back effective demand. Demand is cut through the pruning of social services, particularly those involving income transfer, and through wage freezes. Frozen wages, along with other indicators that the government has brought labor under control, can be expected to inspire the confidence of investors, both domestic and foreign. Other measures, however, such as credit, tax, and tariff policies, commonly favor foreign businesses over domestic ones. Domestic enterprises are absorbed by transnational ones, and a general denationalization and oligopolization occurs. The production system stresses exports, whether of raw materials or of manufactured goods. Domestic production favors consumer durables. Based on imported technology and product lines, its target market is the upper and middle classes. In some cases fully rationalized policies of weeding out national enterprises and, generally, of deindustrialization reversed and nullified the gains of economic development programs that had been in effect over several decades. Meanwhile, progressive forms of taxation gave way to regressive ones, and the easing of currency convertibility and profit repatriation accelerated the flow of capital from Third World to First.

Having successfully completed the first stage of economic transformation, the regime may then turn its attention to the promotion of industrialization, rural modernization through high-technology agribusiness, and infrastructural projects such as highways, ports, and dams. Whereas the early pruning of social services may have resulted in a general contraction of the state sector, that sector soon expands once again, but in different directions, responsive to the interests of the new ruling elite (initially the military) and its constituencies. New state activities may include the establishment of parastatal enterprises, such as weapons production, that generate income and high-level positions for elements of the new elite. Although it was uncommon, some such governments played important entrepreneurial roles and imposed their own guidelines on foreign investors. Brazil, for example, was able to do so and, in general, to greatly modernize its economic system while generating economic growth. At the same time, real wages dropped dramatically. Between 1960 and 1970 every decile of the population except the top one experienced a relative loss of income.[3]

Some counterrevolutionary regimes, generally favored by foreign and international financial institutions, have had considerable early success in curbing inflation and later success in attracting foreign investment, promoting economic growth, and increasing foreign exchange earnings. In the longer run, however, the extensive foreign borrowings, the abandonment of basic food production in favor of export agriculture, and other poorly conceived policies have brought these economies into crisis, in some cases hastening military withdrawal and the return of elected governments.

Virtual Transition: The Chilean Model

Chile's counterrevolution penetrated deeply into all aspects of economic and social life. The combination, for example, of severe repression and precipitous economic decline, particularly in the manufacturing sector, shrank union membership from 41 percent of the labor force in 1972 to 10 percent in 1987. Thus, redemocratization was hard fought, long delayed, and tenuous.

Chile's democratic movement revived the party system and returned its members to elective office under an electoral code that was devised to defeat them. When the Pinochet regime caved in to domestic and international pressures in the late 1980s to stage elections, it was in the belief still that the military and its civilian allies would be able to control the process and the governments produced by it. To their surprise, a set of elections in 1988 and 1989 edged Chile back toward civilian rule. Even so the transition occurred under a constitution drawn up by the Pinochet regime that maintained a "tutelary" role for the armed forces and tilted electoral and legislative processes sharply to the Right. General Pinochet himself retained the role of commander in chief of the armed forces and in early 1998 still refused to step down until he was allotted a seat for life in the senate.

Economic Continuity as the Price of Transition. For a variety of economic and political reasons, the Concertación, a Center-Left coalition that has held office since 1990, has seen itself as having little choice but to pursue in broad outline the economic course set by the predecessor regime. For one thing, it would have been hard to argue with a course so widely seen in global money markets as successful. Following deep recession in the early 1980s, the Chilean economy in the late 1980s had entered a phase of steady growth, and creditors and international financial institutions were already touting the Chilean model. For another, it was necessary to placate domestic and foreign business interests in order to gain their acquiescence in pushing the military back to the barracks and to keep them from disinvesting after the transition.[4]

In fact the policies of the civilian government have approximated the free-market ideal to a much greater extent than did the policies of the Pinochet government. The military government had eliminated

protections for domestic business as well as labor, but it had not deregulated or slashed subsidies across the board. Regulations changed so as to
favor the raw materials export sector, particularly agribusiness, and subsidies slashed from civilian services showed up on the military side of
the public ledger. Ten percent of the revenues from the copper industry
were earmarked for the armed forces, an arrangement the civilian government has not seen fit to challenge.

Military government subsidies also appeared in the form of privatization at below-market values of favored enterprises and nationalization at
above-market values of favored enterprises and conglomerates in financial crisis. Pinochet privatized banks that had been nationalized during
the Allende government, but when deregulated private banks collapsed
in 1981 he bailed out the banking sector by temporarily renationalizing it.

The collapse had come about owing in large part to heavy foreign borrowing, leaving Chile in the 1980s with one of the world's highest per
capita debts. Much of that debt was retired in the late 1980s through conversion of debt for equity in public enterprises. The stock of foreign direct investment in Chile by 1992 amounted to 30 percent of GDP. It was
not until the late 1980s that the military government began to balance its
own books. Meanwhile, further reductions in tariffs and massive devaluation had generated a boom in nontraditional exports.

Pursuing a steadier and more nearly orthodox course, the civilian government has continued to expand and diversify trade and to generate
savings and investment. During Aylwin's four-year term, per capita GDP
grew by almost 20 percent, exports by 14 percent, and investment by 70
percent. The uniform import duty was reduced to 11 percent, and lower
rates were offered through preferential trade agreements pursued with
countries in all parts of the world. Trade relations, in fact, are highly diversified, almost equally divided between Western Hemisphere, European, and Asian partners. Agricultural exports have more than quadrupled since the early 1970s, leaving copper to account for less than 30
percent of export revenues, compared to about 80 percent in the 1960s.

A breakdown of shares of the GDP in 1992 is illustrative of major transformations in the economy. As compared to the late 1960s and early
1970s, the share of mining had remained relatively constant at 61 percent,
but the manufacturing sector had dropped significantly from 25 to 21
percent while that of agriculture, livestock, and forestry had risen somewhat from 7.4 to 7.9 percent. Construction was down from 7.7 to 6.0 percent, and services including banking were up from 26 to 29.1 percent.
Fishing and tourism had also been gaining ground rapidly since the late
1980s.

Foreign direct investment had continued to be strong, showing a 46
percent increase in 1996 alone. The largest portion of new investment, 51
percent, was in the service sector, followed by 19 percent in mining and

18 percent in industry. The U.S. share of total investment for the period 1974 to 1996 was about 40 percent, but in 1996 it rose to nearly 49 percent.

Most of the privatizations that have so transformed the economy since the disruption of democratic rule, involving some 550 enterprises previously in the public sector, occurred during the dictatorship. The process of privatization continues, however; the Frei government in 1997 was seeking to privatize or grant concessions in highways and toll roads, ports, airports, passenger rail service, and waterworks.

Chile's remarkable productivity since the mid-1980s had been attributed in large part to the labor flexibility—generally meaning the near absence of supports—that could only have been brought about by repressive means. The civilian coalition government has since tried in vain to link wage increases to increases in productivity. Nor has it been able to enhance greatly the bargaining power of labor, but it has succeeded in pushing through legislation placing some restrictions on employers' recourse to lockouts and on causes claimed for firing employees. And required compensation in the event of layoffs has been increased.

Likewise the Concertación has had little success in reintroducing progressivity into taxation. The Aylwin government was able to pass a temporary increase for 1991–1993 in the corporate income tax rate from 10 to 15 percent. The government remains more heavily dependent, however, on the regressive value-added tax (VAT). The VAT rate, 20 percent during most of the Pinochet regime, had been dropped to 16 percent just before the 1988 plebiscite. It was raised back to 18 percent by the Aylwin government.

The Privatization of Social Security. Much of the social welfare system that had been constructed by democratic governments was dismantled by the Pinochet dictatorship. In 1981, a new social security system displaced the state-run system that had been in place since 1952. Employees entering the work force after 1983 were obliged to participate. Participation was optional for employees already vested in the older system or persons who were self-employed.

The new system, privately administered but government regulated, was based on the notion of individual capitalization accounts. Neither public nor private employers contribute to the account. It is rather like a private insurance policy, including payment of fees or commissions to the competing Pension Fund Administrators (APFs), except that contributions amounting to 10 to 15 percent of earnings are obligatory and a minimum benefit to contributors is guaranteed by the state.

The system had generated considerable positive attention from governments and employers anxious for relief from pension obligations and from players in capital markets. The funds soon became the largest institutional investors in Chile's capital market, representing about one-third of GDP by the mid-1990s. The funds were the major factor in a national aggregate savings rate that was competitive at that time with the rates of the so-called Asian tigers. Growth in the aggregate of forced savings was matched, however, by growth in individual consumer (particularly credit card) debt.

The pension funds had enjoyed continuous growth in Chile's thriving stock market, but in 1995 they registered a loss, and a public opinion survey that year indicated considerable public skepticism. The real test of the system will come in two or three decades when it is called upon to support an aging population. The idea that it might involve considerable risks and drawbacks is suggested by the fact that the military establishment that created the system opted out of it for its own personnel.

Mixed Blessings.   Chile's first civilian government in seventeen years inherited a fast-growing economy that served as a magnet to creditors and investors. While the private sector was thriving, however, in part on resources and markets previously in the public domain, the public sector had been gutted. As the fiscal deficit shrank during the period of military rule, the social deficit grew. Some of the services previously subsidized by the government were still to be found, at higher cost, in the private sector; others appeared to be unavailable at any cost. And recent economic growth had served to widen the already yawning gap between rich and poor.

The economic system bequeathed by the military regime was one that had been transformed from an import substitution to an export-oriented model. The mix of export products as well as of trading partners had been expanded and diversified. But as in the preindustrial era, exports were mainly raw materials and largely depletable ones. The economy had been rendered highly competitive and thus attractive to foreign investors through the suppression of wages and in general a retilting of the playing field to favor private over public, large over small, and foreign over local enterprises.

Although growth rates in the late 1980s were high, it cannot be said that the military regime had generated the macroeconomic stability required for sustainable growth. In fact, even in growth terms, the economy had been on a roller coaster over the course of Pinochet's rule. Whereas for the dozen years before military rule the economy had grown at an average annual per capita rate of 4.16 percent, the rate for the military period, from 1973 to 1989, was less than 1 percent. Growth spurts in the late 1970s and late 1980s, heralded each time as economic miracles, were miracles in the biblical sense—of rising from the dead. The 6–7 percent growth of the late 1980s, for example, responded to the shock of a 13 percent annual decline in the early 1980s.

It was not until the late 1980s that Chile's per capita income measured in constant dollars recovered its 1970 value. And average wages in 1989 were still 8 percent below those of 1970. The proportion of the population defined as living in poverty had risen from 20 percent to 40 percent, and the wealthiest 20 percent of the population had increased their share of total consumption from 45 percent in 1969 to 60 percent in 1989. Growing poverty and inequality had been reinforced over the period of military rule by a reduction of 20 percent per capita in social spending.

Given the challenges the new elected governments have faced and the straitjackets they have worn, the progress they have achieved in restoring social services and raising living standards is remarkable. The economy's growth momentum has been maintained, averaging 7 percent annually from 1990 through 1996, while inflation has been gradually tamed, dropping to single digits per annum by 1995. The fiscal budget has maintained a yearly surplus, and the savings rate exceeded 28 percent in 1996.

Spending on education, health care, and housing has increased by 10 percent annually in real terms since 1990. To support such programs, however, the government has been largely dependent on regressive taxes, like the 18 percent value-added tax. Between 1987 and 1994 the percentage of Chilean households living below the poverty line dropped from about 40 percent to 24 percent. The lowest pensions and the minimum wage rose about 50 percent between 1990 and 1994, and by 1996 tight labor markets had finally allowed real wages to reach and surpass predictatorship levels. Unemployment in the formal sector was held to 6.4 percent in 1996, though an estimated 40 percent of the work force remained in the relatively unstable, unprotected informal sector.

In sum, since the return of civilian rule, the performance of Chile's economy has been truly impressive, and progress toward the consolidation of civilian rule has been steady. Seventeen years of fearsome dictatorship, however, have taken their toll, especially since many perpetrators of great crimes continue to enjoy impunity and even, in some circles, prestige. Moreover, while great progress has been made in improving the standards of living of the poorest Chileans, the income gap continues to grow, leaving Chile second only to Brazil in income disparity in the Western Hemisphere. In 1996, the cash income of the wealthiest 20 percent of the population was thirteen times that of the lowest 20 percent. Much remains to be done in the rebuilding of social infrastructure and the reweaving of the social fabric. The country remains far removed from the broad-based and free-wheeling, albeit disorderly, democracy that flourished before the imposition of military rule.

For the most part, public debate about economic policy since the beginning of the democratic transition has focused on programmatic detail, including social services, rather than the general structure of the economy, but some critics within the governing coalition argue that the current system is unsustainable. They see it as too subject to the whims of the foreign investors and global markets, too subject to the volatility in particular of markets for primary products, and too exploitative of depletable resources. They advocate the enactment of a coherent industrial policy to advance toward a broader resource-based industrialization. Many see the growth in wine exports, averaging 50 percent a year in the early 1990s, as indicative of what might be accomplished.

Democracy in the New Order: The Absence of Accountability

The pursuit of change on behalf of the disadvantaged or less powerful is by definition an uphill struggle, but the direction of change during most of the twentieth century was toward greater equity, that is, toward giving more people a larger share of the fruits of their labor and a stronger voice in the distribution process. That movement—wherein it was presumed that reform, or social change, meant change toward greater equity, and the wielders of economic power were so embattled as to solicit military intervention in state after state—reached its zenith in the 1960s and 1970s. Thereafter the position of the reformist leaders and movements became increasingly tenuous.

Election to Office, Not to Power

The election to the highest political office of a popular reformer representing a broadly based constituency became possible most often in times of economic crisis. Such a development was an indication that political power and economic power were out of kilter. In the Third World especially, it often meant that economic growth and the elaboration of economic roles had generated a middle class that was attempting to wrench from the traditional power structure its rightful place in policy-making councils. It sometimes meant that a more-or-less democratic system had given political representation to a working class that had yet to be expressed in economic redistribution. Or it meant that a more-or-less counterrevolutionary regime, having arisen most likely in response to an earlier bout with reformism, had run its course or had at least come to recognize the need for an institutional buffer zone between exploiter and exploited and was now willing to share its power, or at least its stage, in exchange for sharing also the blame for inequitable policies.

   The essential point is that the reformers' position was based on moral force—on the evidence of popular support for his or her ideas—rather than on economic power (e.g., ownership or control of the means of production). Organization charts notwithstanding, that generally meant that the reformist president or prime minister lacked the full powers normally associated with the office—most important, control over military and paramilitary forces, including the police.

There have been times and places in which reformist leaders and movements have been able to consolidate their positions and move their societies to a higher level of development. During the first two decades of the twentieth century, for example, José Batlle y Ordóñez, having drawn a generation of European immigrants into his urban-based Colorado Party, was able to turn a politically and economically backward Uruguay into a modern social-welfare state. In India, building upon the inspiration of and the massive popular mobilization carried out by Mahatma Gandhi, Jawaharlal Nehru and the Congress Party were able to achieve far-reaching reform along with national independence. Nevertheless, the very extensive and sophisticated redistributive features built into India's constitution and laws are not much in evidence in the country's shanty-towns and rural villages. Bankers, landowners, and industrialists, their actual power little diminished by reformist governments and legislation, have often been able to prevent implementation of laws running contrary to their interests.

As a rule, the position of the democratic reformer was a most precarious one. The ritual of an election should not normally be viewed as conferring power upon the popular choice. If the winner does indeed appear to be the popular choice, and one who aspires to respond to the will of the electorate, the odds are that real power is not vested in the electorate and that the reformist leader will be straitjacketed by armed forces and/or foreign powers having motives contrary to those of the electorate. An extreme case in the late 1980s was President Vinicio Cerezo of Guatemala, who often seemed a virtual prisoner in the presidential palace.[5] President Cory Aquino of the Philippines and Prime Minister Benazir Bhutto of Pakistan appeared to have rather more latitude but hardly a full range of powers.

Directly or indirectly, First World governments and major donor institutions have often promoted political and economic reform, but within limits—limits guaranteed by flows of aid and credit as well as by First World influence on Third World armed forces. The limits were drawn, for example, in decades past, at the expropriation of foreign-owned assets, the encouragement of rural labor organization, or the trimming of military budgets.

Some reformists rejected the limits and came to be seen, in Cold War terms, as subversives. Others accepted the limits and came to be seen by their own constituencies as sellouts. The sellouts then lost their political bases to the subversives. In the case of U.S. clients in particular, since U.S. policy was more prone to sharp reversals than the policies of other donor states, reformists were subject to a sort of political whiplash when limits were drawn in abruptly as a new administration replaced the old. The consequent fluidity was unnerving to domestic and foreign elites and sometimes led to counterrevolution.

As in the case of revolutionary governments, the most important policy breakthroughs of the reformist government were generally made early on, while supporters were mobilized and optimistic and before opponents had fully marshalled their forces. Reformers generally had more slack in the leash, however, for expanding human rights and civil liberties than for rewarding their constituencies with economic gains and opportunities. To the extent that they were able to raise the purchasing power of the lower classes, they ran the risk of overstimulating the economy, creating shortages for more-affluent consumers, and generating inflation. The risk was particularly great since the increase in effective demand is likely to coincide with capital flight, domestic and international credit freezes, and other expressions of elite displeasure that interfere with production. In the end, the reformist, unable to generate employment elsewhere, often felt obliged to bloat his own bureaucracy.

Even if the reformer were utterly unsuccessful in redistributing income, his intentions alone would have sufficed to mobilize opposition on the right. Meanwhile, the high expectations of his erstwhile supporters would have turned to frustration, frustration likely to be vented in ways newly legitimated by the reformer, such as strikes and street demonstrations. Sooner or later, the police, perhaps with military backing, would turn on the strikers or demonstrators with unguarded fury. The reformist leader then had to decide whether to assume responsibility for repressive measures he did not authorize or admit publicly that he was not in control of the country's security forces. He usually chose the former.

In Latin America and other areas where military governments withdrew from power in the 1980s—making way, in some cases, for genuine would-be reformers—that withdrawal has been considerably less than complete. While the military remains more or less on call, the more immediate task of protecting foreign and domestic elite interests—in particular of ensuring that debt servicing is maintained without threat to the existing economic structure—has fallen to the IMF.

When foreign creditors demand sacrifice as the price of extending further loans, the rich make the usual choice about whether to accept that sacrifice, and the sacrifice is borne by those who have no choice. Civilian elites who can no longer blame the military for such grossly inequitable policies can now pass the buck to the mysterious and seemingly omnipotent IMF.

A party such as the Dominican Republic's Dominican Revolutionary Party (PRD), popular and reformist in its origins, would ordinarily be a source of anxiety for economic elites and a target for military repression—as indeed it was throughout most of its history and as recently as 1978. Because of that history, in fact, it was a much-subdued PRD that assumed the presidency in 1978. Even so, the most modest of its promised welfare advances were thwarted by the austerity measures imposed by the IMF, while the military lurked in the background. Seeing themselves under constant threat—feeling the pull of the short leash—PRD executives, Salvador Jorge Blanco in particular, made concessions to the armed forces, to creditors, and to other foreign and domestic elite interests that even notoriously conservative presidents might have resisted.[6]

Such an outcome, allowing a reformist party to take "power" only to discredit itself, while their own reputations are protected along with their interests, has obvious appeal for economic elites, as for hegemonic powers. In the United States in the 1980s, a government representing the ideological Right finally discovered what more-seasoned conservatives had long recognized, that in a client state a civilian government that is uninterested in acting upon or unable to act upon a popular mandate and unwilling or unable to control military and paramilitary forces is a better hedge against social change than a repressive military government. That learning process was expedited by a Congress that under popular pressure to end support for human rights violations insisted on taking a firm position on both sides of the fence; particularly with respect to Central America, it made the maintenance of a "democratic" civilian facade a condition for the ongoing provision of military aid.

Democracy as Blame Sharing

The end of the Cold War coincided with the new era of electoral democracy, the most far-reaching yet in geopolitical terms; by the late 1990s there were some 118 states claiming elected governments. This was due in part to the disintegration of the Soviet sphere, the accompanying separatist fervor, and the explosion in the number of recognized states. Whatever the motives of those prospecting the new frontiers of East Europe and Central Asia, whether revision of property and investment codes or the facilitation of new forms of expression and participation, the staging of elections launched the reorganization and offered essential legitimation.

This era of electoral democracy may also be the most far reaching in terms of the breadth of participation in voting and in office holding. Suffrage has expanded to such a point that it has become difficult for a government practicing exclusion on grounds of race or gender to claim legitimacy (although many governments are getting away with increasing exclusivity by making citizenship a privilege and not a right). Indeed, here and there in the 1990s, in Haiti and South Africa, for example, electoral outcomes have unmistakably represented the triumph of a long suppressed popular will. But as elections become freer, the elected become less so. In fact, it has been particularly in these cases where electoral outcomes represent real triumph that investors and creditors and the governments and international financial institutions that serve them have laid out in no uncertain terms the dangers that accompany precipitous promotion of equity.

For the Third World in general, the end of the Cold War has meant both liberation and resignation. For the Right it has meant the loss of a cover story, for the Left the loss of a dream. For populations in general, confronting an unregulated globalized capitalist economy, it has meant loss of the prospect of competing successfully under any form of government for a fair share of their countries' riches. Thus, both revolutionary and counterrevolutionary, or militarist-modernizer, movements have shrinking constituencies; and the forces that have constituted at times the political extremes, at times the political options, are left with no marketable alternative to elections. Elected leaders who in times past would have been "tutored" by their military commanders-in-chief are now tutored by ministers of finance.

The most important effect of the termination of the Cold War has been the removal of the control mechanisms of economic decision-making and redistribution from the public venue where the nonrich had achieved representation to the private venue of financial and corporate interests. As elected governments here and there, in First World and Third, in the 1960s and 1970s became accountable to broader constituencies, the weightiest economic interests on the one hand threw their weight behind antidemocratic forces within state systems and on the other hand sought protection for their assets and freedom from regulation beyond the reach of any nation-state. Globalization, made possible finally by technological advances and by the collapse of the alternative models of development, is the completion of the great escape. Redemocratization may have closed the barn door, but the horse was already out.

The upshot has been the appearance of the flowering of democracy around the world, but that is only because the ritual of elections is now unthreatening to wielders of economic power; elected officials have no meaningful involvement in economic decisions. The direction of change has been reversed. Whereas until the early 1990s a reformist leader was understood to be one who was seeking to enhance the power position of the many against the few, a reformist since that time has come to mean one who is doing the opposite—deregulating, or dismantling popular controls over the money movers.

State officials find themselves in a position akin to that of colonial administrators, except that instead of answering to a mother country they answer to a corporate cabal that has no name and no headquarters but an unmistakable and inescapable set of rules. There is indeed competition in this system, but the competition that counts is that of an increasing number of states competing for the favor of a shrinking number of creditors and investors.

The competition is played out in the manner of a South Pacific cargo cult. Like islands exposed suddenly to modern air transport and conspicuous consumption, governments at all levels build landing strips in hopes that riches of exotic origin will come to rest on their turf. And along with ever more elaborate landing strips, enticements include golf courses, industrial parks, tax holidays, and suppressed wages. Such a development strategy promotes and rewards the skills of hustlers and punishes precisely those who would empower local communities to set their own goals and use their own ingenuity to build from the bottom up. The power that emerged triumphant from the Cold War is market power. Virtually all states are now vanquished states, the public sector having succumbed and been colonized by the private sector. But states are not likely to wither away; elite interests are well served by allowing elected governments to assume responsibility for the imposition of austerity policies, ensuring that state resources will be directed to debt service rather than public service, and to absorb the blame for policies punishing the poor.

Notes

1. See James H. Mittelman, *Out from Underdevelopment* (New York: St. Martin's Press, 1988), pp. 129–155; and William Finnegan, "A Reporter at Large (Mozambique—Part II: The Emergency)," *New Yorker*, May 29, 1989, pp. 69–96.

2. Alberto Faya, conversations at Casa de las Americas, Havana, May–June 1993.

3. Albert Fishlow, "Brazil's Economic Miracle," *World Today* (London) 2y, November 1973, pp. 474–494.

4. Carlos Huneeus of the Instituto de Ciencia Política, Universidad de Chile, speaking at St. Antony's College, Oxford University, May 13, 1998, observed that the Concertación had turned the making of economic policy, including labor policy, over to economists. Eight of the ministers in the Aylwin government had doctorates in economics.

5. Adolfo Pérez Esquivel, Argentine Nobel Peace laureate, told this author in May 1989 that, while visiting recently with Cerezo in Guatemala City, he had the impression that there were only two civilians in the presidential palace—himself and Cerezo.

6. For elaboration on the fate of the PRD, see Jan Knippers Black, *The Dominican Republic: Politics and Development in an Unsovereign State* (Boston: Allen and Unwin, 1986).

Suggested Readings

Augustine, John S., ed., *Strategies for Third World Development* (New Delhi: Sage Publications, Inc., 1989).

Boyer, Robert, and Daniel Drache, eds., *State Against Markets: The Limits of Globalization* (London: Routledge, 1996).

Byres, T., and B. Crow, with Mae Wan Ho, *The Green Revolution in India* (London: Open University Press, 1983).

Corbo, Vittorio, Anne O. Krueger, and Fernando Ossa, *Export-Oriented Development Strategies* (Boulder: Westview Press, 1986).

Crook, Clive, "The Future of the State," *The Economist*, September 20, 1997, pp. 55–57.

Fanon, Frantz, *Toward the African Revolution* (Harmondsworth, UK: Penguin Books, 1964).

Fortmann, L., *Peasants, Officials, and Participation in Rural Tanzania* (Ithaca: Cornell University Press, 1980).

Furtado, Celso, *Accumulation and Development: The Logic of Industrial Civilization,* trans. Suzette Macedo (New York: St. Martin's Press, 1983).

Gills, Barry, Joel Rocamora, and Richard Wilson, eds., *Low Intensity Democracy: Political Power in the New World Order* (London: Pluto Press, 1993).

Heady, Ferrel, *Public Administration: A Comparative Perspective,* 2nd ed. (New York: Marcel Dekker, 1979).

Hewlett, Sylvia Ann, *The Cruel Dilemmas of Development: Twentieth Century Brazil* (New York: Basic Books, 1980).

Hyden, G., R. Jackson, and F. Okuma, *Development Experience: The Kenyan Experience* (Nairobi: Oxford University Press, 1970).

Kelly, Phil, ed., *Democracy in Latin America* (Boulder: Westview Press, 1998).

Mittelman, James H., *Out from Underdevelopment: Prospects for the Third World* (New York: St. Martin's Press, 1988).

Needler, Martin C., *Identity, Interest and Ideology: An Introduction to Politics* (New York: Praeger, 1996).

Nyerere, Julius K., *Freedom and Development* (Dar es Salaam: Oxford University Press, 1973).

Papanek, Gustav F., *Lectures on Development Strategy, Growth, Equity, and the Political Process in Southern Asia* (Islamabad: Pakistan Institute of Development Economics, 1986).

Payne, Anthony, and Paul Sutton, *Modern Caribbean Politics* (Baltimore: John Hopkins University Press, 1993).

Ranis, Gustav, "Can the East Asian Model of Development be Generalized?" *World Development* 13, no. 4, 1985, pp. 543–546; and William R. Cline, "Reply," ibid., pp. 547–548.

Robinson, William, *A Faustian Bargain* (Boulder: Westview Press, 1992).

Sassen, Saskia, *Losing Control? Sovereignty in an Age of Globalization* (New York: Columbia University Press, 1996).

Scully, Timothy R., *Rethinking the Center: Party Politics in Nineteenth and Twentieth Century Chile* (Stanford, Calif.: Stanford University Press, 1992).

Serra, José, "Three Mistaken Theses Regarding the Connection Between Industrialization and Authoritarian Regimes," in David Collier, ed., *The New Authoritarianism in Latin America* (Princeton: Princeton University Press, 1979), pp. 99–163.

Sheahan, John, *Patterns of Development in Latin America: Poverty, Repression, and Economic Strategy* (Princeton: Princeton University Press, 1987).

Smith, Lois M., and Fred Padula, *Sex and Revolution in Socialist Cuba* (New York: Oxford University Press, 1996).

Smith, Wayne S., *Portrait of Cuba* (Atlanta: Turner Publishing, 1991).

Valenzuela, J. Samuel, and Erika Maza Valenzuela, *Religion, Class and Gender: Constructing Electoral Institutions and Party Politics in Chile* (Notre Dame, Ind.: University of Notre Dame press, forthcoming).

Walker, Thomas W., ed., *Nicaragua Without Illusions: Regime Transition and Structural Adjustment in the 1990s* (Wilmington, Del.: Scholarly Resources, 1997).

Walker, Thomas W., ed., *Nicaragua: The First Five Years* (New York: Praeger, 1985).

The Medina in Fez, Morocco, has changed little since the middle ages. But small businesses—the informal sector—are seeking assistance now from development agencies.

The expansion of tourism, as on Lake Kariba on the border between Zambia and Zimbabwe, and support for microenterprise has in many areas served to sustain indigenous crafts.

When women control resources, children are healthier.

China—ostracized by most potential trading partners—developed its own "appropriate" technology for modernizing agriculture and industry. The equipment shown here is in Sun Yat-sen province. But while autarchy has been forced upon some revolutionary governments, it is most rarely undertaken by choice.

Fiji is the most modernized of the South Pacific island states. It has experienced rapid economic growth but also growing inequality, ethnic and class strife, foreign intrigue, and even, in 1987, a military coup d'état.

In Tibet, indigenous culture is threatened by Chinese occupation.

A co-op member in the Ecuadorean Sierra. Peasants participate enthusiastically in their local cooperative, even though the approach of co-op promoters from national organizations is often paternalistic and sometimes downright condescending.

The people of Población Victoria San Miguel, one of the largest and best-organized shanty-towns in Santiago, Chile, demonstrated remarkable wit, grit, and collective self-sufficiency even though subject to military repression and discrimination in employment throughout the dictatorship of General Augusto Pinochet. The social glue that sustained the community derived in large part from a network of Mothers' Centers.

PART THREE

Development in Focus: Contemporary Issues and Themes

8 Development and the Gender Gap

Even more than most disciplines and policy areas, that of development is subject to fads. While in the United States legislation calling for targeting assistance to the poorest of the poor and paying heed to the appropriateness of technology remained on the books through the 1980s, the advent of the Reagan administration shifted the focus of consultants and bureaucrats in short order to the promotion of private enterprise. Meanwhile, however, the influence of two new categories of pressure groups, feminists and "greens," was being felt around the world and was being translated by NGOs, with backing in particular by the United Nations, into policy agenda.

Thus, beginning in the 1970s and building to a crescendo in the 1990s, the issue of the gender gap, and of the actual and potential roles of women in development, dominated conferences and symposia, research proposals and position papers, and came finally to be reflected, at least in rhetoric, in major donor foreign assistance programs. The United Nations declared a Decade for Women that closed in 1985 with an international conference in Kenya. It was followed a decade later by an even larger and more momentous conference in Beijing.

Getting the Price Wrong

When all else fails, as it so often does, women around the world somehow summon the strength to raise their children and sustain their communities. But the price is high.

Most of the world's landless farmers are women. Centuries ago in much of what is now the Third World—Africa, the South Pacific, and parts of Europe and Asia—men hunted and made war while women farmed. There is little game left to hunt for food; hunting now is mostly for sport. Some might say the same of war making. At any rate war making has become highly specialized and capital intensive. But women still farm. In Africa, for example, 70 percent of the food crops are raised by women. Women, however, are rarely able to obtain credit in their own names. In cases of divorce, abandonment, or death, the woman is left with no claim, as title to the land was held in her husband's name only.

Women normally work longer hours than men. The notorious "double shift" is not limited to the First World or even to the industrialized world. Women who farm or produce handicrafts or take on odd jobs in the informal sector are subject to it, too. A recent survey in Zaire indicated that men did only 30 percent of the work women did.[1] In the Philippines women were putting in sixty-one hours weekly to men's forty-one; in Uganda fifty hours compared to twenty-three. Women in North India were working two to four hours more than men each day in the tea gardens, not counting time spent on housework and child care.[2]

Women start working younger—at seven or eight years of age—in the home or in the fields. A survey in Burkina Faso showed seven-year-old girls working more than five hours a day, compared to forty-five minutes for boys of the same age. This means, among other things, that girls receive less schooling. Sixty percent of the women of the Third World are literate, compared to 78 percent of the men.[3]

Women work for less. The global standard for women who earn wages or salaries has remained remarkably steady through several decades—at about 60 percent of the earnings of men. In parts of the Third World the gap is much greater. In Nairobi, Kenya, in the early 1980s, half the working women earned less than the legal minimum wage, compared to 20 percent of the men.

Women eat less. The same women who work longer hours from an earlier age and actually produce most of the food must feed the men first. Fathers and male children get priority in both quality and quantity of food. From childhood on, women are also less likely to receive medical attention. Thus in much of the Third World, the female's natural advantage in longevity does not apply. Whereas in the developed world women had an advantage of about eight years, in the Third World generally it was only two years; and in some areas—South Asia, for example— men lived longer.[4]

But is not modernization improving the situation of women? Not necessarily.

The Mixed Message of Modernization

Colonial governments in some respects improved the lot of Third World women. In some places they were responsible for drawing women into formal education systems. In India, the British prohibited the practice of suttee—immolation of the widow on her husband's funeral pyre—and in parts of Africa and the Middle East, British and other colonial administrations sought to protect women from such practices as clitorectomy. On the other hand, in areas where women had decided advantages, the colonial powers brought gender relations into line with their own male-dominant model. Social structure in India's Kerala state, for example, was matriarchal and matrilocal until the British brought practices there into line with those elsewhere in the empire—supposedly for the sake of administrative "efficiency."[5]

Higher technology may exacerbate problems rather than solve them. Despite their doing more of the work (or perhaps because of it?), women have traditionally been valued less and female infanticide has been practiced widely. With the spread to the Third World of amniocentesis, the female population is also being diminished by feticide. In India the proportion of women to men is 927 per 1,000—and dropping. The devaluation of daughters this reflects is not necessarily a vestige of traditionalism, likely to be overcome in time by the spread of modernism. It is in part a product of dowry abuse, wherein the groom's family makes excessive financial demands of the bride's family. Dowry abuse itself may well be a product of modernism.

Like so much else in India, abuse of women is a long-standing tradition. The disturbing and puzzling thing about dowry abuse, however, is that it is a relatively recent phenomenon. It is most prevalent among the urban middle class, and it is spreading fast. Registered cases of dowry death, about 1,000 in 1985, were exceeding 5,000 a year in the late 1990s, and those registered were assumed to be only a small fraction of actual cases.

The dowry system came about, in Hindu custom, because real property could not be passed to a daughter. As the daughter would be relocating to her husband's household, she could inherit only movable goods. The dowry, then, was simply the daughter's inheritance, passed to her at the time of her marriage. The interests of the in-laws were irrelevant to the transaction.

The potential for abuse was officially recognized, however, and the system was proscribed by the Dowry Prohibition Act of 1961. The act was almost universally violated, but it was not until the 1970s that accounts of brides being killed in bizarre accidents, particularly kitchen fires, became so common as to demand the attention of researchers and law-enforcement officials. The concept of "bride-burning," once a reference to the practice of suttee, has since taken on a new meaning. The real story behind the fatal kitchen fire has all too often turned out to be that of a husband or mother-in-law spilling kerosene on the bride's sari and striking a match to it. Along with such "accidents," there has also been an upsurge in suicides. A great many brides have apparently seen suicide as their only acceptable escape from the incessant pressure to drain the livelihood of their parents to satisfy the whims of their in-laws.

Sociologists and others who have studied this trend attribute it in part to the new materialism or consumerism infecting the middle class. For the bridegroom and his family, marriage may become a means of acquiring the shiny new toys—stereos, VCRs, motorcycles, even cars—that they could never afford on their own salaries. And the extortion may go on long after the wedding, as brides rarely feel that they have the option of leaving their husbands. It is socially unacceptable for a bride to return to her parents' household. Indian women are expected to marry and stay married, and apart from a few shelters established by charities or women's groups, there are virtually no alternative living arrangements. Even for female professionals who could afford to rent their own apartments, there are few landlords who would rent to single women.

Formerly prevalent only among Hindu middle-class families in the northern states, dowry demands—and dowry deaths—have spread across lines of geography, class and caste, and even religion. The practice is now common throughout the country, even in areas of Moslem or Christian settlement. In a region where women have traditionally been undervalued, at least in modern times, the steady inflation of dowry demands has led many parents to see female offspring as a distinct liability. Thus the dowry system has exacerbated the problems of female infanticide and, where amniocentesis is available, feticide. It has also contributed to the neglect and ill-treatment of female children. India is one of the few countries where women's life expectancy is markedly shorter than men's.

The only good news with respect to this grim topic is that recognition of the seriousness of the problem has served to mobilize women. Indian women are better organized now and more active politically and socially than they have been at any time since Mahatma Gandhi tapped their energies for the independence movement.[6]

Other aspects of modernization also serve to exacerbate inequality between the sexes as well as between classes. The option of cash cropping, for example, is generally available only to men. Agricultural development programs, whether of international or domestic derivation, have been grossly discriminatory. Membership in co-ops and the availability of extension services have often been restricted to men. Labor-saving devices or technologies passed on by governments or development agencies are usually passed to men, even where the labor to which they apply is women's work. Corn grinders have been made available in Kenya, but women have not been taught to operate them. Likewise oil presses in Nigeria and tortilla-making machines in Mexico became the preserve of men, who have access to cash or credit.[7] Cash crops then claim the best land, leaving only the less-fertile and less-accessible land to women for their food crops. The food crops would have fed the peasant family. The cash crop is more likely to feed the bartender's family.

We have seen that the introduction of cash cropping often leads to greater concentration of landownership and to increasing landlessness among former subsistence farmers. With shrinking plots, the men are forced to migrate—to seek work in the cities or in more prosperous areas as migratory farm laborers. Many never return. This has resulted in a rapid increase in the number of rural households headed by women. These women, as we have seen, will have even more difficulty than their husbands did in obtaining credit and technical assistance and ultimately in holding onto the tiny patches of land left to them. The spreading feminization of poverty means the juvenilization of poverty, too.

In some areas, such as East Asia, where industrial development has been largely in the direction of labor intensity and precision work, women have become very much involved in the formal workforce. In most Third World areas, however, where factory production has wiped out the market for handicrafts, the women so displaced are less likely to be hired than men; women, then, are pushed into the unregulated and notoriously low-paying informal sector.

The Burden Shifting of Structural Adjustment

As we have seen, the long-term trend toward global economic integration, with its accompanying roller coaster of economic growth and decline, has had the effect, in general, of widening gaps between rich and poor countries, between rural and urban communities, between classes and sectors, and between men and women. But the social and economic transformations that have accompanied the reabsorption of the Second and Third Worlds into a First World–centered global system have been particularly hard on women.

The economic restructuring that became the condition for credit first in Latin America and Africa in the 1980s, then in the other parts of the Third World and in the former Soviet sphere in the early 1990s, and in East and Southeast Asia in the late 1990s has had the effect of shifting rewards and resources upward in the social pyramid and outward toward external players while shifting burdens and responsibilities downward to those having the least political clout. At the bottom, where the buck stops, one still finds women.

The set of policy changes demanded by private creditors and multilateral lending institutions, known generally as structural adjustment, constitutes essentially an adjustment of priorities, so that the needs to be met first are those of the banks. Government services take a back seat to the servicing of the debt. As the predominant caregivers—teachers, nurses, social workers—women have been disproportionately disadvantaged by the downsizing of the public sector. In the Ukraine, for example, some 80 percent of the job loss of the first half of the 1990s was experienced by women.

Loss of public service has not only meant loss of the best jobs for some women; for women generally it has meant shouldering more of the burden of service and welfare borne previously in part by the state. Meanwhile, in terms of austerity, when men are also losing jobs and wages are losing value, women have no choice about being breadwinners if there are jobs to be found. Those jobs, however, are most likely to be in low-wage, export-processing industries or in the informal sector—in either case largely beyond the reach of labor unions and labor legislation.

As nongovernmental, nonprofit organizations attempt to fill in caregiving gaps—assistance for the old, the sick, the hungry who have been abandoned by the state—women have assumed leadership of that sector. But the nonprofit sector has scarcely a fraction of the resources previously available to the state. Women have never lacked responsibility. What they lack now more than ever in structurally adjusted states is resources.

Implications for Development

What, then, are the implications for development specialists to be drawn from this assessment? In the first place, targeting the poorest of the poor (as has been mandated by USAID and by the World Bank, though practiced only in a token manner) generally means targeting communities in which the role of women is preeminent. It is precisely in the villages or shantytowns where conditions are most desperate that women are most likely to be the economic mainstays as well as the caregivers of their families and the organizational glue of their communities. This is partly because men can, and often do, flee from their responsibilities to another place or perhaps just into a bottle. Women cannot.

In the second place, targeting women, rather than discriminating against them, benefits the whole family. A number of studies from disparate parts of the Third World have indicated that compared to men, women spend a far greater proportion of their incomes on meeting family needs rather than on personal gratification. Thus, enhancing the income of women means also raising healthier children, male and female. It is not enough, however, for women simply to earn the income if it is only to be seized by their husbands. Women must also be able to maintain control of the income they earn, and in some areas a step in that direction will call for very considerable education, consciousness-raising, and social pressure.

In the third place, it is very generally acknowledged that the population explosion is among the major sources of frustration for development strategy. General education and the issuance of contraceptive drugs and devices through family-planning clinics may be, in the absence of major social change, a very long-term process. More drastic approaches taken to date have even less to recommend them. In India, the Congress Party suffered a terrible backlash from its short-lived efforts to impose sterilization. The Chinese government had more success in imposing its policy of limiting couples to one child but in the process prompted a sharp rise in female infanticide. The only really effective and morally acceptable means now known of sharply limiting family size is the education and liberation, or empowerment, of women.

For women, as for other disadvantaged categories of people, there can be no gains without political struggle, but the good news is that the struggle has been joined. In countries that have undergone successful revolution, women have been prominent among the armed combatants as well as in all other roles essential to the struggle. That mobilization has subsequently been reflected in involvement in policy-making and of varying degrees of improvement in status. In the Soviet Union, women advanced quickly into the professions, becoming particularly prominent in medicine. Professional status, however, has given them no relief from the "double shift."

Revolutionary Cuba has actually tried to deal with the double shift problem. Its path-breaking Family Code, which went into effect in 1975, specifies that marriage partners are to share equally in child care and in carrying out household chores.[8] Legislation is one thing, of course, implementation another. In Nicaragua, where one-fourth to one-third of the combatants in the revolutionary struggle had been women, women's organizations have had a prominent role in the subsequent transformation of society. Just a few months after the triumph of the revolution, however, an eighteen-year-old female military officer told me, with undisguised anger, that male chauvinism had already reappeared in the Sandinista Armed Forces and the women were being pushed out.

Elsewhere the organization of women in the Third World for the advancement of their own cause as well as the causes of human rights, child welfare, and, in general, democracy and social justice has been gathering momentum at least since the 1960s. In Taiwan, for example, where economic development has greatly outpaced political development, feminist organizations have been in the forefront of the campaign for political liberalization.[9] Even in South Asia, where most women have traditionally suffered awful repression and deprivation, some of the most effective national leaders have been women, and women's organizations have been very active in grass-roots development as well as in other aspects of political life.

Globally, women have made remarkable progress in electoral politics at the state level over recent decades, and particularly in the 1990s. Of the 32 women who have served as presidents or prime ministers during the twentieth century, 24 were in power during the 1990s. When Mary Robinson left the presidency of Ireland in 1997 to become the UN high commissioner for human rights, all four of the major candidates to succeed her in the presidency were women. Women's representation in national legislatures increased from 7.4 percent in 1975 to 11 percent in 1995, at which time, according to the Interparliamentary Union, there were only nine countries in the world having no female representation in their legislatures.[10]

Women around the world were finding, however, that participation, even effective participation, at the national level was not enough if the decisions that so impact their lives were being made beyond the reach of the state. The convergence of some thirty-five thousand women on Beijing in 1995 for the Fourth UN conference on women underscored the recognition that to achieve political change at any level women must be organized and mobilized at all levels—from the local to the global.[11] At that and other global meetings, leaders of the women's movement have also made it clear that their agenda is not simply about women's needs but rather about human needs. To the extent that the movement is able to sensitize and mobilize previously nonparticipant populations, it should have a democratizing effect on society in general.

Notes

1. Paul Harrison, *Inside the Third World: The Anatomy of Poverty*, 2nd ed. (Harmondsworth, UK: Penguin Books, 1987), p. 441.

2. Tony Barnett, *Social and Economic Development: An Introduction* (New York: Guilford Press, 1989), pp. 168–169.

3. United Nations Development Program [UNDP], *Human Development Report 1997* (New York: UNDP, 1997), p. 151.

4. Harrison, op. cit., pp. 444–446.

5. Discussions with Sarah Matthew, director of women's programs, Institute for Development Education, Madras, June–July and October–November 1988.

6. While on a Fulbright-funded research program in India in 1998, this author had occasion to meet with leaders of several women's organizations that were dealing with the dowry-abuse problem and to become acquainted with the family of a recent dowry-abuse victim.

7. Barnett, op. cit., pp. 157–158.

8. For more information on Cuba's family code and on the role of women in revolutionary Cuba, see Chapter 5 in Jan Knippers Black, ed., *Area Handbook for Cuba* (Washington, D.C.: Government Printing Office, 1976). See also several books by Margaret Randall, including *Cuban Women Now* (Toronto: Women's Press, 1974) and Lois Smith and Fred Padula, *Sex and Revolution in Socialist Cuba* (New York: Oxford University Press, 1996).

9. Feminist leaders and organizations have been in the vanguard of the democratic movement at least since the flourishing of *Formosa* magazine in the late 1970s. Feminist leaders, including Lu Hsui-lien and Chen Chu, were sentenced to prison when the movement was crushed following the Kaohsiung rally in 1979. The author was able to meet with leaders of the once-again flourishing feminist movement in Taipei in 1988, 1994, and 1995. Lu was elected to the Taiwanese Senate in 1993 and was elected magistrate of Taoyuan County in 1997.

10. Jane S. Jacquette, "Women in Power: From Tokenism to Critical Mass," *Foreign Policy* 108, fall 1997, pp. 23–37.

11. Amat Al-Aleem Assooswa, undersecretary of information of the Republic of Yemen, the highest-ranking woman in that government, told this author that the issue of sending a delegation of Yemeni women to the Beijing Conference proved a highly controversial one, which in itself proved beneficial to the movement for women's rights. Debates about whether or not to send a delegation ultimately engaged women who had never previously enjoyed a public forum and opened up for discussion the broader issue of women's participation in public affairs. Interview at the Ministry of Information, Sana'a, July 3, 1998.

Suggested Readings

Boserup, E., *Woman's Role in Economic Development* (London: Allen and Unwin, 1970).

Chatty, Dawn, and Annika Rabo, eds., *Organizing Women: Formal and Informal Women's Groups in the Middle East* (Oxford: Berg Press, 1997).

Dankelman, Irene, and Joan Davidson, *Women and the Environment in the Third World: Alliance for the Future* (London: Earthscan Publications Ltd., 1988).

Deere, Carmen Diana, and Magdalena Leon, *Rural Women and State Policy: Feminist Perspectives on Latin American Agricultural Development* (Boulder: Westview Press, 1987).

Eisler, Riane, *The Chalice and the Blade* (Cambridge, Mass.: Harper and Row, 1987).

Eisler, Riane, David Loye, and Kari Norgaard, *Women, Men and the Global Quality of Life* (Pacific Grove, CA: The Center for Partnership Studies, 1995).

Jacquette, Jane, *Trying Democracy: Women in Post-Authoritarian Politics in Latin America and Central and Eastern Europe* (Baltimore: Johns Hopkins University Press, 1998).

Kardam, Nuket, *Bringing Women In: Women's Issues in International Development Programs* (Boulder: Lynne Rienner Publishers, 1991).

Karl, Merilee, *Women and Empowerment: Participation and Decision-Making* (London: Zed Books, 1995).

Scott, Catherine V., *Gender and Development: Rethinking Modernization and Development Theory* (Boulder: Lynne Rienner Publishers, 1996).

Summerfield, Gale, and Jiyang Howard, *Women and Economic Reform in China* (London: Routledge, forthcoming).

Tinker, I., and M. Bramsen, *Women and World Development* (Washington, D.C.: Overseas Development Council, 1976).

United Nations, "Report of the Fourth World Conference on Women," Beijing, September 4–15, 1995.

United Nations Development Program [UNDP], *Human Development Report 1995* (New York: UNDP, 1995).

Waylen, Georgina, *Gender in Third World Politics* (Buckingham, UK: Open University Press, 1996).

9 The Fragile Ecology of Mother Earth

Trends in donor policies have always had more to do with First World politics than with Third World needs. Policies and programs serving trade and investment interests have been fairly consistent and have constantly enjoyed a high priority. Other programs, however, have been subject to the wide pendulum swings of foreign policy that reflect a major cleavage in Western, particularly U.S., society. Aspects of policy subject to the pendulum swing—from security interests, for example, to humanitarian interests—may be more nearly expressive than instrumental, designed more for their repercussions in the First World than in the Third. Intended or not, however, repercussions in the Third may be very great indeed. Major donors have generally been unreceptive to Third World solicitations and initiatives, viewing them as threatening to the established order (that is, the order favoring major donors).

Benchmark studies of Third World needs and of foreign assistance efforts and their consequences commissioned by the U.S. Congress or the executive branch over the years (i.e., the Rostow Commission study of 1957 or the Carlucci Commission report of 1983)[1] have generally served to legitimate trends already under way rather than to launch new ones. Some developments have been traceable in part, however, to nonofficial studies, and even to particular books, although such cases have usually involved long periods of gestation. The appropriate technology trend of the 1970s, which survives into the 1990s in the work of NGOs/PVOs despite diminished interest among major donors, owes much to Ernst F. Schumacher's book, *Small Is Beautiful* (1973), as the environmentalist concerns so prominent in the 1990s are traceable to Rachel Carson's *Silent Spring* (1962).[2]

The environmentalist perspective, centering on respect for and protection of the natural, of life in all its abundant forms, as opposed to the artificial—the forms and products and transformations wrought by technology and commerce that consume and overwhelm nature—has maintained soft margins, expanding its range as new concerns are identified. Thus it has drawn very broad support, steadily gaining adherents since the 1960s. By the 1990s, there was hardly an agency or organization having anything to do with development that did not have a division or committee dealing with the environment, and the reorientation of academics, consultants, and even politicians served to build momentum.

Exporting Garbage

In development studies, as in other areas of public discourse, the bandwagon of the 1990s proved to be the garbage truck. One of the many unfortunate consequences of success in the post–World War II drive for rapid industrialization and unlimited production is the generation on a massive scale of waste. Even within the United States, the issue of dumping has aroused regional antagonisms as the more-industrialized Northeast and Midwest shop around in the South and West for communities desperate enough to take in their garbage for a few dollars or a few jobs.[3] And as other local and state governments attempt to protect their constituencies, the difficulty of finding legal means of and locales for dumping makes the waste management industry particularly attractive to organized-crime syndicates.

Nor is the scourge of waste confined to the countries where it is produced. Like other by-products of the industrial age, it slips easily over national borders, becoming a source of friction among neighboring states. U.S. businesses and municipalities, facing ever-higher disposal costs in the United States, are shipping great quantities of waste to Mexico, Central America, and the Caribbean.

The problem would be serious enough if the foul stuff in search of an eternal resting place were relatively benign household waste. Much of it, however, is hazardous industrial waste, and some—the radioactive waste of weapons and power plants, for example—is extremely lethal, posing to air, soil, and groundwater long-term threats that we have only begun to fathom. Furthermore, the more toxic the waste, the more likely that the producers will seek to dispose of it on someone else's turf and that the dangers it poses will be understated. As the private transnational organization Greenpeace has gone to great lengths to dramatize, a great deal of the world's hazardous waste is being dumped in the oceans; this serves to blunt the jurisdictional and liability disputes so often associated with disposal, but it does not prevent the generalized contamination of the world's food chain.

The by-products of industrial development that are not dumped en masse as garbage may be doing even more damage. Hazardous chemical compounds are constantly being released into the air or filtering into rivers, streams, and aquifers. Particles from one such set of compounds, chlorofluorocarbons, have made their way to the protective ozone layer and eaten a hole in it, threatening higher rates of skin cancer, among other dire consequences. (This threat was viewed as serious enough to inspire a superpower treaty, signed by Bush and Gorbachev in 1989, to limit the production of chlorofluorocarbons.)

Meanwhile the cutting and burning of forests and the consumption of fossil fuels release carbon dioxide, which traps solar radiation near the earth's surface. The resulting global warming, the "greenhouse effect," could raise sea levels, inundating coastal cities and swallowing up entire islands. The Worldwatch Institute's annual *State of the World* reported in early 1989 that the five warmest years of this century had been in the 1980s. About 40 percent of this greenhouse effect is attributable to fossil fuel combustion. The United States alone contributes one-fifth of the carbon being added annually to the atmosphere, a consequence in large part of its energy-inefficient transportation system; the average car adds its own weight in carbon to the atmosphere each year. U.S. emissions alone increased by more that 1 percent annually between 1990 and 1998. Some such increases might be attributed to the U.S. economic boom of the 1990s, but pollution levels rose faster in 1996 than did economic output or energy consumption.

Also contributing to the imbalance of carbon and oxygen in our atmosphere has been the rapid depletion of the planet's rain forests. Tropical ecosystems around the world are currently being destroyed at the rate of 25 million acres a year. By 1992, according to the Worldwide Fund for Nature, two-thirds of the world's forests had already been lost.

Much has been written about the clearing of the Amazon Basin. One-fourth of Brazil's forestry reserves had been cut down by 1974. In 1988 the country lost an area of tropical rain forest larger than Switzerland. That same year, an indigenous crusader against deforestation, Francisco (Chico) Mendes, was murdered by cattle ranchers. But the problem of deforestation, with consequent topsoil erosion, upland desertification, and downstream flooding, is of global scope. Papua New Guinea, among the last of the world's region's to be explored and exploited by nonnatives, has about 145,000 square miles of tropical forests. But given that the amount of wood exported annually has more than quadrupled since 1980, local environmentalists estimate that at current rates of depletion, forests of commercial value will be gone by 2020.

The loss of fertile soil, in turn, takes its toll on food production. For the world as a whole, per capita food production in the late 1990s had gained over the levels of the 1970s, but in the least developed countries it had fallen behind, and "food security" had become a major concern. There is no doubt that loss of productive farmland, through industrial and urban development on the one hand and erosion on the other, is one of the several factors leading so many countries to import more and more of their basic foodstuffs.

Sharing Hardships

What does all of this have to do with development? To the extent that development is measured in production and consumption without regard to ecological balance and replenishment, it has everything to do with it. Such development must be seen, along with population growth, as the engine of this ecological crisis; and the crisis offers an intimation of the limits of the process. Furthermore, wherever there are hardships to be shared, the poor get more than their share of them. In an internal memo leaked from the World Bank in 1992, the Bank's chief economist, Laurence Summers, applying cost-benefit analysis, (perhaps ironically) said, "I think the economic logic behind dumping a load of toxic waste in the lowest wage country is impeccable, and we should face up to that."[4]

As the ecological crisis is global, its effects are felt more immediately and more sharply in the Third World. In the first place, much of the Third World is urbanized, if not highly industrialized; it is urbanizing at a faster rate than the First World, and its municipalities are less well equipped to deal with the consequences of such concentration.

Sewerage systems, for example, are almost everywhere inadequate. In São Paulo, a modern city of more than 16 million, less than half the sewage is even collected, and of that less than 5 percent is treated. In the heart of Madras or Mexico City, Santiago or Seoul, Bangkok or Jakarta, breathing is a struggle. In some cities, cement plants and petroleum-refining facilities throw off dust and sulfur. In others, mineral- and chemical-processing plants put arsenic and other toxic compounds into the air. In almost every major city, excepting a very few essentially nonmotorized ones like Phnom Penh and Dacca, motor vehicle pollutants, especially diesel fuel, routinely cause sore eyes and throats, chronic coughing and shortness of breath, and apparently increase the incidence of lung cancer. Illnesses caused by polluted water and air must be discounted against the gains attributable to modern medicine and health-care-delivery systems.

It is estimated that 40 million tons of hazardous industrial waste are produced in Latin America each year. For better or worse, as capital circles the globe seeking cheap land and labor, the Third World is rapidly acquiring more industry, with its attendant liabilities. Whether the fault lies with weak or corrupt host governments or with greedy foreign investors, the precautions against ordinary pollution or against ecological disaster that are less than adequate in the First World are even less adequate in the Third. The kind of accident that devastated Bhopal, India, might well threaten Union Carbide's U.S. plants also, and the 1989 Exxon oil spill in Alaska's Prince William Sound exposed the weaknesses of U.S. regulatory systems; but the fact remains that preventable industrial contamination is even more common in the Third World than in the First.

If the Third World suffers more than the First from environmental degradation, it is in part because First World companies use it as a dumping ground for products they are prohibited from marketing at home. Pesticides, in increasingly common use with the spread of plantation-style export agriculture, have been among those products. They are likely to come home to roost, as residues on the fruits and vegetables shipped back to the First World. But the price to Third World field laborers, blanketed regularly in the stuff by crop dusters, is much greater; they have been suffering in ever-larger numbers from pesticide poisoning. In El Salvador, for example, during the 1970s, 1,000 to 2,000 cases of pesticide poisoning were reported annually. In 1987, 50 children died of it in a single hospital in San Salvador.[5] In several Amazonian villages in the late 1990s, where miners had used mercury in panning rivers for gold, most of the children tested showed levels of mercury contamination (in hair samples) well above those considered to be tolerable by the World Health Organization.[6]

The loss of vegetation and of fertile land ultimately affects us all. But as in the case of most life-and-death struggles, the affluent are not likely to be found on the front lines. The peoples most devastated are the ones who were trying to scratch out a living on land that was already marginal. The first victims of desertification are the nomads around the edges of the Sahara and Kalahari deserts. The first to suffer from erosion are the subsistence farmers on Haiti's already severely eroded hillsides.

Deforestation has disturbing implications for the planet in general. It is estimated that one-fourth of the oxygen in our atmosphere derives from the Amazonian rain forest alone. But for the poor of many Third World countries, the retreat of the trees poses more immediate hardship. The FAO estimates that 86 percent of the wood cut in the Third World is used for fuel. Wood is an inefficient fuel, but for many there is no affordable alternative. As firewood has dwindled in south and central India, "power packs" of cow dung must be used for heating and cooking, but that leaves little to be used as fertilizer. It is estimated that more nitrogen and phosphorous from power packs goes up in smoke than the total Indian production of chemical fertilizer.

The foothills of the Himalayas, particularly in eastern Nepal and in northeast India, are being deforested at an alarming rate. For the wood gatherers, usually women, this means that the hike in search of firewood takes them farther each year from their villages. Population pressure is partly to blame, but the locals have also sometimes found themselves in competition with major lumber companies.

In one such case, in the Indian state of Uttar Pradesh, the people decided to fight back. The Chipko movement, or "tree huggers," as they came to be known, mostly women, vowed to hug the trees so that the lumber companies could not fell them without felling the villagers with them. Similar, more or less spontaneous grass-roots movements representing a coincidence of popular and environmental interests, and building upon the Gandhian tradition of nonviolent activism, sprouted elsewhere in India in the 1980s, but few have been as successful as the tree huggers, who actually forced the lumber company out of their forests.[7]

Another major threat to forest and farmland alike in the Third World has been the relentless spread of large-scale infrastructure projects. Undertaken in the name of development, sponsored by governments, underwritten by loans from the World Bank and the regional development banks, such projects have included roads, railroads, ports, power lines, and, in particular, massive dams. The clearest beneficiaries of these projects, who have mounted impressive lobbying efforts, have been First World or transnational construction companies.

The most immediate losers from these infrastructure operations have generally been indigenous peasants. Such indigenous peoples, generally occupying remote valleys or jungle clearings on the frontier of settlement, may be unintegrated into the national community and utterly lacking in political clout, but they are the vestiges of expertise in ecological balance. The resettlement promised to Mexico's Chinantec and Brazil's Kayapo Indians when plans were drawn up in the late 1980s to construct dams flooding their ancestral lands came as scant compensation. Both groups resisted and two of the Kayapo chiefs were brought to trial under Brazil's Foreign Sedition Act. Ironically, it was for urging a role for local populations in designing the policies that affect them that the Kayapo's chiefs were tried, along with a U.S. anthropologist—under a law forbidding foreign interference in Brazilian affairs.[8]

In the late 1990s, a new spurt of growth in the Brazilian economy was inspiring a wave of large-scale infrastructure projects in the Amazon. Underwritten by multinational agencies as well as by U.S., European, and Asian investment banks, the industrial waterways, railways, roads, and oil and gas pipelines are expected to provide Brazil new export corridors to the Pacific, Caribbean, and North Atlantic coasts. Plans include also ten new hydroelectric dams to provide energy mainly for the expansion of mining operations. Most of this new development is taking place without environmental impact studies or consultation with indigenous groups or political debate in the larger community on the costs and benefits of such projects.[9]

Questions of Equity and Responsibility

An environmental perspective raises fundamental ethical questions about equity and responsibility—about assessing blame and liability, about the setting of priorities, and about the merits and the urgency of competing claims on scarce resources—that are not necessarily set in relief by other perspectives.

Some of these questions pit the First World against the Third: Is it fair or reasonable for the overdeveloped nations to demand of the underdeveloped ones that they forgo certain practices, now seen as detrimental to the global environment, that were crucial to First World development? Should certain of the LDCs choose to forgo such practices, are they entitled to extra assistance to compensate for possible losses in growth or productivity? When it is clear that First World practices are responsible for environmental degradation affecting the Third World, should the responsible countries and companies be held liable in the sense of owing compensation? If environmental degradation threatens us all, do nonnationals have an inherent right to influence the practices of particular countries? If, as is argued, all life on the planet is dependent on the oxygen produced by the Amazon rain forest, should nonnationals be able to pressure the Brazilian government to drop incentives to clearance? If so, perhaps nonnuclear nations threatened by radioactive waste should have a voice in the weapons and power development policies of countries having nuclear capabilities.

As to questions of priority and urgency, many in the development community will have no trouble deciding, in principle, which has the prior claim when the interests of profit are pitted against the interest of environmental preservation. But what about the equally common circumstances that pit the interests of Mother Nature against the interests of clearly needy local populations? Where do justice and reasonableness lie when the urgent needs of large numbers of poor people run counter to those of endangered plant and animal species and, more important, to small numbers of people representing endangered cultures?

Perhaps the most important conflict of interests with respect to environmental issues, however, lies between old and young, or between generations now seeking succor from this planet and generations to which they will leave what's left of it. In this contest, future generations are at a terrible disadvantage: They have no weapons and no vote.

It would be unrealistic to imagine that the great debates about environmental issues, whether they take place at the summit or on the street corner, will have any more influence on the actual allocation or reallocation of resources than have earlier debates on technology and change, the terms of trade, the energy crisis, the income gap, and the gender gap. But we must hope that there is something to be gained through increased awareness of what is at stake.

On April 22, 1990, the twentieth anniversary of the original Earth Day was celebrated in thousands of towns and cities across the United States and around the world. Whereas the first Earth Day, brainchild of U.S. Senator Gaylord Nelson, had been in essence a counterculture event, that of 1990 was a mainstream spectacular; speakers were the biggest names in government and show business, and underwriters included the biggest transnational corporations and conglomerates, including some of the most notorious polluters. At the largest rallies, there was no need for those in attendance even to pick up their own litter; clean-up crews had been hired. For environmentalists, the mainstreaming of the issue represented a major victory of sorts; but some aging hippies were uneasy about being sidelined as spectators while the foxes ceremoniously assumed guardianship of the chicken coop.

Flunking the Millennial Review

The spread of environmental consciousness in the 1990s, as of organization and mobilization, has been phenomenal. And there have been some impressive victories along the way. Just over a decade after French intelligence officers sank its flagship, *Rainbow Warrior,* in the harbor at Auckland, New Zealand, Greenpeace, still shadowing French war ships in the South Pacific, saw the French government back away in 1996 from planned tests and sign the South Pacific Nuclear Free Zone Treaty. The organization had also been highly successful in protecting whales, dolphins, seals, and other sea creatures and was engaged in campaigns against all manner of polluters on land and sea. Meanwhile, Greenpeace had grown from some 1.5 million contributing members to 5 million with affiliates in thirty-two countries.

A milestone of activism and optimism for environmentalists and other nongovernmental, nonprofit organizations was the United Nations Conference on Environment and Development (UNCED) in Rio de Janeiro in 1992. The conference—known as ECO '92—proved to be the largest gathering of world leaders up to that point in history, with more than one hundred heads of state in attendance. Even so, the official conference was probably less significant than the NGO forum that met simultaneously, with activists converging from all parts of the world to bring pressure to bear on their government delegations. The basic document of the conference, an agreement that became known as Agenda 21, encapsulated UNCED commitments with respect to clean air and water and preservation of forests, wetlands, species, and other essential ingredients of the material environment. It also recognized an antipoverty strategy as a basic condition for ensuring sustainable development.

But the despoilers of ecosystems, particularly in the private sector, have proliferated and grown stronger and hungrier. Twenty-first-century technology and post–Cold War politics had made resources that were once remote or protected readily accessible. And governments harnessed to debt servicing schedules had had to accelerate exportation to earn foreign exchange. They were in no position to resist the pollution of their air and water, the erosion of their soil, or the exploitation of their natural resources.

Rio Plus Five

Delegates gathering at the United Nations in New York City in June 1997 for Rio Plus Five, the second world environment summit, a follow-up to ECO '92, found the general mood to be a grim one. Virtually every target that had been set in Rio de Janeiro had been missed, and most of the problematic trends identified in 1992 had accelerated.

Logging firms had plundered forests everywhere almost at will, resulting in the extinction, just since 1992, of more than 130,000 species. Even as the forests that might have absorbed some of the carbon dioxide were being destroyed, emissions, both from motor vehicles in the First World and dirty industry in the Third, were increasing.

Pollution and diversion of water have become major concerns. One-fifth of the world's population lacked access to potable water in 1995, and in the poorest countries 90 percent of urban sewage is dumped untreated into rivers, lakes, and oceans. Fish stocks are dwindling, threatened by pollution as well as overfishing.

The greatest failing in the follow-up to ECO '92, however, was found to have been the neglect of the planet's human resources—the failure to recognize and act upon the intrinsic relationship between human and environmental poverty. Bankrupt governments, for example, are unable to follow through on treaty commitments, as they are unable to resist the propositions of investors.

The United Nations Development Program reported in 1997 that the poorest 20 percent of the world population, which in 1960 received 2.3 percent of global income, now receives only 1.1 percent. And even as gaps widen, the rich nations that had promised in 1992 to increase aid for sustainable development had in fact cut such aid by 20 percent, from 0.33 percent of GDP to 0.27 percent.

The Politics of Global Warming

One of the most important documentary outcomes of ECO '92 was a treaty, ratified by 159 states, designed to reduce pollution from carbon dioxide and other greenhouse gases in order to ward off major global climate change—the so-called greenhouse effect that occurs as pollution in the atmosphere traps solar radiation. The industrialized states agreed in the 1992 treaty to reduce and stabilize their emission of greenhouse gases by the year 2000 at the levels that prevailed in 1990. It appeared that very few were likely to meet that goal. A report produced for the World Energy Council, an independent research group based in London, found that carbon dioxide emissions, largely from the burning of fossil fuels, rose 12 percent between 1990 and 1995.

Climate change, or "global warming," continued to be among the major concerns of environmentalists throughout the 1990s. International conferences on the topic took place in Berlin in 1995 and in Geneva in 1996. But goals that were set were repeatedly missed. The UN conference scheduled for Kyoto in December 1997 was widely seen as something of a last-ditch effort. If the damaging trends could not be deescalated at this point, it might be too late for many low-lying regions to avoid inundation. When the delegates from 160 countries gathered to draw up a treaty, along with the thousands of environmentalists in attendance, more than eight hundred registered industrial lobbyists were on hand to plot derailment. To many of the dedicated environmentalists, this conference produced little more than another inning in the North-South blame game.

Third World leaders were scarcely receptive to U.S. calls for carbon emissions targets; they considered such targeting on their part to be premature, to say the least, until rich countries started cutting their own emissions and pledged to help finance improved technologies in poorer countries. The richer countries by no means put up a united front. And though few bodies drifted to the surface, the battle raged on within some governments, including that of the United States.

The European Union sought fairly stringent controls, whereas the United States proposed to stabilize emissions at 1990 levels. But as U.S. levels had already risen by 8 percent since 1990, many were skeptical of the feasibility even of that proposal. Ultimately, the United States signed on to an agreement to reduce emissions of greenhouse gases to about 7 percent below 1990 levels by 2012, but to achieve that only through market incentives rather than government regulation. The Democratic administration's treaty was not likely under any circumstances to receive serious consideration by the Republican Congress. Earlier in the year, the Senate had unanimously passed a resolution to the effect that it would not ratify a treaty reducing U.S. emissions targets until developing countries agreed to cut theirs.

Assessments of what was accomplished by the conference varied greatly. But that of Mother Nature was unequivocal. She weighed in with her own commentary in early 1998, as El Niño storms—generated by extraordinarily warm ocean currents—relentlessly pounded the Western Hemisphere for months. For the world as a whole 1998 turned out to be the hottest year on record.

Notes

1. U.S. House of Representatives, 101st Congress, 1st Session, Committee on Foreign Affairs, *Background Materials on Foreign Assistance*, Report of the Task Force on Foreign Assistance, February 1989 (Washington, D.C.: GPO, 1989), pp. 257–259.

2. See Ernst Friedrich Schumacher, *Small Is Beautiful: A Study of Economics As If People Mattered* (London: Blond and Briggs, 1973); and Rachel Carson, *Silent Spring* (New York: Houghton Mifflin, 1962).

3. Likewise, peddling the same "economic development" incentives, private-sector prison management companies like the Nashville-based Corrections Corporation of America were approaching the same depressed and desperate communities in search of dumping sites for people. There were more than 1,000,000 inmates in U.S. federal and state prisons in 1999 and, like material waste management, people waste management continued to be a growth industry.

4. Doug Henwood, "Toxic Banking," *The Nation*, March 2, 1992, p. 257.

5. See Tom Barry, *El Salvador: A Country Profile* (Albuquerque: Resource Center, 1989).

6. David Cleary, "Mercury Contamination in the Amazon Basin: Problems and Solutions," seminar presented at St. Antony's College, Oxford University, October 14, 1997.

7. Discussions with D. K. Oza, a senior officer of the Indian Administrative Service, who had done extensive studies on spontaneous grass-roots organization and the influence of Gandhi, Madras, June–July and November 1988.

8. Alexander Cockburn, "Killing Cultures," *Nation* 247, no. 13, November 7, 1988, pp. 446–447.

9. Anthony Hall, International Advisory Group of the G7 Pilot Programme to Conserve the Rainforest, Comments at "Brazil: Toward the 21st Century," Inaugural Conference of Oxford University's Center for Brazilian Studies, December 8–9, 1997.

Suggested Readings

Brown, Lester, Christopher Flavin, and Hal Kane, *Vital Signs, 1996: The Trends That Are Shaping Our Future* (New York: W. W. Norton/Worldwatch Institute, 1996).

Brown, Lester R., et al., eds., *State of the World* (New York: W. W. Norton & Co., 1986).

Brundtland, Gro Harlem, chairperson, *Our Common Future* (New York: Oxford University Press, 1987).

Calvert, Peter and Susan, *Environmental Politics in the Third World: The South, the North, and the Environment* (London: Cassell-Pintor, 1999).

Council on Environmental Quality, *The Global 2000 Report to the President of the United States* (New York: Pergamon Press, 1980).

Dwivedi, O. P., and D. K. Vajpeyi, eds., *Environmental Policy and Developing Nations* (Boulder: Lynne Rienner Publishers, 1995).

Gore, Al, Jr., *Earth in the Balance: Ecology and the Human Spirit* (New York: Houghton Mifflin, 1992).

Hatch, Michael, "Domestic Politics of Global Warming in Germany," *Environmental Politics* 4, no. 3, autumn 1995, pp. 415–440.

Kelly, Petra, *Thinking Green* (Berkeley, Calif.: Parallax Press, 1994).

Meadows, Donella H., et al., *The Limits to Growth* (Washington, D.C.: Potomac Associates, 1974).

Norberg-Hodge, Helena, *Ancient Futures* (San Francisco: Sierra Club Books, 1992).

O'Conner, James, *Natural Causes: Essays in Ecological Marxism* (New York: Guilford Publications, 1997).

Streeten, P., and R. Jolly, eds., *Recent Issues in Development* (Elmsford, N.Y.: Pergamon Press, 1981).

Strohm, Laura A., "The Environmental Politics of the International Waste Trade," *The Journal of Environment and Development* 2, no. 2, summer 1993, pp. 129–154.

Thurow, Lester, *The Zero-Sum Society* (New York: Penguin Books, 1981).

Wright, Angus, *The Death of Ramon Gonzalez: The Modern Agricultural Dilemma* (Austin: University of Texas, 1990).

10 *Food Insecurity: Cocaine and Other Cash Crops*

At the beginning of the 1990s, First World development strategies underwent yet another reappraisal. Politically, the dramatic transformation of the Second World unleashed by Soviet leader Mikhail Gorbachev's campaign for disarmament, democracy, and perestroika and concluded with Boris Yeltsin's dissolution of the Soviet Union in 1991 made it awkward to say the least to maintain a foreign assistance program premised mainly on the Cold War.

If environmentalism, fed by the idealism and energies of the generation coming of age in the 1990s, promised to be the moral equivalent of war, there remained the challenge of how to maintain the budgetary equivalent of war. In itself, the focus on environmental degradation had some promise. Like the previous threat to national security, the threat to the environment is eminently elastic, and the means of countering it are susceptible to "technicalyzing"—that is, the removal from public discourse to bunkers of expertise. Thus it should prove a useful rhetorical cover for the movement of large sums of money from public to private coffers with minimal oversight. Indeed, the amounts proposed for the cleanup of U.S. nuclear weapons facilities rivaled the costs of making the mess in the first place. And the military-industrial complex, the only government dependent allowed to pursue Keynesian models, has not been squeamish about seeking megabucks for cleanups of messes it continues to make. But other Cold War objectives and claims on foreign assistance budgets called for other strategies.

The "War on Drugs" was soon primed to take up some of the slack and serve some of the same purposes as the Cold War—e.g., as cover or justification for the monitoring and suppressing of Third World insurrection.[1] The drug war also served as a rationale for maintaining obsolete or "underutilized" military units and weapons systems and for developing new ones. In an interview reported in September 1990, General Donald J. Kutyna, commander of the North American Air Defense (NORAD), said that the drug war had sharpened skills and boosted morale among his troops. He noted that the drug war gives his men real intercept targets, making it unnecessary to contract artificial ones for practice runs. At least until the Iraqi invasion of Kuwait in August 1990, 42 percent of the Air Force's Airborne Warning and Control System (AWACS) missions were being flown in alleged pursuit of drug smugglers. Kutyna pointed out, however, that that was a costly use of AWACS and urged instead that Congress fund the new, experimental Over-the-Horizon Backscatter Radar system.[2]

Making War on a Cash Crop

In Latin America, the squeeze on imports, forcing retrenchment in industrial development, and the unreliability of prices and markets for traditional primary products, of late including even petroleum, have served to increase the importance of the area's only reliably lucrative cash crop: narcotic drugs. The introduction of new cash crops has always had a destabilizing effect on political as well as economic systems, as it has given rise to new elites having the wherewithal to challenge previously dominant classes. New cash crops also generate new struggles over land tenure and further reduce the land area allotted to food crops, leading to shortages and higher prices for staple commodities. Any promising new source of income can also be expected to complicate relations among neighboring countries and to invite intervention, as foreigners seek to cut themselves in on profits or marketing arrangements or to suppress competition.

All the usual complications and threats, however, associated with new cash crops and industries are magnified in this case because of the peculiar characteristics of the product and the illegality of the traffic. Particularly troublesome have been the steady growth in demand, especially in the United States but more recently in Latin America as well; the remarkable profitability; the high level of violence associated with the trade; the corruption of officials and institutions; the inability of governments to tax or regulate; and the invitation to intervention by the United States. The invitation to U.S. agents, and in some cases even troops, has been in some instances enthusiastic and in others grudging—more or less coerced; but in all cases it involves a certain relinquishment of sovereignty.

U.S. officials, seeing their own society as a victim of narcotraffic (rather than the engine of it), have assumed a right—even a duty—to intercept the trade at its Latin American sources, particularly in the more inaccessible reaches of the Andes and the Amazon Basin, or at pass-through points in Mexico or the Caribbean. But the Drug Enforcement Administration (DEA) regularly offers cover for the Central Intelligence Agency (CIA), and as the Kerry Subcommittee report, released in April 1989, confirms, U.S. agents have also been known to build and use the trade—not only in Latin America, but in Southeast and Southwest Asia as well—for their own official and unofficial purposes.[3] At any rate, the priorities of U.S. agents and troops stationed in Latin American countries are not likely to coincide neatly with those of host governments, much less of the powerless masses.

This focus for U.S. foreign assistance received new impetus in September 1989 when President Bush launched his own "War on Drugs." The war was launched with the extension of $261 million in security assistance to Colombia, Bolivia, and Peru to support antidrug efforts. U.S. Special Forces joined DEA agents in advising the military and police establishments of these countries. If one assumes that rhetorical objectives are taken seriously, this war is even stupider than most. To begin with, security assistance is more likely to strengthen the *narcotraficantes* in the long run than the weak and impoverished civilian governments that must compete with them for the loyalty of military and paramilitary forces. One of the reasons the industry has flourished in Colombia has been the very considerable protection it has received from extreme right-wing factions of the military and police.

U.S. advisers in the early 1990s were training local narcotic squads in Bolivia's Chapare Valley and participating in a major offensive in Peru's Upper Huallaga River Valley. Along the Upper Huallaga, "the law" was the Sendero Luminoso (Shining Path) guerrilla organization. Their enforcement techniques were harsh, but they were said to enjoy the support of tens of thousands of coca-growing peasants in the area because for a "tax" or "dues payment" of 10 percent to 15 percent of the peasant's earnings, the guerrillas represented their interests vis-à-vis the Colombian traffickers and sought to protect them against the U.S.-funded coca-eradication program. Thus, in a sense, U.S. engagement with Sendero Luminoso represented yet another instance of the use of foreign aid funds to cripple labor representation, but the business side of the equation to be strengthened in the process turned out to be the Colombian traffickers.

Narcotraffic, long thriving in Southeast and Southwest Asia as well as in the Andes, spread in the 1990s to encompass many nontraditional suppliers, markets, and transit regions. Many of the reasons are obvious: the rise of powerful new mafias; privatized government thuggery from democratizing countries like Russia and South Africa; deregulation, offshore banking, speed-of-sound mobility of money and other aspects of globalization that free all kinds of big business from government oversight; and the U.S. war on drugs. U.S. policy-makers continue to choose not to understand the fallacy of a supply-side strategy for a war against a cash crop in inflexible demand. So long as demand persists and the "war" keeps profit in the stratosphere, the shutdown of production or transit operations in one area can only mean the opening of new theaters of operation.

In 1997, after U.S. taxpayer investment of some $290 billion in the war on drugs, cocaine and heroine were more readily available than ever. Coca cultivation, according to UN calculations, has doubled since 1985.[4] But the U.S. policy had not failed all stakeholders. It had enabled U.S. military and intelligence agents to sustain their own budgets and to strengthen their Latin American counterparts vis-à-vis underfunded civilian governments and agencies. As one former commander of the U.S. Southern Command put it, "it's the only war we've got."[5]

Candidate Clinton criticized Bush administration drug policies and called for an emphasis instead on education and treatment at home. In office, however, he continued to allocate about 65 percent of the federal drug-control budget to eradication and interdiction programs. In fact, even under a tough-talking Republican Congress, appropriations were dropping. But as the presidential elections of 1996 approached, Clinton, under assault, launched a counteroffensive. Support for Latin American military and police forces, justified mostly by drugs, more than quadrupled from fiscal 1996 to fiscal 1997, at a time when development assistance and support for international organizations were dropping off sharply.

The U.S. Agency for International Development has been drawn into drug control programs to promote crop substitution. Field agents have found it difficult, however, to convince peasants that cut flowers will prove as profitable as cocaine. Many accommodating peasants have nevertheless accepted AID officers' assistance; they plant new crops on land formerly devoted to cocaine and move cocaine production to newer, less accessible, fields.

Trafficking in Food

Those who have carried the antiwar movement to the war on drugs have cited among its atrocities the diversion of limited funds for foreign assistance to programs that strengthen repressive military and intelligence agencies, contribute to the abuse of human rights, and incidentally benefit the narcotraffic industry. But the spread of narcocropping and trafficking is only part of a larger and perhaps more dangerous pattern—one that divorces peoples from habitats and production from consumption and leaves all but a dwindling few in a circumstance of profound dependence.

Security until now has been defined almost exclusively by those who have had the most at stake in absolute material terms—the war makers and the war winners and those whose economic interests they were protecting. But in the 1990s, leaders of some of the most disadvantaged and dependent states have begun to use the term in a different context; they have begun to speak of food security—about the importance of not starving.

Food security is impacted by the degradation of land and the dispersal of population—by land tenure patterns and squatters' rights; by agricultural productivity and crop diversification; by trade, transportation, and comparative advantage; and by food prices and distribution systems. Civil strife takes a heavy toll, and one that endures long past the fighting, as land once sown with maize and manioc is now strewn with land mines. Desertification, salinization, and soil erosion are also serious concerns. But the most important development over the very long term is probably that of what the wagers of drug wars call a cartel. In fact the illegal drug industry, like the legal one, is not a cartel that monopolizes decisions on volume and price but an oligopoly, a limited number of competitors who may cooperate when they deem it in their interest. With respect to food security, the significance is that over time decisions with respect to the production and distribution of food become ever more concentrated in fewer hands ever farther removed from those who need to eat.

The process of transition from subsistence farming to cash cropping and to the multinational agroexport business is as old as international trade, but it has become accelerated in the late twentieth century by globalization and, in particular, the debt service requirement of placing top priority on exportation and the generation of foreign exchange.

Like most other aspects of modernization, the costs and benefits of agroexport have been unevenly distributed. The prospect of a large market, especially a lucrative foreign market, for a product suited to a particular soil and climate enhances the value of the land, inspiring those who already have the larger chunks of it or who for reasons of political or military support are able to buy off, squeeze off, or chase off those with smaller claims. Such centralization of landholdings means the displacement of families and the dissolution of communities. In much of Africa and Asia, as noted previously, as cash crops edge out food crops, women, who have primary responsibility for food crops, are driven to more distant and marginal land. They lose status as well as resources, and their children are likely to be less well fed.

The Agroexport Advantage

Global aggregate figures with respect to food production may be good indicators of growth or profitability of the agroexport industry. They are not good indicators of food security. In fact growth and profitability of the industry may be inversely related to food security. To say that the industry is guided by market forces or the logic of the marketplace does not mean that decision-making has been left to God or to Mother Nature. It means that the interests of profit seekers are left to override the collective voice of community. Food was being exported from Ireland during the great potato famine of the nineteenth century and from the Sudan during the sporadic famines of the 1980s and 1990s.

Now, as in the heyday of European colonialism, comparative advantage dictates that the fertile land in the Caribbean be used in the production of export crops. The advantage at issue, however, has been that of mother country or mother company, not Mother Nature. In fact Caribbean plantations brought immense riches to European planters, pirates, and potentates. But for the indigenous people, hunted down and enslaved, they brought near extinction, reaching a point at which local people had to be replaced as a labor force by enslaved Africans.

At the beginning of the 1990s, after a decade in which the U.S.-brokered Caribbean Basin Initiative was to bring prosperity through more aggressive export promotion, Caribbean countries as a whole were exporting more but earning less, as market gluts brought commodity prices down. They were borrowing less but expending more on debt service. And they were spending more on food but eating less, as real incomes had dropped.

Even as the Caribbean states exported more, what had been for them a trade surplus with the United States became a deficit, in part because they were importing an ever-increasing portion of their food. And Caribbean Community (CARICOM) research indicates that about half of the area's population is undernourished. Even when export earnings keep pace with export volume, those earnings are rarely distributed effectively to the population at large; higher prices for imported food always are.

Notes

1. The priming has had its glitches. A USAID consultant told this author of an occasion in which the burning of coca fields was to be staged as a major media event; camera teams were trucked into the hinterland of Bolivia only to find that no one had brought a match.

2. Tad Bartimus, "Cold War Machine Takes on Drug Runners," *Albuquerque Journal*, September 3, 1990, pp. A1, A4.

3. U.S. Senate Committee on Foreign Relations, Subcommittee on Narcotics, Terrorism, and International Relations. Report on "Drugs, Law Enforcement, and Foreign Policy," released April 13, 1989.

4. Reported at the United Nations "drug summit," hosted by the UN International Drug Control Programme in New York during the second week of June 1998. At that summit, the Lindesmith Center, underwritten by George Soros, reported that opium production was also rising sharply.

5. Coletta Youngers, "'The Only War We've Got': Drug Enforcement in Latin America," *NACLA Report on the Americas* vol 31, no. 2, September/October 1997, pp. 13–18.

Suggested Readings

Agarwal, Bina, *A Field of One's Own: Gender and Land Rights in South Asia* (New York: Cambridge University Press, 1994).

Athanasion, Tom, *Divided Planet: The Ecology of Rich and Poor* (Boston: Little, Brown, 1996).

Davies, Susanna, *Adaptable Livelihoods: Coping with Food Security in the Mahalian Sahel* (New York: St. Martin's Press, 1996).

Dye, Alan, *Cuban Sugar in the Age of Mass Production: Technology and the Economics of the Sugar Central, 1899 1929* (Palo Alto: Stanford University Press, 1998).

Human Rights Watch/Americas, *Bolivia Under Pressure: Human Rights Violations and Coca Extraction* (New York: Human Rights Watch/Americas, 1996).

Lappé, Frances Moore, Joseph Collins, and David Kinley, *Aid as Obstacle: Twenty Questions About Our Foreign Aid and the Hungry* (San Francisco: Institute for Food and Development Policy, 1980).

Marshall, Judith, *War, Debt and Structural Adjustment in Mozambique: The Social Impact* (Ottawa, Canada: The North-South Institute, 1992).

Mitchell, Donald O., Melinda D. Ingco, and Ronald C. Duncan, *The World Food Outlook* (Cambridge: Cambridge University Press, 1997).

United Nations Food and Agriculture Organization [FAO], *The Sixth World Food Survey* (Rome: FAO, 1996).

Wronka, Joseph, *Human Rights and Social Policy in the 21st Century* (Washington, D.C.: University Press of America, 1992).

11 The Homeless, the Stateless, and the Indigenous

Displacement is by no means a new problem. Humanitarian agencies had only begun to deal with the debris of World War II when independence struggles and the revolutionary and counterrevolutionary movements spawned by the Cold War generated new waves of refugees. Compounded by ecological and economic trends and disasters, such spillovers of dispossessed and desperate peoples continued to build during the Cold War years.

The end of the Cold war, however, did not resolve the problem. Rather, it resulted in new calamities and new categories of the displaced. While conflicts provoked or perpetuated by superpower interests were shut down, other conflicts that had been suppressed because of superpower Cold War concerns were unleashed. Newly vindicated or newly fabricated nationalisms tore asunder what had been the Soviet sphere and spread well beyond it. Abrupt shifts in national boundaries, as in trade and investment patterns, generated new waves of refugees and immigrants.

More importantly, however, the displacement of the 1990s was the product of a global economic system unhitched from local popular, or public sector, controls—a system that uproots people and then discards them, that leaves ever more people competing for ever fewer and less remunerative jobs, a system that treats people as just another, potentially disposable, factor of production. Like other endangered species, people in ever greater numbers are finding themselves out of context, stripped of culture, community, and habitat and of historically viable options for sustaining life, profoundly alienated and vulnerable—litter on the mean streets of the global village.

Refugees, Migrants, and Misfits

The U.S. Committee for Refugees, a private organization, reported that there were more than 15 million refugees worldwide in 1989, a figure not counting internally displaced refugees or the more than 700,000 East

Germans who poured into West Germany at the end of the year. Nor did it count the peoples whom the unwilling hosts, for ideological reasons, would not classify as refugees, such as Salvadorans, Guatemalans, and Haitians who fled to the United States in the 1980s. The 1989 figure of 15 million represented a 50 percent increase over a five-year period.[1]

Four countries alone—Israel, Afghanistan, Mozambique, and Ethiopia— had produced more than a million refugees each. There were some 3 million Afghan refugees in Pakistan, displaced by the *mujaheddins'* assault on the Soviet-backed government in Afghanistan. A tenuous resolution in the 1990s favoring the fiercely militant Moslem rebel group known as the Taliban has not inspired a great many Afghans to go home. The extent of its persecution of women has been such as to gut the region's service and nonprofit sectors.

The deprivations of the Palestinian refugees in the occupied territories were compounded in the 1990s by the *intifada* (uprising) and Israeli reprisals and have not been resolved by the misbegotten accords on Palestinian autonomy. Meanwhile, the Iraqi invasion and occupation of Kuwait in August 1990 generated several hundred thousand more refugees—Kuwaitis fleeing their own country as well as foreigners, particularly from the Philippines and South Asia, who had been working in Kuwait or Iraq. The first stop for most of them was Jordan, a poor country that had yet to absorb successfully earlier waves of refugees from Palestine. Ongoing conflict in Iraq and its neighborhood has particularly victimized the Kurds, who—like many other ethnic minorities before— were co-opted and then discarded by U.S. intelligence agencies. Oppressed by the Turks as well, they have sought refuge in Italy and Greece. Some 320,000 Cambodians have been repatriated from camps across the Thai border, but ongoing power struggles among the remnants of the Khmer Rouge, the Sihanouk dynasty, and the Vietnamese-backed Hun Sen regime were generating more refugees in the late 1990s.

The brutal suppression of student-led democratic movements in Burma in 1988 and in China in 1989 has generated new refugees within and from those countries, and several years of civil strife in Sri Lanka have uprooted thousands in that tragic land that nature had dressed only for celebration. Meanwhile, Tibetans, fleeing Chinese occupation, continue to stream into India.

The refugee population in the Horn of Africa and in southern Africa increased by a million between mid-1988 and mid-1989 alone. More than a million Mozambicans fled the terror of the South African-backed guerrilla organization, the Mozambique National Resistance Movement (RE-NAMO). Malawi, one of the world's poorest countries, sheltered at least 800,000 Mozambican refugees. While domestic conflict and famine drove more than a million Ethiopians from their homes, some 350,000 Sudanese and 400,000 Somalis fled to Ethiopia. Meanwhile, about 2 million refugees sought shelter in the Sudan. Thousands also fled in the late 1980s from conflict in Burundi and in Namibia.[2]

By the late 1990s, most of those conflicts and crises had been resolved, but others had arisen. Somalia and the Sudan continued to be wracked by conflict and famine, and Rwanda and Burundi had been the sites of another great political and ethnic bloodletting. In 1994 almost a million people were slaughtered in Rwanda alone in a version of "ethnic cleansing" that left another 3 million homeless. The conflict spilled over into Zaire (now, once again, the Congo), where in 1997 it toppled the long-protected ghoulish regime of Mobutu Sese Seko. Elsewhere in Africa—Liberia and Sierra Leone, for example—long-playing conflict was producing hundreds of thousands of casualties and refugees. Most of southern Africa by the late 1990s was finally enjoying a reprieve from political and ethnic conflict but not necessarily from natural (drought) and man-made (structural adjustment) disasters.

Central American conflict in the late 1970s and the 1980s also produced a multidirectional exodus—from El Salvador to Honduras, from Guatemala to Mexico, from Nicaragua to Honduras and Costa Rica, and from all of those countries to the United States. Estimates of the uprooted in the area ranged from 2 to 3 million, though not all crossed national borders; many remained displaced and dispossessed within their own countries.

In Cambodia, Afghanistan, Angola, and elsewhere, U.S. Cold War policies of nurturing and prolonging conflict and sabotaging settlement efforts played a role in generating ever-more refugees, but such policy choices were particularly ironic in the case of Central America because the final destination of the uprooted from that area was the United States. And the longer the United States sought by force to contain political change there, the greater was the flood of Central Americans across U.S. borders. Such is the price of empire—a price that, among Americans, the celebrants of empire seem least willing to pay.

The end of the Cold War opened up space for a democratic breakthrough in South Africa and for a peaceful settlement in Central America, but it launched a new era of conflict and diaspora in Eastern and Central Europe and Central Asia. The most devastating episode in the disintegrating Soviet sphere has been the violent breakup of Yugoslavia, leaving tens of thousands dead, hundreds of thousands in exile, and millions displaced. We may hope that the worst of the ethnic cleansing is over for Serb, Croat, and Bosnian communities. But short-sighted and self-serving decisions on the part of Balkan leaders and more distant players might still spread the conflagration farther south, where deprived and disgruntled Albanian communities span three states.

It is far from certain that we have seen the last of the dissolution of the Russian empire and the uprooting of its peoples. The stripping away of

the Soviet republics may have been only a first step. Along with Chech-
nyans, Tartars and other non-Russian minorities have demanded states
of their own, and sporadic rebellion has displaced populations along borders with Georgia, Moldova, and other new countries. Likewise ethnic
Russians, subject now to discrimination in new states, may be to tempted
to turn to Mother Russia for support.

At the end of 1995, the United Nations estimated that there were 16
million persons who might be defined under the governing 1967 proto-
col as refugees, that is, persons who had fled their countries under threat
of persecution. But there were another 30 million or so who were displaced and dispossessed and in desperate need of assistance. That is in
addition to an estimated 100 million around the world who are homeless.[3] Many of them are children vulnerable to abuse or enslavement by
traffickers in drugs and sex or to murder by death squads, generally off-
duty policemen in the hire of merchants who want "safe streets" for
their customers.

Even as the need for emergency relief grows, donor contributions, particularly from the United States, to the relevant UN and nongovernmental organizations dwindle off. And no country is now lifting a torch and
issuing an invitation to the "huddled masses." It should not be surprising that the countries that have absorbed the greatest number of refugees
in recent years have been among the world's poorest ones. The richest
are increasingly opting to stay that way by opening borders to money
and resources while closing them to people.

Former refugees from Central America, southern Africa, and the
Balkans were being resettled in their homelands in the 1990s in part because social peace and hope were being restored. But it was also in great
part because the temporary refuge they had enjoyed was being terminated. National policies with respect to immigration or even temporary
residence were becoming ever more restrictive.

That was not to say that foreigners would not be admitted. Indeed,
where economies were booming they would be sought out as "guest
workers." But it would be on terms dictated by states and the corporations they serve rather than by the needs of refugees and migrants. And
those conditions would mean that more and more individuals and families would become caught up in a floating stateless underclass, deprived
of services and earned benefits, of the right to vote or bargain collectively
or even to protest their deportation when their labor was no longer
needed.

The Plight of the Indigenous

Indigenous peoples have suffered disproportionately from externally
provoked aggression against people as well as against nature. In some

cases, they have been intentionally targeted by modern-day conquistadores who coveted their land. In other cases, they have been exploited by combatants—used as cannon fodder in wars they knew little about—or simply wiped out in passing when their ancestral homes got in the way of bombs and bullets and herbicides.

Indigenous peoples have been under assault for centuries, of course, but the plight of unintegrated vestiges of so-called primitive cultures is set in relief as their numbers dwindle. The most common means of measuring development—national aggregate data—tell us nothing about the fate of such peoples. High rates of GNP or per capita growth may well represent the success of conquering peoples or cultures in obliterating indigenous ones.

About 5 percent of the world's population in the late 1990s—some 300 million people representing six thousand nations—were categorized as indigenous. They are distinguished by having a unique language and culture and profound ties to an ancestral homeland.[4] They are in fact the antithesis of a new order that demands mobility and flexibility, instant assimilation to new cultures and virtual cultures. Such multigenerational attachment to, and familiarity with, place has made them at the same time valuable and vulnerable.

The resources rush of the post–Cold War era is pushing such peoples onto ever more marginal lands and subjecting them to new forms of violence, contamination, and deprivation. In Papua New Guinea, where new ventures in logging, mining, and plantation agribusiness have produced growth in the 1990s of up to 14 percent, economists speak of economic miracles. Indigenous peoples speak of loss of language, culture, and personal and community pride.

Cultural Diversity and Biodiversity

One of the great ironies of our times is that even a new appreciation for wilderness has sometimes redounded against the indigenous, as they are perceived and treated as pollutants rather than preservers. Many of the indigenous peoples of the rain forest of North Borneo were driven from their homes when the sultan of Brunei set aside huge tracts as nature preserves. Indigenous peoples were not considered to be a part of that nature and so were prohibited from pursuing the hunting, fishing, gathering, and subsistence farming that had constituted their way of life.

But neither were they considered to be citizens of Brunei. There is no right to citizenship based on birth or longtime residence in the territory. Citizenship is a privilege reserved essentially for those of Malay ethnicity. The 10 to 15 percent of the population that is indigenous is only one of several categories of residents who need not aspire to citizenship in Brunei. The case of Brunei is unusual only in that denial of citizenship is formal and straightforward. Denial of the rights and protections and benefits of citizenship in practice is the norm for the indigenous.

Commonly when indigenous peoples are driven from the rain forest it is because corporate interests crave their wood or their mineral resources. In Burma, it is because a brutal military regime needs a greenwash. A full-scale assault against the Karen peoples that since 1997 has killed more that 2,000 villagers and forced 30,000 from their homes has been inspired by a project that is to be the largest nature preserve of its kind in the world. Featuring a great variety of plants and animals, including tigers, elephants, and rare Sumatran rhinoceros, it is expected to attract millions of tourists.

Some have argued that the only real hope for most indigenous groups lies in assimilation into dominant cultures. But few seem willing or able successfully to negotiate that obstacle course. In multicultural societies, to the extent that assimilation occurs it is likely to be into a deprived underclass rather than into the dominant culture. In the rain forest or in the cities, wherever they are found—with the possible exception of some casinos in the United States—the indigenous are among the most disadvantaged. Along with material poverty, they suffer disproportionately from low levels of education, ill health, and an inclination to self-destructive behavior. This is hardly surprising. Where is one to look for guidance and for a sense of dignity if he is expected to depreciate and reject his own culture?

The loss of cultural diversity, like the loss of biodiversity, is a tragedy for all of us. The loss of cultural diversity also means the loss of biodiversity, because indigenous people are often the only guardians of the secrets of their habitats, of the healing, nutritional, and other exploitable qualities of the flora and fauna of their environments. Fortunately that has been widely recognized, as a great number of scientists have joined nonprofit organizations in seeking to defend the rights of the indigenous, including now their prior rights to products that corporations may seek to enclose in patents under the new concepts and treaties regarding international intellectual property rights. Moreover, with help from UN affiliates and a multitude of NGOs, indigenous groups around the world are organizing and networking in defense of their own interests.

Notes

1. Ambassador Jonathan Moore, U.S. Coordinator for Refugee Affairs, "Update on Immigration and Refugee Issues," statement before the Subcommittee on Immigration, Refugees, and International Law of the House Judiciary Committee on April 6, 1989, *Department of State Bulletin* 89, no. 2148, July 1989, pp. 59–60. See also "Refugees Top 15 Million Worldwide, Group Says," *Albuquerque Journal*, April 25, 1990, p. A7.

2. Moore, op. cit.

3. United Nations Development Program [UNDP], *Human Development Report 1997* (New York: UNDP, 1997), pp. 24–31. See also United Nations High Commission for Refugees, *The State of the World's Refugees in 1997* (Oxford: Oxford University Press, 1998).

4. Douglas Watson, "Indigenous Peoples and the Global Economy," *Current History* 96, no. 613, November 1997, pp. 389–391.

Suggested Readings

Black, R., and V. Robinson, eds. *Geography and Refugees: Patterns and Processes of Change* (London: Belhaven Press, 1993.)

Harris, Nigel, *The New Untouchables: Immigration and the New World Worker* (New York: I. B. Tauris, 1995).

Isbister, John, *The Immigration Debate: Remaking America* (West Hartford, Conn.: Kumarian Press, 1996).

Rabben, Linda, *Unnatural Selection: The Yanomami, The Kayapó and the Onslaught of Civilization* (London: Pluto Press, 1998).

Redfield, R., *The Primitive World and Its Transformations* (Ithaca: Cornell University Press, 1953).

Sell, Susan K., *Power and Ideas: North-South Politics of Intellectual Property and Antitrust* (New York: State University of New York, 1997).

Shiva, Vandana, "Homeless in the Global Village," *Earth Ethics* 5, no. 4, 1994, p. 3.

United Nations High Commission for Refugees, *The State of the World's Refugees in 1997* (Oxford: Oxford University Press, 1998).

United Nations High Commission for Refugees, *Populations of Concern to UNHCR: A Statistical Overview* (Geneva: UNHCR, 1996).

Van Cott, Donna Lee, *Indigenous Peoples and Democracy in Latin America* (Boston: St. Martin's Press, 1995).

12   *Macrodebt and Microcredit*

One of the major obstacles to development by any approach or definition is the debt treadmill. Even before the East Asian meltdown of 1997 occasioned massive bailout loans, developing country external debt amounted to more than $1.4 trillion, 38 percent of combined GNP.[1]

The significance of debt is often misunderstood because it is treated as the outcome of discrete transactions generally resulting from miscalculation or malfeasance on the part of the borrower. In fact, debt is sought and maintained by creditors because it has been discovered that collecting interest is an efficient way to make lots of money without any heavy lifting.

Debt as a building block of social systems involves a great deal more than extending loans and collecting interest payments. It becomes a great divide within communities and states and among nations. Whether individuals or nations, those caught for any considerable period on the debtor side tend to stay there pending far-reaching systemic change, and those who find themselves on the creditor side are able to widen the gap between themselves and their debtors. Several millennia ago the Hebrew peoples recognized the dangers of debt servitude and ruled that every fiftieth year would be a year of "jubilee," in which all debts would be erased.

Like a feudal or colonial relationship, debt may become a very long-term value extraction, or transfer, system. More than that, however, once the debt treadmill itself takes over and new loans become necessary simply to service older ones, debt becomes the maintenance engineer of a power system. At that point the creditor may be able to impose his will with respect to matters utterly unrelated to the debt.

Debt Crisis and Debt Maintenance

From the perspective of creditors and other agenda setters, the debt crisis was essentially an issue of the 1980s. The crisis was not about the size or persistence of debt; it was about debt servicing—about the ability and willingness of debtor governments to make full and timely interest payments whatever the cost to their citizens and national patrimonies.

By the 1980s the debt trap had become particularly burdensome for most Latin American and African countries, but even South Pacific island ministates, only recently drawn into the global economy, had suffered severe setbacks. And countries like India and Yugoslavia that had acquired some space for genuinely national planning and economic innovation had felt obliged, because of debt exposure, to turn to less-independent and less-egalitarian policies.

The modern version of Third World debt servitude began to take shape in the 1950s and 1960s with such industrial white elephants as steel mills. The white elephants of the 1980s—nuclear-power plants, for example—were even hungrier and more dangerous, but other follies and calamities weighed in as well. Corruption, capital flight, and consumption of scarce foreign reserves for luxury imports rather than for capital goods played their part, along with military buildups, energy crises, and, above all, interest obligations.

Extraordinarily large loans were needed in the 1970s to cover the costs of energy, but bankers, awash in petrodollars, were more than anxious to extend such loans; and for the borrowers, accelerating inflation mitigated the sting of interest. In the 1980s, however, when First World inflation rates dropped, "variable" interest rates did not drop proportionately. Those rates have been kept high throughout the debate in part by a U.S. deficit steadily deepened by military spending.[2]

After 1982, rising debt service and the cut in lending to developing countries led to a sharp reversal of net resource transfers. Whereas between 1977 and 1982 long-term lending had contributed to positive net resource transfers amounting to $147 billion to developing countries, net transfers between 1982 and 1988 were negative, shifting $85 billion from Third World to First (see Figure 12.1). Net loss for the highly indebted middle-income countries was even greater, $93 billion, and debt service claimed more than a third of export earnings in the 1980s.[3]

From Crisis to Treadmill

The crisis, from the perspective of the major foreign private banks and the multilateral financial institutions, was most acute in Latin America. That was the region in which private, particularly U.S.-based, banks had the greatest exposure to nonperforming loans and from which rumblings about default, possibly even collective default, were beginning to be heard in the early 1980s.

By the 1990s the crisis was over in the sense that the banks had won an uncontested victory. It was achieved in the first place by breaking up what threatened to be a coordinated approach—to the most anxious, a "debtor cartel." This was done through a relatively generous bailout of one major player, Mexico, and the imposition of a virtual credit freeze

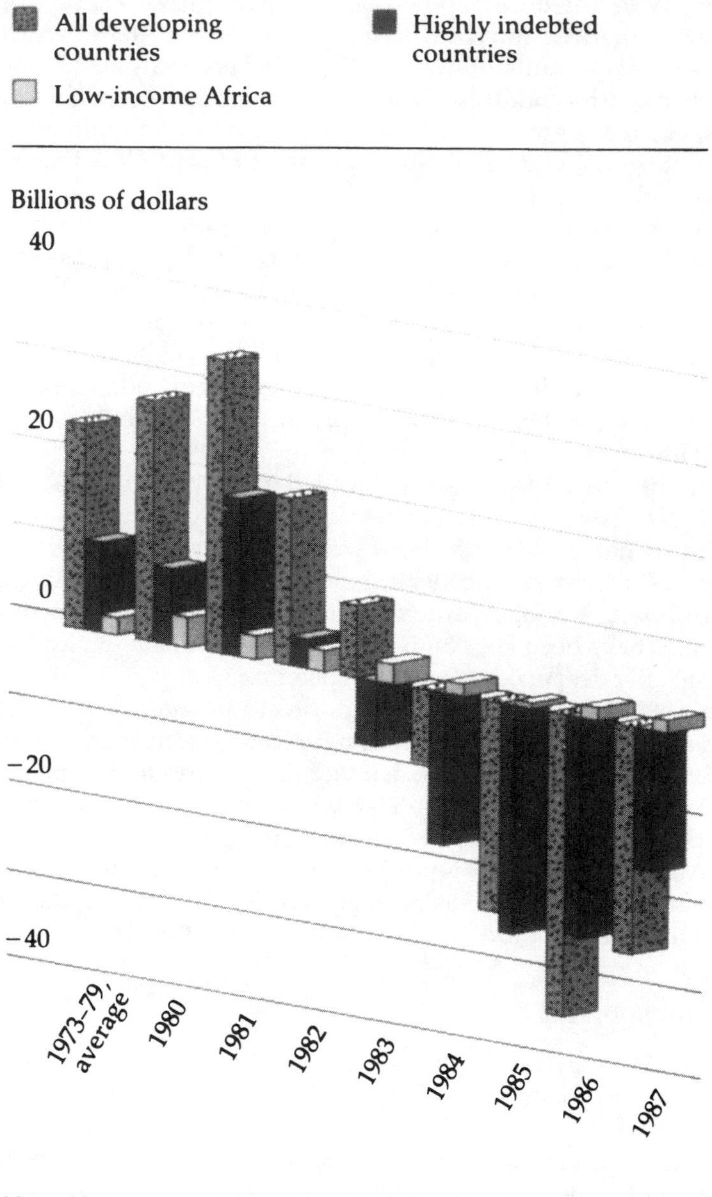

■ All developing   ■ Highly indebted
   countries   countries

□ Low-income Africa

Billions of dollars

Note: Net resource transfers are defined as disbursements of medium- and long-term external loans minus interest and amortization payments on medium- and long-term external debt.

FIGURE 12.1   Net Resource Transfers to Developing Countries, 1973 to 1987.
Source: World Bank, *World Development Report, 1988* (New York: Oxford University Press, 1988), p. 30.

against some of the more obstreperous ones, including Argentina, Brazil, and Peru. In fact, most Latin American countries experienced negative resource flows, reflected in a "growth" rate of -8 percent for the decade. But the clincher in this victory for the banks came with dissolution of the Soviet Union and the alternate market of which it was the linchpin.

The Payoff for Creditors

With the elimination of the competition, such as it was, Western bankers were able to solidify their own cartel in the sense of holding firmly to an agreed-upon set of conditions for the extension of credit. Those conditions, discussed elsewhere as economic restructuring or structural adjustment, ensured that private debt to foreign banks would be underwritten by governments and that top priority in the allocation of national resources would be placed on earning foreign exchange in order to service debt.

Debt service, however, was not to come at the expense of foreign providers of goods and services. Limitations on imports, which might have served to bring trade into balance, were ruled out. In fact, markets were to be virtually unregulated, ensuring for most countries continual trade imbalances and debt buildup. Debt is in turn traded for equity in the most lucrative, or potentially lucrative, of the industries and services that had been operated by the governments. Privatization on a major scale has had the additional benefit, from the creditors' perspective, of withdrawing resources and options from governments, thus weakening them as a counterpoise to the power of creditors and investors.

The Catch-22 for Debtors

It is easy enough to see why creditors continue to loan, but why do debtors continue to borrow and to service debt? In the first place, no credit means no imports; and as we have seen, given domestic power structures and the rise everywhere of middle classes with modern consumer appetites, precious few governments would stand a chance of opting for autarchy and surviving. Even Cuba, which was able to deal with the sudden loss of petroleum in the early 1990s by substituting bicycles for cars and oxen for tractors, cannot revive its high-tech medical and pharmaceutical industries without imports. The Castro government, with great trepidation, is now welcoming foreign investment and seeking integration into the global economy.

In the second place, debtor governments are scarcely inhibited about worsening the financial mess because those who make the mess are not obliged to clean it up. There are both temporal and social dimensions to that kind of transference. The temporal relates to long-term versus short-term accountability. Benefits accrue to the government that takes out the loan and has use of the capital. Burdens fall to some future government, or perhaps future generation.

The social dimension is one of class. When the party incurring debt is a state, the collateral is the collective holdings and earnings capacity—the labor—of its people. When sacrifices are to be made for the sake of debt service, it stands to reason that they will be made by those who have no choice—those incidentally who had no voice in incurring the debt and no access to the money. If the state-holding classes that actually borrowed and spent the money had to repay it themselves, with interest, the system would soon collapse.

The Informal Sector

As modern economic sectors in the Third World have been devastated, particularly since the 1980s, by debt, inflation, loss of markets, and the like, many savvy workers restructured out of their jobs and disgorged onto the streets have learned how to use the unregulated markets of the streets and the illegal sweatshops of the back alleys to survive and in some cases even to prosper. Recent studies in several countries have indicated that half or more of annual GNP derives from the "informal," or unregulated, underground sectors of the economy. This discovery has led some to see the flourishing of the informal sector as a promising wave of the future.

The ingenuity and industriousness of the poor come as no surprise to development specialists who have worked directly with them, but it is hardly edifying to be reminded that people will work longer hours for less if they are desperate enough. The glorification of the informal sector strikes this author as a sort of academic jujitsu—a matter of redefining the problem itself as the solution.

"Informals," or persons who lack the means or connections to do business on the state's terms—the street-smart shoestring entrepreneurs, finding spaces for productive activity in the interstices of underdeveloped and overregulated economies—are familiar throughout the Third World and in much of the First World as well, and almost everywhere they are continually hassled and hobbled by governments responsive to the wealthier business sectors.

In Santiago, Chile, during the dictatorship of General Augusto Pinochet, unemployment was chronic, particularly among the one-third or more of the population who live in shantytowns. A social worker in Pudahuel, an area of spontaneous colonization and low-cost government housing, told me in the early 1980s that of the 340 families she served, only 50 individuals had jobs. Most had no recourse save the informal sector, but there they faced a merciless obstacle course.

In La Victoria, one of Santiago's oldest and largest shantytowns, a community continually persecuted because of its resistance to the dictatorship, a friend of mine tried to open a business as a seamstress in her house. She managed to scrape together the 1,500 pesos (about U.S. $30 at that time) for the license. But she had to wait six months for a visit by a municipal inspector, who told her that her premises were too primitive to qualify. She was never able to open a business, but the license fee was not returned, and she was later fined for not having filed an income tax return for her business. Her brother, a skilled carpenter, tried selling his carved wooden toys on the street, but he could not afford the license required by law of all street peddlers, so the police confiscated his wares and he, too, was subjected to a heavy fine.

Even where governments have shown some sympathy for those in the informal sector, relief from the usual obstacle course has been hard to implement mainly because of the weakness of such governments vis-à-vis the affluent private sector. Luiza Erundina de Souza, elected mayor of São Paulo in 1988, a Marxist representing Brazil's Workers' Party, allowed the homeless to occupy undeveloped property, despite a daily barrage of criticism by the city's conservative newspapers. And she allowed peddlers back onto city streets, though in response to fierce pressures from middle-class shopkeepers she limited their numbers and the areas where they could work.

The thrust of most studies and recommendations in the 1980s regarding the informal sector, at least those attracting major donor support, was to reinforce pressures at the national level for privatization, relief from progressive taxation, easing of currency convertability, and deregulation, including a rollback of official measures designed to protect workers or consumers. The policies proposed for reinforcing the informal sector, for example, by Peru's Instituto de Libertad y Democracia, which received about $9 million from USAID in 1989, were very like those long advocated by foreign investors and creditors and normally imposed by the IMF—policies that have contributed to such levels of unemployment and extremes of desperation in the first place.[4]

Microcredit and Microenterprise

It became clear early on to practitioners of grass-roots development, however, that if the upshot of a focus on the informal sector was to be fewer obstacles or more development assistance for community cooperatives or for small-scale owner-operated enterprises in villages, slums, and shantytowns, the outcome might be very positive. A considerable body of research supports the arguments that small businesses are more productive and innovative than big ones and that a multitude of locally based small businesses constitutes a sturdier base for development than a few large and potentially mobile ones. It was also well understood by those whose development experience was in the field rather than in the penthouse suites or the major donor agencies, whence programming decisions are dropped like high-altitude bombs, that responsible money management is more likely to be found among shantytown mothers than among uptown bankers.

Much of the inspiration for what was to become the dominant tool or market model for grass-roots development in the 1990s came from South Asia. In 1971, Muhammed Yunus, an economist from Bangladesh, returned to his newly independent homeland after studying at Vanderbilt University and teaching at Middle Tennessee State University. He became frustrated that the economic theories he was passing on were of no benefit to the poverty-stricken people around him in Bangladesh. He made a few small loans out of his pocket to women he knew were being exploited by loan sharks and wholesalers, and he became convinced that poor women were very good credit risks.

From that conviction sprang the Grameen Bank. Yunus's own research showed that wealthier people were more likely to default on loans, but he was unable to convince commercial bankers, so for a time he simply took out personal loans and then lent the money out. Finally, in 1983, he persuaded the government of Bangladesh to let him open a Grameen, or village, bank. The bank favored women because they had been found to be more likely to repay the loans and more likely to spend the proceeds on their children.

Borrowers were required to form groups of five, who elected among themselves a president and a treasurer. The groups were to meet weekly to discuss their business problems and exchange ideas. They became known as solidarity groups in that loan repayment was a commitment of the group, and group solidarity was conceived as the functional equivalent to collateral. Along with commitment to loan repayment, the groups committed themselves to sixteen principles for the promotion of family and community well-being.

The concept spread very quickly through Bangladesh. By 1997 the Grameen Bank was serving some 36,000 villages, lending $1 million a day (94 percent of the borrowers were women) and employing 12,000 people.[5] It also spread quickly to other parts of the world. A similar program launched in Bolivia in 1984 by former Peace Corps volunteer John Hatch, known as the Foundation for International Community Assistance (FINCA), was soon to spread through Latin America. In the early 1990s, under the leadership of Maria Otero, the well-established and extended development organization, Acción International, began to champion a microcredit-microenterprise program. The concept also sparked interest in the United Sates in the late 1980s, where the Full Circle Fund of Chicago, catering to inner-city women, became one of the earliest and most successful converts to the model.

By the late 1990s, the model of small loans for small business had spread to more than fifty countries, with some sixty thousand participants in the United States alone. Of course as the Grameen-inspired programs spread, there appeared variations and mutations. The principles that govern solidarity groups are modified to address local needs and conditions, and many new programs now offer more in the way of training and technical assistance than in credit. There is increasing pressure now to draw in male borrowers with larger enterprises and to shift savings and benefits from nonprofits to banks.

The success of this approach owes much to the fact that it appears to reinforce rather than threaten dominant trends, paradigms, and value systems. That is, it is supportive in principle of banking, business, and individual entreprenuership as opposed, for example, to the cooperative and communal approaches to income generation that were popular in the 1960s and 1970s, and it serves to bring previously marginalized peoples around the world into monetized and credit-generated systems that ultimately further the process of globalization.

And therein lies the rub. Success has built-in contradictions. Successful people become celebrities. Successful places become tourist attractions. Like successful people and places, successful programs run the risk of becoming caricatures of themselves. Microcredit and microenterprise programs are now supported by a multitude of foundations and by major national and multinational donors like USAID and the World Bank. That means among other things that they exert a powerful pull on funds and personnel away from other kinds of grass-roots development programs.

The promising jujitsu is that major donors may have been tricked by economically correct language into supporting programs that actually promote equity and empowerment of the poor—that is, by shifting the initiative within organizations and agencies to those who are serious about such empowerment. The danger, though, is that if such programs come to be dominated by institutions and interests that do not share the inspiration of the founders, they might come to have the effect of channeling public funds into the private coffers of the not-so-truly needy or, worse, of dissolving community solidarity rather than reinforcing it and of drawing ever greater numbers into long-term indebtedness.

Notes

1. United Nations Development Program [UNDP], *Human Development Report 1997* (New York: UNDP, 1997), op. cit., p. 191.

2. Susan George, *A Fate Worse Than Debt: The World Financial Crisis and the Poor* (New York: Grove Press, 1988).

3. World Bank, *World Development Report, 1988* (New York: Oxford University Press, 1988), pp. 27–32.

4. Hernando de Soto, *The Other Path: The Invisible Revolution in the Third World* (New York: Harper and Row, 1988).

5. Muhammed Yunus, lecture at United Nations Headquarters, New York, January 31, 1997, as prelude to the opening in Washington, D.C., on February 2 of the global "summit" on microcredit.

Suggested Readings

Brecher, Jeremy, and Tim Costello, *Global Village or Global Pillage: Economic Reconstruction from the Bottom Up* (Boston: South End Press, 1995).

Danaher, Kevin, ed., *Corporations Are Gonna Get Your Mama* (Monroe, M.: Common Courage Press, A Global Exchange Book, 1996).

Ekins, Paul, and Manfred Max-Neef, *Real-Life Economics: Understanding Wealth Creation* (London: Routledge, 1992).

Elliott, Larry, and Dan Atkinson, *The Age of Insecurity* (London: Verso, 1998).

Feinberg, Richard, and Ricardo French-Davis, eds., *Development and External Debt in Latin America: Basis for a New Consensus* (Notre Dame, Ind.: University of Notre Dame Press, 1988).

Grieder, William, *One World, Ready or Not. The Manic Logic of Global Capitalism* (New York: Simon & Schuster, 1997).

Lissackers, Karin, *Banks, Borrowers and the Establishment: A Revisionist Account of the International Debt Crisis* (New York: Basic Books, n.d.).

Mander, Jerry, *The Case Against the Global Economy and for a Turn Toward the Local* (San Francisco: Sierra Club Books, 1996).

Oxfam International, "Multilateral Debt: The Human Costs," Oxfam International Position Paper, Oxford, 1996.

Payer, Cheryl, *The Debt Trap: The International Monetary Fund and the Third World* (Harmondsworth, UK: Penguin Books, 1974).

Phillips, Kevin, *The Politics of Rich and Poor* (New York: Harper Perennial, 1990).

Results Educational Fund, *The Micro Credit Summit Declaration and Plan of Action* (Washington, D.C.: Results Educational Fund, 1997).

Even in the more prosperous and more highly modernized cities of the Third World, such as Carcas, Venezuela, large sectors of the population are left behind.

Growing income gaps mean that alongside luxurious new housing development there is also a mushrooming of shantytowns, like this one along the Paraguay River in Asuncian.

Salvadoran peasants, resettled under the protective arm of the Catholic church, tend their fields on the slopes of the volcano Guazapa, ignoring the military's counterrevolutionary offenses. Where donor countries perceive "security" interests, developmental goals are sure to be subverted.

Focus on the informal sector has served to camouflage the real extent of unemployment and underemployment, but it has also inspired new development initiatives, like microenterprise. (Salvador, Bahia, Brazil)

Deforestation in the Amazon and other extensive rainforests has accelerated dramatically in the 1980s and 1990s.

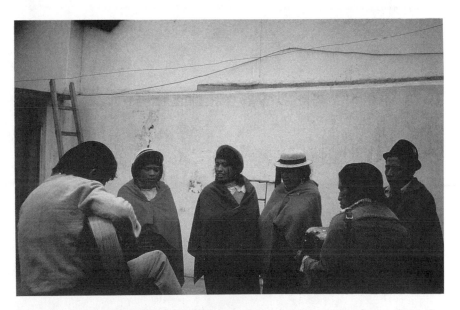

Quechua speakers in the Ecuadorean Sierra prepare a musical program for a radio station run by the Catholic Diocese of Riobamba. The radio programs are one aspect of the efforts of Monseñor Leonidas Proaño to educate, organize, and empower the Indians of the Sierra, efforts that have been a source of alarm to the economic elite of the area.

Export-processing industries, like Mexico's maquiladoras, offer capital a sort of extraterritoriality, free generally of tariffs and of labor legislation and unions. The labor force for such industries consists mainly of young women, expected to give more and demand less.

Albania—Donkeys remain an important part of the transportation system around Druja, 15th century stronghold of Albanian national hero Skanderbeg.

PART FOUR

The Process and the Protagonists: Paradoxes of Development

13 *The Process: Games Developers Play*

In earlier chapters we have dealt with differing perspectives on the part of theorists as to the nature and causes of underdevelopment and thus as to what should be the priorities of development programs and the approaches of development agencies. These broad discrepancies at the macro level of analysis reflect differences in values and thus in goals between categories of donors as well as between some categories of donors and their clients or partner organizations. Arguments with regard to efficiency or prospects for success must ultimately deal with the question, For whom? The answer to that one is dictated not by facts but by values.

In development, however, as in most public-policy areas, the question of values and thus of ultimate goals is not often dealt with straightforwardly. In fact, in any given program, there may be as many goals as there are institutional or even individual actors. In the case of many programs—particularly the most ambitious in terms of funding and personnel—the most crucial issues are not openly discussed at any level: not between executive and legislative branches or among supposedly cooperating agencies, not between donor and host governments, and most certainly not between donor agencies and client organizations or communities.

Thus, the ambiguities, inconsistencies, and outright but unacknowledged conflicts are pushed out of the assembly rooms and boardrooms and into the field. The goals of the game are left to be deciphered and the outcome determined by the dynamics of the process.

The unfolding of the development process, as it reflects the interplay among donor agencies and clients—often having conflicting needs and objectives—and the crossfires and minefields that field agents must negotiate, will be addressed in these chapters in a set of paradoxes. These paradoxes are drawn from the author's observations in the course of field research in various regions, including Latin America since the 1960s, South and Southeast Asia in the mid- to late 1980s, and Eastern Europe, Eurasia, and Africa in the 1990s. An account of the uncertain course of development for and by the indigenous in the Ecuadorean Sierra is woven throughout.[1] I believe, however, that these paradoxes characterize the problems of development anywhere, including in the pockets of poverty in the United States. They are very general, impressionistic, and irreverent; they are also meant to be provocative and to serve, perhaps, as seeds of "appropriate" theory.

> Paradox No. 1: *In public affairs, no matter how bad things appear to be, they're actually worse.* Governments and other institutions almost always try to cover up their mistakes and misdeeds and put the best face on what they have done or are doing.

Publicized rationales for policy initiatives often cover for undisclosable motives. Moreover, even when motives are relatively benign, agencies can be expected to exaggerate their successes and minimize their failures. Finally, even where publics or clients cannot avoid being less sanguine, bureaucrats tend to become convinced by their own propaganda or their own reports of successful project completion.

One need look no further than Watergate or the Iran-Contra scandal to see that beneath any government disclosure, voluntary or otherwise, lies another layer of undisclosables.[2] Nor is such mendacity confined to the U.S. government or to the superpowers. In the 1980s alone, France had its *Rainbow Warrior* sabotage, Great Britain its suppression of *Spycatcher* and its Falkland War cover-ups, and Japan its Recruit Company bribe scandal.

In the 1990s, scandal became so widespread in the Third World and the ex-Soviet sphere that countering corruption came to be among the stated goals of major development agencies. Of course, it was *not* often stated that much of the newly evident corruption responded to the models and incentives offered by the West—that is, out-of-control and transnational political campaign finance, deregulation of financial transactions, and the acceleration of privatization and other lures to instant enrichment. Even more scandalous in some cases have been the motives underlying the choice of which manifestations of corruption to highlight and which to sweep under the rug.

Because the concept of development is at the same time extraordinarily elastic and puffed up with positive connotations, "development" often becomes a cloak for programs with less-felicitous objectives. The British, for example, in conjunction with the World Bank, launched the Kariba hydroelectric project, which was heralded as a major contribution to the industrialization of Zambia. The Zambians were so thoroughly sold on the project that they even helped to pay for it, even though they were not to see the first payoff from their investment for thirty-five years and even though a Rhodesian company was to be appointed agent for construction.

Only later did it become clear to the Zambians that the Rhodesian company was in virtually complete control of local decision-making and that they had simply been conned. It turned out that the overriding objective of the project was to circumvent UN sanctions against the government of Ian Smith, providing huge amounts of cheap electricity to the blockaded Rhodesian regime.[3]

Misrepresentation is common also to nongovernmental institutions of First World or Third, and even relatively innocent organizational self-aggrandizement can frustrate relations among donors, field agents, and clients. When my contingent of Peace Corps volunteers arrived in Chile in 1962, our host country organization, *Techo* (Roof), which promoted community development in some of Santiago's sprawling shantytowns, briefed us on the facilities it had established and the projects we would be working with. We were told, for example, that in Población La Victoria the organization was operating nine clinics. A careful survey of the area by volunteers failed to turn up a single clinic. When we reported back to the staff that there were no *Techo* clinics in La Victoria, they responded, "Of course there are, they are right here in the files."

> Paradox No. 2: *Were it not for wrong reasons, there would be no right things done.* Development, even more than other political processes, makes strange bedfellows. The necessity of coalition building dictates that legislation or program planning benefiting the powerless must appeal also to some sector of the powerful.

The same foreign assistance programs that were sold to the U.S. Congress in earlier decades as means of winning hearts and minds away from so-called godless communism were being marketed in the 1990s as trade promotion. Even programs for the promotion of "food security" in famine-prone regions were justified, despite the obvious inherent contradiction, as a means of expanding stable, long-term export markets for U.S. grains.

The Food for Peace program was and is a case in point. Of course there were those among its proponents who were genuinely concerned about hunger in the Third World, but the program owes its existence for the most part to those whose interests are closer to home. U.S. food aid was introduced in the 1950s largely to expand markets for U.S. grain. Thus, the grain is not normally given away; it is sold to foreign governments, which in turn resell it on national markets, often at prices the poor majority cannot afford. If, on the other hand, the grain is sold cheap, it may undercut the narrow profit margins of local farmers, driving them out of business.

Moreover, food aid, like any other kind of aid, may be used for political purposes: to promote certain policies or bolster certain allies. The Ford administration, for example, used the Food for Peace program in 1974–1975 to bulwark Chile's murderous General Augusto Pinochet after Congress had cut off military assistance to his regime. Finally, such aid is under any circumstances a mixed blessing, as it diverts attention from the need for land-tenure and farm program reforms both in client countries and at home. Hunger, whether in First World or Third, does not normally reflect lack of food production or productive capacity but rather maldistribution of land, income, and opportunity. To the extent that periodic shortages, leading to famine in particular locales, are due to lack of food production or productive capacity, the deepening of long-term dependence on imports serves only to exacerbate the problems of supply and distribution as well as of inflation and debt.

Likewise, land reform has stemmed from various instigators and purposes. Ecuador's land reform of 1964 was an outgrowth, in part, of the Kennedy administration's Alliance for Progress, which was in turn a response, in part, to the Cuban Revolution. The 1964 reform law provided that *huasipungueros,* or peons, were to receive title to the land they worked if that land was not being efficiently used or if workers were being exploited. The law was feared and staunchly opposed, of course, by some *hacendados,* or landowners. Nevertheless, it was favored—some would even say instigated—by many of the modernizing landowners who wanted to rid themselves of the medieval ties of obligation and to liquefy their assets in order to invest in industry or in construction in the cities. Some particularly well-connected landowners profited handsomely by inducing the government to pay in cash an inflated price for their land. The even more powerful barons of the northern coastal plantations also favored the 1964 agrarian reform law because it generated a larger pool of migratory wage laborers for seasonal work.

The most popular projects at the grass-roots level in the 1990s have been those involving microcredit and microenterprise. They appeal to development professionals because they can be an effective means of channeling assistance to the poorest, of generating income and promoting self-sufficiency, and even of nurturing community solidarity and activism. But a major reason why such programs have caught on at a time when development assistance in general is dwindling is that they borrow the language of business (individual entrepreneurship, etc.) and so can be persuasive to legislators and bureaucrats who might instinctively oppose programs that sounded like socialism or charity.

Bankers, for the most part, initially scoffed at the idea of microcredit, and they still shrink from loaning to the poorest, but those who deal in international finance can see the virtues, from their perspective, of using public or nonprofit funds to draw the resources of otherwise marginalized peoples into the mainstream money economy. And for bankers operating at the local level, the payoff may be more immediate. Nonprofit NGOs promoting microcredit programs are not allowed to compete with banks but rather become feeders for them.

Nonprofits, for example, are not allowed to handle the savings generated by microenterprises, so commercial banks become the beneficiaries, even as they shrink from the risk of making loans. Inspired by the successes of the microcredit programs of California-based Katalysis and its local partners in rural Honduras and by the increased trade generated by microenterprise, Bancomer Honduras began putting up stalls in village marketplaces. They found that the rural people who had been associated with microcredit-microenterprise programs were more comfortable now with the idea of banking and had more to save. Moreover, in response to another trend of the 1990s, they had become more concerned about being robbed on the way home.[4]

> Paradox No. 3: *To every solution there is a problem.* In development work, there are no happily-ever-afters. That is partly because in a nonrevolutionary situation—that is, where the material and institutional resources of most of the elite remain intact—the "haves" will soon figure out how to turn even a new law or program designed to benefit the "have-nots" to their own advantage. Thus, those who would promote the interests of have-nots cannot be caught napping; they must focus always on ends rather than means.

The idea of establishing partnerships between First World donor agencies or NGOs and Third World NGOs is not really a new one. Albuquerque-based Futures for Children came into being in the 1970s as the partner of an organization established in Colombia in the 1960s. But partnerships—which ideally are supportive relationships, generally including technical assistance, between independent organizations—were being strongly promoted in the late 1990s by most multilateral and bilateral major donors and avidly sought by most NGOs. In fact, for many kinds of programs, major donor funding had become contingent upon the establishment of partnerships.[5]

The concept of partnership, moreover, had blurred and blended and merged to a large degree with that of networking in the construction or nourishment of a well-functioning, productive "civil society." The more ambitious programs of the World Bank and its affiliates, USAID, the Inter-American Foundation, and many other agencies involved promoting collaboration among NGOs, private enterprise, and municipal or other authorities in a particular locality.

There are many reasons for the current popularity of this particular approach to problem solving, but a major one is that it makes a virtue of necessity; the first problem to be solved is that of a shrinking resource base for what might have been publicly funded development programs. In other words, as First World foreign assistance and Third World public budgets shrank, would-be problem solvers sought to follow the money—to tap into the coffers of corporations, including major foreign investors.

The problem with this solution, of course, is that corporations are in the habit of taking money in rather than giving it away and that corporate decision-making practices are not bottom-up and participatory.

To the extent that corporations do become involved in such partnerships they can be expected to hold their material investments to the minimum required to control the outcome so as to maximize corporate interests. Corporate contributions to educational programs, for example, are generally conditional, directly or indirectly, on curricular changes seen as advancing corporate interests—that is, essential training for their work forces. That is not to say that the changes called for would necessarily be contrary to community interests, but the process would not likely be "participatory" or otherwise empowering to nonprofits and noncorporate citizens. Moreover, programs dependent on the support of municipal governments may lack "sustainability." Constituencies and program preferences of municipal governments may be subject to change with each election.

In the case of land reform, peasants often exchange the problems of feudalism for the problems of capitalism. In the process of redistribution in Ecuador, the landlords, in most cases, kept the best plots—those on level land with an adequate water supply. For the majority of the former *huasipungueros,* there was no way to support a family on the tiny plots of vertical land they were left with. According to the census of 1974, half the country's landholdings were of less than 3 hectares.[6]

In the absence of a further major change in the landholding pattern, the problem of shrinkage can only get worse, as the peasant subdivides his tiny plot among his seven or eight children. Thus the cycle remains a vicious one. The peasant can't afford seed, so he is forced to hire out his labor, to migrate for several months of the year to the cities or the coastal plantations. The children left behind must help their mothers tend the crops. Unable to stay in school, they fail to acquire the skills that might enable them to earn a decent wage in the city. Marcelo Torres, director of projects for Ecuador's Agrarian Reform Institute (IERAC), said that although the reforms of 1964 and 1973 were to have eradicated all forms of "precarious" tenure, new forms, such as sharecropping and land rental, have since appeared.

Some of the Andean peasants migrate to the cities, increasing the pressures on the limited urban market for housing and jobs. One of the motives of the Ecuadorean government in launching its land reform program was to keep the peasants on the land, reducing the pressures of urbanization and increasing production so that the peasants could feed themselves as well as the urban population. But even under the best of circumstances it would be difficult to increase production on the typical peasant's arid, eroded plot. And the "best of circumstances" do not prevail. In general, the credit—essential for any kind of improvement—that was available to the landlord is not available to the peasant. In fact, over the past decade, the importation of basic foodstuffs has been increasing sharply.

The colonization of newly opened lands in the Oriente (the Amazon Basin) and in the Santo Domingo zone, between the Sierra, or high Andes, and the coast, has eased the pressure to some extent. But the life of the pioneer in such areas has not been easy. Apart from the land itself, the government has been able to offer very little. José (Pepe) Aguilar, director of the regional office of the Ministry of Agriculture and Ranching (MAG) for the Santo Domingo zone, complained that the zone is sorely lacking in roads, potable water, electricity, basic health care, schools, technical assistance, credit—everything. Furthermore, most of the accessible land in the zone has now been claimed. Recent arrivals have to serve as wage laborers for those who are already landowners, resulting in a new social stratification. Some of the new migrants simply become squatters on land that has already been claimed, generating social tension and increasing pressures on the government.

In tandem with the proliferation of *minifundios*, or tiny plots, in the Sierra and the colonization of the jungles, there has been a reconcentration of land in the richer, more productive area of the northern coast. Plantation owners, producing largely for export, welcomed the termination of the semifeudal *huasipungo* system, as the new tenure pattern provided them an ample supply of cheap wage labor. By the same token, however, they firmly resist any further development of the Sierra that would enable the peasants to support themselves fully on their own farms. They also, of course, resist paying the export or import taxes that would finance such development in the Sierra. As the migratory laborers begin to organize and demand higher wages, plantation owners can be expected to revise the balance between capital and labor intensity. With increasing modernization and mechanization, the danger is that in some two decades the country will have a very high proportion of workers who have neither land nor jobs.

Agrarian reform is usually presented in egalitarian terms, but even when governments mean well, development programs for the rural sector are more readily accessible to the larger landholders and often exacerbate inequality. The green revolution, regularly cited as one of the great successes of the international development agenda of the 1960s and 1970s, made available new varieties of seeds and fertilizers, new technologies, and new lines of credit, but only to farmers who could afford to invest in them and who were already successful enough to be considered creditworthy. The farmers who have been able to take advantage of the program, while becoming richer, have also become more dependent.

Meanwhile, the enhanced value of land has induced the larger landowners to covet more of it, especially land held in precarious tenure arrangements, like sharecropping, by subsistence farmers. Thus, with the green revolution, India, previously subject to famine and required to import much of its food, has become self-sufficient in food production. Ironically, though, while food is more abundant, some Indians are surely eating less; the miracle of productivity has led to more concentrated landownership and increasing numbers of peasants who are landless.

On the idyllic island of Bali, the Indonesian government, in 1984, introduced an agrarian reform program. With government encouragement and assistance to those who could afford to be innovative, cash crops, particularly vanilla and cloves, were supplanting subsistence crops, and peasants who previously worked their own land were becoming tenants or wage laborers on the land of others. Even in the South Pacific, which has suffered less in general from modernization than other Third World regions, cash cropping for export is changing patterns of lifestyle and of diet. Polynesians, Melanesians, and Micronesians, who used to have balanced diets of fresh fruit, root crops, and fish, are now eating canned meat, Wonder Bread, and granulated sugar and are suffering from heart disease, high blood pressure, and diabetes. And Western development specialists, in an uphill battle against Western foodstuff exporters, are engaged in educating the island peoples about the virtues of their native diets.

Paradox No. 4: *Development programs are given impetus, not by underdevelopment, but by the fear of development that is not programmed from above.* As a rule, there is very little money for development until those who have the money and the power feel threatened—precisely by the self-activation of the poor.

All development specialists maintain that their aim is to promote self-help. It appears, however, that the primary objectives of the best financed programs are the channeling and control, if not the suppression, of the initiatives of the poor.

The big influx of development money—from AID, the World Bank, and evangelical missionaries—that came into Ecuador in the mid-1970s clearly came in response to a major mobilization of Indians in the Sierra, encouraged by the Catholic church and propelled by a belated recognition of the legal options signified by the 1964 land reform. By 1977 the peasant movement had begun to dissolve.

There are, however, many better-known examples of this paradox—like the campaign by AID in the early 1960s to suppress the Peasant Leagues of the Brazilian Northeast or, more recently, the so-called economic aid—some $700 million annually in the 1980s—directed to Central America or the "money bombs" dropped on the Mexican state of Chiapas since the Zapatista uprising of 1994. That desperately poor, largely Mayan, long neglected state received $2.7 billion from the World Bank between 1995 and 1997, about 20 percent of the bank's budget for Mexico. The Mexican government complains bitterly about the funds spent by NGOs from Europe and the United States in calling international attention to the plight of the indigenous peoples of Chiapas, but Mexico's federal government spent $1.3 billion in 1996 alone on strengthening anti-Zapatista groups and communities and local governments in Chiapas's conflict zones.[7]

Brazil's Northeast contains the country's greatest concentration of poverty generally and of rural poverty and powerlessness in particular. The area, which had 24 percent of the population but accounted for only 11 percent of the national income in 1960, remained basically feudalistic in political and socioeconomic structure and was subjected to periodic droughts that resulted in widespread starvation and emigration. The area's peasants had been untouched by the rise of populism and other developments that had expanded the urban political base and had received no benefits or protection from the extension in the 1940s of minimum-wage and union-recognition laws to the rural sector. The illiterate majority of the peasants lacked even the minimum fee for membership in the patrimonial political system—the vote.

Nevertheless, a group of tenant farmers in the state of Pernambuco had organized a mutual benefit association in the early 1950s, and when the landowner and his political allies tried to disband it in 1955, the peasants sought the support of a federal deputy named Francisco Julião. From that embryo, the movement, which came to be known as the Peasant Leagues, swelled to a following of about 100,000 at its peak in 1961. The challenge or the threat of the political awakening of the rural masses drew the attention of Brazilian nationalists as well as of the U.S. government.

Brazil's President João Goulart, along with the parties, unions, student and church groups, and other elements of the so-called leftist-nationalist movement that supported his government, responded to the challenge by joining in the fray to organize and service the peasants in hopes of drawing them into his political base. A new Rural Workers Law, promulgated in March 1963, facilitated that process. In the meantime, funding for a comprehensive approach to the problems of the area, through a new agency, had cleared the Brazilian Congress in December 1961. The Superintendency for the Development of the Northeast (SUDENE), brainchild of economist Celso Furtado, answered directly to the president and enjoyed administrative autonomy. In addition to its own responsibilities in the planning and execution of development projects, it was empowered to coordinate the delivery of both national and foreign technical assistance to the area.

U.S. administrations of liberal bent are always ambivalent, and the Kennedy administration was no exception. Thus there were those in policy-making circles who were serious about promoting redistributive reforms in Brazil and elsewhere, but the heavyweights in those circles were convinced that dealing with what they perceived as the "threat of revolt" in the most impoverished region of Latin America's largest and most populous state had to be the first critical test of the Alliance for Progress.

The U.S. effort there was to have two interrelated purposes. First, as part of the larger strategy to undermine the Goulart government, it aimed to assist "democratic" (pro-U.S., anti-Goulart) political leaders in defeating Leftists or other supporters of the central government.

The second purpose—undermining, containing, repressing, or destroying those organizations that gave aid and comfort to a peasant movement the United States could not control—called for manipulations at the grass-roots level. U.S. strategy on both levels spelled direct confrontation with the agency through which foreign assistance was to be channeled.

After sending a special mission to the Northeast in 1961 to draw up recommendations, the United States entered into the so-called Northeast Agreement with Brazil on April 13, 1962. The United States committed a total of $131 million, of which $760,000 was to be in dollars and the balance in local currency under PL 480 (the Food for Peace program). Thirty-three million of this amount was to be earmarked for immediate action, or "impact," projects, and $98 million was reserved for long-range development projects. The Brazilian Northeast became the only subnational region in the world to merit its own AID mission.

The Northeast Agreement turned out to be, from the start, a disagreement and an utter failure in terms of both its stated and its unstated goals. U.S. attempts to co-opt political leaders and to influence the outcome of elections in the area through timely allocations of impact aid were generally unsuccessful, as were efforts to contain the peasant movement and to generate parallel organizations under covert U.S. control. Those U.S. efforts did, however, deprive SUDENE of anticipated support from the political center and drive it farther to the left. Thus the undermining of SUDENE, undertaken initially as a consequence of that agency's refusal to subordinate its own objectives to U.S. interests, had become an end in itself, and the designation of SUDENE as anti-American became a self-fulfilling prophecy.

It was only after the military coup d'état of March–April 1964, which replaced the elected civilian government with a military dictatorship, that the Peasant Leagues and other popular organizations of the Northeast were suppressed and a purged and reconstituted SUDENE adopted a policy of full cooperation with the U.S. AID mission.[8]

Brazil endured twenty years of militocracy before it saw the return of civilian rule, and it was not until the mid-1990s that the country appeared to be politically and economically stable. Prosperity, however, was narrowly distributed. The gap between rich and poor remained among the worlds' widest and continued to grow. And the central government, in Brazil as elsewhere beholden first to foreign creditors and investors, was obliged to trim rather than expand public benefits and services.

That is not to say, however, that there was no arena for social activism and no prospect of social progress. In Brazil as elsewhere, many of the NGOs that had previously focused their efforts on organization and advocacy at the national level had redirected their attention to the local level, strengthening community-based groups and enabling them to participate more effectively in local government. In the city of Curitiba, for example, an energetic mayor and a strong environmentalist movement had generated a system for recycling garbage that had become a model for cities around the world. In Porto Alegre, capital of the state of Rio Grande do Sul, a government elected by the broadly based Workers' Party (PT) had been able to get local businesses to pay higher property taxes in support of municipal services. In the late 1990s representatives of the World Bank, the IDB, and other major donors were drawn to Porto Alegre to observe the city's "participatory budgeting" process in action.[9]

A major innovation of the development business in the 1990s has been the aforementioned focus on partnership, or social networking for the strengthening of "civil society" at the local, or municipal, level. No doubt much of the revitalization to be seen here and there at that level reflects the funding by development agencies of incentives to that end. It is also the case, however, that in many communities genuine participation was being achieved by unaided local efforts, bringing popular parties or coalitions into government, and that foreign agencies, seeing the bandwagon on the move, have hastened to get on it—and sometimes even into the driver's seat.

Paradox No. 5: *Credit is extended to ~~only~~ mostly those who do not need it.* The lenders' interpretation of creditworthiness generally results in discrimination against those whose holdings and ambitions are modest.

In development, as in other realms of political and economic competition, there are no happily-ever-afters. There are, however, important changes and periodic causes for celebration. The blossoming of the village banking, or microcredit, movement is such a cause. The four thousand funders and promoters of poverty lending programs around the world who gathered on February 2, 1997, in Washington, D.C., for the Microcredit Summit pledged to extend their programs so as to reach 100 million of the world's poorest families by the year 2005.

In light of the achievements and the momentum of this movement I had thought that I might actually be able to "retire" this paradox that appeared in the first edition of this book. On closer examination, however, it appears that full retirement would not be warranted because those who are serious about poverty lending should be made aware of the tendency to "mission creep." Like the managers of development banks in earlier decades, managers of village banks sooner or later begin to think like bankers.

Scarcity of credit for those who need it most has long been among the gravest problems afflicting development programs in general and rural development in particular. Land reform programs are often stymied by the unavailability of credit for *minifundistas* and new settlers and thus result in a general decline in agricultural production.

The poorest peasants are often afraid even to seek loans from private banks for fear that the bank will seize their land. Such fears may be unwarranted in particular cases, but they are not irrational. Likewise, peasant communities have been hesitant to enter into contracts with government agencies; they are not confident that they understand all of the ramifications of such contracts, and they fear they might somehow be tricked.

When peasants do seek loans, they often find that banks will not honor their titles or their land-sharing or swapping arrangements among themselves. In Ecuador, peasants who want to sell land must get permission from the agrarian reform agency, IERAC. IERAC urges them to sell to owners of adjoining land or at least to others in the community, but peasants often prefer to make their own arrangements. Thus among themselves they enter into extralegal "commitments to sell." Banks, even if they were disposed to extend credit to peasants, would not recognize such extralegal arrangements. Extralegality, of course, is not their only problem.

In the Santo Domingo zone, IERAC may, under certain circumstances, sell to squatters the land they have cultivated. But the squatters cannot then get credit because banks refuse to recognize their titles. Banks also refuse to recognize collective ownership of land, even though the traditional Indian *comuna* was sanctified by law in 1937 and its provisions for participation and benefits for all community members were strengthened by legislation passed under the Hurtado government.

It is unfortunate but hardly surprising that private banks are rarely accessible to peasants. What is more discouraging is that even the Banco de Fomento, Ecuador's national development bank, generally refuses to make loans except to those who do not need them. Like any private bank, it is preoccupied primarily with recovering its resources, and it expects repayment in full with interest. For that reason, it was necessary to establish FODERUMA, Development Fund for the Marginal Rural Sector, as an organ of the Banco Central (Central Bank). FODERUMA does not really expect repayment, but it may direct its resources only to a very few communities; only the poorest are said to be "FODERUMAbles."

Similar problems present themselves in the establishment and the functioning of cooperatives. Until recently, almost all development agencies promoted cooperatives, although most co-ops fail—at least in their function of raising incomes. In the first place, members must make investments. Therefore, those who most need help are not able to participate. For most purposes a co-op may be organized with as few as eleven members. Furthermore, cooperatives must maintain community services, draining scarce resources and making it all the more difficult for members to realize economic advantages. Investment can rarely be the solution when the problem is lack of money.

Finally, when a cooperative does succeed, it is likely to divide the community by generating new inequities. In Ecuador, there have been a few agencies, like IERAC and the literacy campaign, that at times and in places—primarily the Sierra—promote a return to traditional forms of organization, involving entire communities, rather than cooperatives. But they have encountered a great deal of resistance, because the oligarchy views such *comunas* as the seeds of communism.

The unavailability of credit for those who need it most is a major problem throughout the Third World and in parts of the First World as well. Development and agriculture economists at the Universitas Udayana of Denpasar, in Indonesia, told me in 1984 that while the government provides credit for some cooperatives and resettlement projects, none is extended to the neediest, as it is assumed that they would not be able to pay it back.[10] In Indonesia, as elsewhere, co-ops usually fail. Dividends are rare, as co-op managers reinvest the meager earnings, and members, seeing no economic advantage, soon lose interest.

The poorest of the peasants, unable to obtain credit from government or from private banks, or to get ahead through membership in cooperatives, are forced to rely on traditional paternalistic—and generally exploitative—relationships. A. L. Mendiratta, serving the UN Food and Agriculture Organization in New Delhi, noted that in the 1980s rural bondage, based generally on inherited debt, was still to be found in parts of India. Such bondage had been outlawed, but peasants are poorly informed of their legal rights and poorly equipped to exercise or defend them. Defiance of landlords is risky under any circumstances, and the Indian government is unprepared to serve as an alternate patron.[11]

In Malawi, beginning in the late 1960s, the government, with a major transfusion from the World Bank's International Development Agency, undertook patronage of a set of four ambitious rural development projects. A major feature of the projects was to have been the extension of credits to peasant farmers. As it turned out, however, fewer than 5 percent of the farmers actually received any of the funds. Most of the funds were allocated to capital development and management costs, including luxurious offices and generous salaries and expense accounts for a top-heavy bureaucracy. At least one of the projects, the Lilongwe Land Development Project, received considerable praise in development-management circles, as infrastructure construction was completed roughly on schedule and productivity was increased. Participatory and distributive benefits, however, were not evident. Distribution figures for 1975 indicated that Malawi's peasantry, amounting to 95 percent of the population, received only about 11 percent of the income generated by agricultural production.[12]

Pockets of poverty in the First World have also found credit hard to come by, and agencies created to deal with the problem often manage to overlook it. In New Mexico in the late 1980s, the institution that was to serve as an agricultural development bank was making its largest loans to the developers of resort hotels.

There can be no doubt that the originators of village banking have been dedicated to serving the poorest. But like people and places and theories, programs that gain celebrity status, that are widely praised and copied, are in danger of seeing their essence transformed, of becoming caricatures of themselves. FINCA, one of the earliest poverty lending programs, now has some 2,500 banks serving 70,000 borrowers in fourteen countries on four continents. It nevertheless makes a point of reserving eligibility to borrowers—mostly women—who earn no more than the equivalent of $2 a day, twice the level fixed by the World Bank as indicative of absolute poverty. FINCA's founder, John Hatch, maintains that only about 10 percent of the agencies promoting microcredit hold to such an earnings ceiling.

Most of the newcomers to the movement have been subject to "mission drift," to lending more to the less needy, and to men as well as women. They believe, wrongly according to Hatch, that making larger loans to larger, male-managed businesses enhances their prospects for success, or "program sustainability." In fact, apart from the issue of risk—rich men have consistently proved to be greater credit risks than poor women—commercial banks are beginning now to compete with microcredit agencies for the more promising loans to medium-sized businesses.[13]

> Paradox No. 6: *Third World governments are weakened by the lack of pressures.* Pressures on such governments are fierce and incessant, but they are virtually all from one side—the side of the rich. For long-term effectiveness, development programs must build up countervailing pressures.

Victor Paz Estenssoro, perennial president of Bolivia, attributed the survival of the Bolivian revolution in its early years to the existence of the peasant militias. He told me about the visit of one such militia from a village on the altiplano to his office early in his first presidency. A spokesman for the group said the village desperately needed a telephone and a bridge to link it to the road to La Paz. Paz said, "I am very sorry, but you must understand; there are so many demands, and so few resources. There is no way I can help." The peasant leader then said, "Mr. President, do you remember how the counterrevolutionaries hanged President Villarroel from a lamppost? Well, when they come for you, you can call us on our telephone and we'll come running over our bridge and save you." Paz said they got their bridge and their telephone.[14]

In Ecuador in the early 1980s, President Osvaldo Hurtado was trying to plant the seeds of popular organizations, but it was still the *camaras*—chambers of industry and agriculture—who dominated politics. Almost all the professionals in the field of rural development in Ecuador at the time, including the militants of the government of Hurtado, acknowledged the need for another kind of agrarian reform; they conceded that even with the greatest imaginable luck and success the programs under way would not touch the structural obstacles to social change. But it would be neither fair nor realistic simply to blame the government.

With the sudden death of President Jaime Roldós in 1981, Vice President Hurtado had been propelled into the presidency before his time. He was only forty-one years old. More important, his party was relatively new and small, holding fewer than 20 percent of the seats in the single-chamber legislature, and had had little opportunity to build a popular base. Furthermore, his style—that of a soft-spoken political science professor—was puzzling to a populace accustomed to demagoguery. Finally, his administration's lack of ideological definition, though in some ways an asset, allowed critics on the left to label Hurtado a technocratic elitist, while those on the right called him a crypto-Marxist. Supporters of the government believed that it would be an accomplishment of the greatest importance if Hurtado managed to stay in power until the next scheduled elections.

Such debility was not a problem simply of that particular government, but of any Ecuadorean government, and especially of any government that proposed to incorporate the "marginalized" poor into the mainstream of national society. Rarely has a civilian government exhibited firm control of the armed forces, and no Ecuadorean government ever managed seriously to tax the oligarchy. Revenue accruing to the state from the oil boom of the 1970s had begun to provide a measure of autonomy for the government, even though 50 percent of the oil royalties were earmarked for the military. But the international petroleum glut of the early 1980s and the precipitous drop in prices left the new civilian government with heavy commitments and scant resources.

The president's administrative assistant, Ramiro Rivera, said that the country had to consider a new approach to land reform sometime in the future, perhaps in two or three decades, but the current political system simply would not permit it. The electorate in the early 1980s appeared to be abandoning traditional parties in favor of center to center-left or populistic ones. But real power does not lie with the electorate. It lies, as noted, with the chambers representing agribusiness and industry. Not only would the *camaras* react with hostility to the prospect of new structural reforms, they were still aggressively striving to roll back previous ones.

Ricardo Izurieta Mora Bowen, president of the National Federation of Chambers of Agriculture, said the *camaras* considered it their "duty" to put a stop to the policies that were ruining the economy. In addition to their objections to the Hurtado government's price controls on dairy goods and other agricultural products, their complaints focused on the agrarian reform legislation as codified in 1973. The reform of 1964 was not so bad, Izurieta said, because it removed the "irritant" of the *huasipungo* system and improved the "image" of the *hacendados*. But the codification of 1973 had left landowners insecure. Whereas under the 1964 law, land could be seized if it was unused for ten years, the modification of 1973 allowed the government to seize land that had been out of use for only two years. Izurieta conceded that the Hurtado government was not going out of its way to enforce the law, but as long as the law remained on the books the federation would see it as a threat; thus, the federation was trying to get it repealed.

Agribusiness had not failed to notice that the codification of 1973 was carried out under a military government. Izurieta said that only a minority of extremists within the *camaras* actually wanted to provoke a coup. The strategy of the majority appeared to be to keep the government intimidated by the threat of a coup without actually provoking one.

In order to deal with such extraparliamentary pressures as well as to prevail in parliament and to activate somnambulant bureaucrats—in order to address the needs of the nation as a whole—the government must be subject to counterbalancing pressure, effective pressure from the nonaffluent. No one was more conscious of that than Hurtado himself. His development programs were long-term ones, looking perhaps to the year 2000, but it appeared that all were designed to generate popular organizations that could at some point begin to serve as a balance. In the meantime, Hurtado called the military chiefs in regularly for briefings on the sad state of the economy—in hopes that they would see little promise in taking over a government that was broke.[15] He succeeded in serving out his term and turning over the office to another duly elected president; his was the first government in twenty years to do so.

In fact, it might be argued that the seeds of popular organization planted by the government of Hurtado in the early 1980s and cultivated more intensely by the government of Rodrigo Borja and by a multitude of local and international NGOs in the late 1980s were beginning to bear fruit well before the arrival of the new millennium. Indigenous organizations from the starkly diverse coastal, Andean, and Amazonian regions had formed a relatively tight and politically creative network and in the 1990s, for the first time in the country's history, were electing their own representatives to municipal and parliamentary bodies.

Paradox No. 7: *The primary beneficiaries of rural development programs are the cities.* Development money settles mostly in the cities, where offices are maintained, supplies are purchased, and salaries are earned and spent.

Ouagadougou, capital of what was then Upper Volta (since renamed Burkina Faso), offered an extreme example in the late 1970s of the urban backwash of rural development. There were endless horror stories coming out of the Sahel about creeping desertification and its wake of famine and starvation; but Ouagadougou was booming. There were no tourists at all, but Ouagadougou, I was told, at that time had the highest per capita concentration of development specialists in the world. Almost any Third World capital, however, will illustrate the point.

There has been progress in Ecuador, even among the indigenous peoples in rural areas, since the beginning of banana exportation in the 1950s. Such progress has been indicated by increased consumption of commercial products and, more important, by advances in health, including a decline in infant mortality. Nevertheless, Ecuador remains a dual society, with an enormous gap in living standards between Indians and non-Indians as well as between urban and rural areas.

Ecuador's most obvious progress over the past several decades has been in social mobility—that is, the growth of the middle class. The income represented by economic growth has accrued mostly to the middle and upper classes. As banana money modernized Guayaquil, oil money has modernized Quito, and precious little of it has trickled into the countryside.

Likewise, development money, including money allocated to rural development, has been spent mostly in the city. The offices of most development agencies, including those dedicated to rural development, are located in major cities. Field agents in most rural development programs venture only infrequently and briefly into the field. Their supplies are purchased and their salaries are earned and spent, for the most part, in the cities.

Increasingly, since the International Labor Organization's Andean Mission (Misión Andina) of the 1950s, development has come to represent a major industry for Ecuador. In the late 1970s and early 1980s, the Inter-American Development Bank was investing an average of about $100 million annually in development; the World Bank $50 to $100 million; AID $15 million; the United Nations Development Program $3 million; the UN World Food Program $3 million; the Peace Corps $2.5 million; the World Health Organization $1.4 million; the UN Food and Agriculture Organization $1.4 million; the Organization of American States $1 million; and the

UN Fund for Population Activity $1 million. Lesser amounts were being provided by Japan, West Germany, the United Kingdom, France, and Israel.[16]

Private development agencies also constituted a big business in Ecuador. There were at least 40 private development agencies, as such, from the United States, not to mention service, charity, and religious organizations that sponsor development programs. Don Swanson, a former Peace Corps volunteer who directed Consultants for the Development of Latin America (ASDELA), one of the major private development organizations (NGOs) in Ecuador, identified 300 NGOs in the country without counting some 9,000 community-level "popular organizations." The nationally based Information Service for Private Organizations (SIOP), which conducted a survey of private development and welfare organizations, identified 500.

Finally, the array of development agencies of the Ecuadorean government, all known by their acronyms, constituted a veritable alphabet soup. There were at least 60 ministries, agencies, or institutions involved in one way or another with development.

For Quito, the development boom has kept the airport busy throughout the year. It has filled office buildings, hotels, restaurants, and taxis. It has consumed tons of paper and generated a great many professional and clerical jobs. It has generated elegant proposals, plans, and evaluations. But all development programs, whether public or private, foreign or national, are top-heavy. The development boom fizzles out at the city limits.

That is not to say that there has been no development in the rural areas. But given the hundreds of millions of dollars invested and the manpower assigned to the effort, the level of development activity in the areas where it is needed most must be said to be disappointing.

> Paradox No. 8: *The most reliable guardians of any ecosystem are those who do not have the option of leaving.* Contemporary corporations, like colonialists before them, deplete, despoil, and depart.

The global village is swallowing up the last of its hinterland. It reached out, in the early 1990s, and almost overnight took in Papua New Guinea. Even in the most rugged and remote regions of the highlands of Papua New Guinea, long ignored or avoided by the carriers of Western civilization, jungles, farmland, and rivers that provided subsistence over the millennia to indigenous populations are being exploited and despoiled for logging, mining, and plantation agribusinesses that have produced growth rates of up to 14 percent. Environmentalists estimate that, at current rates of depletion, forests of commercial value will be gone within twenty years. While economists speak of miracles, the indigenous Papua New Guinea people are losing much more than land and livelihood; they are losing languages, cultures, and personal and community pride.

Caribbean islands were exploited for centuries to the comparative advantage of European pirates and potentates. Their original inhabitants were annihilated, and several generations of Africans and East Indians were enslaved or indentured to produce sugar, coffee, spices, and tropical fruits for European markets.

Starting half a millennium ago, with the first onslaught of European exploration of the Amazon, Brazil's cycles of boom and bust development have set in relief the limits of development as exhaustive production. Unlike the indigenous peoples who had lived in a state of equilibrium with their environment, European colonialists tended to exploit the resources of a newly claimed area until they were depleted and then to move on. Among the resources to be nearly depleted early on, along with the turtles and manatee of the Amazon, were the indigenous peoples, enslaved to stoke the sugar boom in the plantations of the Brazilian Northeast.

Like the colonialists and neocolonialists before them, today's globe-hopping corporations deplete, despoil, and depart. But whereas for a time in the 1960s and 1970s many governments had the incentive and the constitutional authority to regulate rates of depletion of national resources and to limit levels of despoilation of the environment, governments now hamstrung by treaties on trade and investment and harnessed to debt-servicing schedules are in no position to resist the pollution of their air and water, the erosion or toxification of their soil, and the exploitation of their national resources. Moreover, technological advances and ravenous appetites of capital markets in the 1990s have made it feasible to reach into wilderness regions until recently left alone. Thus the resources rush has pushed the indigenous onto ever more marginal land.

Indigenous peoples are more than ever under assault, but they are also more than ever fighting back, and with greater prospects of success, owing to United Nations-nurtured global alliances among such groups and between them and environmentalist networks. The pollution of indigenous lands by oil companies—Texaco in the Ecuadorean Amazon, Shell Oil in Nigerian Ogoniland—and the stripping of rain forests in Malaysia and Brazil have come to global consciousness because of persistent and media-savvy resistance by the indigenous peoples themselves.[17]

Such resistance often carries great risk and sacrifice. Union leader Chico Mendes was murdered in December 1988 for trying to protect the livelihood of indigenous and mestizo rubber tappers against accelerated ranching and logging in Acre and Rodônia, on Brazil's borders with Peru and Bolivia. But a few years later, leaders of the Kayapó tribe, with help from foreign social and natural scientists and ultimately from the media, were able to put a stop to work on the Kararao project, a massive dam complex that would have flooded the homelands of eleven tribes in the Amazon Basin's Xingu River Valley.

In Papua New Guinea, where the exportation of wood—unprocessed logs—has more than quadrupled in less than two decades, officials who have tried to expose corruption by the foreign logging companies and to require practices ensuring sustainability of the forests have been subject to brutal assaults. But some tribal leaders have shown extraordinary resourcefulness in renegotiating disadvantageous contracts. In one community, tribal negotiators pointed out that company staff manning a dam and power station might become uncomfortable around villagers with their bows and arrows and poison-tipped spears if those villagers were resentful. The company then saw the wisdom of reopening negotiations.

On the slopes leading from the Cobaria River toward the Sierra Nevada de Cocuy, near the Colombian border with Venezuela, the U'wa people, numbering only a few thousand, who now live on one-tenth of their ancestral lands, wait for the incursion of the oil prospectors. Until now the oil culture has kept its distance—about 160 kilometers to the east. There the Caño Limón oil field, held in partnership by U.S.-based Occidental and Anglo-Dutch Shell, with the Colombian state company, Ecopetrol, as a junior partner, hovers over some 1,200 million barrels of oil. Within the compound are all the comforts of a modern country club: swimming pools, tennis courts, gymnasiums, restaurants, shops, helicopter pads.

The compound is protected by miles of steel fences with 3-meter-high coils of razor wire as well as by several army brigades, subcontracted, so to speak, from the Colombian government. The company pays a "war tax" for protection from guerrilla groups that regularly bomb and mine their pipelines to the Caribbean coast. There is no protection, however, for occupants of the frontier war zone around the compound. Along with ecological degradation and social disintegration—the Guahibos, indigenous to the area, have been reduced to begging—violence is escalating. Kidnapping, disappearance, torture, murder, and massacre are routine and are attributed both to the guerrillas and to military and paramilitary forces.

At current rates of output, the Caño Limon field is expected to be approaching exhaustion in about ten years, so Shell and Occidental did seismic studies in surrounding areas and found that an area known as Samoré, encompassing much of the U'wa territory, holds as much oil as Caño Limón. They then sought and received license from the government to exploit Samoré. As one of Colombia's eighty-four recognized tribes, the U'wa have rights to their land but not to subsoil minerals. Colombia's constitutional court ruled in February 1997 that the government and the companies were violating the rights of the U'wa. But that judgment was overruled within weeks by the higher administrative court, leaving a political standoff between the oilmen and the U'wa.

In the Caño Limón area, the oil companies have straightened the river, dug new lakes, and filled in preexisting ones. They are proud of what they see as their mastery over nature, an attitude as alien to the mind-set of the U'wa as the U'wa's unwillingness to be bought off at any price is to the oilmen. To the U'wa, it is not only habitat, livelihood, culture, and identity that are at stake; it is their collective purpose, guardianship of the sacred earth that sustains them and all life.

The ultimate weapon of the U'wa, employed in the sixteenth century when the Spanish first encroached on their territory, is mass ritual suicide. They have threatened to employ it again—to throw themselves off of the formidable escarpment known since the sixteenth-century episode as the Cliff of Death—if the oil companies move into their territory. The power of such a stance was literally brought home to Rodrigo Villamizar, Colombian former minister of mines and petroleum, when his son asked, "Daddy, are you going to make the Indians jump off the cliff?"[18]

Notes

1. Much of the research reflected in Part 4 was conducted in Ecuador in June, July, and August 1982, courtesy of a Fulbright-Hays grant. It consisted primarily of interviews with about 100 development agency officials, field agents, and community leaders. For an elaboration of findings and sources, see J. K. Black, "Ten Paradoxes of Rural Development: An Ecuadorean Case Study," *Journal of Developing Areas* 19, no. 4, July 1985, pp. 527–555. A Fulbright-Hays grant also underwrote my research in India in 1988. Other research efforts represented here were funded by Mellon Foundation grants.

2. It appears now that the "arms for hostages" aspect of the Iran-Contra scandal, which the Reagan administration took such pains to deny, was itself a cover. Evidence continues to mount that while the arms shipments to Iran were indeed related to hostages, they were not to be in exchange for the *release* of hostages held in the mid-1980s. Rather, the arms shipments appear to have been part of a deal negotiated in the fall of 1980 between the Ayatollah Khomeini's camp and Reagan's wherein Iran was to *hold* the U.S. Embassy hostages until election day, ensuring Carter's defeat. See Christopher Hitchens, "Minority Report," *Nation* 250, no. 21, May 28, 1990, p. 731.

3. David Morrell, *Indictment: Power and Politics in the Construction Industry* (London: Faber, 1987).

4. Conversations with Jerry Hildebrand, president of Katalysis, Stockton, California, March 1998.

5. Typically, a major multicultural or bilateral donor might match the grant of a First World NGO to its Third World partner and/or the major donor might fund a program of technical assistance by the First World NGO to its Third World partner or partners.

6. Instituto Nacional de Estadística y Censos, *Resumen Nacional: 11 Censo Agropecuario, 1974* (Quito: Instituto Nacional de Estadística y Censos, 1979), p. 1.

7. Conversation with Jan Rus, U.S.-based scholar who lived and worked in Chiapas in the 1990s, University of California at Riverside, February 13, 1998.

8. The best of several books dealing with the nature and consequences of U.S. foreign assistance to northeast Brazil in the early 1960s is Joseph A. Page, *The Revolution That Never Was: Northeast Brazil, 1955–1964* (New York: Grossman, 1972).

9. Jeffrey Rubin, Institute of Advanced Studies, Princeton, "Decentering the Regime: Grassroots Democratization in Brazil and Mexico," lecture at St. Antony's College, Oxford, April 28, 1998.

10. I. Detut Nehen and K. G. Bendesa, Facultas Ekonomi, Universitas Udayana. Personal interview, Denpasar, July 4, 1984.

11. A. L. Mendiratta, United Nations Food and Agriculture Organization. Personal interview, New Delhi, July 19, 1983.

12. Alifeyo Chilivumbo, "On Rural Development: A Note on Malawi's Programmes of Development for Exploitation," *African Development* 3, no. 2, 1978.

13. Conversation with John Hatch, founder of FINCA, Washington, D.C., March 24, 1998.

14. Conversations with Víctor Paz Estenssoro, Albuquerque, spring 1978.

15. Conversations with Osvaldo Hurtado, Albuquerque, April 1985.

16. U.S. Agency for International Development, Ecuador, "Briefing Book," 1981.

17. "Human Impacts on the Environments of Brazilian Amazonia," conference coordinated by Darrell Posey, Linacre College, Oxford University, June 5–6, 1998.

18. John Vidal, "A Tribe's Suicide Pact," *Manchester Guardian Weekly*, October 12, 1997, pp. 8–9.

Suggested Readings

Bryant, Coralie, and Louise G. White, *Managing Development in the Third World* (Boulder: Westview Press, 1982).

Chambers, Robert, *Rural Development: Putting the Last First* (Harlow, UK: Longman Scientific and Technical, 1983).

Church, Frank, "Farewell to Foreign Aid: Why I Voted No," *New Republic*, November 13, 1971.

Firth, R., and B. Yamey, *Capital, Savings, and Credit in Peasant Societies* (London: Allen & Unwin, 1964).

Fiszbein, Ariel, and Susan Crawford, *Beyond National Politics: Partnerships for Poverty Reduction* (Washington, D.C.: EDI World Bank, 1996).

Ghai, Dharam, and Jessica M. Vivians, eds., *Grassroots Environmental Action: People's Participation in Sustainable Development* (London, Routledge, 1992).

Grindle, Merilee, *Politics and Policy Implementation in the Third World* (Princeton: Princeton University Press, 1980).

Hoyer, Hans, *Open Minds: Reflections on Human Development and South-North Issues* (Colombo, Sri Lanka: Plan International, 1996).

Institute for Development Studies, "The Power of Participation: PRA and Policy," Policy Briefing Issue 7, Sussex (1996).

Korten, David C., and Felipe B. Alfonso, eds., *Bureaucracy and the Poor: Closing the Gap* (West Hartford, Conn.: Kumarian Press, 1981).

Korten, David C., and Rudi Klauss, *People-Centered Development: Contributions Toward Theory and Planning Frameworks* (West Hartford, Conn.: Kumarian Press, 1984).

Lipton, M., *Why the Poor Stay Poor: Urban Bias in World Development* (Cambridge: Harvard University Press, 1977).

Mulwa, Francis Wambua, *Enabling the Rural Poor Through Participation* (Eldout, Kenya: AMECEA Gaba Publications, 1994).

Nef, Jorge, "Development Theory and Administration: A Fence Around an Empty Lot?" *Indian Journal of Public Administration* 27, no. 1, January to March 1981, pp. 8–22.

Reilly, Charles A., *New Paths to Democratic Development in Latin America: The Rise of NGO-Municipal Collaboration* (Boulder: Lynne Rienner Publishers, 1995).

Schumacher, Ernst F., *Politics, Bureaucracy, and Rural Development in Senegal* (Berkeley: University of California Press, 1975).

Stout, R., *Management or Control* (Bloomington: Indiana University Press, 1980).

Watson, Douglas, *The New Civil War: Government Competition for Economic Development* (Westport, Conn.: Praeger, 1995).

White, Louise G., *Creating Opportunities for Change: Approaches to Managing Development Programs* (Boulder: Lynne Rienner Publishers, 1987).

14 *The Protagonists: Donors, Clients, and Field Agents*

Development specialists are surely no less committed to their professed missions than are other categories of professionals. But, along with the material and psychic rewards sometimes accrued, there are frustrations and obstacle courses that would try the patience of any saint.

An American who has spent more than twenty-five years trying to promote development in Latin America says that development work is rather like shoveling smoke. No mandates are unambiguous or irreversible; no precise boundaries can be drawn; no projects are ever concluded; no results are definitive; and no assessments are entirely reliable.

Development is intensely political. What is true of policy-making within a national context is true also in a profession or field of endeavor like development. Pressures on decision-makers of donor and client governments as well as of bilateral and multilateral agencies and even of well-funded NGOs are incessant, but they are mostly from those who have the most to gain or lose politically or materially in the enterprise. Thus, those who would pursue development as bottom-up empowerment, along with trying to catalyze change or protect constructive change processes in particular communities, must at the same time seek to build a transnational mobilizable constituency for their approach.

Many of the frustrations are inherent in the role of honest broker between the powerful and the powerless. In programs involving big money and big bureaucracies, the serious developmentalist, as opposed to the careerist or timeserver, will often feel like an infiltrator, able to pursue the agency's professed goals only in a surreptitious manner and forced to see his or her best efforts continuously ignored or sabotaged. Agency decision-makers, responding to the political climate that most directly affects their funding or career prospects, often override their own professional staffs and even highly paid consultants. It has not been uncommon, for example, for political appointees of the World Bank or the regional development banks to override the virtually unanimous recommendations of their professional staffs. The reverse is less common but also possible; on occasion, when the political leadership, executive or legislative, shows genuine concern for the unpowerful, it finds itself ignored or sabotaged by less-committed bureaucrats.

Even if the development specialist can count on the backing of his own agency, he must still negotiate the rapids of host country, regional, or local politics. At the local level, one can expect to encounter political reaction, loss of credibility, brain drain and budget drain, bureaucratic turf skirmishes, and overqualified, undergratified would-be field agents. And there is no guarantee that client communities will be appreciative or responsive. Still the business of development grows and attracts the best and brightest.

> Paradox No. 9: *The experts are always wrong.* The theories and models that guide the work of experts utilize a limited number of factors and do not allow for the unexpected. Especially when one is working in an unfamiliar setting (and experts by definition are), the unexpected always happens; in fact, if development is to be sustainable, the unexpected *must* happen.

There is a great deal of literature in circulation now on the need for culturally sensitive, ecologically sound, participatory approaches to development (empowerment, the buzzword of the 1980s, was replaced in the 1990s by sustainability), and some small agencies and PVOs are demonstrably serious about it, but the big bureaucracies and high-tech or high-priced consulting agencies are not likely to be. In the first place, big bureaucracies are the creatures of political systems. They must answer first of all to the powerful, not to the powerless.

At the University of Michigan in the early 1960s, a graduate student from Venezuela, on leave from a position in his country's very reputable Ministry of Planning, explained to his fellow students how the ministry used cost-benefit analysis in making decisions on road building: "First you calculate the cost of materials, labor, purchase of right-of-way, and other expenditures, and you place that figure below the line. Then you calculate the additional income the farmers will earn through the new access to markets, multiply by the number of years the road will be serviceable, and place the product above the line. If the resulting figure is greater than 1, you build the road."

A student interjected, "But what if the figure is less than 1?"

The Venezuelan responded, "You recalculate the farmers' earnings or extend the estimated years of serviceability until the result is more than 1."

"So you always build the road?"

"Of course. We wouldn't be doing the study unless somebody important wanted the road built."[1]

The very nature of bureaucracy militates forcefully against participatory, bottom-up processes. Bureaucracies need to be able to report results—preferably quantifiable results—within a preordained and generally very limited time frame (e.g., the fiscal year). Furthermore, both concrete, or material, results and timing should be as planned or predicted. In the case of a transfer of responsibility to local counterparts or to a client organization, the process is complex and imprecise, calling for constant reappraisal, and specification of timing at the outset would probably be counterproductive.

In fact, of all the forms the termination of a program may take, a definitive intentional transfer of responsibility to community-level clients is among the rarest. Ordinarily the required reports should be of a nature that calls for further appropriations and an ongoing program. Program maintenance, the minimal objective of the institutional imperative, calls for reinforcing dependency. Likewise most consultants who claim expertise in management or technical skills are in the business of marketing those skills for money, often big money, and they are not likely to be interested in building local capacity against which they would have to compete for further contracts. Even the nonexpert, serving in a not-for-profit capacity, who has set out from the beginning to train counterparts and work himself out of a job, will often find it stressful to acknowledge that he is no longer needed and to turn his pet project over to others.

Finally, for the project manager with layers of supervisors to report to, the worst possible outcome—the development most threatening to his career—is for things to get out of control. For the client community, though, "getting out of control" is the very essence of empowerment.

The control of individual projects by bureaucrats and consultants, especially foreign ones, may result in completed projects, but it is not likely to result in the enhancement of local capacity. Nor is it likely to produce results that are well attuned to local needs. An experience of former Peace Corps volunteer Chris Searles in Swaziland in the 1970s highlights the problem. The Mbabane Urban Extension Project, to which he was assigned, involved physical and policy planning for a squatter slum with a population of about 14,000. The plans to be produced were to address land use, roads, water, sewer, and community facilities.

The expatriate-dominated project team included a U.S. architect, a South African planning firm, and a British-based multinational engineering firm. The team failed utterly to adjust plans and procedures to the local context. The master plan that was drawn up called for the strict land-use zoning common in the industrialized West, but lacking any traditional or legal basis in Swaziland, where even the concept of private property was alien. Not only did the project fail to build local capacity, but it failed even to produce a usable product. The $30,000 plan was simply discarded.

Similarly in Tunisia in 1987, in the same scorched area, on the fringes of the Sahara, where the troglodytes (cave dwellers) have for centuries found relief from the relentless heat in their naturally cooled underground dwellings, I was shown a cinder-block housing development erected in the 1970s and funded, in part, by USAID. The development simmers unoccupied in the blistering sun—an instant ruin, a monument to the arrogance of the experts who are unwilling or unable to learn from the people they would serve.

Partnership programs, a solution of the 1990s to the perennial tendency to build dependencies rather than helping people to escape them, have generated a problem of their own. In funding Third World NGOs directly, rather than through umbrella organizations in the First World, experts serving the major donors felt that they were nurturing responsibility and accountability. But major donor support often forces changes in organizational structure that make the organization top heavy and vulnerable when the donor eventually pulls the plug. Reporting requirements make it necessary for the Third World NGO to hire its own high-priced experts—accountants, lawyers, and such. Such high overhead for professional personnel threatens spontaneity, entrepreneurialism, and creativity as well. Development programs that are stymied by institutional constraints, such as the need to maintain control, or by constraints of self-interest, such as hesitance to generate competing capacity or expertise, are likely also to suffer from paternalism.

Paradox No. 10: *Rural development is a process whereby affluent urban-dwellers teach poor peasants how to survive in the countryside without money.* All development programs and agencies are to some extent paternalistic.

The worst that might be said of a development agency is that it is paternalistic. All agencies, even religious, service, and charity groups, consider themselves to have been transformed since the 1960s or 1970s and say that they are not patronizing like the rest. But changing rhetoric is one thing; changing behavior patterns, particularly institutional and bureaucratic ones, is quite another.

Development specialists, for the most part, are loath to acknowledge the traces of arrogance in the operations of their own agencies but are highly sensitive to the insensitivities of other agencies. Several administrators and field agents have pointed out to me the tendency of developmentalists (in other agencies, of course) to speak to peasants in professional jargon they could not be expected to understand or to speak down to them, as if they were children. This problem was impressed on me in a personally embarrassing way in a small village in Ecuador's highland province of Chimborazo, where I appeared with the provincial director of a highly reputable development agency before a group of campesinos. He introduced me and said that "*la doctorita*" is here to find out "if you are disposed to develop yourselves or if you are apathetic and lazy like your grandparents."

Distinguishing between *desarrollo* (development) and *desarrollismo* (developmentism), Monseñor Leonidas Proaño, bishop of Riobamba, said that *desarrollismo* is paternalistic. It presumes to promote change without asking the people what they need, without building on their own experience, without involving them and allowing them to take initiatives.

By way of illustration, he cited a project of the Andean Mission in a village in Chimborazo. Mission representatives arrived one day with two big healthy rams. They rounded up the villagers and asked them to bring some of their own scrawny rams for comparison. They then told the villagers that they should take the healthy rams on loan and breed them. Villagers later told the bishop that had they been consulted they would have told the mission representatives that the healthy rams would die because the area lacked water and good grazing land.

By contrast, Proaño said, *desarrollo* is above all development of the person—of his ability to think, to decide, to invest. Beneficiaries must be the subjects of their own development.

Proaño noted that traditionally the Catholic church has stressed hierarchy and ritualism. The faithful were expected simply to do as they were told. Several international conferences, however, including those at Medellín, Colombia, in 1968, and at Puebla, Mexico, in 1979, have stressed the role of the Church as a community. When he first came to Riobamba in the early 1950s, Proaño said, he found the Indians—under a system of near slavery—greatly intimidated, afraid to speak to the *patrón* (landlord), to government officials, to any non-Indian, much less to a bishop. Now they are discovering that they can express themselves without fear. But true liberation from exploitation, social marginalization, and deculturation is far from being realized. Indians, he said, are still expected to go to the back of the bus.

Intimidation, of course, is the flip side of paternalism. Thus Pedro Chango, president of a Catholic student organization in Chimborazo with chapters in thirty communities, said that the primary function of his organization is consciousness-raising: instilling self-confidence and inspiring self-expression.

Among the perennial obstacles to development in the Sierra, according to Raúl do Valle, a Brazilian World Bank economist on loan to the Ecuadorean government in the early 1980s, are development agents who do not know how to relate to communities and communities that do not know how to prioritize and present demands. Raúl Gangotena, executive director of the National Pre-investment Fund (FONAPRE), conceded that integrated rural development, which was such an important theme of the Hurtado government, remained little more than a theme. Bureaucrats, he said, have generally been unwilling or unable to bridge the cultural gap, to stimulate participation, or to respond to community initiatives. As a consequence, there were no mechanisms for involving supposed beneficiaries in the planning process, or even in implementation. At the same time, the bureaucrats were unable to carry out even the simplest projects, such as the building of a school, without community participation. Thus the Indians, customarily suspicious and skeptical, for good historic reasons, saw the false starts and failures of the bureaucrats as confirmation of their skepticism.

Another problem closely related to paternalism is that of ethnocentricity. Carlos Moreno, director of the Education Ministry's literacy campaign in Chimborazo, told of a UNESCO pilot project in literacy in the early 1970s that failed miserably because its imagery was utterly alien to life in the Andean highlands. The image representing the word "mama," for example, was a tall thin blond in Western dress. Pedro Bagua, an Indian leader in Chimborazo's predominantly evangelical canton of Colta, commented that along with all the programs designed to teach Indians about non-Indian culture, there should be a program to teach non-Indians—at least those involved in development—about Indian culture.

The supposedly unsophisticated may, of course, have a great deal more to teach the cosmopolitan than the mysteries of their cultures. N. Cristescu, rector of the University of Bucharest, told the author of an occasion in the late 1980s when his car developed problems as he was driving in the vicinity of the Romanian village of Bragadiru. At the village mechanic's shop where his car was being fixed, he found that ordinary car engines that ran on gasoline were being converted to use diesel fuel, which was cheaper and, in Romania, easier to filch from government supplies. Cristescu said that he mentioned the incident later to European scientists who allowed that such conversion was not possible. "Not possible," perhaps, for his scientifically trained friends, Cristescu said, but it was being done very successfully in a remote Romanian village.

In a similar vein, David Korten reported that engineers of the Philippine's National Irrigation Administration (NIA), in the Laru Project, received more advice from local farmers than they really wanted. The project proposed to strengthen the NIA's capacity to work with communally owned and operated gravity-fed irrigation systems, but project engineers were dismayed to find that local farmers objected strongly to the materials they chose for dam construction. The farmers won a Pyrrhic victory when the dam, constructed over their objections to the engineers' specifications, washed out soon after completion.[2]

Once again in the 1990s, fashion was dictating the promotion of community participation, the involvement of the community in the assessment of needs and the planning of projects as well as in implementation. But for the largest bilateral and multilateral funding agencies, accustomed to dropping projects and money in the manner of high altitude bombers, participation is likely to mean, at most, allowing a "focus group" to express itself on the merits of projects preordained in broad outline in faraway offices or patching a popular but minor project onto a much larger one, the local benefits of which are less apparent, in order to implicate or pacify the affected community.

Phil Moeller, a consultant with the World Bank and other agencies for some three decades, says that participatory methodologies practiced by NGOs had finally filtered up to some of the major donors in the 1990s. They were being incorporated systematically into training programs and applied in fieldwork. When Moeller met with peasant leaders in Chinese villages on behalf of the Asian Development Bank (ADB), he found that farmers in the area had no interest in the freeways for which the Chinese government sought funding; instead, the farmers were very much interested in rural roads, particularly leading from village gates to all-weather roads. Thus the ADB factored $10 million for rural roads into a $150 million freeway project.[3] It might be argued, however, that the allocation responding to peasant needs was tokensim, serving to justify the larger sums allocated without pretense of participation.

Participation may also be achieved by a major donor through buying into a program or project already in operation, catalyzed perhaps by foreign or local NGOs. Indeed, for most kinds of projects, building and supporting existing organizations and efforts is generally more responsible and conducive to sustainability than starting from scratch organizing and perhaps competing with and undermining existing capacity. There is a fine line, however, between supporting and controlling, and donor agencies all too readily, regardless of good intentions, slip to the wrong side of that line. Donor agencies need success stories to report to their benefactors, and there is always a temptation to absorb and lay claim to a demonstrably vibrant program. I was told, for example, of a highly successful World Bank biodiversity program in the Ukraine. It was already successful, however, more so from the perspective of its organizers and more attuned to local realities, before the World Bank moved in and took over.

Paradox No. 11: *The more important an agency's mission and the more efficient its performance, the sooner it will be suppressed.* If an agency with an important mission, like land reform, has any success at all, it will generate a reaction from the privileged classes. If it has no success, it will lose credibility among its supposed beneficiaries. Worse still, it is to be expected that such agencies will generate reaction and lose credibility with beneficiaries at the same time.

As a rule, the fate of a state development agency is much like that of a progressive presidency: The longer it has been in existence, the less effective it will be. Furthermore, each new government naturally wants to leave its own mark on the bureaucracy and has little incentive to strengthen the programs of previous governments. Thus new governments and external funding sources will begin to cultivate new agencies.

But old agencies never die; they only appear to be dead. They slump into a low profile. Enough is retained in the budget for paying the salaries of bureaucrats but not enough for fulfilling their missions. Thus the professionals with the most initiative (or perhaps the most ambition) move to the new agencies or to the private sector, and the rest remain, demoralized and less productive.

In Ecuador, by the beginning of the 1980s, initiative and support had become concentrated in a few relatively new agencies, like the Secretariat for Integrated Rural Development (SEDRI), National Preinvestment Fund (FONAPRE), and the Development Fund for the Marginal Rural Sector (FODERUMA), and in the Education Ministry's literacy campaign. Agencies like the Agrarian Reform Institute (IERAC), and even the all-encompassing Ministry of Agriculture and Ranching (MAG), had become encrusted, defensive bureaucracies. For the latter agencies, budget problems were getting worse every year. When I left the office of IERAC in Santo Domingo in mid-1982, I wanted to call a taxi, but that wasn't possible; the office's telephone service had been cut for failure to pay the bill.

FONAPRE, an offspring and technically a dependency of the National Development Council (CONADE), was created in the early 1970s through a grant from the Inter-American Development Bank (IDB). Its pivotal role was that of conducting feasibility studies for all categories of public investment, including government contracts with private firms and with foreign and international banks and agencies.

Representatives of FODERUMA, established in 1978 as the development arm of the Central Bank, sat on a permanent committee with SEDRI and MAG. Other rural development committees, involving additional agencies, were formed on a project basis. Obviously, as Políbio Córdoba, of the Central Bank, pointed out, where FODERUMA was involved, it had the last word because it controlled the money. But SEDRI, established in 1980, soon came to occupy center stage. It was designed by CONADE largely as a means of circumventing the Ministry of Agriculture. Its director, Fausto Jordan, acted, for most purposes, as the Hurtado government's minister of development.

SEDRI's major functions were those of designing projects, soliciting external funding—primarily from USAID, IDB, and the World Bank—and coordinating the efforts of other agencies and ministries. Jorge Andrade, a SEDRI official in the Santo Domingo zone, noted that the various ministries were far from pleased to relinquish authority, initiative, and even budget to another bureaucratic entity.

Relations between SEDRI and IERAC were particularly cool. A few years earlier IERAC had been the agency with authority, initiative, and money, and with enthusiastic employees. By the early 1980s IERAC had lost its sense of mission; its function, Andrade said, had become technical rather than social. IERAC Project Director Marcelo Torres said IERAC had been paralyzed by lack of government support for its mission. Officials of SEDRI had chosen in general to view integrated rural development as a follow-up to the structural change of agrarian reform already carried out by IERAC. IERAC officials, however, saw it differently. They believed that IERAC had been intentionally weakened by successive governments in response to pressure from landowners. And they viewed the work of SEDRI as a nonstructural, noncontroversial alternative to agrarian reform—the way of least resistance.

IERAC officials in Chimborazo complained that they were expected to serve 100 communities with three professionals and two vehicles, and they had to beg for money for gas. Attempts to redistribute land usually got tied up in courts for several years. If they were ultimately successful, IERAC had to pay the landowners in cash, whereas the peasants bought the land from IERAC over a five-to ten-year period. Thus, a transaction on a single hacienda might absorb a large proportion of IERAC's budget—a powerful disincentive to aggressive discharge of the agency's mandate.

In the Santo Domingo zone, IERAC's task of surveying the land and issuing titles had been immensely complicated by spontaneous colonization, and IERAC had often been blamed for the ensuing chaos. Colonizers were entitled to claim only cultivated areas, and IERAC could sell to squatters if original claimants were not cultivating the land adequately. But as in the Sierra, well-connected landowners usually got their way in court. Amidst the chaos, said Estrella Velez, IERAC director for the Santo Domingo zone, IERAC had found it virtually impossible to regulate the size and shape of plots or to insist on soil conservation, reforestation, or other ecologically sound practices. Lacking the budget and personnel for follow-up technical assistance, IERAC referred peasants with newly acquired land to its stepparent, MAG; but MAG was inclined simply to refer them back to IERAC.

MAG was in a sense the pariah of the Ecuadorean bureaucracy. From intellectuals, political leaders, development professionals, peasants, even from its own personnel, it was rare to hear an appreciative word about the ministry. A former MAG official at the vice-ministerial level commented that the ministry could disappear overnight and the country would never notice—despite the fact that, in principle, MAG's authority and responsibilities were enormous. In many rural areas, at least for purposes of implementation, MAG was the government. Its role, or potential role, was eminently political. Among other things, for example, it was required to oversee elections for the officers of all co-ops and *comunas*.

While younger and smaller agencies could be characterized as having a sense of mission, or a sense of mission lost, MAG was too old and too big for any such characterization. Within MAG there was considerable friction and competition, most of it derived from differing regional or methodological orientations. Roque Alvarez, director of MAG's *Desarrollo Campesino* (Rural Development) program in Chimborazo, observed, for example, that MAG technicians who served the northern coast tended to defend the interests of agribusiness while those in the Sierra were more likely to be sympathetic with the peasants. For the most part, however, MAG's reputation derived from those bureaucrats who were viewed—rightly or wrongly—as serving their own interests, and in general the ministry was held in low regard by landowners and peasants alike.

MAG employees were said to treat their jobs as sinecures rather than as opportunities for service. Worse yet, in the Santo Domingo zone, accounts of corruption were rife. Pepe Aguilar, director of the MAG office for that zone, felt that the ministry's reputation was undeserved. The government's development programs, he said, were unintegrated and inadequate. Foreign and domestic development funds were being channeled into isolated projects, like those of SEDRI and FODERUMA, *"lunares en la cara de la pobreza"* (moles on the face of poverty), while MAG's provincial offices, which had to deal with all the rest, were understaffed and underpaid. "We are left," he said, "with overwhelming responsibilities and no resources."

Paradox No. 12: *Sophistication in development processes is acquired and program continuity maintained not by donor institutions but by client organizations and individuals.* Objectives and approaches of major international agencies and of state agencies of First World and Third are adjusted in accordance with shifts in elite political climate rather than in response to experience or outcomes in client states or communities.

Since the productive life of a state development agency is very short, we see little there in the way of institutional learning. Nor is there much disposition in First World international agencies to learn from experience in the Third World; for policymakers of such agencies, it is far more important to stay attuned to policy trends in donor states. And the priorities of state agencies, in First World or Third, change somewhat with each change of administration. Nevertheless, there is continuity and there is learning.

Development, in theory as in practice, is a slave to fashion. The unpowerful of the Third World have seen wave after wave of First World development specialists seeking to do good or to do well. They have heard earnest admonitions to embrace change or stability, democracy or security, secularism or religion, nation building or community building, exploitation of resources or preservation of them.

Fashion in the post–Cold War 1990s was a product above all of Pax Capitalista—a passion for trade. Developing countries had become "emerging markets." Client states, collaborating businesses, and NGO contractees had become "partners" and "stakeholders." And people in need had become "customers," who were being urged to assume "ownership" of donor-funded projects.

Abrupt changes of philosophy and of objectives on the part of a foreign donor institution or of a state agency will have reverberations all the way down to community-level organizations or projects, but some threads of continuity may be retained despite the hardships and the odds. Returning to Santiago, Chile, in 1977, thirteen years after having served there as a Peace Corps volunteer, and four years after a particularly brutal military counterrevolution had destroyed most popular institutions, I found that *Techo,* one of the host-country organizations volunteers had worked with, had been "intervened"—taken over by the dictatorship to serve its own purposes.

It turned out, however, that all that had been taken over was the name, the physical assets, and perhaps the links with private and foreign funding sources. The people—shantytown dwellers who had been the institution's supposed beneficiaries and its raison d'être—were gone. *Techo's* most important organizational component, a garment production co-op, had simply slipped out from under the institutional umbrella, changed its name, and continued its operations.

The co-op had recently fallen on hard times, though. It might have maintained itself indefinitely without subsidy or technical assistance, but the utter lack of political standing and thus of legal protection was harder to withstand. When customer firms wrote bad checks or simply refused to pay for merchandise delivered, the co-op had no recourse. "In Chile now," the manager said, "there are no courts for poor people."

Much of the continuity throughout the Third World in the planning and execution of development programs must be credited to a growing body of development professionals—dedicated and enthusiastic individuals of the highest motivation and of great experience. These professionals—working locally or internationally—are not bureaucrats because they do not serve institutions or governments as such. They move freely between national and international organizations and between the public and private non-profit sectors. What they serve is the mystique of development, and they are the repositories of much of what has been learned about the process.

Charlie Reilly, who has devoted more than thirty years to development work through the Inter-American Foundation, the Inter-American Development Bank, and the Peace Corps, says most projects are demand driven, supply driven, or discourse driven. The participatory, or civil-society approach, he says, is discourse driven, but for more than forty years there has been more discourse than development on that track.

The half-full, as opposed to half-empty, side of that glass, however, is that while supply- and demand-driven projects flash and fade kaleidoscopically, the discourse of development as the inalienable right of the circumstantially disadvantaged and unpowerful to fulfill their individual and collective potential—in the manner that suits their strengths and purposes, encouraged and supported but not led or manipulated by outsiders—is one that will not die. It's an idea whose time comes around again and again, and even in the 1990s under cover of the pursuit of profit, the pursuit of justice had found niches in which to thrive. In fact, one of the reasons why bottom-up, people-centered, participatory development was in vogue again was that political developments in the 1990s had given voice to many of the same individuals who had been rolling that stone uphill since the 1960s.

Small, private, voluntary, or nonprofit development agencies tend to be more inventive and innovative than large public ones; the former are more likely to have the flexibility to experiment with new models and approaches. The existence of such private agencies is often precarious, and there may be little direct cooperation between public and private agencies, even though private agencies seek to influence public policy and public agencies stand to profit from the experimentation of private ones.

Nevertheless, continuity is often achieved through the process of absorption—not only of projects, but more importantly, of people. Individuals who have cut their professional teeth in the more competitive and innovative world of the nongovernmental agencies are a great resource to governments that aim to chart a new course. Projects initiated by foreign and international agencies may also be absorbed. USAID Director John Sanbrailo said that at least forty projects or organizations initiated by AID and its predecessor agencies had been adopted by the 1980s by the Ecuadorean government. A number of the Ecuadorean government's more resilient programs and dedicated development specialists were veterans of the Andean Mission, a multifaceted program launched by the International Labor Organization, with the participation of several other UN-affiliated agencies in Ecuador, Bolivia, and Peru in the mid-1950s.

Some of the more promising government programs have grown from the seeds of volunteer efforts. The Hurtado government's literacy campaign, for example, was new to the government, but it built upon many years of experimentation and learning. The country's first literacy program was launched by the Ecuadorean journalists' union in 1944 and was carried on, without financial support, until 1960. The Ministry of Education established a Department of Adult Education in 1960, but during the 1960s and early 1970s it undertook only a few isolated, poorly conceived, and poorly funded projects.

Meanwhile in the early 1970s, a group of unemployed professionals founded a voluntary association, the Volunteer Educational Service (SEV), to promote literacy training. The group was assisted by the University of Massachusetts, under contract with AID from 1970 to 1973 to put into use the philosophy and methodology of Paulo Freire. The Inter-American Foundation became involved in 1972 and, with continuing assistance from AID, carried on the program until 1976.

Carlos Moreno, one of the founders of SEV, joined the Ministry of Education in 1976. After the change of government in 1979 the ministry conducted an aggressive literacy campaign. Moreno directed the very successful program in Chimborazo, a program in which content and method were determined by the campesinos themselves. The commitment of the Ecuadorian government to literacy and to other essentials of grassroots development had waxed and waned over the course of the 1980s and 1990s as the pinnacles of power, such as they are, changed hands. But with ongoing assistance from the Inter-American Foundation, Moreno continued to serve the people of the Sierra. In the late 1990s, he was codirecting yet another grassroots service organization.[4]

Paradox No. 13: *In the Third World, there is a need for technicians who are less well trained.* For the most part, those who invest their time and money in acquiring professional status do not do so in order to work in muddy shoes.

In the early 1960s, acute shortages of the well-trained were common. Juan Bosch, former president of the Dominican Republic, told this author that in 1963 he was unable to find a single Dominican electrical engineer to head up his new state electrical corporation.[5] By the 1980s, in the Dominican Republic, as in much of the Third World, training in technical and professional fields often outstripped demand and resulted in the infamous "brain drain." (An UNCTAD report estimated that as early as 1970 the value of the trained manpower resources transferred to the United States from the Third World exceeded the entire U.S. nonmilitary foreign aid budget for that year.[6]) The problem remains, however, that professionals do not normally choose to work—much less to live—in uncomfortable surroundings among slum dwellers, urban squatters, or the rural poor.

Given the medical school requirement of one year of rural service and the national glut of doctors, there was no shortage of physicians, as such, in Ecuador's rural areas in the 1980s. But the doctors were reputedly ill prepared and disinclined to do the kind of work that was required among the rural poor. It is widely believed that trained nurses, of whom there was an acute shortage, would do a better job.

There should also be a greater effort to train indigenous peoples in medical fields. In the province of Chimborazo, which had the nation's highest proportion of Indians, there was only one physician in 1982 who was an Indian. Even though it would be most difficult to provide adequate medical care in the Sierra without personnel who speak Quechua, Carlos Moreno, director of the education ministry's literacy campaign in Chimborazo, reported that the efforts of his ministry to teach doctors on rural service a basic medical vocabulary in Quechua had been a failure. The doctors don't learn, he said, because they are not interested.

The same problem is readily noted in other fields: One need not be an agronomist to help establish a cooperative, but one must have the patience to become acquainted with the community. Rural people customarily speak of the officials of the Ecuadorean Ministry of Agriculture as *"hombres sin piernas"* (men without legs) because, it is said, they never get out of their jeeps.

Although various foreign assistance programs still stress professional training, none of the development agents I consulted in Ecuador considered the lack of professional or technical training as such a significant problem. The problem among administrators, according to Raúl Gangotena, executive director of FONAPRE, was not so much lack of training as lack of sensitivity and motivation. As to would-be or should-be field agents, most of them simply are not. One development professional commented that MAG's agricultural extension program had always been carried out by Peace Corps volunteers. The Ecuadorean "counterparts" who should be taking over from the volunteers rarely even venture into the far-flung, sometimes nearly inaccessible, villages where the volunteers work. After more than twenty years of Peace Corps programs, MAG and other ministries that engaged in rural development seemed more dependent on the volunteers rather than less.

Many explanations have been offered for the reluctance of field agents to go to the field. Understaffing, underfunding, and bureaucratic inertia are among the most obvious. Racism and fear have also been suggested. Some agents have not bothered to conceal contempt for or exasperation with the Indians. Others have simply been fearful of venturing into Indian villages. One IERAC official commented that the highland Indians were inscrutable; they would welcome you to the village, she said, then block the road and burn your car.

Another explanation is early burnout. A Peace Corps volunteer who said he had spent most of his time "being stood-up by MAG" observed that MAG employees who are assigned to extension work in peasant communities usually get less done and become discouraged more quickly than do those in other types of assignments. Tasks in the field are difficult to define and success is hard to measure. It is easy to understand how even those who begin their work with great enthusiasm might conclude after a few years that, as a MAG soil engineer told me, "the campesinos are not interested in development; they don't want to learn." It seems likely, however, that when bureaucrats see such apathy they are gazing at a mirror image.

In the final analysis, the career and lifestyle ambitions of Ecuadorean professionals are no different from those of professionals elsewhere. For the university trained, working in muddy shoes simply does not represent the pinnacle of a career, nor does it appear to be the fast track to the pinnacle. The well-trained are hardly to be blamed for wanting to live well. But surely there are those who would find a lesser degree of training, a less-than-professional salary, and the opportunity to serve a privilege. In this, the literacy campaign may have blazed a trail. It has had outstanding success in training indigenous peoples to work in their own communities.

Technical training has become a major component of most rural development programs worldwide. Bill Douglas, a former Peace Corps volunteer in Nepal and in the 1980s a USAID officer in Kathmandu, maintained, however, that such training has created almost as many problems in Nepal as it has solved. The most highly trained are reluctant to work in the countryside, while middle-level training of villagers tends to raise their ambitions and cause them to leave their own villages. Furthermore, Douglas said, when Nepalese receive their development training outside the country or from foreigners, they learn the concepts and the jargon of development professionals, and their own local perspectives are lost or suppressed; they even find it difficult to communicate with their own people.[7]

> Paradox No. 14: *Distance unites.* Exploitation and racial and class discrimination may well be built into national and international systems, but the expression of these evils with which the poor must live on a daily basis is local. Thus, a requirement for changing traditional relationships may be the intervention of agents who are not local.

It seems well enough recognized as we approach a new millennium that our planetary mobile home is a small and crowded one and that, if distance does not protect us from other peoples' wars, diseases, ecological disasters, and financial meltdowns, then for our own sakes we dare not let distance limit our concerns. Moreover, globalization of markets has meant globalization of economic policy-making and thus of job insecurity and community vulnerability. Common interest has more to do now with class and sector, gender and generation, than with geopolitics; thus organization and networking must as well.

If leaders of government, multilateral institutions, business, and banking are to gather regularly in intergalactic summits, like those meeting in Davos, Switzerland, in the 1990s, NGO leaders, promoting development for the benefit of the unpowerful, have no choice but to follow suit. But those who would represent the humble at the global level cannot reach the podium without standing on the shoulders of millions who are active in their own communities. And community activists are intolerably vulnerable unless they are seen as enjoying the support of a broader network.

In the pursuit of grass-roots development, there has always been a need for the "outside agitator." In modern times, change agents—who perhaps have new ideas and skills but, more importantly, have external linkages—have included missionaries, immigrants, trade unionists, university students, and more recently NGO and development agency volunteers.

It is no accident that those development agents who have the will to live among the rural poor and who, for the most part, are accepted by them are so often young foreigners. Foreigners, and particularly young ones, are able to cross the lines of class in a manner that would be far more difficult for nationals (or for the same young foreigners in their own countries). In this sense distance unites. By the same token, at least until recently it has been easier for Indians of the Sierra, for example, to deal with national officials in Quito than with local or cantonal officials.

Furthermore, there needs to be a bridge between campesinos and development agencies that have the resources but neither the contacts with nor the confidence of the people. For now, these foreign volunteers living in rural villages are practically the only agents who have the ability and the will to serve as such a bridge.

The arguments against using foreigners, particularly from the United States, in national development programs in the Third World are many and often sound. But the most obvious and most common argument—that Peace Corps volunteers are, after all, agents of a neocolonial power and of the particular administration that happens to be in office—probably is not sound, except in the most narrow sense.

While some U.S. administrations, particularly that of Richard Nixon, have attempted to suppress the Peace Corps or to change drastically its functions, the Peace Corps as a whole appears to have changed little in approach and objectives since its course was first charted by Sargent Shriver. That is probably due in no small measure to the large proportion of midlevel contemporary Peace Corps officials who were among the founding generation of volunteers. Thus the programs of the Peace Corps in many countries even in the 1980s were more nearly reflective of a Kennedy administration than of a Reagan one.

Beyond that, however, it is arguable that Peace Corps volunteers are not, in practice, agents of anyone other than themselves. Like other kinds of "field agents," they tend to become "free agents"; that is, their performance in the field is determined in greater measure by their own imaginations and value systems and by their own personal interpretations of what their roles should be than by the objectives of funding or supervisory agencies.

A common complaint by Peace Corps and host country supervisors about the volunteers is that they tend to "do their own thing." Volunteers freely admit that is the case, and in general, "their own thing" has meant doing more rather than less—abandoning agencies that served middle-class interests to work with the poorest of the poor, shunning routine bu-reaucratic roles for mobilizational ones, organizing and enabling com-munities to bring pressure to bear on foot-dragging bureaucracies or elected officials, and denouncing corruption.

Most of the several dozen volunteers who participated, through inter-views or questionnaires, in a survey this author conducted in Ecuador in 1982 said or implied that when they perceived differences between the objectives, wishes, or demands upon them of Peace Corps supervisors, host agency supervisors, and residents of their communities, they would be most likely to respond to their communities.[8] Further observations have convinced me that the more complex the superstructure of supervi-sory agencies, the more leverage is available to the field agent. The more leverage available to the field agent and the more intense and prolonged the contact between agent and beneficiary community, the more closely the project will respond to the aspirations of that community rather than to the objectives of the sponsoring bureaucracies.

Paradox No. 15: *In the land of the blind, the one-eyed man is a subversive.* Know-ing too much or caring too much in modern and traditional societies alike is apt to make one an "enemy of the people."

Killing the messenger is an old and honored tradition. At the very least, the telling of unpopular truths may make one a social pariah; and in the development business, the agent who insists on allowing the real world to encroach on a program designed to meet the needs of the official world may soon find himself unemployed. In development work, however, the paradox takes on additional meanings.

Simply informing underprivileged populations of their rights and urg-ing them to seek redress are likely to subject them to new dangers. In fact, if a solution that seems obvious to the development agent is not being tried, it may well be because locals are aware of dangers to which the nonlocal agent is oblivious. After all, to elites whose insecurity is exag-gerated by the enormity of what they have to lose (e.g., El Salvador's "fourteen families"), it matters little whether those who seek to enhance the bargaining position of the poor are motivated by goals that might be designated developmental rather than revolutionary.

A redistribution of goods or benefits on any basis other than charity (that is, on any basis that challenges rather than reinforces preexisting power relationships) will be threatening to elites. Dom Helder Camara, archbishop of Olinda and Recife and spiritual leader in the 1960s of the opposition to Brazil's military dictatorship, said of his country's ruling elite, "When I feed the hungry, they call me a saint. When I ask why they are hungry, they call me a Communist."

One of the advantages of involving nonlocals in the development process is that whether such agents represent foreign governments, international organizations, or national institutions, such as the Church or the national university, they will probably be less vulnerable than members of a local underclass to reprisal by landlords or other local elites. Their links to nonlocal institutions would normally offer them at least a modicum of security. Furthermore, even if they remain very vulnerable indeed, the odds are that they will be relatively oblivious to such risk. In this sense, then, ignorance may really be bliss.

In India's rural areas, minimum-wage laws are rarely enforced. Peasants do not have the time, information, or resources to take landlords to court. Nor is the government prepared to take on the new roles that would be necessary if the legislation were to be made effective. In general, the issue is joined only when outsiders, most often university students, assist in educating and organizing the peasants. Even then, success is by no means ensured, and the price of failure may be high. Landowner reprisal against reform-mongering has often been swift and brutal.

When nonlocal agents, however, become aware of risks—for example, after underclass mobilization has generated fear and anger among elites—they may pull out, leaving locals even more exposed and vulnerable. In many areas that have seen strife, locals are keenly aware of this potential sequence of events and thus less than receptive to the message of the well-meaning but naïve or uninformed development agent. Nevertheless, the seasoned development agent has a responsibility to take such vulnerabilities into account, to discuss them fully and straightforwardly with client communities, and to subject clients to no more risk than the agent and his nonlocal colleagues are prepared to take.

There are some, of course, who with their eyes wide open choose to invest their prestige and external connections in an effort to lend support and protection to peoples already endangered. Renowned poet Ken Saro-Wiwa was well aware of the likely reprisals for calling attention to the contamination of his homeland by the operations of Shell Oil Company in the Niger River Delta in Nigeria. Saro-Wiwa and eight other Ogoni community leaders were executed by Nigeria's military government in 1995. Likewise Archbishop Oscar Romero, assassinated in 1980 for his outspoken commitment to the poor of El Salvador, and Monsignor Juan Gerardi, auxiliary bishop and head of the Guatemalan archbishopric's human rights bureau, assassinated in 1998, had good reason to know that a meaningful life is the kind you get crucified for.

Monsignor Gerardi was murdered two days after he published a fourteen-hundred-page report, *Guatemala: Never Again*. He had seen the report, which estimated that Guatemala's long "dirty war"—a war essentially of the army against the indigenous people—that left 150,000 dead,

50,000 disappeared, and more than a million displaced and dispossessed, as a step in the "retrieval of the collective memory." "The truth hurts," he said in presenting the report, "but it is necessary."[9]

In countries now undergoing reconciliation, it appears that a great many people prefer not to revisit the awful past, not to acknowledge cognizance as to why and how it came about and who was responsible. But a reconciliation without atonement is a reconciliation of the privileged and the wretched, the armed and the unarmed, the abusers and the abused. Where perpetrators of atrocities enjoy impunity, free even of open condemnation of their misdeeds, whole populations are left in a state of suppressed anxiety, a state hardly conducive to the participatory underpinning of democracy and development.

There is a final possibility that should be mentioned. Given the fact that the motives of external donors and/or of host governments may be less than forthrightly stated, the field agent who takes seriously the publicly stated goals of a development project (i.e., community organization for self-help) may on occasion find himself isolated. If the field agent pursues a strategy of empowerment when the donor's purpose was actually pacification or control, the agent may find his project being sabotaged by his own supervisors or by other agencies of his own government or the host country government from which he had expected support.

Moreover, the development specialist, or field agent, may find that the information or skills he is expected to pass on to host country authorities or counterparts are likely to be used in a manner utterly at odds with his own objectives or the stated purposes of the program. In such a case, he may find it necessary to redefine his own role or to sabotage his own project.

A Peace Corps volunteer working in the public administration program in Monrovia, capital of the West African state of Liberia, in the late 1960s said, "Look, the fellow I'm working for is a crook; that's all there is to it. Here I am teaching him modern methods of administration and accounting. What do you do when you make that kind of person more efficient? You teach him how to steal more money, that's what."[10]

Notes

1. This exchange took place in the classroom of Political Science Professor Martin C. Needler at the University of Michigan in 1963.

2. David C. Korten, "Rural Development Programming: The Learning Process Approach," chap. 18 in David C. Korten and Rudi Klauss, eds., *People-Centered Development* (West Hartford, Conn.: Kumarian Press, 1984).

3. Conversation with Phil Moeller, Washington, D.C., March 18, 1998.

4. The Inter-American Foundation is one of the few U.S. agencies that might be considered a "learning organization." It has made a point of learning from its mistakes as well as from its achievements. Its staff members have formed a strong

bond to defend the essence of the institution against political tides that threatened to wash it away, and like veterans of Peace Corps service, its field-tested professionals have sought to infect larger and more bureaucratic agencies with their passion for empowerment.

5. Former President Juan Bosch, personal interview, Santo Domingo, January 12, 1988.

6. Tony Barnett, *Social and Economic Development* (New York: Guilford Press, 1989), p. 214.

7. William Douglas, USAID, Nepal, personal interview, Kathmandu, July 8, 1983.

8. Of the seventeen volunteers who sent me completed questionnaires, eight said they would respond first to their Ecuadorean communities, two to their own judgment or conscience, three to Peace Corps supervisors, two to host agency supervisors, and two did not know to whom they would respond.

9. Bertrand de la Grange, "Right Blamed for Guatemala Bishop's Killing," *Manchester Guardian Weekly*, May 10, 1998, p. 15.1.

10. Efrem J. Sigel, "The Peace Corps As a Development Service," *International Development Review* 10, no. 1 (10th Anniversary Issue), March 1968, pp. 34–38.

Suggested Readings

Bates, R., "People in Villages: Micro-Level Studies in Political Economy," *World Politics* 31, 1978, pp. 129–149.

Bryant, Coralie, and Louise G. White, *Managing Rural Development: Peasant Participation in Rural Development* (West Hartford, Conn.: Kumarian Press, 1980).

Burbidge, John, *Beyond Prince and Merchant: Citizen Participation and the Rise of Civil Society* (New York: PACT Publications, 1997).

Chambers, Robert, *Managing Rural Development* (New York: Holmes and Meier, 1974).

Gorman, Robert F., ed., *Private Voluntary Organizations as Agents of Development* (Boulder: Westview Press, 1984).

Hancock, Graham, *Lords of Poverty: The Free-Wheeling Lifestyles, Power, Prestige, and Corruption of the Multi-Billion Dollar Aid Business* (London: Macmillan Press, Ltd., 1989).

Heginbotham, Stanley, *Cultures in Conflict* (New York: Columbia University Press, 1975).

Hirschman, Albert O., *Development Projects Observed* (Washington, D.C.: Brookings Institution, 1967).

Hyman, Eric L., "Making Foreign Aid More Relevant and Effective Through a Small-Scale Producers Strategy," *Journal of Environment and Development* 2, no. 2, summer 1993, pp. **TK–TK.**

Jedlicka, A., *Organization for Rural Development: Risk-Taking and Appropriate Technology* (New York: Praeger, 1977).

Korten, David, "Community Organization and Rural Development: A Learning Process Approach," *Public Administration Review* 40, September–October 1980, pp. 480–512.

Nelson, J., *Access to Power: Politics and the Urban Poor in Developing Nations* (Princeton: Princeton University Press, 1979).

Reeves, T. Zane, *The Politics of the Peace Corps and Vista* (Tuscaloosa: University of Alabama Press, 1988).

Riddell, Roger, "Grassroots Participation and the Role of NGOs," background paper, United Nations Development Program, New York, 1992.

Scanlon, Thomas J., *Waiting for the Snow: The Peace Corps Papers of a Charter Volunteer* (Chevy Chase, Md.: Posterity Press, 1997).

Tendler, Judith, *Turning Private Voluntary Organizations into Development Agencies: Questions for Evaluation* (Washington, D.C.: Agency for International Development, April 1982).

Wynia, Gary, *Politics and Planners: Economic Policy in Central America* (Madison: University of Wisconsin Press, 1972).

15   *On Motives and Consequences*

We have seen that development professionals and field agents are sometimes overcome by a feeling of helplessness. They may find that the priorities of their supervisors deviate greatly from the professed mission of the agency, or that their own projects appear to be veering off in a direction that was never anticipated. In fact, the process of development, involving a complex interplay of interests and motives and impersonal forces, has many authors and many points of departure.

Outcomes reflect far more than any particular identifiable set of motives. For development professionals, as for community leaders, such complexity is sure to mean frequent bouts with disappointment and failure. But it also means opportunity; and what looks at one point like failure may be merely a pause, or a new staging area for a better calculated assault against the barricades.

> Paradox No. 16: *There is no such thing as a system that doesn't work. Every system works for somebody.*

At least in the United States, and more recently in other donor states, budgeting exercises inevitably mean that development assistance will come under assault. The most common argument for slashing development aid is that it does not work—that is, that it does not serve to eradicate poverty, raise standards of living, or move people from welfare or other dependency to positions of self-sufficiency. But it often turns out that those who on the outside have been most critical of development assistance, like President Ronald Reagan and his Republican colleagues, are quick to expand it once they are in decision-making positions. The same might be said, of course, of many other targets of opprobrium, such as fiscal deficits.

Systems often fail, year after year, even decade after decade, to serve the interests or meet the goals that were their ostensible raison d'être. But that does not mean they are serving no interests. Relationships, activities, and expenditures would not form a pattern and ultimately an enduring system if they did not serve interests. If a system, then, does not appear to serve its purported interests, it behooves us to ask whose interests are being served.

As noted earlier, USAID literature during the Reagan administration highlighted the fact that some 70 percent of the aid supposedly intended for Third World development was spent in the United States for goods and services. In the late 1990s, defense of U.S. development assistance before a wary Congress stressed its advantages in the promotion of U.S. trade. Other bilateral donors may be less crass about it, but all to some degree use the system to promote business interests. Of course, development assistance in some times and places also serves the interests of the indigent, but it would not have become the mammoth and enduring system that it is were it not serving elite interests as well.

Many systems serve a variety of interests. In fact, the most enduring ones are probably those to which many categories of actors stake some claim and which are available for co-optation or expropriation when power balances shift. The supposed agenda setters or beneficiaries are often preempted, but the fact that there are unmet expectations and diversions from stated goals gives the would-be beneficiaries some leverage where and when the time is right.

Contrary to its projected image, the World Bank is not a philanthropic institution. It is a bank, and like most banks it normally serves the interest of a power elite. In the late 1990s, however, it finds itself being marginalized by those it served so well. Having served, along with the IMF and other multilateral and bilateral institutions, to leverage national policy changes over the course of two decades that made direct foreign investment easier and more profitable, it now finds itself sidelined. Lending at scarcely half of capacity, bypassed by some 97 percent of the capital flows to developing countries, and unable to collect on its loans to the poorest countries, the bank has begun to shore up its public image, badly battered at least among Third World-focused NGOs, by calling attention once again to the perils of poverty. We are entitled to hope that for a while this will mean a redirection of funding as well as a refinement of discourse. It may be, though, that the poverty the bank is concerned about is its own.

While a high profile campaign, Jubilee 2000, is being waged by the British Council of Churches, Christian Aid, and a great many other large and small NGOs in the United Kingdom in support of debt "forgiveness" for the poorest countries, the multilateral banks are calling for debt "relief." There is an appealingly pristine simplicity to the proposition; it would cut out the middleman—that is, the essentially bankrupt Third World government—saving time and red tape while saving said government from having to make agonizing decisions. Instead of passing funds from First World taxpayers (mainly limited now to wage and salary employees) to governments of developing countries on the condition that they service debts, it would pass the funds directly from First World tax-payers, or more cynically yet, from charitable donors, to the banks. In effect, it would amount to a hijacking of funds that should otherwise be allocated to development or humanitarian assistance to cover debts that would otherwise have to be written off.[1]

Even where development and relief or humanitarian assistance programs are genuinely and unambiguously intended to benefit the most destitute, they often find themselves embedded in symbiotic fashion in a larger system in which they have little leverage—the very systems, in many cases, that are generating the wars and famines and displacement and otherwise intolerable conditions to which they are responding.

On a beach-fringed green-carpeted inlet of one of Hong Kong's many beautiful bays, the Whitehead Detention Camp squats like an intentional offense against nature. In the early 1990s, before the forcible deportations got underway, it contained some twenty-four thousand Vietnamese boat people. There was no ambiguity about the purpose of the camp—no pretense of relief or charity or even of Communist-style "reeducation." It was straightforwardly a detention camp, a maximum security facility, run by the colony's corrections department.

The few TV sets, soccer balls, and other sources of distraction in the camp had to be supplied by charity or relief organizations. Under the umbrella of the United Nations High Commission for Refugees (UN-HCR), such organizations, both local and transnational, offered a modicum of health care, psychological counseling, adult education, and other social services, but their activities were restricted and closely monitored by corrections authorities. (Until 1990 even the teaching of English was forbidden. Authorities finally gave in after it became clear that prohibition was futile. Ever larger numbers of detainees were hiding books under their pillows and studying English by flashlight at night.)

Relief workers and organizations were not allowed to acquire a liaison function between prisoners and wardens, much less to represent individually or collectively the interests of inmates. The offenses most likely to cause an organization to be banned from the camp were talking to journalists and allowing photographs to be taken. The authorities knew all too well that in this case, even more than most, a picture would be worth a thousand words. The UNHCR once took a stand on behalf of the rights of inmates to post slogans demanding freedom, and a few of the Tiananmen Square-inspired statues of liberty, systematically pulled down earlier by authorities, had been erected again, but such expression was tolerated only so long as there were no media to play it up and transmit it.

The Catch-22 for those who cared enough to offer some services or amenities to the refugees was that they served only at the sufferance of correction authorities and they were unavoidably co-opted into the policing system. The UNHCR was expected to keep the organizations under its umbrella on a short leash. Likewise, administrators of relief organizations were obliged to rein in their volunteers. Even the volunteers had to be concerned about the limits beyond which action or free expression on the part of refugee clients would result in the termination of programs and the banning of agencies. Sooner or later everyone who worked directly with the refugees faced the dilemma of whether to act as a censor or to risk reprisals ultimately damaging to the people they were trying to help.

The UNHCR has been stretched to the limits over the last two decades, playing a crucial and sometimes heroic role in serving the needs of the most helpless and endangered. But those who would serve the most vulnerable sometimes, in effect, find themselves trapped by the vulnerability of their wards into helping to sustain a sinister system. On several occasions refugee camps run ostensibly by the UNHCR have been run in fact by guerrilla groups, warlords, or other categories of paramilitary forces. In the late 1970s and 1980s, for example, after the Vietnamese chased Pol Pot from power in Cambodia, the Khmer Rouge was able to use the main refugee center for Cambodians, just across the Thai border, as a resupply and staging area, a source for willing or unwilling recruits, and a captive population to "represent" when negotiations got underway.

Likewise, in the mid-1990s, deposed Hutu military and paramilitary leaders who had set off a wave of genocide in Rwanda were able to use UNHCR refugee camps in Zaire as a political and military base, terrorizing dissidents within the camps and staging raids back into Rwanda. UN High Commissioner Sadako Ogata in vain sought foreign military assistance to protect civilians. She ultimately hired the Presidential Guard of Zairean president Mobutu to provide security for the camps.

Fearing destabilization as a consequence of armed raids staged from the camps across the border, the now Tutsi-controlled government of Rwanda encouraged Laurent Kabila to lead a rebellion against the Mobutu government. As Mobutu was then using the camps as his staging area, Kabila felt free to pilfer supplies for his own forces from the UN agencies. In the end the UNHCR and other relief agencies stood by helplessly as the war was waged around them.[2] Fortunately, it was brief. Mobutu's demoralized forces were soon overcome by Kabila's, who renamed the country Congo.

Expenditures for disaster relief have mushroomed from a total in 1971 of about $200 million to $8 billion in 1994. UNHCR expenditures have risen from $544 million in 1990 to more than a billion each year since 1992. Relief agencies put more money into Africa now than does the World Bank. But while Western governments are willing to risk sending in relief agents (several hundred are killed each year), they are less willing to risk serious diplomacy and unwilling to risk troops. Caregivers thus regularly become suppliers and pawns in other people's dangerous games.

The low-intensity conflict (LIC) that has become the stereotypical face of war over the last two decades of the twentieth century has generated steady demand for relief efforts. But LIC is a poor fit with common definitions and understandings of war. Although effects inevitably spill over borders, LIC is essentially intra- rather than interstate, and it has less to do with the attainment of specific objectives than with system maintenance. The attendant suffering cannot be ignored, but real relief can begin only with the end of conflict.

In the Sudan, war has been the norm for all but about a decade of the last half of the twentieth century. The war, presented simplistically as between Muslim Arabic north and Christian Black-African south,[3] was prefigured by the carelessness of European colonialism, but it was reignited and sustained by the Cold War and has since acquired a momentum, or organic continuity, of its own. The switching loyalties of hegemons, as between the Khartoum government in the north and the Sudanese Popular Liberation Army (SPLA) rebels in the South, has made little difference to the victims.

The government in Khartoum, often unable to sustain the most basic services, has always managed to find the resources to arm its troops and, more importantly, its ethnically based militias in order to carry on the war against the south. Depopulation and famine are not merely by-products of war; they appear to be among the strategic objectives. Bombing, looting, and pillaging villages; stealing cattle; and burning crops in the same areas year after year maintains famine and steadily depopulates. It happens that the areas most often targeted for devastation are also the areas otherwise most valuable in terms of subsoil resources, including the petroleum in which Chevron has already expressed interest. Displaced farmers have no choice but to go in search of food, but relief agencies in a sense contribute to the depopulation, as the refugee camps and feeding stations they set up on the periphery of the targeted, richer areas serve as a draw to the desperate.

Meanwhile, famine has been beneficial to the larger-scale grain farmers, as scarcity keeps their prices high while the cost of labor drops.[4] Sudan has remained a grain exporter through almost two decades of recurrent famine. The exports are required for earning foreign exchange to service debt and to import arms.

Clare Short, British cabinet minister for international development, caused a stir in May 1998 when she suggested that the public was developing "compassion fatigue." She noted that while there had been an increase in recent years in humanitarian aid there had been a decrease in aid for development. "If it is all humanitarian," she said, "we are just going round in an endless cycle that never reaches a solution. The cycle is fantastically destructive."[5] Alberto Navarro, director of the European Community Humanitarian Office, countered that humanitarian and development efforts are two sides of the same coin, and he warned that frustration with the limitations of humanitarian aid must not lead to an emphasis on trade rather than aid. Indeed, even in the spring of 1998, as 350,000 Sudanese were said to be facing starvation, Sudanese grain was fattening cattle in Europe.

> Paradox No. 17: *The more important the decision, the fewer and less well informed will be those involved in making it.* Decisions viewed as most crucial to the system (e.g., war and peace)—or as most crucial to the fortunes of its leaders— will be made by those having general responsibility rather than by those having expertise on the issue.

Among the costliest decisions ever made have been those that have given shape to the modern mosaic of nation-states. Most such decisions have been made at the highest levels—by conquistadores and kings, by alien colonizers most likely unaware and most certainly unconcerned that in drawing frontiers they were cutting across tribal homelands and ancient kingdoms and giving rise to endless conflicts. Spanish and Portuguese rulers divided Latin America between them along an imaginary line drawn by a pope who had never set foot in the New World. The carving up of Asia and Africa by northern European empire builders was equally arbitrary, resulting in the erosion of preexisting political community and the fabrication of externally oriented economies. It remains difficult to travel from one national capital to another in Africa without going by way of London or Paris.

One would like to believe that such high-handed decisions, having dire consequences for so many, must be a thing of the past. Certainly the revolutionary technological advancements in transportation and communications, information gathering and processing, and the proliferation of agencies and institutions of education, research, and "intelligence," should make ignorance on the part of decision-makers less readily excusable. Furthermore, decision-making in most modern governments is formally structured so as to ensure power sharing and accountability. But the availability of good information and the mandating of socially accountable decision-making procedures by no means assures that they will be used. In fact, it is precisely when they are most needed—when the stakes are highest—that they are least likely to be used.

In the United States at the beginning of the 1980s, an administration determined for ideological and partisan reasons to seek military solutions to political and economic crises in Central America not only studiously avoided the counsel of nongovernmental specialists in the area but made a point of purging or reassigning State Department and other governmental area-specialists and replacing them with specialists in counterinsur-

gency and guerrilla warfare. Before the end of the decade, it had been revealed that Reagan's coterie, in pursuing the Iran-Contra affair, had defied and deceived the Congress as well. The effort so conceived and implemented involved the expenditure of billions of dollars, much of it
supposedly economic aid extended in the name of development; the upshot for the Central American states, however, was economic devastation
rather than development and the loss of more than 150,000 lives.

As indicated by the case of the U.S. role in Central America in the
1980s, one of the reasons why the most ambitious development programs—as measured by the money and manpower invested—fail so dramatically is that "development" may be only a cover for the pursuit of
crasser interests. But even where decision-makers have the general welfare in mind, the attachment of the highest priority to a program or project and/or the allocation to it of extraordinary sums generally means
that it will be tightly controlled from the top. Even where counsel is
sought from beyond the constricted circle of policy-makers—on highly
technical matters, for example—those consulted will sense a need to tai-
lor their reports to what they presume superiors want to hear.

Egypt's Aswan High Dam, planned with Western funding in the 1950s
and completed with Soviet funds and technical assistance in the 1960s,
was such a project. The effort to control an entire river basin system was
also to serve as a reaffirmation of Egyptian nationalism, as a means to regional hegemony, and as a pyramid of sorts, guaranteeing immortality to
its sponsor, Gamal Abd al-Nasser. The need to control flooding, to generate power for industry, to secure year-round navigation, and to regulate
water supplies so as to increase food production and fish catch had long
been recognized. But the urgency attached to the high dam project, due
in large part to national and international political considerations, ensured that preexisting studies and alternative plans for the development
of the Nile Basin would be ignored and drawbacks of the new project
would be underestimated. Nasser sought through the project to
strengthen his socialist movement by breaking the monopoly of the traditional Nile River fishing oligarchy, to extend his influence over the Sudan, and ultimately to underscore Egypt's economic and political independence from the West.

There were, to be sure, some very positive outcomes of the dam project, especially in the short term. Periodic flooding was overcome, water
stored in the reservoir could be released as needed, river transportation
became more dependable, and the fish catch from the reservoir was impressive. But many of the expected benefits were not realized, and there
were innumerable unanticipated negative consequences.

Drainage problems on cultivated land were intensified, for example;
salinity and the incidence of schistosomiasis in newly irrigated areas
were greatly increased. As silt previously deposited in the delta was

captured instead by the reservoir, downstream soils were impoverished. Furthermore, the reduced amounts of fresh water and silt reaching coastal areas decimated the sardine industry. Finally, more than 100,000 Nubian villagers had to be relocated owing to construction and flooding of the reservoir. The housing and agricultural lands provided to them failed to meet minimum needs and expectations, and this formerly self-sufficient people was rendered dependent on Egyptian government and foreign assistance.[6]

To be sure, miscalculation is common even in less-ambitious schemes, and outcomes rarely coincide with intentions, but one of the saddest things about this case is that so many of the unanticipated costs and adverse effects might have been avoided if the best scientific and technical assessments had been systematically sought, uninhibitedly offered, and faithfully heeded. In fact, the politicization of the project was such that across a broad range of issues and objectives, essential elements and possible pitfalls were overlooked, costs were consistently underestimated, and benefits were exaggerated.

Mistakes were belatedly acknowledged in the case of the very ambitious project of the Yaceta Dam on the Paraná River, serving Paraguay, Brazil, and Argentina, which was built in the 1990s with support from the World Bank. In 1998 World Bank president James Wolfensohn offered a public apology to environmental organizations operating in the area for the bank's failure to heed their counsel and thus to avoid needless contamination.

The Yaceta Dam is a neighbor of the Itaipú, the world's largest, but Itaipú was not long to enjoy that status; by the late 1990s, the Chinese had launched the construction of the Three Gorges Dam. For this project, which was to submerge one of the world's most spectacular landscapes and to displace more than a million people, the Chinese government was soliciting no advice and offering no apologies.

Such narrowly shared and seemingly ignorant decision-making sometimes reflects simple corruption. An irrigation minister in the Indian state of Bihar in the 1970s, charged with controlling floods along the tributaries of the Ganges and improving irrigation, appointed unqualified henchmen to the highest administrative and engineering posts. Through them he milked the system, manipulating tender requirements, for example, to favor contractors offering kickbacks. Levels of competence were disregarded and construction standards were not enforced. Consequently, the barriers protecting the river valleys collapsed under flooding, ruining crops and leaving millions homeless.[7]

Idiosyncratic and uninformed decision-making, however, need not imply corruption or the intrusion of "high politics." Unfortunately, top-down approaches are the rule rather than the exception for large national and international bureaucracies. The World Bank, in the mid-1970s, emerged from a housing project in Manila with egg on its face, as world-wide attention was drawn to the mobilization of community groups opposed to the project. The bank had helped to create a National Housing Authority, which then undertook an urban upgrading effort in the large Tondo slum area. The 4,500 squatter families that were to be relocated, making room for port facilities for foreign firms, and the remaining residents who were to pay higher rents were not even informed in advance of the plans being made, much less consulted about them.[8] One of the reasons why the bank favored such large, authoritarian-oriented institutions as implementers is that project officers were pressured to commit large sums over a brief period.

Paradox No. 18: *Before a people can determine its own future, it must take back its past; that is, it must reinterpret a history constructed by its oppressors.*

Brazilian educator Paulo Freire has observed that the oppressed internalize their oppressors' opinion of them and ultimately become convinced of their own unfitness. Thus liberation must begin with a realization of self-worth.[9] Most systems of pronounced inequality, especially those in which inequality is compounded and reinforced by racial or ethnic difference, are traceable to armed conquest. Previously self-governing and self-sufficient tribes or nations may have been subjugated and transformed into slaves or serfs on what was once their own land. Or they may have been pushed off the land and left with little recourse but to compete for menial work at meager pay.

Over time the violent roots of such exploitative systems are progressively obscured from subsequent generations of the conquered. The systems acquire a measure of legitimacy through the implantation of the myth that differential reward and punishment and limitations of access to wealth and power rest somehow on divine will or on merit. Challengers of the myth are seen as troublemakers or even "subversives." Thus any movement that embraces empowerment as means or end must begin by discrediting the prevailing myth and replacing it with one—which may or may not be based in historical fact—that serves to enhance individual and collective self-esteem.

Such myths or, in highly elaborated form, ideologies often incorporate imported parts—the ideals of liberalism, for example, or the explanatory power of Marxism—but for the cultivation of a broad base it appears essential that the raw materials be homegrown; that is, the empowering myth must be also a popular history that draws upon elements of religion or culture distinguishing the underclass from its oppressors and that revives popular heroes or incidents of courageous confrontation or successful counterattack against the conquerors or their progeny.

Indigenismo, or nativism, in Mexico and the Andean highlands, Black Power in the Caribbean, and Negritude in Sub-Saharan Africa have offered psychological sustenance to oppressed underclasses. They have also, on occasion, provided momentum and a sense of direction to otherwise sporadic or unfocused expressions of social unrest. Popularly based independence movements in Africa and Asia sought to underpin their new nations with the symbolism of precolonial civilizations. Ghana and Zimbabwe, for example, took their names from ancient African empires.

Mahatma Gandhi, in mobilizing the peoples of the South Asian subcontinent to throw off British rule, employing a relentless campaign of nonviolent civil disobedience, drew upon the works of Tolstoy and Thoreau, upon elements of Western liberal and socialist thought, and upon Christianity. But the integrating principles of his philosophy, particularly the centrality of truth seeking and the conviction that moral ends could be achieved only through equally moral means, he drew from Hinduism; and his concept of a democratic society was that of decentralized village self-rule through the ancient *panchayati* system—ideally a system drawing upon the participation of all members of the community. To him, national liberation meant the uplifting of all the people—women as well as men, and the untouchables, whom he redesignated "harijans," or children of God. It also meant the investment of new pride in indigenous cultures. The grounding of his campaign in indigenous values, customs, and symbols turned the Congress Party into a broadly based movement. The spinning wheel, in particular, at which Gandhi himself worked regularly, came to symbolize the cottage industry that had been highly developed in precolonial times. Such industry had been systematically suppressed by the British, and Gandhi taught that it had to be revived to break the colonial chains of dependency.[10]

Movements for liberation, democratization, civil rights, human rights, and cultural preservation make it clear that whenever and wherever a people's pursuit of dignity and choice calls for throwing off oppression, the oppressed reach into their collective past and draw from it the heroes and heroines, legends and slogans, arts and skills, and organizational principles that set them apart and draw them together.

Nicaragua's Sandinistas gave historical depth and nationalistic significance to their revolutionary struggle by assuming the mantle of the martyr Augusto César Sandino, who led the struggle against occupation of the country by the U.S. Marines in the 1920s and 1930s. Likewise, the Zapatistas, who made their revolutionary debut in the Mexican state of Chiapas in 1994, adopted the mantle of Mexico's great popular revolutionary hero, Emiliano Zapata. Zapatismo, the first postmodern insurrection-by-internet, is not really a revolutionary movement in the sense of seeking national power. Rather, it is a movement—armed but for the most part nonviolent—in pursuit of human, civil, and cultural rights, not war so much as "poetry by other means," and for strength and unity it draws heavily on the imagery of the resurgent Mayan culture.[11]

The struggle of Black South Africans, led by the African National Congress, to bring majority rule—Black rule in the place of apartheid—to their country was long and hard. But they did it their way: They sang and danced their way to power. In so doing, they engendered a spirit so contagious that scarcely a year after the historic election of 1994, a song with deep African roots—"Shosholoza" in Zulu, "Tshotsholoza" in Xhosa—which was adopted by a previously segregated rugby team, had become a virtual national anthem, hugely popular with Whites as well as Blacks and in itself serving to heal and unify.

The indigenous peoples of the Ecuadorean Sierra have come a long way over the past several decades toward freeing themselves from the bondage of conquest and reclaiming the initiative in shaping their own destinies. In this struggle they have encountered both resistance and assistance from the official world of development, and they have selected from it the ideas, skills, and technologies that suited their purposes. But it seems clear that their greatest assets in this struggle have been drawn from their own ancient traditions.

The *minga*, for example, the gathering of volunteers for communal labor on projects expected to be of general benefit, has been responsible for a flourishing of public works—roads, buildings, potable water systems—in Chimborazo and elsewhere in the 1990s. It is true that this amounts to unpaid labor for provisions that in higher-rent districts would surely be undertaken by the state at taxpayer expense. But the fact remains that in the Sierra, without the *minga*, such works would not be undertaken at all. Furthermore, there is a deeply spiritual and unifying significance to the *minga*. It reflects the commitment of the individual to the group and the conviction that such commitment will ultimately be rewarded by the Pachamama, or Mother Earth.[12]

Popular history or revindicating myths may be at the service of rogues, of course, as well as of statesmen. Until about thirty-five years ago, the peoples of highland Papua New Guinea thought they were the only people in the world. The first airplane that arrived, bearing Australian explorers, was seen as a great silver bird bringing back the blanched ghosts of their ancestors. The technologically advanced gadgetry they bore could not have been fabricated by mortals, so it was believed to represent the magic of the spirit world. The appearance there and elsewhere to previously isolated populations in the South Pacific of these miraculous artifacts gave rise to the so-called cargo cult, which assumed that the great silver birds bearing gifts from ancestors could alight only on specially prepared landing strips.

As highlanders and other poor country people of Papua New Guinea flocked to the capital city, Port Moresby, in search of work, they found jobs scarce and the miraculous artifacts generally unobtainable by legal means. Thus illegal means—robberies, accompanied by rape, beatings, and other behaviors characteristic of intertribal revenge warfare—have become all too common. Some of the cleverest leaders of outlaw gangs have devised a means—a kind of stone-age Marxism—for justifying their actions. Their argument is that the dramatic disparity in wealth between themselves and the white foreigners comes about because the gifts sent by their ancestors are being hijacked and monopolized by the foreigners. In burglarizing, therefore, they are only taking back what was rightfully theirs.[13]

> Paradox No. 19: *Maintaining stability at the apex of a sharply graduated social pyramid requires perpetuating instability at the base.* To maintain their position, those at the top must keep those at the bottom fighting among themselves. Structural change therefore requires an unaccustomed unity among the underclasses and deepening cleavages among elites.[14]

In political discourse, "stability" may have any one of three meanings. It may mean (1) the routinization of political and social change in the absence of conflict; (2) the absence of conflict and the absence of change; or (3) the absence of structural change, even if such change must be staved off through conflict. When *stability* is used as a term of art—that is, for political or diplomatic effect—the implication is generally that it is intended to mean the absence of conflict. In fact, however, national elites and/or colonial or hegemonic powers often fall back upon the old principle of divide and rule; that is, they generate conflict or the threat of it in order to establish or maintain dominance.

Tribal and ethnic animosities were not invented by colonial and neocolonial powers; but those powers have often played upon them and exacerbated them to their own considerable advantage. In fact, where social stratification or political centralization did not in itself provide a Herodian class, or co-optable elite, colonial or neocolonial powers often found it necessary to rule through a racial or ethnic minority. Such minorities are more readily manipulable, as they may be able to maintain a privileged position in their own societies only through external support.

In Haiti, the first modern state born of a slave revolt, U.S. forces occupying the country from 1915 to 1934 suppressed Black leadership and ruled through a facade leadership of the French-oriented mulatto minority. In the heart of Africa, in the territory that has become the states of Burundi and Rwanda, European colonialists and neocolonialists have long used the great ethnic divide and historic animosity between the Hutu and the Tutsi to their own advantage, advancing their claims against each other. All too often they have exacerbated rather than mitigated the hostilities that have led time and again—most recently in the mid-1990s—to genocide.

The migration of labor, voluntarily or otherwise, has always given rise to intra-working-class hostilities that elites could play upon as a distrac-

tion from equity, or class, issues. The transplantation of labor for plantation economies, particularly slaves from Black Africa and South Asian laborers distributed around the territories of the British Empire, has left
deep ethnic divisions that seem to invite manipulation by domestic elites
and foreign powers. In Fiji, for example, the British and, since independence in 1970, other aid donors have sought to reinforce the dominance
of the indigenous chiefly oligarchy, even as the population of South
Asian origin was overtaking the islanders numerically. When a coalition
headed by South Asians and having a nationalist, prolabor, and antinu-
clear orientation won national elections in 1987, the United States—edg-
ing out Great Britain in its hegemonic role—apparently encouraged military officers responsive to the chiefly oligarchy to stage a coup in order to
reassert ethnic Fijian preeminence.

In South Africa, it is no accident that the Afrikaners referred to Blacks
as "plurals" and went out of their way to "accommodate" separate tribal
identities. Many of the policies designed to separate Whites, Asians, and
Coloreds from Blacks also aimed to segregate Blacks from Blacks. Designated leaders of Black homelands, for example, acquired a vested interest
in the system and were expected to feel threatened by Black unity leading to a unified state.

In courting Mangosuthu Gatsha Buthelezi, chief minister of KwaZulu,
the Zulu homeland, the Nationalist Party succeeded to some extent in
deepening divisions within the numerically dominant Zulus and between the Zulus and less numerous Black tribes even as the African National Congress (ANC) and other groups sought to unite Black South
Africans in active opposition to the White minority's power monopoly.
ANC leader Nelson Mandela charged that it was government policy to
keep members of Buthelezi's political organization, Inkatha, fighting
ANC supporters in Natal province, where more than 5,000 people died
during the last half of the 1980s. Such conflict appeared in the townships
around Johannesburg in August 1990 and in little more than a month had
claimed 800 lives. The ruling party also sought through such tactics to
convey to Western trading partners the impression that the social conflict
that plagued their society was not a consequence of apartheid but rather
of traditional intertribal hostility.

The unity of the White population, however, has always been tenuous
at best, and the Afrikaner leaders fell into the trap that has so often desta-
bilized minority rule—that of violent overreaction to relatively nonviolent opposition. Such overreaction alienates passive or tentative allies
who enjoy the perquisites of minority rule but prefer not to be associated
with its brutal underpinnings.

For some decades, the English-speaking press had been a source of
persistent, hard-hitting criticism of the Nationalist government. In general, members of South Africa's English-speaking minority had been

quick to dissociate themselves from the crude racism of the more numerous Afrikaners, descendants of Dutch and French Huguenot settlers,
who maintain their own distinctive language. But one need not doubt the
selfless courage of some and the sincerity of many to note that, until recently at least, English-speaking liberals were the most comfortable
group in the country. Enjoying the comforts and privileges of being
White, they also had the luxury of clear consciences; they could protest
their liberalism and blame the brutalities of the system on the Afrikaners.

The intensified strife of the 1980s, however—overwhelmingly government violence against unarmed protesters, often children—left no viable
space for passive scorn. While official violence served to unite and mobilize Blacks, it served to detach definitively from the Nationalist Party
camp many of its tentative, uncomfortable allies. Along with the English
speakers, there was increasing alienation among Afrikaners themselves,
especially those of the generation coming of age. And finally, the gratu-
itous violence made it more difficult for Western allies to continue to do
business as usual. Trade embargoes and disinvestment finally began seriously to threaten major business interests.

Such tidal changes in public opinion and political alignment led the
government in early 1990 to release Mandela, the country's most revered
political prisoner, and to begin formal talks with the African National
Congress. Well into the period of transition to majority rule, unrecon-
structed security forces continued to subsidize the sabotage operations of
Buthelezi and the Inkatha movement in order to portray South Africans'
struggle as essentially Black-on-Black. The deadly struggle still underway in KwaZulu-Natal province, between ANC and Inkatha Zulus, had
spilled over in the mid-1990s into metal-working areas of the East Rand,
or the East ridge, above Johannesburg. There migrant workers, ANC and
Inkatha, from Kwazulu-Natal were housed like sardines in separate hos-
tels in Black townships such as Tokoza, Vosloorus, and Katlehong; their
battles, fought with guns, knives, machetes, and explosives, had en-
gulfed the surrounding communities.

Entire communities—or remains of communities—were under the
control, so to speak, of gangs representing one or the other of the warring
parties, and even for "civilians" trying desperately not to be involved,
being caught on the wrong side of a demarcation line could cost a life.
More than sixteen thousand people were killed in the East Rand during
the first half of the 1990s. Courageous Peace Committee mediators, absorbed after 1994 by Mandela's all-encompassing Reconstruction and
Development Program, did not pretend that peace had been achieved—
only that there was a tense and fragile kind of stability in the conflict
zone.[15]

With the elections of 1994 and the adoption of the color-blind constitution of 1996, the battle for an end to apartheid had been won; but even

though the most blatant manifestations of racial prejudice have been delegitimated, it remains to be seen whether far-reaching socioeconomic change will follow. With respect to egalitarianism, the standards set by "the West," and even by Black-ruled Africa, are not so very high. Nevertheless, for the first time in almost half a century, momentum is clearly on the side of empowerment for South Africa's Black minority.

> Paradox No. 20: *Treating the symptoms may prolong the disorder.* Even with the best of intentions, a development program that simply meets immediate needs rather than enabling communities to organize sustainable means of meeting their own needs is likely to kill local initiative and build dependency. Sometimes, of course, pacification (rather than empowerment) appears to be precisely what was intended.

A major component of the development programs of the United States and the Western European bilateral donors as well as of multilateral institutions and NGOs in the post–Cold War period has been that of building a "civil society," a network of autonomous service, advocacy, charitable, and development organizations, in the formerly Soviet sphere. The argument has been that the only organizations and institutions allowed to function during the Cold War were vehicles of government that would be demobilized in the new order and that under any circumstances Western donors would be loath to support. It was also clear that economic restructuring would be generating new hardships—unemployment, hyperinflation, and so on—just as governments were shedding most social services and safety nets and that there was no buffer zone of religious and philanthropic institutions to mitigate such hardships.

There were, however, a great many relatively new and poorly funded but locally generated organizations throughout the area, born of the democratization struggle or of the socioeconomic crisis that burgeoned well before Western programs were in place. Naturally, some such organizations included leaders or members who had previously been active in government-dependent organizations. In many cases, such organizations have been overlooked, taken over, or incautiously or intentionally undermined.

In launching a program or extending one into a new area, there are many considerations as to whether it is advisable to build on or support existing organizations or develop new ones. It may be that existing organizations are the problem, that they are divisive or elitist, for example, and tend to obstruct rather than promote development. In general, however, prospects for the sustainability of a program should be better if it is undertaken by an organization already rooted in the community rather than one with shallow and essentially external roots.

In Albania's grim and hungry days of the early 1990s, after the collapse of the old regime and before the country had been discovered, so to speak, by the West, a number of Albanian organizations, many of them groups of women who had pulled together for mutual support in the worst of times, united to form the NGO Forum. When Danish donors launched their new Foundation for a Civil Society, they initially intended to strengthen the NGO Forum, but they soon decided that they wanted to fund other groups as well. In time, they were in fact competing with the forum. Even though—or perhaps because—the initiative for grants and programs within the Foundation for Civil Society remained with the Danes rather than passing to Albanian administrators, other donor agencies looking for partners tended to favor the foundation. With funds, personnel, and creative energies drained off to the foundation, the NGO Forum began to wither.

It is hardly surprising that investors in development, like investors in commercial operations, favor organizations with shallow roots. Foreign donors want to know who they are dealing with, and they want to be able to communicate with prospective partners as freely and fully as possible. So they are drawn to development organizations whose founders or administrators have traceable roots, or at least good connections, in the West more so than the East, or First World rather than Third. Returning expatriates have the further advantage of being fluent in the language or languages of donor countries and perhaps even in the latest jargon of development. And for those donor organizations that are intent on maintaining control of the programs and projects they fund, client country partners with shallow roots are preferable because they are less likely to suffer loyalties divided between foreign donors and host-country constituencies and to exhibit confusion about who they answer to.

There is also a tendency to follow the pack. Like journalists who know they must be onto a marketable story if it's the one all the other journalists are chasing, aid donors tend to pile onto each other rather than looking for undiscovered home-grown organizations. NGO umbrella groups that are strictly donor products, like the main one operating in the late 1990s in Prague, may prove more efficient in the short term. But donors, particularly major donors, are fickle.

The development boom in the ex-Soviet sphere has begun to fizzle. Funders are pulling out and host-country organizations are desperately seeking new partners and funding sources. Some Western NGOs, like Washington, D.C.–based VOICE International, are responding to the needs of this new phase by preparing guides to funding sources or offering training in how to prepare project proposals and approach funders. Moreover, Third World, or host-country, partners are taking advantage of international meetings, such as the Microcredit Summit in Washington, D.C., in 1997, to network and learn from each others' experiences with foreign funders. But like eucalyptus economies, eucalyptus NGOs, which put down shallow roots and grow quickly by drawing off nutrients from organisms of local origin, can leave a country or region more underserviced and vulnerable than ever when they pull up stakes and leave.[16]

Monseñor Leonidas Proaño, Ecuador's bishop of Riobamba, said that an important difference between *desarrollo* (development) and *desarrollismo* (developmentism) is that *desarrollismo* treats the symptoms of poverty without dealing with its structural roots. Proaño, spiritual leader of the Catholics of Chimborazo and a "liberation theologist" of international reputation, said that most development agencies, like most political parties, are in the business of co-opting indigenous leaders and dividing, rather than uniting, communities.

Monseñor Proaño was, in the 1970s and 1980s, one of Ecuador's most controversial figures. He is considered a radical, he said, because he speaks of social justice. One high-ranking official of the U.S. Embassy told me in no uncertain terms that Proaño was a Communist. Another asked, with lowered voice, if he was "his own man." Proaño would answer that he is not his own man, but rather a servant of Christ. He noted that Christ showed a preference for working with the poor, that he surrounded himself with the poor and chose his disciples from among them. "We try to live that teaching here," he said.

Proaño held office hours every weekday afternoon, and the humble premises of his bishopric in Riobamba were indeed filled every afternoon with the poor seeking guidance in dealing with their everyday problems. The bishopric promotes the organization of *comunidades de base*, grassroots Christian communities in which the peasants discuss their problems and propose means of dealing with them. The bishopric also sponsors various organizations and educational programs and a radio station that transmits in Quechua. Proaño's preference for ministering to the poor has gained him the enmity of local landowners as well as of governments, domestic and foreign. He and his followers were widely accredited or blamed for the peasant mobilization that got under way in the mid-1970s.

In fact, that mobilization was catalyzed indirectly by the 1964 agrarian reform law. The law was enforced only sporadically, and IERAC, the agency charged with its enforcement, was meagerly funded and kept on a short leash. IERAC was not authorized to institute expropriation proceedings until the *huasipungueros*, on their own, "denounced" their *patrones*, or landlords. Any employee of IERAC who tried to inform peasants of their rights or encouraged them to denounce their landlords was subject to disciplinary action. Nevertheless, word of the legal option spread among the peasants and by the early 1970s, according to Antonio Jurado and Armanda Philco of IERAC's Chimborazo office, IERAC offices in the Sierra were swamped with denunciations.

Meanwhile, after the bishops' conference in Medellín in 1968, the Catholic church decided to divide its own lands among the peasants who worked them. The redistribution program was to be carried out through the efforts of the Campesinos' Labor Federation (CEDOC), organized by a very conservative faction of the Church. The work was later carried on by the Ecuadorean Institute of Development Studies (INEDES), which grew out of CEDOC, and, in turn, by the Ecuadorean Agricultural Service Center (CESA), which grew out of INEDES.

In terms of methods and objectives, both CEDOC and its offspring organizations were moving across the political spectrum toward the left and identifying more and more with the Indians rather than with the founders of the original CEDOC or with the Church. Nevertheless, the peasants working with CESA began to organize on their own and ultimately took over control of the movement. Ramón Espinel, who worked with CESA in the early to mid-1970s, said that the non-Indians who had launched the movement, not knowing how to respond to this usurpation of their role, became demoralized and divided, and many resigned.

The quixotic president of Ecuador, José María Velasco Ibarra, under assault from both the Right and the Left, decided to court the peasants and, in 1969, began more serious enforcement of the agrarian reform law, especially in the rice-producing coastal areas. The military conspirators who prematurely terminated Velasco Ibarra's fifth term, in February 1972, were ideologically inconsistent, but following up on his revolutionary rhetoric, the new president, General Guillermo Rodríguez Lara, in 1973 codified the agrarian reform laws and, in the process, strengthened them. Moreover, the government, temporarily solvent as a consequence of the new oil-exportation bonanza, greatly increased the budget and authority of IERAC.

Rodríguez Lara soon backed away from the promotion of reform, and the junta that replaced him in 1975 proved very conservative. Nevertheless, the peasant mobilization begun in the late 1960s continued to build until it reached a peak of militance, particularly in Chimborazo, in 1975 and 1976. In response to this mobilization, the World Bank, building on a project already started by AID, underwrote a major program of integrated rural development, which was later absorbed by SEDRI. Meanwhile, there was an enormous influx into Chimborazo province of Evangelical missionaries, who invested large sums in their own unintegrated development efforts.

Evangelical missionaries had begun to establish a base in Chimborazo, in the canton of Colta, in the 1940s. Their operations grew in the 1960s, but it was in the 1970s, particularly the mid-1970s, that missionaries arrived in large numbers with large sums of money to distribute. For communities that were prepared to convert, the missionaries and their technicians built potable water systems, community centers, schools, and clinics. An Ecuadorean development specialist in the Sierra noted that the missionaries took over the management of infrastructure projects that were already under way, wilting campesino initiative and dissolving campesino organizations. The Evangelicals' Indian converts also adopted a different frame of mind; they became passive, willing to wait for handouts that, in fact, were coming, but only to Evangelical communities. A Peace Corps volunteer working in Colta observed that the Evangelicals were highly materialistic and paranoid about "communism."

The upshot of this influx of missionaries was the demobilization of the peasant movement. Many Ecuadoreans suspect that was hardly coincidental. They note that most AID funds and other foreign assistance programs also favored the Evangelical communities. The Ecuadorean Institute of Cooperativism (ICE), funded predominantly by the German Konrad Adenauer Foundation, was one of many agencies that tended to favor Evangelical communities. Its provincial director, Vicente Cardoso, who had worked for many years with AID, told me that "with co-ops, people get what they need and are satisfied—not rebellious or revolutionary."

Among the Evangelicals working in Chimborazo were fourteen sects, united for practical purposes in the Gospel Missionary Union. One of the sects operating in Colta, known as *Hoy Cristo Jesus Bendice (HCJB)*, transmitted radio programs in Quechua from the village of Majipamba. It also had a transmitter in Quito that was among the strongest in the world, exceeding even the power of the Voice of America. Radio operations in Majipamba were turned over to indigenous Evangelicals, but the contract stipulated that the parent organization might take it back if locals strayed from the gospel according to *HCJB*.

The bête noir of Catholics and nationalists throughout Ecuador until it was expelled from the country in 1981 was the missionary organization known as the Summer Institute of Linguistics (SIL). Suspicions of covert operations masquerading as evangelism or development subsequently focused on an organization called World Vision. Whereas SIL was based in the Oriente, World Vision worked mainly in the Sierra.

Frank Boshold, director of the World Vision program in Ecuador in the early 1980s, said that World Vision had come to Ecuador in 1978 and had been growing each year since. Its local budget for 1982 was $1.5 million and Boshold expected it to continue to grow. In Chimborazo, World Vision had five "development" promoters on salary overseeing more than thirty projects. Each project was also monitored by community leaders who received token payment.

Boshold conceded that World Vision was often accused of being a CIA front. He maintained that the organization received no government money, although USAID and other funding agencies contributed to some of the same projects or the same communities.[17]

The people of Chimborazo were still rigidly divided into Catholic and Evangelical camps in the early 1980s. The Catholics maintained that the

Evangelicals were apathetic, and the Evangelicals said the same of the Catholics. It seemed, though, that there was a great deal of mobilization and consciousness-raising taking place in both communities. The events of the 1970s suggest that, in the short run, efforts to divide and pacify may be effective; the long run, however, is another matter.

> Paradox No. 21: *He who pays the piper does not necessarily call the tune.* At any rate, development is a complicated process, deriving from many different sources and motives—an art rather than a science and a creature of fortune as much as of planning. No one, not even those who pay the bill, can control it.

Of course there are mixed motives among those who support development programs. It would be most naïve to suppose, for example, that those who underwrite the foreign policy of the United States are greatly concerned about the welfare of Ecuadorean campesinos.

There is always a danger for would-be change agents, as for supposed beneficiaries of development programs, of being co-opted and manipulated. But for people of good will to withdraw from the development process or deny themselves the use of development resources is hardly a solution. Those whose motives are covert, or at least less than forthrightly stated, will continue their work under any circumstances. And there is also the possibility that in the development game the agents and agencies of occult motives are deceiving themselves—that projects that are begun for the purpose of pacification, for example, may result ultimately in further mobilization instead.

It is quite common for agents in the field, or even agency directors, to have motives very different from those of the governments they are presumed to represent. Even USAID, which has been drawn into U.S. efforts in several countries to destabilize democratic governments, is a multifaceted agency with as many motives as it has officers, field agents, and contractees. Along with projects undoubtedly designed to propagandize, divide, or pacify, it also funds many projects having the potential of promoting *desarrollo* as opposed to *desarrollismo*. And even those that are launched as *desarrollismo* may eventually be turned inside out by their intended beneficiaries. Paul Fritz, deputy director of AID-Ecuador in 1982, said that the agency's most effective programs happen by serendipity—through informal contacts and response to "targets of opportunity," which have nothing to do with whatever Washington happens to be pushing.

Furthermore, funding agencies, for better or worse—most development specialists would say for the better—do not necessarily monitor what their contract organizations are doing. The International Volunteer Service (IVS), for example, a small development agency that recruits worldwide for trained technicians to work at the village level in developing countries, was, in Ecuador in the early 1980s, funded in part by US-AID, but IVS's contractual accountability consisted only of one annual global report. USAID country officers had a veto over taking IVS volunteers, but they had nothing to say about the in-country program. Hank Beder, IVS country director, supervising about six volunteers, said that AID had initially requested quarterly reports, but that, in fact, he had only spoken with AID officials three times in four years and that at times AID seemed to lose track of the fact that there was an IVS program in Ecuador.

Another agency that has been colonized by professionals dedicated to the mystique of development is the Inter-American Foundation. Despite the zigs and zags of U.S. policy from one administration to another and despite the long-term thrust of U.S. policy toward Latin America, the Inter-American Foundation has consistently pursued a course that might be called liberational or empowering.

Both the Inter-American Foundation and AID, as previously noted, underwrote a literacy program in Ecuador based on the philosophy and methodology of Paulo Freire—and they did so during the administration of Richard Nixon! Carlos Moreno, who directed the program, had easy responses for its critics. When the Left charged that he and his colleagues were promoting imperialism, he asked, "By spreading revolutionary ideas among the peasants?" When the Right charged that they were fomenting revolution, he challenged, "With AID funds?"

The Inter-American Foundation contributed to the literacy campaign in Chimborazo in the 1980s through a program known as *Pan para la Educación* (Bread for Education). Bakeries were established and operated collectively by and for individual *comunas*. Earnings were used for maintenance of the bakery, for the purchase of books, paper, and other educational tools, and for other community projects. The literacy program itself held that there are three kinds of illiterates: (1) those who cannot read and write; (2) those who can read and write, but don't understand their own reality; and (3) those who see reality but don't do anything about it.

Programs of *desarrollismo* posing as *desarrollo* may indeed divide and pacify in the short term, but any program that involves collective action is hostage to many wills and subject to abrupt change of direction. Thus CEDOC, organized by conservatives for the purpose of controlling the campesinos, had come under the control of campesinos and had become split between the Catholic Left and the Marxist Left. U.S. Embassy officials admitted through gritted teeth in 1982 that an Ecuadorean labor union organized by the American Institute for Free Labor Development (AIFLD)—a strange bedfellow creation of the AFL-CIO, AID, and the CIA—had slipped under the umbrella of the country's major Marxist federation.

Even the supposedly pacified Evangelicals of Chimborazo had ceased to be passive. Moreno said that whereas a few years earlier the Evangelicals scorned all secular music, in the early 1980s some *conjuntos* (ensembles) of young musicians began to compose their own songs of social protest. Under a contract with *HCJB*, the Ministry of Education used its powerful transmitter in the literacy campaign; it also hired five Evangelicals from Majipamba to design radio programs. An Education Ministry official complained to Moreno that their radio programs were becoming overly critical of the government; one of the offensive scripts had said that the government was obligated to respond to the needs of the campesinos, and that if it failed to do so the campesinos should take matters into their own hands.

Moreno said that the Evangelicals had become better organized than the Catholics, and that some of the U.S. missionaries had left due to pressure from indigenous Evangelicals. The indigenous community of Chimborazo remained divided in the 1980s, but some leaders both of Catholic and Evangelical communities were attempting to bridge the gap and to reach out to poor mestizos as well.

The demonstration effect of seemingly modest development projects is often very strong. Once a few schools have been built or a few co-ops organized, once a potential source of assistance has been identified, the energy that propels the process generally comes from the peasants themselves. The Sierra Indians I encountered in no way fit the stereotype of sullenness, shyness, or lethargy. After I had explained, in one small village, that my mission was only of research, one of the villagers approached me and asked, "Are you sure you can't do anything for us?" I replied regretfully that I could not. Nodding toward the Peace Corps volunteer who had accompanied me, the villager asked, "Then what can he do for us?"

Furthermore, development programs often reinforce each other and acquire political significance through unforeseen multiplier effects. Ecuador's literacy campaign has been given impetus by agrarian reform. Since the agrarian reforms of 1964 and 1973 have taken effect, peasants often find themselves involved in legal transactions; they want to be able to read in order to make sure that they are not being cheated. Now that they are learning to read and now that they have the vote (they say that the exclusion of illiterates from the franchise until 1979 had nothing to do with literacy; it was simply a cover for excluding Indians), they are getting together to study and discuss the platforms of the various parties.

The relatively new Party of the Democratic Left (Izquierda Democrática—ID) was already the strongest party in Chimborazo in 1982 and was competing fiercely with Popular Democracy (Democrácia Popular—DP), the Christian Democratic heir of the rural following of the near-defunct Conservative Party—in other rural areas as well. Attempting to compete with the governing DP, ID in 1981 and 1982 launched a number of rural development projects of its own. For efforts in political instruction to have credibility, party leaders had found it necessary to offer the peasants something they needed.

Rodrigo Borja, national ID party leader, and Arnaldo Merino, federal deputy and leader of ID in Chimborazo province, expressed the belief that all development efforts are worthwhile among a people who need so much and that all contribute in one way or another to the general process of mobilization. They also believed, incidentally, that peasant mobilization would, in the long run, favor their party. In fact, it appears that it did; Borja was elected president of Ecuador in 1988 with particularly strong support in the Sierra.

Pedro Bagua, a leader of the indigenous Evangelicals of Colta province, said that after much study and discussion, his people decided that ID was the right party for them. He saw the party's goal, and his own goal for his people, as socialism, and he believed the party was the best vehicle for development, because through it his people could go directly to the parliament with their demands. Bagua developed his various skills—in language, medical arts, teaching, and leadership—through association with the Summer Institute of Linguistics and with the Evangelical mission in Colta. He said that the sources of assistance and the motives of benefactors are unimportant. "The campesinos," he said, "know how to take advantage without being co-opted."

Paradox No. 22: *Any program that pretends to promote organization and self-help on the part of have-nots runs the risk of being successful.*

For the challenge of development, there is no final analysis. No matter the investment of skill and good will, there are no guarantees of success in the short run, or even the long run, for development programs. By the same token, however, acceptance of defeat is often premature. Most whose motives in the development quest are open and straightforward, especially those who would serve the unpowerful, will sooner or later find themselves blindsided by other agents or agencies that have more power and resources at their command and have, perhaps, mixed motives. But in the longer term the outcome of the interaction on a development agenda will have more to do with the motives and skills, determination, and commonality of purpose of the would-be beneficiary community than of the purported benefactors. Indeed, unless the process becomes the beneficiaries' own, it hardly qualifies as development.

Ecuador's Andean province of Chimborazo has seen many ups and downs, advances and setbacks, in the process of development—especially development as the empowerment of the long-suppressed indigenous majority—since the 1960s, when a modest land reform began to unsettle a centuries-old feudalistic system. An important landmark along the way was the election in 1992 of Mariano Curicama as mayor of the town of Guamote. He was only the second indigenous Ecuadorian to be elected mayor in the country's 177-year history. Even more significant, he was enabled to assume office and to accomplish a great deal through the collaborative efforts of the indigenous community.

Curicama is one of the few residents of Guamote to have graduated from high school. He was studying in the provincial capital, Riobamba, at a time of ferment, when indigenous leaders were organizing rural workers to pursue their rights through land reform. He became a member then of the Union of Indigenous Communities of Guamote (Union de Comunidades Indígenas de Guamote—UCIG), a small but growing body.

During the 1980s, as previously noted, the Ecuadorean government's new Secretariat for Integrated Rural Development (SEDRI) sent out teams of specialists to work in rural areas. The team assigned to Guamote hired Curicama to be their chauffeur, but he turned out to be much more. As he was well connected in the indigenous community, he came to be something of a liaison between that community and the technicians of SEDRI and subsequent development promoters.

The municipality of Guamote, comprising a capital of the same name and 119 other communities, sits some 9,500 feet above sea level in the shadow of Chimborazo, the imposing, extinct volcano that gives the province its name. Some 90 percent of its population are indigenous Quichua speakers, and most live in poverty. Ninety percent of the population lack running water, and 63 percent lack electricity. The 45 percent who are illiterate were formally denied the right to vote until 1979, but most of the indigenous were effectively excluded from citizenship until the 1980s.

In 1988 Quichua speakers from several communities in Guamote ran for and were elected to the governing board of the municipality. They were outmaneuvered during that term by mestizo council members, but their participation had set an important example, and indigenous communities approached the elections of 1992 with new determination. Eighty communities met in a general assembly to select their leaders their own way, through questioning of aspirants and lengthy discussions, and ratified those choices some months later by casting ballots in the officially sanctioned elections.

The results were a mayoral victory for Curicama and the election of indigenous members to five of the seven council seats. Mestizo businessmen who were accustomed to controlling the municipality were prepared initially to resist, but Curicama threatened convincingly that his people would depopulate the town and regroup in the hills to govern themselves. The businessmen relented and were eventually won over.

The most dramatic accomplishment of the new municipal leadership has been the construction of a road linking highlands Guamote with the Amazonian town of Macas. But since 1992 Guamote has also seen the renovation of its marketplace; the purchase of tractors, bulldozers, and other heavy equipment; and the construction, among the many communities, of new harvest storage facilities, pipelines for running water, classrooms and playgrounds, and seventy new health outposts.

Curicama's first term record was such that even the business leaders who earlier tried to prevent him from taking office supported his candidacy the second time around. But he is by no means making himself available for co-optation by the preexisting power structure. Rather, he has underpinned his leadership and his development efforts with a dense new network of indigenous organizations and with the regeneration of ancient models and habits of participation.

A Popular Indigenous Parliament (Parlamento Indígena Popular) has been organized, drawing representatives from communities and grassroots organizations throughout the municipality. Other peasant and community organizations on the order of the UCIG have been created or expanded, nurtured, and drawn into participation in decision-making processes in the municipality. Representatives of such organizations have been invited to attend municipal council meetings. The Popular Indigenous Parliament even participates in budget planning for the 120 communities of Guamote.

Sectoral council meetings have been scheduled throughout the municipality, bringing local government officials into direct contact with community leaders, problems, and projects. All of Guamote's public works have been carried out through the use of *mingas,* the contribution of labor for the general good of the community, an ancient Inca tradition intended to promote social bonding as well as material benefit. Curicama and his council have also promoted *minga*-type collaboration among neighboring communities and the sharing of expensive machinery and heavy equipment among municipalities.

Curicama and his colleagues understand very well the power to be found in organized numbers, and they have not hesitated to use unorthodox means of getting the attention of otherwise distracted cabinet members in Quito—for instance, traveling to the capital with an entourage of five hundred community leaders. Curicama sees all this not as the end game but as a beginning, a five-hundred-year plan for overcoming the bitter legacy of the last five hundred.[18] But, at least for the people of Guamote, it is now their plan and theirs to implement.

Notes

1. Clare Short, British minister of international development, in a lecture at Keble College, Oxford University on May 21, 1998, warned about the opportunity costs of debt relief, noting that much of the British contribution, including a recently allocated £10 million to Mozambique, would come out of her development budget.

2. John Pomfret, "Agencies 'Helped Spark Congo Conflict,'" and "Charities Get Caught Up as Tools for War," *Manchester Guardian Weekly,* October, 5, 1997, p. 17.

3. Ethnic groups that are largely Muslim and not necessarily in rebellion, such as the Nuba and the Fur, have also been targeted by government-backed militias who coveted their land.

4. Observations of Professor David Keen of the London School of Economics, who was engaged in research in the Sudan in the late 1980s, Oxford University, May 29, 1998. See his book, *The Benefits of Famine* (Princeton: Princeton University Press, 1994).

5. Clare Short, cited in Anthony Bevins, "Does This Picture Make You Flinch? Clare Short Says Graphic Images Like This Stop People Caring," *The Independent* (London), May 29, 1998, p. 1.

6. John P. Metzelaar, "The Itaipú and Aswan High Dams: Two Generations of Dams Compared" (unpublished), November 1989.

7. Paul Harrison, *Inside the Third World: The Anatomy of Poverty,* 2nd ed. (Harmondsworth, UK: Penguin Books, 1987), pp. 372–373.

8. Stephen Hellinger, Douglas Hellinger, and Fred M. O'Regan, *Aid for Just Development* (Boulder: Lynne Rienner Publishers, 1988), pp. 131–134.

9. Paulo Freire, *Pedagogy of the Oppressed* (New York: Seabury Press, 1970).

10. K. Seshadri, *Indian Politics: Then and Now* (Delhi: Pragatee Prakashan, 1976), pp. 57–66.

11. Yvon Lebot of L'Ecole des Hautes Etudes en Sciences Sociales, Paris, lecture on the Zapatista movement, Exeter College, Oxford University, May 12, 1998.

12. Charles David Kleymeyer, ed., *Cultural Expression and Grassroots Development* (Boulder: Lynne Rienner Publishers, 1994).

13. As explained to the author by political scientist Yaw Saffu, of the University of Papua New Guinea, Port Moresby, July 1985.

14. Plato, in the eighth book of the Republic, made the latter point. "You cannot make a successful revolution," he said, "if the ruling class is not weakened by internal dissension or defeat in war." Cited in Karl R. Popper, *The Poverty of Historicism* (Boston: Beacon Press, 1957), p. 62.

15. The author toured the East Rand with members of the Peace Committee in mid-1995.

16. Observations based on meetings with numerous leaders and supporters of NGOs in Central Europe and the Balkans, July–August 1996.

17. World Vision has come under suspicion in other areas as well, such as Fiji—where its operations, like those of U.S. aid programs, were highly supportive of political factions that staged a coup d'état in 1987—and Central America. The organization withdrew from the administration of a camp for Salvadoran refugees in Honduras after being accused of turning two refugees over to the Salvadoran government.

18. Daniel E. Stanton, "On the Road to Development," *Grassroots Development* 21, no. 1, 1997, pp. 24–30.

Suggested Readings

Andrain, Charles F., *Political Change in the Third World* (Boston: Unwin Hyman, 1988).

Breslin, Patrick, *Development and Dignity: Grassroots Development and the Inter-American Foundation* (Rosslyn, Va.: Inter-American Foundation, 1987).

Brockett, Charles D., *Land, Power, and Poverty: Agrarian Transformation and Political Conflict in Central America* (Boston: Unwin Hyman, 1988).

Brundtland, Gro Harlem, Chairperson, World Commission on Environment and Development, *Our Common Future* (New York: Oxford University Press, 1987).

Foster, G., *Traditional Cultures and the Impact of Technological Change* (New York: Harper and Row, 1962).

Goulet, Denis, *The Cruel Choice: A New Concept in the Theory of Development* (New York: Atheneum, 1977).

Gran, Guy, *Development by People: Citizen Construction of a Just World* (New York: Praeger, 1983).

Hirschman, Albert O., *Getting Ahead Collectively* (Elmsford, N.Y.: Pergamon Press, 1984).

Institute for Development Studies, "Poverty, Policy, and Aid," *IDS Bulletin* 27, no. 2, 1996.

Keen, David, *The Benefits of Famine* (Princeton: Princeton University Press, 1994).

Kleymeyer, Charles David, ed., *Cultural Expression and Grassroots Development* (Boulder: Lynne Rienner Publishers, 1994).

Lernoux, Penny, *Cry of the People* (Harmondsworth, UK: Penguin Books, 1982).

Martin, Hans-Peter, and Harold Schumann, *The Global Trap: Globalization and the Assault on Democracy and Prosperity* (London: Zed Books, 1997).

Oxfam International, "Debt Relief and Poverty Reduction: New Hope for Uganda," Oxfam International position paper, Oxford, 1996.

Salmen, Lawrence F., *Listen to the People: Participant-Observer Evaluation of Development Projects* (New York: Oxford University Press, published for the World Bank, 1989).

Schuman, Michael, *Towards a Global Village: International Community Development Initiatives* (London: Pluto Press, 1994).

Uphoff, Norman, *Local Institutional Development: An Analytic Sourcebook with Cases* (West Hartford, Conn.: Kumarian Press, 1986).

16 Conclusion: Leaning on the Limits

Some years ago Representative Dante Fascell, chairman of the U.S. House Foreign Affairs Committee, quipped that foreign assistance is a means whereby the poor of the rich countries contribute to the rich of the poor countries. It is also, of course, yet another means whereby the poor of the rich countries further enrich their own pampered elites.

Few of our readers will be surprised to find that there is a dark underside to the aid game, as played by the overdeveloped states and the multilateral financial institutions they control. But is that all there is? With respect to big-money, high-visibility, major-donor programs, optimists will find little encouragement in these pages.

Responses to popular insurrection in Central America in the 1980s and in the Mexican province of Chiapas in the 1990s make it abundantly clear that collective self-help, or empowerment, remains the provocation rather than the objective of most major economic assistance programs. As demonstrated repeatedly in other times and places, the big money for development purposes kicks in only when the wealthy and powerful come to feel that the organization, or mobilization, of the poor and oppressed threaten their interests. The only category of U.S. economic aid that grew dramatically during the 1980s was that of Economic Support Funds (ESF). As explained by the State Department, ESF monies "provide the resources needed to stem the spread of economic and political disruption and to help allies in dealing with threats to their security and independence"[1]—allies at the time like Marcos in the Philippines, Pakistan's General Zia, Liberia's Sergeant Samuel Doe, and Zaire's multimillionaire Mobutu.

Perhaps we should find some satisfaction, therefore, in the fact that so much of the money appropriated for development is simply stolen. In the final analysis, if economic development is to mean more than occasional spurts of economic growth, if it is to mean a higher standard of living and a greater measure of self-reliance for the majority, it will not be accomplished by placing the military and economic might of the world's greatest power at the service of those who have perpetually blocked just such development. It should be apparent at any rate that where "security" interests are engaged, economic aid is directed toward pacification, not pump priming, much less empowerment.

The Heist of the Peace Dividend

By the end of the century, the Cold War was history. Many of the policies and programs that had been justified by it, however—including economic aid as pacification on behalf of tyrants—were not. And while the constituencies for what had been Cold War policies remained intact and in some respects emboldened, those that had supported development assistance for the poor did not. That is, those who had supported economic aid as Cold War courtship of hearts and minds had no further reason to support it.

The good news at the end of the Cold War is that some of the most expensive and destabilizing weapons programs, such as Star Wars, have been downsized and some of the most damaging engagements—conflicts on several continents—have been allowed to taper off. The bad news, though, is that there is to be no peace dividend for social reconstruction and development. On the contrary, governments of the wealthier states that had been the major donors, seeing their own social programs succumb to the assaults of an ascendant private sector, find it harder to defend foreign aid. Having pledged at ECO '92 to increase aid for sustainable development from 0.33 percent to 0.7 percent, the rich nations had instead cut ODA by 1997 to 0.27 percent.

As the overall U.S. foreign aid package shrank, funds that had previously supported community development efforts were being siphoned off to sustain "security" programs now threatened by the lifting of the Cold War cover.

The strengthening of Third World military and paramilitary organizations and surveillance and suppression of peasant rebellion, for example, would be carried out through the escalating "War on Drugs." That, too, was to be characterized as foreign aid. Moreover, even where major donor foreign economic assistance is not providing support or cover for political or military undertakings, its objectives are likely to be set with a view toward the debt exposure of commercial banks, the infrastructure needs of private investors, the institutional imperatives of donor agencies, or the interests of other economic or bureaucratic elites.

The Clinton administration in 1997 lifted a two-decade-old ban on the sale of advanced weapons to Latin America. The Cold War cover is no longer needed. The policy is justified straightforwardly as trade—support for the U.S. arms industry.

But what about food aid? Surely it is genuinely meant to address the problem of Third World hunger. Not so, say the Food First folks.[2] Food

aid is above all aid from the U.S. taxpayer to the U.S. grain farmer. Moreover, like any other kind of aid, it may be used for political purposes: to
promote certain policies or to bolster allies. Finally, it may distort domestic and international markets and divert attention from the need for land-
tenure and farm program reforms both in "beneficiary" countries and at
home. Hunger, whether in First World or Third, does not normally reflect
lack of food production or productive capacity but rather maldistribution
of land, income, and opportunity.

Then what about agrarian reform? Indeed the green revolution has
been a great success—to the extent that productivity was its goal. If the
goal, however, was feeding the hungry or strengthening of the position
of poor peasants, the outcome has been very much the reverse. For the
most part, new products, technologies, and credits have been available or
usable only for the already-affluent landowner, and enhanced land values have intensified struggles that peasants were sure to lose. Nor are its
gains likely to be sustainable, since the approach has featured importation of seeds, fertilizers, pesticides, and modern farm machinery.

The miracle seeds, genetically engineered, cannot be used for future
crops, so the farmer remains dependent upon the company supplying
the seeds—for most farmers a foreign company. According to John Kin-
ney, whose Talavaya Center, a nonprofit conservancy and seed bank in
Espanola, New Mexico, won the 1985 UN environmental program
award, 70 percent of the world's open-pollinated (as opposed to genetically engineered) crops have become extinct in the last fifty years because
of the spread of the hybrids. And if the hybrid plants are stronger, so are
the bugs; many have become immune to commonly used pesticides.

Perhaps what is needed, then, is a simple transfer of money, in huge
amounts, from the First World to the Third. That has, in fact, taken place,
at least on paper, and the upshot is the international debt crisis—for the
Third World, a combined foreign debt in the mid-1990s of more than 1.4
trillion dollars.

In this drama, there is plenty of blame to spread around—to public and
private sector elites of First World and Third. The people who can claim
no share of the blame are the same ones who claimed no share of the benefits. They are also the ones who will bear the cost. As the rich make the
usual choice as to whether or not to accept sacrifice, the unavoidable sacrifice is borne by those who have no choice.

The Specter of Globalization

For much of South America, the debt and the "austerity" regimen (i.e.,
higher prices and interest rates, lower wages and longer working hours,
fewer subsidies and fewer services, and a fire sale of government assets)
imposed by the creditors' enforcer, the International Monetary Fund, ac-

complished in the 1980s and 1990s what in the 1970s required military rule: the freezing of socioeconomic and political relationships, or even a rollback of previous political and economic gains by the working or would-be-working classes. Ruling elites in the Third World are placed in the enviable position of being able to claim that they would like to adopt more equitable policies but are prevented from doing so by the IMF, the WTO, and other international financial organizations and trade agreements.

The flotsam of modernization that threatens to bury all hope of development in Latin America and East Asia floats even more incongruously over South Asia and Africa. In Kinshasa, sleek modern skyscrapers, monuments to Mobutu's creditworthiness, hover mockingly over a society that for at least two decades before his displacement and subsequent death in 1997 was in near-total disintegration. When I visited in the late 1970s, I was warned not to venture out onto the city streets. If I failed to have my pockets picked by hungry civilians, I was told, I would surely be mugged by marauding soldiers, whose pay was then several weeks in arrears.

Even Second World countries, before disassembling their own faulty development models, had become entangled in the First World's debt trap.

The new Moscow stock market, up 150 percent in 1996, became one of the world's most attractive "emerging" markets before it plunged again in 1998. The IMF, which had extended more than $9 billion in loans by 1997, was reasonably content at the time with the performance of the Russian economy. The debt was being serviced in a timely manner; but IMF conditions had called for a withholding of government salaries and pensions totaling almost $7 billion, and teachers, scientists, miners, and soldiers had reported delays of up to a year in disbursement. Meanwhile, a loaf of bread that had sold for 25 kopeks in the late 1980s was selling for about 2,500 rubles—a 10,000-fold increase—in the late 1990s, and average family income had dropped twofold. Russia's mortality rate, having increased by 40 percent between 1990 and 1994 to 15.7 per 1,000, was a rate unprecedented in the twentieth century in peacetime and in the absence of major famines and epidemics.[3]

Is there a way out? There might be if First World policymakers and officers of the multilateral financial institutions could be held to their protestations about commitment to democracy. There might be incorporated into international law a ruling to the effect that a people cannot be held liable for debts incurred by a government not of their choosing. There might be general accord on a strategy, like that attempted in vulnerable isolation by Peru's president Alan García, and Zambia's president Kenneth Kaunda in the mid–1980s to limit debt servicing to a modest percentage of annual foreign exchange earnings. In fact, were reason or fairness to prevail, there might be many plausible exits. But the Age of Aquarius missed its cue.

If multinational banks and corporations are to insist on freedom from all prior restraints against the movement of capital or against any categories of business venture (as guaranteed by the Multilateral Agreement on Investment nearing completion by OECD negotiators in 1998), might they not be held accountable for the hardships and human rights abuses occasioned by their ventures? A lawsuit pending in 1998 in the U.S. District Court for Central California had far-reaching implications. Judge Richard A. Paez held that those filing on behalf of Burmese peasants, alleging community displacement, impressment into unpaid labor, and other abuses committed in the construction of a natural gas pipeline, are entitled to sue UNOCAL Corporation, a U.S. company, in U.S. courts for abuses alleged against that company's governmental business partner. UNOCAL, however, was already looking into moving its headquarters to Malaysia.[4]

None of our theoretical models offers a creditable vision as to how current trends and relationships, so often inimical to the interests of people and other living things, are to be transformed. So long as national borders pose no obstacle to the movement of capital and autarchy remains virtually universally unfeasible or unappealing, it is hard to see how nationalistic and/or egalitarian policies could fail to provoke severe punishment.

I find some hope, however, and a good deal of irony in the boomerang effect—that is, in the belated recognition on the part of First World leaders that their policies are self-defeating. Even the long co-opted leadership of the AFL-CIO finally noticed that the U.S. policy of keeping labor in client states weak and disorganized (and thus cheap) was depriving U.S. workers of their jobs. It cannot forever escape the attention of First World farmers and industrialists that the bankrupting of one world region after another by Western financial institutions is depriving them of customers.

In the aftermath of the East Asian financial crisis of 1997, culminating in a competitive one-downmanship of currency devaluation, Western leaders appeared to be telling China to hold fast to its nonconvertible currency and to undertake Keynesian-style pump priming (taboo elsewhere in the globalized free market) on a grand scale to strengthen its domestic market. Just as early Marxists imagined that in a socialized world it might be necessary to maintain a market economy somewhere in order to calculate realistic prices, capitalists of this new order may be wondering if a contained, protected, or planned economy should be preserved somewhere so as to establish a bottoming-out point for wages and currencies.

Furthermore, the ultimate limits to a pattern of development characterized by unfettered growth are posed by a fragile and already dangerously contaminated environment. It remains to be seen whether the global community will take the steps necessary to decelerate the destruction, but the issue at least has been joined.

In the immediate post–World War II period, when scholars were laying out rationales for the public underwriting of private overseas development, it was argued that democracy would mitigate the extremes of free-market distribution; now it is suggested that the requirements of the free market must temper the extremes of democracy. The globalized economy removes options not only from the state as oppressor but from the state as the heretofore only vehicle for organized expression of the popular will.

The "free market" then assumes something of the mystique of divine right, a right that may be expressed as trickle-down supply but not as burst-from-below demand. In such an ambience, charity, which accepts inequity and builds dependency, readily finds its place, but empowerment, which breaks dependencies and proclaims rights, does not.

What then might be said for the prospects for a bottom-up, "empowerment" approach to development? Does a deck so heavily stacked leave any space at all for maneuver by those who hold no aces? There are those who would say that nonrevolutionary development programs—that is, programs designed to induce changes gradually, from the bottom up, to improve the standard of living and the problem-solving capacity of the poorest without immediately and obviously threatening the perquisites of the affluent—are at best foredoomed to failure, at worst sheer hypocrisy, intended to fail. On my more pessimistic days I am one of them. Nevertheless, it must be recognized that most revolutionary movements also fail and that, whether they succeed or fail, they are almost certain to be very costly in lives and in human suffering. Furthermore, no social arrangements are permanent, not even the redistributive benefits of successful revolution. Thus, for those of us who, for reasons of realism, pacifism, or cowardice, are not likely to engage in direct instigation of revolution, there must be some alternative to acceptance of a shamefully inequitable status quo.

In the long run, if the nonaffluent anywhere are to slow the erosion of their rights and living standards and to reestablish some sort of equilibrium in the global economic system, popular organization will probably have to bypass national governments, now impressed into the service of global capital, and confront global economic power with global people power. But any such development may have to await the propagation of a revolutionary new paradigm in the social sciences or a global depression of dimensions none would wish to contemplate. It would seem that, for a near term, those who see development as unshackling the disadvantaged, enabling them to pursue their own interests, have little choice but to focus their attention and energies on the grass roots. To the extent that national governments turn their backs on their own people, local governments and communities have no choice but to take up the slack. At some level, we can be sure that creative energy is potentially at the service of ordinary people. For the development specialist, the challenge is to find that level and to ascertain what might be done to unleash those energies.

Obstacles into Assets

It might be argued that the very grimness of prospects for meaningful political and economic change at the state level at the end of the 1990s makes grass-roots development efforts all the more essential and perhaps even inevitable. It has been said that necessity is the mother of invention. Crisis often gives rise to creativity and to mobilization for the common good.

Even in the United States, as the federal government shed responsibility for assistance to economically depressed areas and sectors, communities were reaching inward and rediscovering the strength to be found in common purpose and collective action. In north-central Maine, several rural communities lacking a physician pooled their money to send one of their own to medical school. Eugene, Oregon, reeling from the collapse of the timber industry, has turned to a strategy most recently tried and abandoned in the Third World: import substitution. A similar and similarly successful program, starting with the matching of local buyers and sellers, has been undertaken in Duluth, Minnesota. This revival of localism has infected even the New South, where leaders have finally despaired of competing not only with each other but also with the Third World in cutting taxes and labor costs to lure industry. In September 1989, the Southern Governors' Association unveiled its new strategy of "growth from within." Along with assistance to local businesses, the governors pledged to stress the enhancement of infrastructure and of education and training programs.

As material resources shrink, communities can and must begin to turn obstacles into assets. The foolhardiness of wasting natural resources has been widely recognized in this new era of ecological sensitivity, and yet in societies at all levels of development we continue to waste the most valuable resource of all: people. Teenagers, for example, in so many different places and circumstances, are regarded as a burden, if not as a threat. We allow them no useful role in society and then blame them for their alienation. Likewise, the increased longevity that is among the clear triumphs of postwar global development becomes a liability as the elderly are shunted aside into categories of dependence, their hard-won wisdom yet untapped. Thus an obvious first step in turning obstacles into assets would be to liberate the many categories of people who, for reasons of age, race, sex, or economic misfortune, have been prevented from fulfilling their potential and enable them to make the transition from alienation or dependence to being valued contributors to community well-being.

In fact, even as the relentless onslaught of modernization shrinks the global village, absorbing land and resources and threatening traditional livelihoods, one hardly finds a depressed area, rural or urban, where some vigorous collective self-help efforts are not under way. The United Nations has identified more than a million popular organizations with community development potential in the Third World. And as U.S. government funding levels for development programs, as such, slip, other governments and nongovernmental organizations move into the breach. Moreover, increasingly organizations launched for other purposes assume developmental roles. By 1990, for example, ninety U.S. cities had adopted sister cities in Nicaragua alone, and many were providing crucial development assistance.[5] In northern New Mexico, the prospect of assistance from the privately funded National Heritage Trust in renovating old churches has served to mobilize a number of Hispanic and Native American communities. The program provides resources for hiring technical expertise and assistance in bringing in volunteers from outside the community, but community members make all important decisions and supervise work in progress. In many instances, successes in these efforts have inspired communities to identify other needs and undertake, collectively, to meet them.[6]

Real development, of the sort we are calling empowerment, will never be neat and orderly and predictable. For better or worse, consequences do not derive directly from any identifiable constellation of motives. But the same uncertainty that makes development work so frustrating also makes it intriguing, challenging, and promising.

Likewise, such development cannot be unthreatening. No matter that change be sought by peaceful means or that initial goals be modest and nonpolitical. The empowerment of "have-nots" is by definition threatening to "haves." (The most insecure people and nations are those that have the most to lose.) Its very successes will continue to attract donors and agencies whose motives are hidden and less than benign.

Investing the Tribute

Should those who would serve the interest of the poor and/or of the public at large then disassociate themselves entirely from the development game as played at the lofty levels where big money is dispensed? Is it necessary to escape the official world in order to deal effectively and beneficially with the real world? I think not.

Few who have suffered extensive exposure to the development aid business would deny that its approaches are often flawed, that it tends to kill initiative and promote dependency among supposed beneficiaries and to foster a gravy train mentality within its own ranks, that its undertakings are often useless and sometimes downright harmful, and that its resources are often ensnared by kleptocratic leaders rather than trickling down to those in need. Indeed, it is sad, but unmistakably true, that unscrupulous leaders appeal time and again to the most generous humanitarian instincts of their own constituencies in order to promote the most lurid and self-serving schemes. But why should that be surprising? What business or profession with grand schemes and high status and megasalaries at stake escapes opportunism and corruption? And the aid business responds, above all, to the most powerful and ambitious governments and the private interests they represent.

Of course, the richer, more powerful countries seek access to the poorer ones mainly in order to exploit them. How naïve it would be to assume otherwise. And, of course, such exploitation is carried out in the name of noble cause—in centuries past, most commonly saving souls; in the late twentieth century, development. That would not cease to be the case if people of selfless good will pulled out of the enterprise. For good or ill the development game will go on as long as the power elite expects to gain from it.

The challenge, then, for those who would turn the tables—to meet the needs and strengthen the positions of the unaffluent and unpowerful—is to take advantage of the cover story. If hypocrisy is the tribute vice pays to virtue, the tribute must at least be invested well. Investing the tribute is the converse of subverting good intentions or misappropriating human kindness. It is hardly a new idea. If the Spanish conquistadores of the sixteenth century thought the priests who accompanied them to the New World would be content with saving souls, Father Bartolomé de las Casas must have given them a jolt; he managed to sell the idea that if the souls of the Indians were worth saving, their bodies should be, too. Ironically, now that development is the cover story, some of the most effective, empowering development work is being done by the long-established churches.

Investing the tribute is a strategy that shows more promise in development than in most fields for a number of reasons. It is a profession that attracts the idealistic as well as, and probably more than, the opportunistic. Though other qualifications may be stressed in recruitment, those most conducive to endurance and long-term satisfaction in the line of duty are compassion, empathy, patience, initiative, and a sense of humor. Thus, whatever the disposition of decision-makers, the ranks are likely to be filled with infiltrators who insist on taking the cover story seriously. It is also a far-flung business, and the farther afield the agent ventures from policymakers and supervisors, the more likely it is that he or she will be "turned" by the supposed beneficiary community and become an agent of their interests. Furthermore, development is a most complex and multifaceted business, one that allows more than most for creativity and serendipity and jujitsu. If the complexity facilitates deviation *from* stated goals, it allows also for deviation *to* stated goals, even where overriding objectives are unstated and less benign than stated ones. And finally, those who would invest the tribute have a host of potential allies. The real protagonists of development—the economically deprived communities of the Third World—may be virtually overlooked in the planning and implementation of a development project, but sometimes, just when the outsiders begin to think they are fully in control, the locals will mobilize and take concerted action, proving that it has been their game all along.

Notes

1. Frances Moore Lappé, Rachel Schurman, and Kevin Danaher, *Betraying the National Interest: A Food First Book* (New York: Grove Press, 1987), p. 15.

2. Ibid., pp. 84–115.

3. Andrei Grachev, former adviser to Soviet leader Mikhail Gorbachev, lecture at St. Antony's College, Oxford University, October 20, 1997. See also Katrina Vanden Heuvel, "Russia Waits," *The Nation,* October 21, 1996, and M. Elaine Mar, "The Dying in Moscow," *Harvard Magazine,* September–October 1996, p. 23.

4. Lucien J. Dhooge, "A Close Shave in Burma: UNOCAL Corporation and Private Enterprise Liable for International Human Rights Violations," *University of North Carolina Journal of International Law and Commercial Regulation,* no. 24, spring 1998, pp. 1–69.

5. The author became familiar with the extensive Sister City programs in Nicaragua in the course of leading a Sister City election observation delegation there in February 1990.

6. Participants in such programs, particularly in the U.S. Southwest, but from all parts of the world as well, congregate each fall at the Peter Van Dresser Workshop on Village Development, which takes place at the Ghost Ranch Conference Center in Abiquiu, New Mexico, to exchange ideas on development needs and approaches.

Appendix: Black's Laws of
Public Affairs and
Paradoxes of Development*

A. Life

1. No matter how bad things appear to be they are actually worse. Governments and other institutions cover up their mistakes and put the best face on what they have done or are doing.

2. In the land of the blind, the one-eyed man is a subversive.

3. A meaningful life is the kind you get crucified for.

4. The essence of waste is to sell out when no one is buying.

5. There is no such thing as "opting out." There are only two ways to relate to the system: as subject or as object—participant or victim.

6. Opportunities ordinarily go to opportunists.

7. Being right too soon is more damaging to a career than being right too late.

8. There is no such thing as a system that "doesn't work." Every system works for somebody.

9. Things can always get worse.

10. Most henhouses are guarded by foxes.

11. Without idealism, one has no destination. Without ideology, no anchor. Without pragmatism, no rudder.

12. Truth is a lonely traveler, the bastard at every family picnic.

13. Never trust anybody who is not aware that you can do him in.

14. We are all either carpetbaggers or migratory laborers now. Some can live any place they want to. Others just want a place to live. But all of us have lost our moorings.

15. History is written by the winners; the losers write the songs.

16. The buck stops short.

17. I am not a pessimist; I am an optimist starting from a low base camp.

18. Thinking for oneself is always an act of defiance.

19. There are no happily-ever-afters, but there are ideas whose time comes around again and again, and some seem to come around stronger each time.

20. If it is possible to do irreparable harm, might it not also be possible to do irreparable good (e.g., to devise the policy, create the organization, leave the record, write the book or the song or the phrase that won't die)?

21. One must know the future in order to predict the past; history is periodically reconstructed to meet the needs of new power holders.

*"Black's Laws," by Jan Knippers Black, comprise an ever-growing list begun in 1982. The list published here was copyrighted by the author in 1998 for classroom use at The Monterey Institute of International Studies.

22. The future is not what it used to be, because the past keeps changing. To get back to the future—the Age of Aquarius—envisioned in the 1960s and 1970s, we must recover lost road maps, paradigms interpreting the past and the potential of civilization.

23. In matters social and political, there is no such thing as the status quo; if things aren't getting better, they're getting worse.

24. Friendship is an expendable resource; the more of it you use, the less you keep.

25. Do the right thing; just don't get caught at it.

26. The sincerest expression of appreciation is a fat paycheck.

27. It is dangerous to make waves when you are in a small boat.

28. Success and greatness lie on different tracks. One does not achieve success with powerful enemies; one does not achieve greatness without them. The good thing about going for greatness is that you don't have to compete with the opportunistic and the unscrupulous.

29. Success is in sync with particulars of time and place. Greatness rises above them.

30. It doesn't matter where you start; what matters is which way you're headed. No matter where you're headed, you have to start from where you are.

31. Debts of gratitude are generally defaulted.

32. In the age of artificial intelligence and virtual culture, we are more than ever in need of real values.

33. Knowing who you are makes it easier to identify your enemies.

34. Don't let people mistreat you; they'll never forgive you for it. Forgiveness is easier for the abused than for the abuser. For the abuser, forgiving anybody, including himself, must begin with acknowledging guilt and assuming responsibility.

35. Wisdom does not travel on the fast track; by the time it catches up with you, you've nothing to do with it except pass it on.

36. With enough enlightenment, self-interest can be the functional equivalent of ethics.

37. Accommodating to a problem is not the same as solving it.

B. Politics

38. With the help of a great many adjectives (limited, tutelary, illiberal, etc.), democracy has become almost universal.

39. Everybody favors democracy to a point: down to the precise point where he is situated on the social pyramid.

40. Bipartisanship is a conspiracy of the elected against the electorate. A ruling party does not seek to share credit, only blame.

41. A government lacking a serious opposition party or movement is a kleptocracy.

42. A "smoking gun" will not be picked up as long as its owner has more big guns. Official history screens out revelations opinion makers and the public are not prepared to entertain.

43. People who believe they have freedom of expression probably have not tried to use it.

44. Impotence also corrupts.

45. The game for those at the top of the social pyramid is to keep those at the bottom fighting among themselves.

46. All elected governments are ultimately centrist. A government launched from either end of the political spectrum is pulled toward the center as its term progresses.

47. A policymaker may become a statesman only when he is permanently out of the loop.

48. Reform can be achieved only at the expense of the reformer. Especially in small group politics, the initial challenger becomes the scapegoat in the denouement phase of acceptance of change.

49. The poorer the country, the more luxuriant the presidential palace; the less serious the function of legislators, the greater their perks.

50. An administration that sets out to prove that government doesn't work always succeeds.

51. Ethnic chauvinism is the program of the runner-up. The leader who has a majority doesn't need it.

52. A coalition of the ruthless, the opportunistic, the fearful, and the apathetic is almost unbeatable.

53. There is an inverse relationship between the value of elections and the cost of candidacy. Would that "free elections" were.

54. When legislators start gaining tenure, professors start losing it.

55. We know that unemployment has gotten out of hand when the state loses its job. "Democracy" poses no threat to elites when economic decision-making has been outsourced.

56. Mobile money means immobilized political leadership.

57. Economics without politics is religion. Politics without economics is entertainment. Disciplines were invented to keep academics talking past each other and to ensure that academic discourse never touched a nerve.

58. Dictatorship is a frame of mind—the vindication of an attitude, not one-man rule but a license that makes petty dictators out of everyone who serves the system.

59. The difference between the major parties in the United States is that the Democrats do with chagrin what the Republicans do with glee.

60. The Right believes in the "power elite" but doesn't talk about it; the Left talks about the power elite but doesn't believe it (if they believed it, they'd know better than to talk about it).

61. The only effective balance of power is a balance between political and economic power—that is, the power of money and the power of organized people. The role of government is not to mediate between private and public interests; it is to represent and advance the public interest.

62. The more democratic the government, the higher the insurance premium it must pay to antidemocratic forces. To reassure merchants and mercenaries inclined to plot against governments they can't control, political leaders beholden to the poor must be even more generous to the rich than their elitist adversaries.

63. A liberal is one who is radical about the past, ambivalent about the present, and delusional about the future.

64. Politics is not a parlor game; it is the action at the top of the food chain.

65. Anybody who thinks there's plenty of room at the top hasn't tried to get there.

66. In truly democratic elections, all money is foreign.

67. Buying candidates is not an improvement over buying votes; the latter at least gave something to the electorate.

68. Globalization is the unfettering of capital at the expense of the fettering of government.

69. Where there are large gaps in wealth and power, adherence to law is optional for those at the top.

70. The mantle of office for elected leaders in the 1990s is a straitjacket. Election to office does not mean to power.

71. Power is the only protective mantle of office. The rituals and trappings that remain after power has been stripped serve only to make the naked emperor look sillier.

72. Without extremists, there are no moderates. Moderates who play along with one extreme in the elimination of the other are suckers; they soon find themselves as a targeted extreme with no "moderates" to protect them.

73. Reward and responsibility are opposite ends of a seesaw; whenever one slips upward in the social strata, the other slips downward.

74. There is no general principle too sound, no religious or secular value too sacred to be used by the strong to abuse the weak. The only defense against abuse is de facto equality.

75. Politics is the art of marketing private interest as if it were the public interest or, conversely, of marketing the public interest as if it were cover for the private.

76. "All else being equal" is oxymoronic. All else is never equal, playing fields are never level, and mainstreams are monitored by big boats. Mainstreaming of an agenda or program should not be considered until its constituency has a well-armed navy.

77. Collective survival is the only kind.

C. Economics

78. When belts must be tightened, it is always around the narrowest waists.

79. The post–Cold War economic model constitutes a synthesis of East and West: privatization of gains and socialization of losses.

80. High-level economic planners, like high-altitude bombers, have the luxury of obliviousness to the consequences of their actions.

81. For communities as for nations, comparative disadvantage lies in being unable to produce what they consume or to consume what they produce.

82. For states as for households, debts are less likely to get out of hand if the same folks who contract them and enjoy the benefits have to endure the hardships necessary to service them.

83. Risk capital is the kind invested in politicians; if those funds are invested well, other investments are insured.

84. When prescriptions are the same for patients with very different maladies, chances are the needs being met are those of the doctors.

85. What are free trade and free love free of?—security, responsibility, equity, and concern for the future.

86. It's a good bet that those calling for short-term sacrifice for the sake of long-term gain are taking their cut in the short term.

87. For employees, "flexibility" means the right to work whenever the boss wants them to and to receive in payment whatever the boss wants to give them.

88. An economic theory that offers only the ahistorical promise of market-regulated trickle down in the long term is of little use to those waiting to be trickled on.

89. It's remarkable how stoically some (e.g., international bankers) can endure the pain of others.

90. The most vulnerable economies are not those with too little foreign capital but those with too much. An open door to foreign capital becomes a revolving door.

91. Globalization is not just about geography; it's about leaving nothing of value beyond the reach of the market. There ought to be something left that you can't buy: body parts, the presidency, or the right to pollute.

92. The laws of free-market economics are just another set of laws that the powerful are not obliged to obey.

93. Corporations no longer compete for consumers but rather for investors/stockholders and credit ratings, based not on product but on stock values.

94. Competition in the global marketplace is not so much between corporations as between localities, and the objective is to cut costs, not prices.

95. Downsizing and outsourcing mean that your job has gone to China.

96. The ultimate collateral in the case of private loans to client states, guaranteed by donor states, is the labor of the peoples of both donor and client states.

97. In the global village, real prices are international, real wages are local.

98. The eucalyptus economy features transplanted high-yield ventures with shallow roots that grow rapidly by drawing off nutrients from their surroundings, thus starving older native species.

99. Streaker capital (e.g., portfolio) streaks in and out of revolving doors of eucalyptus economies.

100. The "informal sector" is not a reserve category; it is everybody except the relative few favored by the transplanted modern economy. The informal sector was "discovered" by economists in the same sense in which Columbus discovered America: It was there all along.

101. If the trickle-down approach to economic redistribution fails, there is always mugging.

102. CEOs who beat the drums loudly about jobs are concerned first of all about their own.

103. Limited liability for the corporate world means unlimited liability for the rest of us.

104. The trouble with money is that it attracts the wrong kind of people.

105. Privatizing usually means using public assets and public moneys to promote private interests. A government may nationalize failing enterprises (i.e., to bail out private owners), but it can privatize only successful or potentially successful ones.

106. Economics and religion have switched realms and roles, as between the physical and metaphysical and between legitimation of and confrontation with power. Economics has even taken over the miracle business.

107. Economic miracles, like religious ones, are most often about rising from the dead. Economic miracle makers have to destroy economies before they can resurrect them.

108. There is a built-in adjustment mechanism in the job market. When job loss becomes extreme, many who had worked in production, trade, and services will be hired back as policemen, security guards, and prison wardens.

109. Homelessness is not a consequence of poverty; the poorest communities take care of their own. It is a consequence of wealth poorly distributed.

110. If property is theft, intellectual property is delusion.

111. A partnership between the for-profit sector and the nonprofit sector is like the partnership between a con artist and his mark.

112. Bankers collect by hook or by crook. When creditors cannot collect from indigent borrowers, they collect instead from well-meaning innocents. Donations to debt relief for the poor are, in effect, reimbursements to lenders for debts they would otherwise write off.

113. The most addictive and abused narcotic on the market today is money; the system has a three-trillion-dollar-a-day habit—and will kill to maintain it.

D. Government and Bureaucracy

114. Nothing succeeds like failure. Rather than admit to failure, a public agency will attribute deterioration of the situation to inadequate funding and solicit more.

115. Nothing fails like success. A successful community (as in drawing tourists), institution (as in drawing funds), or person (as in drawing celebrity) risks becoming a caricature.

116. Charity and volunteerism constitute a special tax on the caring.

117. A state lottery is a special tax on the stupid.

118. There is an inverse relationship between the social value of a task and the funds available to support it; likewise, an inverse relationship between the value of what one does and what one gets paid for doing it.

119. One who takes seriously the mandate a bureaucracy professes will be labeled an innocent or a rogue.

120. Running government like a business means underpaying workers and overcharging consumers and taxpayers in order to generate maximum profits and benefits for a few.

121. Any gain in comprehensiveness is offset by a loss in specificity. If you classify all documents or lock up all lawbreakers, the ones that shouldn't get out surely will.

122. If a representative of the king sits on the board, his vote constitutes a majority.

123. The poorer the people served, the poorer will be the bureaucracy and the bureaucrats who serve them.

124. The grander the theft, the less the penalty. The first thing a really good thief steals is the government.

125. Revenues earmarked for the nonaffluent become a substitute for, rather than a supplement to, funds for that sector from the general operating budget.

126. The crucial issue is never whether to tax or spend or regulate but rather who to tax, who to regulate, and who to spend on.

127. Research findings tend to reflect the interest of research funders. Those who would control policy must control also the research, analysis, and evaluations used to sell it.

128. Services and benefits limited to the poor are not sustainable politically. No service will be run at a high level of efficiency over a long period of time unless all classes are dependent on it (e.g., public education, health, transportation). That's why the enduring legacy of revolution is public service.

129. The ultimate in chutzpah is to deny to the other—for his own good—what one claims for oneself. For example, the U.S. military/Congress deny "socialism," subsidized services such as health care. Industrialized states deny industrialization. The secure deny security.

130. A government that consistently overborrows is undertaxing.

131. Good leadership is not defined by tight reins or loose ones but by knowing who to rein in and who to let loose.

132. The nation-state has become a state of denial.

133. In the new East, phones don't work because of outdated technology; in the West they don't work because of updated technology.

134. Government is a protection racket that doesn't deliver.

135. Professionalism is shared guilt. Like bipartisanship and multilateral operations, it provides collective justification for malfeasance.

136. The bathwater may or may not go, but when the throwing out starts, baby goes first. Lean and efficient government is an illusion. When government budgets are slashed, services are cut before salaries, and the first employees to be cut are the least well paid and the least readily expendable.

137. A government that calls for volunteerism is admitting defeat.

138. A government that shrinks from direct taxation will not simply close up shop; it will stop at nothing short of mugging people on the streets to raise revenue.

139. Both the war on drugs and the war on immigrants are wars of attrition, relying on body counts—a supply-side approach to a demand-driven problem.

140. Privatizing social security amounts to putting the winnings of almost a century of civilization on the roulette table and spinning the wheel.

141. Globalization does not necessarily mean that government is shrinking, just that it has been outsourced.

142. Any fool can sell what belongs to him. The trick, as governments and corporate cannibals are discovering, lies in selling off what belonged to others.

E. International Affairs

143. The most insecure individuals, classes, and nations are those that have the most to lose.

144. An empire extends itself until it is overextended, thus bringing on its own demise.

145. Exploited outlanders, pouring into the metropolis as refugees, immigrants, or guest workers, eventually take over.

146. The strength of nationalism is in inverse proportion to the security of sovereignty.

147. In war, it is equally dangerous to be a big loser or a big winner.

148. There is a Catch-22 for modern-day Machiavellians: If they are fully successful in selling the cover story, they lose out to true believers.

149. In the U.S. foreign affairs lexicon, liberals are true believers in development, conservatives true believers in empire, and moderates, or pragmatists, true believers in profit.

150. A terrorist is a patriot who lost; a patriot is a terrorist who won.

151. Security does not lie in a wall or a missile or a gun. It lies in the reasonable expectation of being able to maintain dignity and human connectedness from day to day.

152. There are no winners in wars of attrition, only losers in disproportionate numbers.

153. All weapons (missiles, secrets, evaluations, statistics) eventually fall into the wrong hands.

154. The Soviet system of workers against consumers left the majority frustrated and blaming the system. The U.S. system of each against all leaves a sizable minority in despair, blaming themselves.

155. When refugees are too numerous, rather than being protected by the system, they become protection for the system—a protection from tight markets and enlightened politics.

156. Rich countries stay that way by taking in resources from poor countries but keeping the people out.

157. In all too many cases being a refugee has come to mean being imprisoned away from home.

158. When two become one, it's generally one or the other.

159. Once "security" is deemed to be the problem, the "solution" will destroy what's left of it.

160. War is expensive but always affordable; peace has to be self-supporting. Why is a peace process always more fragile, easier to sabotage, than a war process?

161. There are no stakes too small for people to fight over.

F. Communications

162. The size of the market for snake oil depends on the size of the snake peddling it. Any theory is marketable if it is packaged with an adequate portion of carrots and sticks.

163. Purveyors of disinformation become convinced by their own propaganda.

164. Every good term deserves another. In public discourse, any term with a strongly positive connotation will soon be used to denote its opposite as well. Thus, a new term must be introduced to convey the original meaning.

165. A "gaffe" is the unintentional utterance of an uncomfortable truth. Only children and comedians get away with speaking the truth.

166. The less one has to say, the more likely one is to have a forum—and vice versa. The primary role of a spokesperson is stonewalling.

167. The rationale for a policy initiative is usually the opposite of the reason for it; the rationale is intended to neutralize those who would otherwise oppose it. Thus, those who would maintain privilege must sell their proposals as essential to the public interest.

168. The first news is the worst news. Subjects tend to be introduced into public discourse by those whose interests are at stake. Especially in crisis situations, the first news, often taken from government press releases, is the least reliable.

169. Plagiarism is the sincerest form of flattery.

170. The pen is mightier than the sword but not in close combat.

171. Objectivity is achievable only by the mindless.

172. If they bother to deny it, it must be true.

173. Among the things the have-nots have not is a forum.

174. The purpose of communication is to obscure misdeeds and motives. Thus the communications superhighway is paved with fertilizer, and truth is roadkill.

175. Lightweight people and arguments float to the top.

176. An argument that cannot be made effectively on logical, ethical, or pragmatic grounds will be made on technical grounds or camouflaged in technicalese.

177. Those who are stingy with truth are sure to be defeated by those who are generous with lies.

178. The longer an agency has been in operation and the more eroded its functions, the greater the budget of its public relations department.

179. In journalism and scholarship, having the "right" sources and the wrong information is a lot safer than the other way around.

180. Computer simulation is the modern functional equivalent of reading tea leaves or gazing into crystal balls. Findings flow from the assumptions or needs of the programmers.

181. Truth is inconvenient to power.

182. High salaries normally amount to hush money.

183. The great value of truth lies in its rarity.

184. A social critic is a whistleblower on the system.

185. Modern media have greatly simplified the problems of conceptualization. Heroes and victims, the famous and the infamous, the outspoken and the outrageous all blur into the single concept of "celebrity."

186. The rich pretend to know more than they do; the poor pretend to know less.

187. Words are prostitutes—for sale to the highest bidder. *Sovereignty* came to mean license for governments to oppress their own peoples; *culture:* for men to abuse women; *efficiency:* for owners to exploit workers; *development:* for richer countries to drain poorer ones; *globalization:* for the private sector to suppress the public one; and *free markets:* for big business to gobble up small business.

G. Gender and Ecology

188. The greater the risks and the smaller the rewards of leadership, the more likely it is that leadership roles will be filled by women.

189. The only reliable guardians of any ecosystem are those who do not have the option of leaving. Like the colonialists of centuries past, today's second-coming capitalists ("There may be no tomorrow; get yours now") deplete, despoil, and depart.

190. For the global pacesetters of the 1990s, ecodevelopment has meant recycled rhetoric and disposable people.

191. The rich North has exported to the poor South its production models, its consumption habits, its polluting technology, and its garbage. Now it seeks to export as well the blame for environmental degradation and the responsibility for reversing it.

192. When hardships are to be shared, the poor can count on getting more than their share; they can also count on a generous allotment of advice and blame.

193. History is about gods and kings and warriors. All the rest is women's studies.

194. As masters of the spiritual realm, men have assumed responsibility for life after death and before birth; women only have to worry about the part in between.

195. Most consequences are unintended.

196. How many women does it take to change a light bulb? One-third. For women to change anything they must constitute about one-third of the decision-makers.

197. Species and cultures come to be valued only when they are almost extinct.

198. The last resort of an endangered species or embattled population is a high level of fertility.

199. The surest way to achieve high GNP growth rates in a relatively underdeveloped region is to harvest all the resources and replace the indigenous population with rich foreigners.

200. Violence results from power inequities. Thus the only real solution to the problem of violence is the empowerment of would-be victims.

201. Protection is dangerous. The greatest danger to most people comes from their protectors (women from men, citizens from police, government from the military). Protection implies dependence, dependence implies inequality, and inequality invites violence.

H. Development

202. Were it not for wrong reasons, there would be no right things done. The necessity of coalition building dictates that measures benefiting the powerless must appeal also to some sector of the powerful.

203. The more important the decision, the fewer and less well informed will be those involved in making it. Decisions viewed as most crucial to the system (e.g., war and peace) will be made by those having general responsibility rather than by those with expertise on the particulars of the crisis.

204. Those who pretend to promote democracy, human rights, or bottom-up development always run the risk of being successful.

205. Before a people can chart its own future, it must reconstruct its past—that is, it must reinterpret a history fashioned by its oppressors.

206. The reigning development model of the 1990s is a modernized version of the cargo cult: build landing strips, golf courses, and sports stadiums (or garbage dumps and prisons); depress wages and declare tax holidays; and riches of exotic origin will drop on you.

207. Development programs are given impetus not by underdevelopment but by fear of uncontrolled development. As a rule, there is very little money for development until those who have the money and the power feel threatened—precisely by the self-activation of the poor.

208. The experts are always wrong. When one is working in an unfamiliar setting (and experts, by definition, are), the unexpected always happens. In fact, if development is to be sustainable the unexpected must happen—that is, the project must get "out of control."

209. The failure of development—that is, the perpetuation of poverty and inequity—is a consequence not of policy failures but of policy decisions.

210. Saddling a project with secondary purposes may defeat its primary purpose. (If job creation is a secondary purpose in a construction project, for example, the project can never be completed; workers must continually sabotage it.)

211. The more complex the plan or the technology, the more there is to go wrong.

212. The more money in the project, the more pages in the plan, the more certain the disaster. Money attracts scoundrels and encourages corruption, and complexity conceals the scams.

213. Low-income housing is never low enough.

214. The "feasibility" of a development project depends more on its paternity than on its promise.

215. Rural development is a process whereby affluent urban dwellers teach poor peasants how to survive in the countryside without money. All development programs and agencies are to some extent paternalistic.

216. The more important a development agency's mission and the more effective its performance, the sooner it will be suppressed. If an agency with an important mission, such as land reform, has any success at all, it will generate a reaction from the privileged classes. If it has no success, it will lose credibility among its supposed beneficiaries. Most likely, such agencies will generate reaction and lose credibility at the same time.

217. In the Third World, there is a need for technicians who are *less* well trained. For the most part, those who invest their time and money in acquiring professional status do not do so in order to work in muddy shoes.

218. Distance unites. Exploitation and racial and class discrimination may well be built into national and international systems, but their expression is local. Thus, changing traditional relationships may require the intervention of agents who are not local.

219. To every solution there is a problem. In development, as in politics generally, there are no happily-ever-afters. The "haves" will soon figure out how to turn any new law or program designed to benefit the "have-nots" to their own advantage. Thus, those who would promote the interests of have-nots cannot be caught napping; they must focus always on ends rather than means.

220. Credit is extended mostly to those who do not need it. The lenders' interpretation of creditworthiness generally results in discrimination against those whose holdings and ambitions are modest. Even in microcredit programs, pressure is building to shun the poorest and move upmarket.

221. Sophistication in development processes is acquired and program continuity maintained not by donor institutions but by individuals and client organi-

zations. Objectives and approaches of major donor institutions shift in accordance with elite political climate rather than in response to experience or outcome in client states or communities.

222. Third World governments are weakened by the *lack* of pressures. Pressures on such governments are fierce and incessant, but they are virtually all from one side—the side of the rich. For long-term effectiveness, development programs must build up countervailing pressures.

223. Treating the symptoms may prolong the disorder. Development programs that simply meet immediate needs rather than enable communities to meet their own needs are likely to kill local initiative and build dependency.

224. The primary beneficiaries of rural development programs are the cities. Development money becomes concentrated in the cities, where offices are maintained, supplies are purchased, and salaries are earned and spent.

225. He who pays the piper does not necessarily call the tune. Development is a complicated process, an art as much as a science, a creature of fortune as much as of planning, and no one, not even those who pay the bills, can control it.

226. The easiest way to solve a problem is to redefine it. Time was when doing without (austerity) and unemployment (the informal sector) were seen as the problems. Now they are being touted as the solutions.

227. The poor have always understood what the rich have not had to: that there is greater security in community than in cash.

228. A development agency that is not in trouble probably isn't doing its job. That is the case especially if the goal is empowerment, because power is relational—the prize in a zero-sum game.

229. It is easier to promote something new than, like Sisyphus, to keep pushing the same stone uphill. Maybe that's why the only development model older than time—community self-help—keeps being rediscovered and renamed.

230. International financial institutions have been remarkably successful in chasing away poverty—from the vicinity of their conference hotels.

231. A successful popular grass-roots organization will soon find a competitive and better-funded organization stealing its limelight and its constituency.

232. Evaluations have to be written, but they do not have to be read.

233. The laboratory for appropriate technology and sustainable development is always the country that has no choice.

234. Responsibility shared is responsibility shunned. When it is spread across continents and hemispheres, scores of branch offices and bureaucratic levels, it becomes almost impossible to track.

235. Given a disjuncture between the objective and the capabilities and inclinations of the instrument, the latter always prevails.

236. Real democracy is most likely to be found where the resources aren't; big money draws big thieves.

237. The difference between charity and development is that charity builds dependency; development breaks it.

238. A set of people becomes a community when the whole is more than the sum of its parts.

239. Decision-making by "stakeholders" is a form of corporatism—a step forward from feudalism but a step backward from democracy.

240. The great appeal of diplomacy and development is that it is always easier to solve someone else's problems.

241. Culture as explanation is a cover for ignorance. By attributing values and behaviors to culture, westerners are absolved from trying to understand and hence need only to overcome. Thus culture as explanation for underdevelopment leads not only to blaming the victims but also to suppression of the wellspring of regeneration and empowerment.

242. Appropriate theory, like appropriate technology, need not be either old or new, high or low, simple or complex. It need only be accessible and useful to those who need it most.

243. One of the requirements for reducing poverty and income gaps in the Third World is to reduce them in the First World. The First World countries that have been most serious about reducing poverty overseas are the ones that first committed themselves to reducing it at home.

Index